STUDIES IN EARLY M...
POLITICAL AND S...

Volume 7

THE ENGLISH
CATHOLIC COMMUNITY
1688–1745

POLITICS, CULTURE AND IDEOLOGY

Studies in Early Modern Cultural, Political and Social History

ISSN: 1476–9107

Series editors

Tim Harris – Brown University
Stephen Taylor – Durham University
Andy Wood – Durham University

Previously published titles in the series
are listed at the back of this volume

THE ENGLISH CATHOLIC COMMUNITY 1688–1745

POLITICS, CULTURE AND IDEOLOGY

Gabriel Glickman

THE BOYDELL PRESS

First published 2009
The Boydell Press, Woodbridge
Reprinted in paperback and transferred to digital printing 2013

ISBN 978 1 84383 464 9 hardback
ISBN 978 1 84383 821 0 paperback

The Boydell Press is an imprint of Boydell & Brewer Ltd
PO Box 9, Woodbridge, Suffolk IP12 3DF, UK
and of Boydell & Brewer Inc.
668 Mount Hope Ave, Rochester, NY 14620-2731, USA
website: www.boydellandbrewer.com

A catalogue record for this book is available from the British Library

Contents

Illustrations

Acknowledgements

In the course of writing a book that required me at times to adopt a peripatetic lifestyle, I have incurred many great debts to those who supported my efforts in a personal, academic and practical capacity. In a publication that grew originally out of my PhD thesis, the greatest of these is owed to my former supervisor, Dr Mark Goldie, who has offered inexhaustible interest, engagement and good humour, ever since taking on the challenge of my BA dissertation in 2000. I am also deeply beholden to Professor Howard Erskine-Hill, whose interest in the mental landscape of Jacobitism and Catholicism was an exhilarating guide since my earliest introduction to the subject. My editor Professor Stephen Taylor offered advice, encouragement and generosity with his time that I simply could not have done without: I extend the most grateful thanks. I would also like to recognise the support of my commissioning editor Peter Sowden. The creation of this book was achieved in the course of a lectureship at Hertford College, Oxford, and the lively, original atmosphere of this institution served to inspire. Grateful acknowledgements go to my colleagues Dr Toby Barnard, Dr Christopher Tyerman, Dr David Hopkin and Professor Roy Foster. The undergraduate historians present between 2006 and 2009 provided a no less vital form of camaraderie.

Through the circuit of conferences and seminars, or even simply over email, I have had access to the thoughts of a number of distinguished academics within the field of early modern and Catholic studies. I would especially like to thank Professor Michael Questier, Dr Bill Sheils, Dr Hannah Smith, Professor Edward Corp, Professor Maurice Whitehead and Dr Susan Rosa. The *Historical Journal, Eighteenth-Century Thought*, the Early Modern Research Seminar in Cambridge, and the Catholic Record Society conference provided important early platforms for the dissemination of my work. While undertaking research, I have had the privilege to work alongside Andrew Nicoll of the Scottish Catholic Archives, and Fr Ian Dickie, formerly of the Westminster Diocesan Archives, a supporter of my efforts to whom I owe so much. For their immense hospitality as well as their kindness in giving access to exceptional manuscript collections, I must thank the monastic communities at Downside and Douai. I should especially acknowledge Dom Philip Jebb, guest-master of Downside, while Geoffrey Scott, Abbot of Douai, has already established a reputation as a formidable scholar in the field of recusant history, and I owe much to my conversations with him. Elsewhere, my visits to Broughton Hall stand out as a defining memory of the past few years, and I am indebted to the friendship of Henry and Janet Tempest. I would also particularly like to thank Andrew and Rosalind Starkie, my hosts in Newcastle, as well as Dr Richard Sharp and the late Robin Gard, who were both kind enough to share their wealth of knowledge on the cultural and religious background of the north-east. I acknowledge the kind permission of Her Majesty the Queen for my citations from the Royal Archives at Windsor, and His Grace the Duke of Norfolk for my use of the manuscripts held at Arundel Castle.

A number of peers have enhanced my knowledge and enjoyment of the subject through their conversation. In Cambridge, Dr Anthony Brown, Dr Niall MacKenzie and Dr John Bew were especially noteworthy. I must also mention Kendra Packham of Downing College, Cambridge, and Geoff Baker of Keele University. Outside the historical field, I should especially cite Nicola Lawton, Adam Bailey, Rebecca Lavender, Polly Evernden, Angela Pathmanathan, Miranda Malins, Katherine Schon and Mary Flannery. My mother, my father and my brother were all signally important to the work in different ways. The academic ethos within my family has been the cardinal inspiration.

Gabriel Glickman

Abbreviations

AAW	Archives of the Archbishop of Westminster, Kensington
BL, Add. MSS	British Library, Additional Manuscripts
CRO	County Record Office
CRS	Publications of the Catholic Record Society
CSPD	*Calendar of State Papers Domestic*
ESC	English Secular Clergy
EPSJ	English Province of the Society of Jesus
HMC	Historical Manuscripts Commission
LPC	Liège Procurators' Correspondence, in the Archives of the English Province of the Society of Jesus, Farm Street
OSB	Order of St Benedict
SCA	Scottish Catholic Archives
SJ	Society of Jesus

Introduction

The direction of recent scholarship has started to restore religious controversies to the heart of our understanding of eighteenth-century England,
calling into question the older image of a secularising 'age of stability'. In the
light of works by Stephen Taylor, John Walsh and Jonathan Clark among
others, it is now far less likely that historians would assent without debate to
the notion that 'by comparison with previous generations, the Englishman
of the early eighteenth century displayed little religious fervour'.[1] Yet, in
spite of the vigorous exchanges roused by these revisions, the community
of English Catholic recusants has evaded attention, and the lack of study
has perpetuated an older view that dismissed them as silent spectators in
the nation's rise to imperial grandeur. In the verdict of J.R. Jones, recusants remained an 'inert, defensively-minded and intellectually negligible'
minority, shut out from the discourse that dominated the English public
sphere.[2] To John Owen, they were an 'impoverished' group, who 'played
no part in national politics'.[3] To Linda Colley, Protestant self-assertion was
part of the genetic make-up of the Hanoverian kingdom, and those who fell
outside the pale risked being cast to the margins.[4] Indeed, the study of recusants over the larger early modern period has been reduced, all too often,
in one recent judgement, to 'an historiographical sub-field or occasionally a
ghetto'.[5] At best, the examination of English Catholicism has been deemed
less significant than the study of *anti-Catholicism*. Such an emphasis cannot,
however, be dismissed as the product of an incorrigible Protestant Whiggery.
Hitherto, the trends of 'recusant history' have largely reinforced the view of
Catholic exclusion from the Augustan public domain. In challenging the
current state of neglect, this book will seek to show why a systematic inquiry

---

[1] John B. Owen, *The Eighteenth Century 1714–1815* (London, 1974), p. 194; J.C.D.
Clark, *English Society 1660–1832: Religion, Ideology and Politics during the Ancien Régime*
(2nd edn, Cambridge, 2000); Stephen Taylor and John Walsh, 'The Church and Anglicanism in the "Long" Eighteenth Century', in *The Church of England c.1689–c.1833.
From Toleration to Tractarianism*, ed. John Walsh, Colin Haydon and Stephen Taylor
(Cambridge, 1993), pp. 1–64.
[2] J.R. Jones, *The Revolution of 1688 in England* (London, 1972), p. 80.
[3] Owen, *The Eighteenth Century*, p. 45.
[4] Linda Colley, *Britons: Forging the Nation 1707–1837* (London, 1992), pp. 19–25, 45–
6.
[5] Ethan H. Shagan, ed., *Catholics and the 'Protestant Nation'* (Manchester, 2005), p. 1.

1

into the recusant world represents an important addition to our awareness of the closing phase of early modern England.

Before and after the Glorious Revolution, the official records of the English state would seemingly confirm the social and political isolation of the Catholic minority. After the passing of *Regnans in Excelsis*, the papal bull of excommunication against Elizabeth I in 1570, the recusant community was set on a collision course with the political, military and ideological needs of an embattled Protestant power. Dramatised by a patriotic narrative that stressed deliverance from the Armada, the Gunpowder Plot and (in contemporary eyes) the diabolical papist hands behind the Great Fire of London, the call to arms against Rome's 'Whore of Babylon' became a stimulant in high diplomatic considerations, a motif of political literature, and the inspiration behind a body of penal laws threatening in theory, if not in practice, to eradicate the faith. One of the definitive treatises on the theme, Andrew Marvell's *Account of the Growth of Popery and Arbitrary Government in England* (1677) helped to entwine the Catholic name with images of foreign brutality, assaults on personal liberty, and a loss of moral moorings. These deadly vices distinguished 'such a thing as cannot, for want of any other word to express it, be called a religion'.[6] Yet, penal laws and pamphlet fulminations do not convey the complete picture. Uniquely among the Reformation states of northern Europe, the British kingdoms fostered an enduring Catholic minority, incorporating families with high social status and a glittering Medieval ancestry, shaped and formed by polemical contact with their Protestant compatriots, and strong enough to survive some of the most convulsive political dramas to fall upon the early modern state. On the eve of the Glorious Revolution, the community has been posited at a size of 60,000; vestiges of the Elizabethan habit of 'church-papistry' may have rendered it substantially larger.[7]

As they breathed the air of emancipation after 1829, Catholic scholars duly marvelled at the endurance of their community, through unimaginable vicissitudes. 'Faith of our fathers living still/ In spite of dungeon, fire and sword' saluted Frederick William Faber, and the heroic narrative of the Victorian 'Second Spring' addressed the fortunes of the suffering righteous, on their march towards triumph and redemption.[8] For most hagiographers,

6   Andrew Marvell, *Account of the Growth of Popery and Arbitrary Government in England* (1677), p. 5; Tim Harris, 'London Crowds and the Revolution of 1688', in Eveline Cruickshanks and John Miller, eds, *By Force or Default? The Revolution of 1688–9* (Edinburgh, 1689), pp. 44–65; Michael A. Mullett, *Catholics in Britain and Ireland, 1558–1829* (London, 1998), pp. 74–82.

7   J.M. Bossy, *The English Catholic Community 1580–1870* (London, 1976), chs 5, 7–8; P.R. Newman, 'Roman Catholics in pre-Civil War England: The Problem of Definition', *Recusant History*, 15 (1979), pp. 148–52.

8   Bede Camm, *In the Brave Days of Old* (London, 1899); John Morris, *The Troubles of our Catholic Forefathers* (3 vols, London, 1882–1887).

however, the decades that followed the Glorious Revolution at best added nothing to this illustrious lineage, and at worst threatened to undermine all the suffering glory and martyrdom that had enlivened an earlier phase of resistance to the Reformation. Among the patriarchs of Catholic historical scholarship, E.H. Burton and J.H. Pollen spoke of 'depression, lost hopes and discouragement', and saw their eighteenth-century forbears waning towards extinction – through their own tepid character as much as the antagonism of the state.[9] Cardinal Newman viewed the old guardians of English recusancy as 'gens lucifuga': the people who shunned the light.[10] Such opinions combined to smother any evidence of Catholic engagement with the Georgian realm beneath an emphasis on the 'barren wilderness' of spiritual affliction: a final time of trial before the Victorian assemblage of Italian missionaries, Irish immigrants and Oxford converts could confer a miraculous kiss of life. With Catholic sources lying unexplored, and over-arching generalisations persisting unexamined into the twentieth century, the pitfalls of this sort of scholarly treatment have been well-phrased by Eamon Duffy:

> Catholic history, as it has been written by Catholics, has been constantly plagued by a sort of historical myopia, a lack of proportion in which 'the sufferings of our Catholic forefathers' have been wrenched out of the context of the wider community, to which even Catholics belonged.[11]

Among Catholic commentators, the impact of the 'Second Spring' school was to install a virtual mirror image of the old Whig historical narrative, setting recusants in a context of permanent 'otherness' and opposition, with their culture drawn apart from the underpinning values of English society.

The attempts to challenge this black-and-white image of the past marched in step with a liberalising mood, in deference to the tenets of the Second Vatican Council, which informed the writings of revisionist historians, such as Duffy, John Bossy and Hugh Aveling. The construction of a post-Reformation Catholic community was attributed not simply to diehard conservatism, but linked to the revivifying methods of the Counter-Reformation, imported by missionary priests from the Tridentine seminaries.[12]

---

9   E.H. Burton and J.H. Pollen, edition of John Kirk's *Biography of English Catholics in the 18th Century* (London, 1909).

10 Quoted in Leo Gooch, '"The Religion for a Gentleman": The Northern Catholic Gentry in the Eighteenth Century', *Recusant History*, 23 (1996–7), pp. 543–68, at p. 543.

11 Eamon Duffy, '"Over the Wall": Converts from Popery in Eighteenth-Century England', *Downside Review*, 94 (1976), pp. 1–25, at p. 25.

12 Bossy, *Community*, pp. 11–74. Eamon Duffy, ed., *Challoner and his Church: A Catholic Bishop in Georgian England* (London, 1981); J.H.C. Aveling, *The Handle and the Axe: The Catholic Recusants in England from Reformation to Emancipation* (London, 1976).

With the old liturgy all but exterminated by official crackdown, it was the resources of continental education, religious conversion and a devotional literature centred on exemplary personal morality that kept the communion alive through troubled times. Construed in the same light, the Georgian era could be rediscovered as a period of 'modest growth', generating a rise of approximately 30 per cent in the numbers of the flock.[13] Although Catholics were not incorporated into the 1689 Toleration Act, they nonetheless benefited from the breaking of the Anglican machinery of enforcement, and the mid-century church of Richard Challoner, Vicar Apostolic for London, was seen to have presided over a time of philanthropic industry; a missionary force adopting methods of organisation akin to the Dissenters.[14] Bossy saw English Catholicism as part of the 'varieties of Nonconformity', one shade in the widening rainbow of English religion, and he set about 'exploring the functions of the Catholic community within a general corpus of Dissent', stimulating comparisons with the Quakers, Methodists and Presbyterians.[15] Revisionists accentuated the preaching traditions and pastoral strategies that allowed English Catholicism to flourish in an authentically native hue, before the Victorian transformation. The sacrifices of the martyrs were no longer made the prerequisite for Catholic success.

Stripping away the layers of confessional history has allowed us to appreciate the extent of Catholic involvement in the life of eighteenth-century Britain. It was a Catholic poet, Alexander Pope, whose *Essay on Man* defined the temper of an early English Enlightenment; a Catholic architect, James Gibbs, who returned baroque forms to the London skyline; a Catholic composer, Thomas Arne, who produced the score to *Rule Britannia*.[16] Yet, because of the overwhelming revisionist concentration on religiosity and sociability, the rewriting of Catholic history has thus far failed to reach the domain of eighteenth-century public affairs. Indeed, there remain three essential points of commonality between revisionist and 'Second Spring' interpretations, which have prolonged the exclusion of recusants from mainstream narratives of the Hanoverian realm. Firstly, both schools viewed the traditional public leadership of English Catholicism – the recusant landed gentry – in a state of near-terminal decline. 'Second Spring' scholarship hailed the achievements of English missionaries, saints and martyrs, but its authors had little veneration for the seigniorial religious framework, with its faintly anti-clerical sprit of lay activism, and their works propagated a narrative of cultural degeneration for the old squires who had controlled

---

[13] Bossy, *Community*, pp. 11–15; Aveling, *Handle and the Axe*, pp. 3–5. Duffy, '"Poor Protestant Flies": Conversions to Catholicism in Early Eighteenth-Century England', in D. Baker, ed., Studies in Church History, 15 (London, 1978), pp. 289–304.

[14] Bossy, *Community*, pp. 278–92; Duffy, ed., *Challoner and his Church*, pp. 1–26.

[15] Bossy, *Community*, pp. 301–401.

[16] Terry Friedman, *James Gibbs* (London, 1984). See Chapter 4 for Pope and Arne.

the church, scarred by tales of apostasy, bankruptcy and decadent retreat.[17] Twentieth-century authors also looked to trace a 'revolt of the plebeians' against feudal confinement, and recaptured Georgian England as an age of transition for Catholics, when the extension of the faith into new frontiers of national life brought a foothold amongst the urban poor and 'middling sort'.[18] Hence, revisionist writers did not challenge the picture of social change painted by the traditionalists; they simply brought it forward by a century.

Secondly, both schools accepted as a consequence of gentry decline the disenfranchisement of the recusant community as a *public* force in eighteenth-century England, the slow silencing of the political voice. From the heart of the Second Spring, Cardinal Manning, mocked the lay elites for subscribing to a view of political life akin to the disposition of 'the Seven Sleepers'. He added: 'If anything they are Charles I royalists. But there is no Charles I left.'[19] A century later, Bossy agreed that, with no access to public office, the majority of Catholics in Georgian England simply came to the conclusion that 'politics was a danger to the soul and in particular none of their business'.[20] The religious life and basic sociability of the Catholic community may have been more dynamic and creative than the old archetypes assumed, but it was not seemingly to be found in the affairs of state.

Finally, traditionalists and revisionists alike concurred as to the cause of this shift to the political sidelines. For both schools, the delusions of the 'Charles I royalists' found their most fatal expression in attachment to the doomed romance of the Jacobite movement: clinging quixotically against wisdom and experience to James II, his son and grandson, in their attempts to restore the deposed hereditary line of the house of Stuart.[21] Even before the decisive blow to Jacobite hopes at the battle of Culloden in 1746, the temptation of following a Catholic prince had brought stark consequences for the English recusant leadership. For half of the Catholic peerage, Jacobite allegiances entailed an experience of exile. For those left at home, the cause of the 'Pretenders' ushered in a period of extreme instability, brought to a head by the 1715 rebellion, and the sight of recusant magnates going to their deaths by public execution. Thereafter, 'privations, social pressures and

---

[17] R.C. Wilton, 'Early Eighteenth Century Catholics in England', *Catholic Historical Review*, n.s., 4 (1924), pp. 367–87, at p. 387; Edward Norman, *Roman Catholicism in England from the Elizabethan Settlement to the Second Vatican Council* (Oxford, 1985), p. 3.

[18] Bossy, *Community*, pp. 280–90; Aveling, *Handle and the Axe*, pp. 284–307; J.A. Williams, 'Change or Decay? The Provincial Laity 1691–1781', in Eamon Duffy, ed., *Challoner and his Church*, pp. 27–54.

[19] E.S. Purcell, *The Life of Cardinal Manning* (2 vols, London, 1890), II, p. 630.

[20] John Bossy, 'English Catholics after 1688', in Ole Peter Grell, Jonathan I. Israel and Nicholas Tyacke, eds, *From Persecution to Toleration: The Glorious Revolution and Religion in England* (Oxford, 1991), pp. 369–87, at p. 380.

[21] Bossy, *Community*, p. 287.

enforced asceticism' are believed to have reduced English Catholic loyalties to a state of forlorn nostalgia, pinned intransigently but ineffectually to the private domain.[22] The common conception of the recusant Jacobite has not diverged greatly from the caricature of reckless vainglory presented by Scott's Hugh Redgauntlet: his zeal blinded to the implausibility of a Catholic monarch being restored to the British throne. The legacy of the experience was a formal estrangement from the political nation that lasted until 1779, when church leaders acknowledged the right of George III.[23] This was not promising terrain for a recusant revival, and most Catholic historians have accordingly seen the Stuart cause as the last hurrah of a defeated and disabled gentry class, whose confusion of archaic allegiances with religious conscience threatened to reduce their co-religionists to a 'dwindling remnant' in the English nation.[24] A community in the grip of such recidivist feelings has not been judged capable of serious engagement with the public sphere. To the Jesuit historian, Thomas Clancy, the period after 1688 can at best be characterised as 'a good century for Catholic music, but a bad century for Catholic thought'.[25] The gentry mind, if not the changing body of the English recusant community, was set for a period of 'shunning the light'.

It is the contention of this book that current judgements on the eighteenth-century recusants have accepted too readily the Whiggish and confessional narratives of Catholic cultural degeneration, and therefore stand in serious need of revision. In aiming to release the Catholic gentry from scholarly caricature, I will seek to produce a sustained examination of how recusants viewed, imagined and represented the world around them, looking at how they justified their choices in politics and religion, and rediscovering their engagement with public affairs in Britain and Europe. In throwing open the private archival remains of the gentry community, I will aim to highlight the hidden diversity and sophistication of Catholic debate, as laid bare in vigorous intramural exchanges. Alongside the revival of interest in Georgian religion, the avenue for a reappraisal has been opened up by wider reinterpretations of eighteenth-century British politics, the fruits of which suggest that to be a Catholic would not have been the catalyst for inevitable personal ruin. Historians taking their cue from John Kenyon have looked again at the political sensibility of Augustan Englishmen, exposing the clefts

---

[22] Murray Pittock, 'Jacobite Ideology in Scotland and St Germain-en-Laye', in Eveline Cruickshanks and Edward T. Corp, eds, *The Stuart Court in Exile and the Jacobites* (London, 1995), pp. 113–23, at p. 119.

[23] M.A. Goldie, 'The Scottish Catholic Enlightenment', *JBS*, 30 (1991), pp. 20–62.

[24] A.C.F. Beales, *Education under Penalty: English Catholic Education from the Reformation to the Fall of James II* (London, 1963), p. 260.

[25] T.H. Clancy, *A Literary History of the English Jesuits: A Century of Books 1615–1714* (London, 1996), p. 233.

created by the Revolution of 1688, and the intellectual anxiety that underlay the 'polite and commercial' society.[26] Justin Champion and Andrew Starkie have revealed how the English Protestant identity – far from being an aggressively unifying force – was riven by disputes of political theology, evident not just between Church and Dissent, but *within* the Anglican corpus.[27] Paul Monod, Daniel Szechi and Eveline Cruickshanks among others have drawn attention to the vitality and endurance of English Jacobite discourse, across the religious divide.[28] While its political significance remains a matter of pronounced controversy, it is increasingly accepted that the Stuart cause was an intellectually capacious phenomenon, offering a language of opposition to the expanding post-Revolution state that moved beyond anguished jeremiads against the removal of the rightful monarch. In turn, Colin Haydon has shown how expressions of 'anti-popery' reflected genuine fears among some Protestant congregations of an imminent Jacobite triumph, bound to a belief that the recusant community was alive and growing.[29] The loss of the Catholic voice is somewhat anomalous, when the Catholic *issue* remained potent for several decades beyond the Revolution.

A new study of eighteenth-century Catholicism would build upon a slew of recent works re-examining the history of the community in an earlier period, to rectify what Ethan Shagan has termed 'the paucity of dialogue between Catholic and Protestant history' and visualise a community shaped as much by the politics of the early modern nation as its own spiritual priorities.[30] Alison Shell and Anne Dillon have drawn attention to the rich interior life of Catholic England, enshrined in its devotional and martyrological literature, but also made apparent in literary controversy across the public domain.[31] Michael Questier has argued that Elizabethan and Jacobean Catholicism was more than a narrowly sectarian presence, with gentry and aristocratic leaders exploiting their court connections to intervene in national politics, pressing an agenda that linked toleration at home to the

---

[26] John Kenyon, *Revolution Principles: The Politics of Party, 1689–1720* (London, 1977).

[27] Justin Champion, *The Pillars of Priestcraft Shaken: The Church of England and its Enemies 1660–1730* (Cambridge, 1992); Andrew Starkie, *The Birth of the Modern Church of England: The Bangorian Controversy, 1716–1721* (Woodbridge, 2007).

[28] See especially Eveline Cruickshanks and Jeremy Black, eds, *The Jacobite Challenge* (Edinburgh, 1989); Paul Monod, *Jacobitism and the English People* (Cambridge, 1989); Daniel Szechi, 'Constructing a Jacobite: The Social and Intellectual Origins of George Lockhart of Carnwath', *Historical Journal*, 40 (1997), pp. 977–96; Howard Erskine-Hill, 'Literature and the Jacobite Cause: Was there a Rhetoric of Jacobitism?' in Eveline Cruickshanks, ed., *Aspects of Jacobitism* (London, 1981), pp. 49–69.

[29] Colin M. Haydon, *Anti-Catholicism in Eighteenth-Century England c.1714–80* (Manchester, 1993).

[30] Shagan, *Catholics*, p. 12.

[31] Anne Dillon, *The Construction of Martyrdom in the English Catholic Community* (London, 2003); Alison Shell, *Catholicism, Controversy and the English Literary Imagination 1558–1660* (Cambridge, 1999).

building of Catholic alliances in Europe.[32] A fuller understanding of pre-1688 Catholicism would therefore consider not just coded wills or concealed chapels, but the disputes of a divided public sphere, uncovering the political calculations that reached into the highest ranks of the realm. In exposing the splits within the Protestant nation, episodes from the abortive Spanish Match to the Personal Rule of Charles I had convinced recusant magnates to resist the allure of seclusion and re-engage with the public domain. As Shell has surmised, the extent of their political commitments 'problematizes any simple idea of Catholicism as an opposition culture' in early modern England.[33] Moreover, as my opening chapter aims to show, the material and intellectual prosperity of the Catholic gentry equipped them to keep their interests alive through the Civil War, the Cromwellian Protectorate, and the frenzy of the 1678–79 Popish Plot. Without due evidence to the contrary, it is less than feasible to assume that old Catholic stratagems simply disappeared with the Glorious Revolution.

The received wisdom – that English Catholicism had been thoroughly stripped of any public pretensions after 1688 – has arisen primarily because historians have been looking in the wrong places. In recent years, a set of local and family studies, many appearing in the journal *Recusant History*, have started to prise away the old picture of Georgian Catholic life, showing how new missionary activity rested upon the wealth and resilience of the traditional gentry patrons.[34] As these works have revealed, neither the physical evidence of gentry households, nor the records of recusant estates cohere with the image of a class in decay. However, the missing element is any study of the *mental* framework to recusant gentry life, any attempt to trace the development of the political imagination beyond the Revolution of 1688. The problem lies not with lack of sources but lack of scholarly attention. Existing Catholic bibliographies have confined themselves largely to works *about* Catholicism – devotional literature and theological controversy – rather than the wider corpus of literature written by recusants.[35] It is certainly true that Catholic political pamphlet literature was less prolific after the fall of James II. In 1687, 147 recusant books had emerged from the press: between 1689 and 1700, only 95 can be identified, with not one

[32] Michael C. Questier, *Catholicism and Community in Early Modern England: Politics, Aristocratic Patronage and Religion, c.1550–1640* (Cambridge, 2006).

[33] Shell, *Catholicism*, p. 10.

[34] Gooch, 'Religion for a Gentleman', pp. 543–68; P. Jenkins, 'A Welsh Lancashire? Monmouthshire Catholics in the 18th Century', *Recusant History*, 15 (1980), pp. 176–88; P. Roebuck, ed., *Constable of Everingham Estate Correspondence 1726–43* (Yorkshire Archaeological Society, 136, 1976).

[35] T.H. Clancy, *English Catholic Books 1640–1700* (Chicago, 1974); F. Blom, J. Blom, F. Korsten, and G. Scott, *English Catholic Books 1701–1800: A Bibliography* (Aldershot, 1996).

addressing the issue of civil or political loyalties.[36] But there were many ways other than formal treatises for a religious minority to make its case, with poetry, martyrology and the writing of history operating as out-workings of recusant political thought. Moreover, confining research to the printed word fails to take account of the persistent usage of manuscript circulation as a forum to convey news and shape opinions: a feature of sociability before the Revolution that persisted in private networks into the new century.[37] The more recondite handwritten sources, including monastic records, commonplace books, and autobiographical reflections, shed light on the formation of a self-conscious English Catholic community. Any scrutiny of political ideas must also consider the great mass of unstudied private correspondence preserved in recusant archives, voicing a commentary on the time. The reality is not that the Catholic *voice* disappeared after 1688, purely its conventional means of public expression.

The unexplored Catholic hinterland was as much geographical as intellectual. Early modern recusant lives were not confined to the restricted space offered within their own nation, and no accurate picture of the community can be formed without considering the expatriate zone of English Catholicism: the diaspora that stretched from France and the Low Countries, across Italy and the Iberian Peninsular. The infrastructure of Jacobite exile rested on an older nexus of English colleges, seminaries and convents, established after the Reformation and thriving in centres such as Paris, Douai, Lisbon and Louvain.[38] An education spent in exile had introduced transnational horizons to successive generations of recusant families, rendering it possible for well-connected English émigrés to enter into the life of the continental *ancien régime*, imbibe its ideas and assimilate elements of its public discourse. The experiences of the recusant community would therefore be shaped by the controversies of church and state within and between the kingdoms in which they settled. Time abroad could never entail a complete escape from their native kingdom, nor a severance from its politics. The European diplomatic and cultural pressures on the British state, re-emphasised in recent works by Tony Claydon, Brendan Simms and Andrew Thompson, ensured that English Catholics living close to the elite worlds of France, Spain and the Austrian Empire could be subject to renewed attention from their own government.[39] However, an equally piercing scrutiny appeared from continental authorities, spiritual as well as temporal. By virtue of their position

---

36 Information collated from Clancy, *English Catholic Books*.

37 Harold Love, *Scribal Publication in Seventeenth-Century England* (Oxford, 1993).

38 Peter Guilday, *English Catholic Refugees on the Continent, 1558–1795* (London, 1914).

39 Tony Claydon, *Europe and the Making of England 1660–1760* (Cambridge, 2007); Brendan Simms, *Three Victories and a Defeat: The Rise and Fall of the First British Empire, 1714–1783* (London, 2007); Andrew C. Thompson, *Britain, Hanover and the Protestant Interest, 1688–1756* (Woodbridge, 2006).

on the frontiers of the Catholic world, the choices made by English recusants posed serious pastoral and political questions for the cardinals, nuncios and pontiffs of the Holy See.

Piecing together the fragmented archival material, it is made evident that English Catholics drew their concerns from a far wider well of intellectual experience than has been hitherto appreciated. Some recusants, as Bossy uncovered, may have *acted* in a fashion comparable to Dissenters, but this does not mean that they thought of themselves as such. In England, a public domain troubled by questions of legitimacy, rights and titles was made potentially just as accessible to Catholics as to Anglicans and Nonconformists. By fixing their ideas alongside the concerns that influenced compatriots of *all* stripes of opinion, we can start to recast the community not as pariahs, but *participants* within the debates of the kingdom. Futhermore, in their efforts to mediate between their conflicting allegiances as Catholics, Englishmen and potential Jacobites, recusant writings dramatised the questions of identity experienced across a greater swathe of eighteenth-century Europe, when pressures towards absolutism and uniformity had created similar experiences of defeat, disaffection and self-appraisal within the Huguenot, Jansenist, Pietist and Scottish Episcopalian communities.[40] Faced with the pressures of public affairs in their own country and across the continent, recusants could not afford to lapse into secluded isolation: the exposition of what it meant to be an English Catholic could not simply be passed in silent contemplation through manor chapels. Contrary to the image of seclusion, recusant lives were penetrated by the debates that gripped the European mind: questions of monarchy and nationhood, the efficacy and limits of religious coercion, and the function of temporal and spiritual powers in human affairs.

The direction of historical inquiry has therefore opened up a fresher context in which to recover the political, cultural and ideological exchanges of the neglected recusant community. In exploring these possibilities, this book is centred on the records of over twenty Catholic lay families and a wide base of clerical material, much of it originating in Europe and brought back to England to escape the tumults of the revolutions after 1789. I have concentrated on the papers of the Vicars Apostolic (who held nominal authority over the domestic mission) and the secular clergy in England, France, Scotland, Portugal and the Low Countries, together with extant records of the English Jesuit superiors active in Rome and Spain, and the rich Benedictine collection originating in Paris and Douai. This evidence is supported by the papers of the exiled Jacobite court, records of the British government and correspondence among the various cardinals and nuncios who provided points of liaison between the recusant community and the

---

[40] Bernard Cottret, *The Huguenots in England: Immigration and Settlement c.1550–1700*, trans. Peregrine and Adriana Stevenson (Cambridge, 1991); Emmanuel Le Roy Ladurie, *The Ancien Régime: A History of France 1610–1774* (London, 1996 translation), pp. 251–56; G.D. Henderson, *Mystics of the North-East* (Aberdeen, 1934).

Holy See. These manuscripts are complemented by the tracts, treatises and scholarly disquisitions produced by the Catholic printing presses in London, Douai, Paris and St Omer. As will be seen, Catholic commentators viewed public affairs very much as their own business, and refused to adopt the tone of a crushed and hounded minority. If religious controversy did retain its place into the eighteenth century, then the alternative perspectives unearthed from these sources demand to be heard.

The seven chapters of this book aim to offer a new synthesis for the study of eighteenth-century English Catholics: examined through their own writings, reflections and correspondence, but also in their involvements with the outside world encountered on both sides of the Channel. The re-examination begins with the Glorious Revolution. The paradox surrounding English Catholics after 1688 was the fact that most recusants still saw themselves as viscerally loyal to their kingdom. Indeed much of the shock – to non-Jacobites – of the 1715 rising was occasioned because the rebel leaders represented some of the most prominent and 'integrated' Catholic laymen resident in the English shires. The origins of this enigma can be located in the longer ideological experience under the Stuart polity, the old habits of mind, rhetorical stratagems and thwarted ambitions that cast a shadow over the Catholic imagination beyond the fall of James II. Chapter One will show how recusant literature after the 1660 Restoration had been exercised by controversies over the validity of state oaths, principles of allegiance and expositions of how a religious minority could reach a *modus vivendi* with their compatriots. Attachment to the reigning dynasty had been identified as the most likely route to acceptance within the English realm: but it was an approach made increasingly precarious as the Catholic leanings of the dynasty and the rising shadow of Louis XIV returned religious anxieties into the public domain, to bring about a fatal loosening of allegiance towards James II. In the crisis of 1688, Catholics were therefore caught between partisan solidarity towards a deposed royal co-religionist and the formative discourse of loyalty that had been built up to cultivate a Protestant nation. The chapter will show how recusant leaders took the gamble of trying to reconcile these conflicting imperatives, making a case for the house of Stuart that was framed by the older language of patriotism and moderation, to contest the conquest and 'usurpation' of a Dutch prince. The legacy of the experience was that Catholic politics had been re-founded on a fragile, audacious premise: a call to arms, not merely to start a counter-revolution, but legitimise it to the hostile national majority.

By turning a contingent of lay leaders into exiles and fugitives, the upheaval of 1688 threatened to unleash transforming social, as well as political, consequences, for the recusant community. The country of the penal laws and the Protestant succession certainly presented too cold a prospect for the émigrés who followed James II into France. However, as my second chapter will show, most of the gentry who remained possessed the resources to reconstruct their lives in post-Revolution England, and the squires worked to negotiate between the conflicting demands towards integration and separatism in an unpromising environment. Within the community, the creation of closely interwoven marital networks, imaginative management of family estates, and participation in the commercial world sustained the old patrician leadership against the social and economic privations threatened by the state. Looking outwards, family alliances with local Tory and Whig magnates could guarantee a measure of protection against anti-papist activity from government or the mob. However the refiguring of the political domain after 1688 brought repeated reminders of Catholic vulnerability. The reluctance of recusant squires to lay down their arms in 1688, the exodus of so many of their brethren into exile and the Protestant confessional wording of the state oath created a climate of suspicion that was embodied in the imposition of new legal bars and constraints. Moreover, the recusant heartlands were subject to increasing pressures from the burgeoning Stuart diaspora, and the affluent enclaves of English Catholic society developing on the other side of the Channel. Within a year of the Revolution, Jacobite partisans were starting to resume contact with kinsmen left at home, and aiming to transmit a case for adherence to the Stuart cause into English manors and chapels. Although active conspiracy was confined to the militant northern counties, a larger culture of Jacobitism was domesticated within Catholic gentry households, nourished by spiritual sensibilities, and informed by a tradition of royalist action harking back to the Civil War. The religion of 'prayers and roast beef' as it was dubbed by Alexander Pope, may have longed for civil tranquillity, but this yearning was set against the belief that the goal could never be achieved without a Stuart restoration.[41]

The third and fourth chapters examine the Catholic conflicts, discussions and disputes generated over English politics, firstly among the Jacobite exiles in St Germain, secondly within recusant opinion-forming networks inside the British Isles. Not every recusant was a Jacobite, and English Catholics never held a monopoly over the counsels of the Stuart cause. However, the political vision generated from St Germain was so closely bound to the hopes of recusant England that the study of Catholic opinion must begin with the ambitions stimulated in exile. 'Court' Catholic Jacobitism could be a revanchist doctrine, hailing James II as a martyr and sanctioning warfare on the succeeding 'usurpers'. But the zeal of the Jacobite conscience would be subject to repeated challenges: occasioned first by military defeat, and latterly by the work of a small but articulate minority in Catholic opinion who declared in favour of the Revolution – their efforts climaxing with an abortive bid for an oath of allegiance to George I in 1716. At St Germain, the pressure for a fresh Jacobite engagement with English opinion was

---

[41] Alexander Pope, *Correspondence*, ed. G.E. Sherburn (5 vols, Oxford, 1956), I, p. 457.

evident as early as 1692, when a party of recusant courtiers sought to over-throw doctrines of Catholic absolutism, in favour of an alternative, patriotic case for a restored monarch reigning over subjects of a different faith. The terms of this debate ramified into England. Far from sending the community into atrophy, the fragility of political life after 1688 opened up sweeping debates over recusant relationships with the temporal power, the chance of re-establishing a Catholic role in public affairs and the possibility of accom-modation with Protestant compatriots.

On both sides of the Channel, Catholics confronted the vital ideological task of appealing to the sensibilities of a nation against the prejudices of its political and dynastic order. Chastened by defeat, Jacobite statesmen nurtured the Stuart 'Pretender' on a contemplative form of Catholicism, compatible with liberty of conscience, constitutional politics and greater distance between temporal and spiritual estates. In England, Catholic Jaco-bite and Hanoverian pamphleteers jousted for ownership of the language of patriotism, public virtue and the 'ancient constitution'. A larger body of recusant writers sought to keep their dynastic voice oblique, and appropriated a Whiggish patriotic rhetoric to fashion a case against state coercion, which reaffirmed a Catholic love of England even where it declared discontent with court and government. On both sides of the dynastic divide, recusant engagement in English politics carries implications for the study of eight-eenth-century patriotic culture. Challenging the common argument that emerging ideas of British nationhood were bound up with state formation in London, Colin Kidd has suggested that the identifying vocabulary could be adopted by 'fringe' groups, such as the Scots to seek fuller participation in the life and liberties of the polity and criticise the political mainstream for its failure to live up to its own proclaimed ideals.[42] The same idea can apply to the religious as well as the geographical periphery. My fourth chapter will argue that the civic humanist ideology of 'Britishness' voiced especially by the opponents of Sir Robert Walpole created the space for Catholics to accentuate their own national feeling in a stand *against* the government. Pope was merely one of a cohort of Catholic authors who endeavoured to find a language of patriotism that could be voiced without submitting to the full claims and obligations of the Hanoverian state. Between violent resist-ance and full acceptance of the 1689 settlement was a capricious domain, a dangerous path of navigation for even the most agile of religious consciences. But in spite of exclusion from public office, there was evidence enough to suggest that being a Catholic presented no barrier against being a Briton.

While the early chapters of the book concentrate on English political debates, the latter half covers wider terrain. Many of the internal divides

---

[42] Colin Kidd, *Subverting Scotland's Past; Scottish Whig Historians and the Creation of an Anglo-British Identity, 1689–1830* (Cambridge, 1993), pp. 205–15.

in Catholic opinion were configured by political and religious splits created in Europe, with their roots in the decision of the Austrian and Spanish monarchies to support the overthrow of James II, as a means to halt the forward march of his French ally. The attempts to formulate an oath of allegiance to William III, Anne and George I were fomented by a section of pro-Austrian opinion within the Catholic community, endeavouring to capitalise on diplomatic accord between London and Vienna. The idea gathered momentum outside the recusant world due to the ambitions of Whig statesmen seeking to eradicate points of contention with their continental Catholic allies. In turn, the oath design was bitterly opposed from the exiled religious houses in Paris and Douai, where a Jacobite political ideology had been nurtured on the original alliance between France and the Stuarts, and endured despite the Bourbon tilt towards George I after the death of Louis XIV. The significance of European considerations in framing the domestic agenda raised the profile of English recusants inside their own nation. However, the continental context was not easy to negotiate, when 'Catholic interest' had fragmented between rival dynasties and power blocs, with the papacy itself notably prone to vacillation. Recusant politics in England and abroad should therefore be viewed against the background of what has been called Europe's 'crisis of conscience': the final collapse of the principle of Catholic universalism as a cultural ideal and a motivating force for military action.[43] Recusant debate over foreign affairs therefore possessed spiritual as well as diplomatic ramifications. Historian rediscovering 'the politics of piety' in eighteenth-century Europe have all-too-often overlooked the fact that some of the most vociferous sources of contention arose not between but *within* confessions, as different groups contested the meaning, implications and leadership of the faith within the world.

As my fifth and sixth chapters show, Catholics present within the inner sanctum of the Jacobite movement experienced an especially problematic relationship with the court of Rome, starting with the clash between the diplomatic needs of the Stuarts and the papacy, but exacerbated by deeper conflicts of interest. The exiles in Europe were brought face to face with the dangerous contradiction imported into recusant politics throughout a century of public engagement: in order to cultivate the sympathy of a Protestant nation, they had to create distance from the confessional models promoted in Catholic Europe, and steel themselves to reject the calls for unity, orthodoxy and obedience that emerged from the more ardent voices in the Holy See. By the middle of the 1690s, disenchantment in Europe had emboldened Jacobites to seek English affections by disavowing the temporal power of Rome and repudiating the absolutist image of a Catholic kingdom presented by Louis XIV. The commentary of the secular clergy chaplains at St Germain combined calls for religious toleration with a manifesto built

---

[43] Paul Hazard, *La crise de la conscience européenne (1680–1715)* (Paris, 1935).

upon principles of civic patriotism, driving the spiritual obligations due to an international church further from the needs of the regal state. Authors from the exiled colleges in Paris and Douai campaigned to cut back the authority of the Holy See and grant Jacobite princes power of appointment over Catholic ecclesiastics in the British Isles. The priests Benet Weldon and Charles Dodd looked to sanction their claims through historical scholarship, describing an English Catholic church that grew under the jurisdiction of Saxon princes, and did not therefore need the Henrician break to create dignified distance from the 'court of Rome'. Increasingly, the language of persuasion to fellow Englishmen was moving close to a case for resistance to the Holy See.

Voiced by recusants in England, this was a provocative argument. Written by members of the diaspora, it could be even more contentious. In the eyes of religious authorities in France and Rome, the writings of diaspora Jacobites were starting to submit a challenge not just to Hanoverian England, but to the regimes that hosted them in Catholic Europe. The result was a spate of allegations of heresy, a claim that figures close to the Jacobite entourage were associating with radical dissident groups, and threatening disruption to civil and ecclesiastical foundations alike in the countries where they settled. Prominent English Catholics were identified with the actions of the proscribed Jansenist movement in Paris: on three occasions between 1705 and 1718, claims were levelled against errant doctrines preached at the heart of the exiled Jacobite court and the English colleges in Paris and Douai, while the émigré community in St Germain reeled under threat of arrests, denunciations, and *lettres de cachets*. Later, the court tutor Andrew Michael Ramsay was turned away from the city of Rome, due to his espousal of the theologically distinct but equally illicit quietist creed of Archbishop Francois Fénelon. The interrogation placed upon recusants for being insufficiently 'English' in their native kingdom was more than matched in force and intensity by the claim that they had become less than truly Catholic when they moved among their co-religionists abroad.

The final chapter to the book identifies the heterodox element in the English Catholic world as a ramification of the larger conflict in church-state relations gathering pace in France. Through the political entanglements of the seventeenth-century, French 'Gallican' doctrines had established a hold over the recusant imagination: not a uniform movement, but the common banner for a corpus of writings that emphasised the temporal freedom of kingdoms from papal control and laid down a bulwark against 'ultramontane' doctrines preached in Spanish and Jesuit circles. However, Counter-Reformation France was a house divided, with its universities, seminaries and cathedrals caught between competing claims to represent true Catholic orthodoxy, and, by the time of the Glorious Revolution, the model offered for English recusants was becoming increasingly problematic. Gallican doctrines had been thrown into crisis in the 1690s by the attempted reconciliation between their figurehead Louis XIV and the Holy See, by the king's decision to recast himself as a champion of Catholic orthodoxy, and his attempt to purge the realm of heretical beliefs. The culminating stage of this strategy, the anti-Jansenist bull Unigenitus, caught a large array of French priests and scholars in the web of inquisition, and began a process that turned Gallican ideas into a doctrine of patriotic opposition, crystallising in the Paris *Parlement* in the reign of Louis XV. This book contends that, like most of their French coevals, the English émigrés were never guilty of harbouring the theological 'errors' of Jansenism. However, in their promotion of certain *avant-garde* pious and mystical traditions within the Gallican Church, their critique of absolutist kingship and their reappraisal of papal powers, they *had* been driven closer to the reforming circles made subject to suspicion. Moreover, I suggest that, under pressure of inquisition, the original English Gallican critique was not extinguished: instead, it fragmented into a loosely bound reformist movement within the Jacobite diaspora, entering the commentaries of émigrés such as Simon Berington, George Flint, Nathaniel Hooke and Thomas Southcott, who moved within the orbit of the exiled court. The reaction to the conflicts in France was voiced in a genre of utopian political fantasies, discourses on religious toleration and blueprints for an alternative, non-absolutist form of kingship, composed in exile, but brought back across the Channel into the correspondence of recusants at home.

It is the contention of this work, therefore, that Catholic scholarship in England can only be understood as a response to the conflicts experienced on the continent. If the eclecticism of the Catholic exiles' world has not subject to a full historiography, this book responds nonetheless to a recent scholarly movement that has reconsidered the provenance of eighteenth-century enlightenment traditions, calling into question the assumptions implicit in the older scholarship that divided the world into 'believers' and secularists, and all-too-often disregarded the permutations present within 'believing' communities.[44] Studies by Roy Porter, Derek Beales and T.C.W. Blanning have sought to unearth the role of national and religious traditions in the making of enlightenment culture, pushing back the primacy of secular internationalism, and pinpointing the *Christian philosophe* as a significant protagonist in European intellectual life. This reassessment has allowed historians to locate a genuine movement towards 'Catholic Enlightenment' in German and Italian territories.[45] In recent years, reassessments

---

[44] Dale Van Kley, 'Piety and Politics in the Century of Lights', in Mark Goldie and Robert Wokler, eds, *The Cambridge History of Eighteenth-Century Political Thought* (Cambridge, 2006), pp. 119–45.

[45] T.C.W. Blanning, 'The Enlightenment in Catholic Germany', in Roy Porter and Mikulas Teich, *The Enlightenment in National Context* (Cambridge, 1981), pp. 118–26; Ole Peter Grell and Roy Porter, *Toleration in Enlightenment Europe* (Cambridge, 2000); Derek Beales and Geoffrey Best, *History, Society and the Churches: Essays in honour of Owen Chadwick* (Cambridge, 1985), pp. 1–10.

of French and Irish Catholicism by Dale Van Kley and Thomas O'Connor have unravelled the old caricature of the Jansenist influence as 'a Calvinist Trojan horse within the precincts of orthodoxy', showing instead how the variety and sophistication of the heresy responded to fundamental challenges levelled at western Catholicism, when the jurisdictional clashes of popes and kings collided with calls for moral and pastoral resurgence within the Church.[46] Some of these ideas have been sporadically applied to British Catholicism. Geoffrey Scott has drawn attention to cosmopolitan influences among the eighteenth-century Benedictine Congregation, while Eamon Duffy and Joseph Chinnici have identified the later Catholic Relief movement under George III as a mouthpiece for 'enlightened' propositions.[47] Mark Goldie has illustrated a contemporary 'Scottish Catholic Enlightenment', broad enough to encompass a radical 'Foxite' trajectory among some former Jacobite supporters.[48] This book will, however, argue that a 'Catholic Enlightenment' cut far deeper into the English recusant imagination than these accounts have suggested, with its origins to be found much earlier in the century. Moreover, its rise was not contingent on the renunciation of old political loyalties. When the reformist movement had developed in the communities of the diaspora, the Stuart cause did not have to fail to allow the regeneration of the English Catholic intellect.

The reformist tilt to English Catholicism did not represent the only voice within recusant and Jacobite communities – it was certainly a contested stance. However, I suggest that for three key reasons, an idea of irenic patriotism became the dominant position within English Catholic thought over the course of the century. Firstly, notions of wider toleration and distance between church and state moved in harmony with the impulses of the Catholic minority fighting against Protestant pressures in England. The wellspring for the radical tendency in the Jacobite diaspora was an older Erasmian humanist persuasion in recusant scholarship, with its rhetorical roots in the dialogue between seventeenth-century loyalists and French Gallican theorists seeking to justify detachment from the 'court of Rome'. The same idea inspired the private commentaries of recusant squires such as Stephen Tempest, Sir Robert Throckmorton and John Belson. Secondly, the potential for conflict with continental Catholic orthodoxy was inherent

---

[46] Thomas O'Connor, *Irish Jansenists 1600–1670* (Dublin, 2008), p. 15. See also O'Connor, *An Irish Theologian in Enlightenment France: Luke Joseph Hooke, 1714–96* (Blackrock, 1995); Dale K. Van Kley, *The Jansenists and the Expulsion of the Jesuits from France, 1757–1765* (New Haven, 1975).

[47] Joseph Chinnici, *The English Catholic Enlightenment: John Lingard and the Cisalpine Movement, 1780–1850* (Shepherdstown, 1980); Eamon Duffy, 'Joseph Berington and the English Catholic Cisalpine Movement, 1772–1803' (unpublished PhD thesis, Cambridge University, 1973).

[48] Geoffrey Scott, *Gothic Rage Undone: English Monks in the Age of Enlightenment* (Downside, 1992), pp. 127–56; Goldie, 'Scottish Catholic Enlightenment', pp. 20–23.

in the life of the recusant community, when in the judgement of one of its pre-eminent historians, 'most of its virtues, and nearly all of its peculiar ethos' derived from an unusual minority status in national life.[49] The overwhelming scholarly stress on the tensions besetting Catholics in the English kingdom has not yet been matched by an examination of the gulf created with European co-religionists by the compromises in recusant life. Finally, essential elements of the reformers' manifesto enjoyed the ear of an exiled Jacobite court straining to prove its fitness to rule a Protestant kingdom. The Pretender James Edward Stuart himself acknowledged the personal influence of Archbishop Fénelon, and experienced in his own household some of the tensions aroused over the principle that 'It should never be my business to study how to be an apostle, but to become a good King to all my people without distinction.'[50] Together, these tendencies could put up barriers against 'ultramontane' pressures emerging from Europe.

English Catholic thought after 1688 has been misconstrued – where it has been examined at all – because it has invariably been viewed in the restrictive context of gentry decline and Jacobite defeat, losing sight of the wider intellectual hinterland in which the leading recusants operated. Now, reinterpretations of the political, religious and intellectual history of eighteenth-century Britain and Europe have created an opportunity to unpeel the old, unspoken and inhibiting caricatures, and reclaim the study of English recusants for a fuller political and cultural history. My contention is that the thoughts generated by conflict in the diaspora left a legacy over the English Catholic mind that endured long after the collapse of the Jacobite movement: dislodged from the cause of the Stuart Pretenders, the manifesto of patriotism, toleration and reformist kingship came to influence a later discourse of engagement with the British polity. The irenic and cosmopolitan sensibility galvanised by the Jacobite reformers was reinvigorated in the 'liberal' rhetoric that arose within the reign of George III and shaped the language of the campaign for Catholic Emancipation. Drowned out by the triumphalist din of a Victorian revival that changed the complexion of the faith in England, this mood had dwindled into a lost mental world by the time of the Catholic 'Second Spring'. But for two generations, the old apparatus of recusant thought had combined with influences gleaned from the experience of exile, to create the origins of an authentic 'English Catholic Enlightenment'.

---

[49] Aveling, *Handle and the Axe*, p. 335.
[50] Anon., *A Letter from an English Traveller at Rome to his Father, of the 6th of May, 1721. O.S.* (London, 1721), pp. 7–8.

1

English Catholics and
the Glorious Revolution of 1688

The events that started in December 1688 became rapidly ingrained in the public mythology of the English state. The 'Protestant' wind that blew William of Orange towards the throne of the three kingdoms, the humiliating exit of James II and the subsequent reassertion of parliamentary right were serenaded as the hallmarks of deliverance from the twin pillars of 'Popery and Arbitrary Government'. Raised as a landmark moment for the constitution, the Glorious Revolution was perceived to have set the dogma of Rome against the will of freeborn Englishmen to bring the final triumph of Protestant over papist, tarnishing the co-religionists of James II with obscurantism and defeat. In recent years, the stress on religious conflict within the Revolution has yielded before an alternative historical emphasis. Some of the strongest works have explored the 'conservative' and 'reluctant' qualities of the event, considered the countervailing role of temporal patriotism against eschatological piety, or reasserted the primacy of high politics over clashes of ideas. Scholars of the continental scene have stressed the new king's record as a defender of Catholics in his native territories, to suggest that William's enthronement dampened, more than it inflamed, the confessional passions of the realm.[1] Yet contemporary witnesses were somewhat less sanguine. The Prince of Orange's banners proclaimed 'the Protestant religion' as a spur to action, his preachers hailed a godly triumph, and his coronation formally endorsed the conviction that Catholic governance was 'inconsistent with the Safety and Welfare of this Protestant Kingdom'. The immediate effect was that an even greater number of Catholics left the

---

[1] Jonathan I. Israel, 'William III and Toleration', in Ole Peter Grell, Jonathan I. Israel and Nicholas Tyacke, *From Persecution to Toleration: The Glorious Revolution and Religion in England* (Oxford, 1991), pp. 129–70; John Morrill, 'The Sensible Revolution', in Jonathan I. Israel, ed., *The Anglo-Dutch Moment: Essays on the Glorious Revolution and its World Impact* (Cambridge, 1991), pp. 73–104; W.A. Speck, *Reluctant Revolutionaries: Englishmen and the Revolution of 1688* (Oxford, 1988), pp. 241–51; Steven C. Pincus, '"To protect English liberties": The English Nationalist Revolution of 1688–1689', in Tony Claydon and Ian McBride, eds, *Protestantism and National Identity: Britain and Ireland c.1650–c.1850* (Cambridge, 1998), pp. 75–104.

shores of England in 1688–1689 than during the convulsions of the 'Popish Plot' ten years earlier.[2]

For recusants, the Revolution was a terrible and tumultuous moment, recalled in verse lament as the descent from 'perverted order to confusion', leaving a desperate flock 'Famished with want', the 'Wilds and Deserts to tread … for Zion is no more'.[3] Behind this refrain was indeed the 'confusion' of a shattering political irony, splendidly phrased by Hugh Trevor-Roper, that when Catholics thought they 'had found their ideal king … the English perversely chose that occasion to adopt the Jesuit doctrine that orthodox subjects may depose a heretic ruler'.[4] The outcome was a formal estrangement from the political nation that lasted for almost a century: a calamity that seemed to contemporaries equally portentous as the reverses suffered by the dwindling faithful of Tudor England. Yet in all the vexed debates that have surrounded the expulsion of James II, the place of English recusants has been neglected: Catholic victimhood has been accentuated over Catholic activity, with only sporadic attempts made to discover how the community responded to a king who had restored them, briefly but consequentially, to the centre of national affairs. Moreover, the absence of a Catholic perspective marks the point of departure for recusants from mainstream histories of England's 'long eighteenth-century': in most verdicts it is the beginning of an ideological slumber, and a fall into ritualised seclusion. Lingering support for the Stuarts has been dismissed as an atavistic affair, an intoxication that ended when wiser heads recovered their political sobriety, and which in any case proved unable to stop the march of retreat from the public domain.

Responses to the fall of James II allow us to re-examine the accepted narratives surrounding English Catholicism at the beginning of the eighteenth century. This chapter will call upon material dispersed through recusant archives, to prise out the reasons why Catholic leaders maintained their allegiance to the deposed king – and the way in which they justified their choice, to themselves and to the wider nation. I will begin by surveying the 'physical' impact of the Revolution on the gentry leadership that governed the Catholic community: the social, political and military contingencies that left a wide section of the recusant elites branded as Jacobites even before the coronation of William III. The chapter will then look further back to probe the roots of an *ideological* response to 1688, arguing that Catholic attitudes should be located inside a longer lineage of thought, a struggle for national recognition set down in poetry, tract and drama that gathered intensity after the Restoration. In 1685, they could view the crowning of a Catholic monarch as the climax of a favourable direction in politics, a vindication for those who had held up the banner of Civil War memories

---

2   Aveling, *Handle and the Axe*, p. 241.
3   Thomas Southcott, *The Prayer of Jeremy Paraphras'd*, in *Miscellaneous Poems and Translations, by several hands* (1712), pp. 109–16.
4   Hugh Trevor-Roper, *Historical Essays* (London, 1957), p. 112.

and endured the instability of political life. But the Catholic strategy was blown apart by two developments that came to a head after 1685. Firstly, the rising absolutism of Louis XIV's France, which destroyed the credibility of the Gallican model of Catholic monarchy favoured by English recusants. Secondly, the aggressive activism of convert lords on the council of James II severed the royal programme from the will of an older Catholic leadership, and destroyed the key tenet of their political argument: an alliance with the Tory Anglican defenders of throne and altar. Both trends exposed the limits of English obedience to the Stuart throne, the basis on which Catholics had grounded their conception of temporal and spiritual allegiance. The rhetorical stratagems conceived by recusants to seek acceptance from the public domain were overturned in the crisis descending on the three kingdoms, and the result was to leave a long shadow over Catholic life into the following century.

The onset of exile

The clergymen of the Scots College, Paris, were among the first to monitor the wave of refugees, flooding into France in 1689, and desperately seeking shelter. 'Daily multitudes of gentlemen of all employment arrive', wrote Charles Whyteford, alongside 'hundreds of poor Catholics, begging for charity'.[5] The accounts of clerics inside the British Isles took on a darker tone. 'All night in the city burn innumerable bonfires' ran one report from London. 'At one there was his holynesse, a great crosse … burnt in effigie, at another the King, Queen and prince now burnt.'[6] Testimony abounded of recusant homes ransacked – including the residences of the Privy Councillors, the lords Dover and Melfort – and priests whipped through city streets.[7] London was no longer a safe place to be a Catholic, and carriages moving by night conveyed the devotional apparatus of threatened chapels to mansions such as Broughton Hall in the West Riding of Yorkshire: an attempt to salvage precious symbols of a crumbling religious revival.[8] The Scottish bishop Thomas Nicolson despaired: 'I can see no way through this labyrinth.'[9]

If this did not, in the end, prove to be England's Protestant answer to the St Bartholomew's Day massacre, memories of Titus Oates and the Popish Plot nonetheless combined with the breakdown of control in the cities to

---

5   Charles Whyteford to William Leslie, 21 January 1689, SCA, Blairs, I, 126/3.
6   Charles Whyteford to William Leslie, 7 March 1689, SCA, Blairs, I, 126/11.
7   Anon. to Lewis Innes, 15 December 1688, SCA, Blairs, I, 119/6; Charles Whyteford to William Leslie, 21 January 1689, Blairs, I, 126/3.
8   Note in Stanford papers, 1697, Tempest MSS (private collection); G. MacDonald, 'The Lime Street Chapel', *Dublin Review* (1927) 180, pp. 261–5, and 181, pp. 2–6.
9   Thomas Nicolson to Lewis Innes, 11 December 1688, SCA, Blairs, I, 119/2.

convince recusants that they were witnessing the start of a virulent war of religion. A proclamation purporting to be from William of Orange enjoined Protestants to seize, disarm and imprison their Catholic neighbours, and the response was to spread the wave of looting and civil disorder into the provincial strongholds of the 'old faith'.[10] The chapels established by the Throckmortons at Coughton Court and the Yates of Harvington were demolished; William Massey of Puddington reported aggressive poaching on his estate.[11] The seemingly anti-Catholic credentials of the new regime did not take long to establish themselves. By April 1689, penal legislation was being revived, with restrictions on travel, a proscription on the priesthood and the tendering of oaths to forswear essential tenets of Catholic doctrine.[12] William Blundell of Little Crosby, an old royalist soldier, faced a series of humiliations throughout the year. In May, his servants were attacked and his horses stolen; two months later, he was conveyed to Liverpool and detained for six months without trial.[13] The wife and daughters of Robert Brent, a Catholic barrister and advisor to the king, were thrown into gaol for two months: the same justice awaited the lords Montgomery, Langdale, Salisbury and Peterborough.[14] By August 1690, the London lawyer Daniel Arthur lamented that 'all England over … most of ye papists of any note are either in prison or under confinement, according as they are looked upon more or less obnoxious'.[15] A force of anti-Catholicism that had torn a king from his throne had reached to the very doors of the recusant squirearchy.

A significant number of Catholics refused to let the regime of James II fall without a struggle, and in some of the strongest recusant heartlands, a fierce insurgence ensured that the enthronement of William of Orange was not as bloodless as its advocates liked to suggest. Under the auspices of Colonel John Gage, the winter of 1688 had seen Catholic troops amassed across the north and west, with the intention of producing thirteen organised regiments.[16] From the attempt to capture Chester by Viscount Molyneux in December 1688, to the defence of Powis Castle by Welsh recusants in May

---

[10] John Carswell, *The Descent on England* (London, 1969), p. 201.

[11] Robert Fleming to Sir Daniel Fleming, 27 December 1689, HMC, *Le Fleming*, p. 231; Narcissus Luttrell, *Brief Historical Relation of State Affairs from September1678 to April 1714* (6 vols, Oxford, 1857), I, pp. 485–6, 490; Michael Hodgetts, 'The Yates of Harvington, 1631–1696', *Recusant History*, 22 (1994), pp.152–81, at p. 173.

[12] Daniel Arthur to Henry Browne, 21 April 1689, AAW, Browne MSS, 7.

[13] Margaret Blundell, ed., *Cavalier: The Letters of William Blundell to his Friends 1620–1688* (London, 1933), pp. 255–65.

[14] Lady Anne Lytcott to James Edward, 26 November 1718, HMC, *Stuart*, VII, p. 573; Luttrell, *Brief Historical Relation*, I, pp. 499, 560; Daniel Arthur to Sir Henry Browne, 28 October 1689, AAW, Browne MSS, 15.

[15] Daniel Arthur to Daniel Arthur (his son), 1 August 1690, AAW, Browne MSS, 41.

[16] Commission papers, *CSPD 1687–9*, pp. 282, 285, 289, 311; Shevson to Shrewsbury, 13 June 1689, *CSPD 1689–90*, p. 146; Rishton to Roger Kenyon, 30 April 1689, HMC, *Kenyon*, p. 211.

1689, those who had found themselves in arms duly resisted the new order.[17] Yet, pitched against the military might of the victorious powers, and with no support forthcoming from the Jacobite forces in Ireland or Scotland, such gestures appeared increasingly futile, and recusant eyes turned to the continent. The onset of a journey into exile is testified in fragments from family papers: in the monthly household accounts of Powis Castle, the signature of the earl is discreetly replaced by that of his son, Lord Montgomery.[18] The extent of the exodus may be gleaned from the lists of those newly resident in St Germain, where the royal family re-assembled their court.[19] With 220 families present by by 1690, and over 40,000 subjects ultimately scattered across Europe, the Catholic flight from the three kingdoms brought a significant demographic dispersal. To one émigré, the court page John Stevens, 'I shall ever esteem it the most glorious action of my life that I made myself one of this number', who had not 'bowed their knees to Baal'.[20]

A large proportion of the émigrés would be formed by the 'wildgeese', penniless Irish soldiers exiled after the battle of the Boyne, but the parochial records of St Germain also show a substantial number of men and women of high social status living in close proximity to the royal household.[21] Prominent among these were fourteen noblemen, half of the complete Catholic peerage, including the courtier lords Waldegrave, Stafford and Teynham and the earls of Powis and Dover, members of the Privy Council. The dowager duchess of Norfolk and the sons of the earl of Salisbury swelled the ranks of noble-blooded Catholics.[22] Later, the two sons of the poet laureate John Dryden brought a taste of a lost literary grandeur from Stuart London.[23] Catholic aristocrats took flight because of their close association with the defeated court. Yet the voyage was also undertaken by sundry leaders of the recusant squirearchy: a salient example of private individuals caught up in the cataclysm of state affairs. Exiles from Sussex included the poet and playwright John Caryll of West Harting and Henry Browne, the descendant of Elizabethan courtiers and diplomats. From the midlands, Giffords of Leicestershire, Booths of Herefordshire, Holmans of Northamptonshire and Plowdens of Shropshire joined the venture abroad. Biddulphs, Perkinses, Fermors

---

17 Luttrell, *Brief Historical Relation*, I, p. 489; *CSPD, William and Mary, 1689*, p. 111.
18 Household accounts of William, Earl of Powis, 1686–1700, BL, Add. MSS, 38,864, fols 56–7.
19 'List of Englishmen with King James', *CSPD, William and Mary, 1690*, p. 375.
20 Robert H. Murray, ed., *The Journal of John Stevens* (Oxford, 1912), pp. 13–14.
21 Natalie Genet-Rouffiac, 'Jacobites in Paris and St Germain-en-Laye', in Eveline Cruickshanks and Edward Corp, eds, *The Stuart Court in Exile and the Jacobites* (London, 1995), pp. 19, 24.
22 Major-General Thomas Maxwell to Henry Browne, 31 March 1691, BL, Add. MSS, 39,662, Browne letter-book, p. 46; Sir Daniel Arthur to Browne, 25 March 1691, BL, Add. MSS, 37,662, pp. 57–8.
23 Charles Dryden to the countess of Perth, 16 October 1697, SCA, Blairs, II, 21/6; John Dryden to Charles Dryden (n.d.), Lambeth Palace Library, Main Series, 933/44.

and Lytcotts emerged from the gentry households of the Thames valley.[24] From the north, two branches of the Strickland family, of Sizergh and Catterick, entered St Germain, while three of the wealthiest landowners – Bartholomew Walmesley and Sir Gervase Clifton from Lancashire, and Thomas Swinburne from Northumberland – also linked their fortunes to James II.[25] Old social networks were reflected and renewed in the national gathering of refugees around England's 'shadow' throne.

The expatriates were united in an analysis tersely expressed by one Jacobite correspondent in April 1691: 'we pray hard one of the new prayers for the king's safe return, for if he fail we are undone'.[26] This belief drove their lives into disruption. Lord Thomas Howard was drowned in 1691, in a frantic attempt to recover his children from England, and it was Henry Browne's anguish that exile meant severance from his daughters: the family lawyer recommended that they be sent to board with a governess since 'there is little possibility of sending them over to their mother, and noe speedy probability of her coming to them'.[27] Many of the émigrés, such as Lady Browne herself, knew very little French. Others, like Colonel John Gifford in Bruges, lacked any place of residence, clustering instead wherever the urgently-boarded vessels left them:

> I have been forced to pawne some of my things to make us Lodge and Eate, it is now tenne days since we have been in this condition … we are forced to live in a publike house for no private house will take Lodgers. We all long to be somewhere in order to serve our King, but I believe this is not the place.[28]

The exiled court would place a serious strain upon its own resources, in its efforts to bring the means of subsistence to dislocated followers.

In contrast to earlier religious disruptions, such as the 'Popish Plot', the force of the Revolution had fallen upon the laity, rather than the priest-

[24] C.E. Lart, *Jacobite Extracts from the Parish Registers of St Germain-en-Laye* (2 vols, 1910–12); Edward Corp, *A Court in Exile: The Stuarts in France, 1689–1718* (Cambridge, 2003), p .139; Richard Fermor to Henry Browne, 16 December 1691, BL, Add. MSS, 37,662, pp. 31–2; Francis Plowden to Browne, 20 March 1691, BL, Add. MSS, 37,662, p. 50; Richard Biddulph to Browne, 23 September 1691, BL, Add. MSS, 37,662, pp. 283–4.

[25] Royal Licence for Thomas Swinburne June 1698, Newcastle, Northumberland CRO, Swinburne MSS, 509; Walmesley account book, 1689, Preston, Lancashire CRO, Walmesley MSS, DDPT/1; John Betham to Lewis Innes, 17 September 1689, SCA, Blairs, I, 127/1; Henry Hornyold, *Genealogical Memoirs of the Family of Strickland of Sizergh* (Kendal, 1928).

[26] Anon. to Henry Browne, 3 April 1691, AAW, Browne MSS, fol. 78.

[27] Cokayne, *Complete Peerage*, IX, p. 626; Arthur to Browne, 21 October 1691, AAW, Browne MSS, 54; Papers of Thomas Howard, Arundel Castle, Howard of Norfolk MSS, Howard family documents 14/1–31.

[28] Colonel John Gifford to Sir Henry Browne, 6 May 1691, BL, Add. MSS 37,662, p. 112.

hood of recusant England. A total Catholic population of only 60,000 encompassed approximately ten per cent of the English gentry and peerage, and these elites had held the recusant world together, with their marriages, common sociability, and education in continental religious houses.[29] Now, a missing squire, a rise in furtive activity or a heightened level of surveillance would make their political vulnerability painfully evident to tenants and neighbours. Even many families who did not voyage abroad concealed secrets. The Gorings of Sussex were reported to be hiding a fugitive 'Irish knight' from the army of James II in their mansion at Highden in November 1690.[30] In the northern counties, those who had entered into Gage's regiments found themselves turned involuntarily into Jacobites by their failure to disband. Lord Gerard of Brandon, the new Lord Lieutenant in Cheshire, observed that 'All the young gentlemen among the papists have absented themselves': an ominous sign for 'I fear this design is laid so deep that all the care and conduct imaginable will not prevent a great deal of mischief'. Circumstances impelled him, he said, to prepare for a state of religious warfare, raising 'Protestant soldiers' to be 'vigorous in the Protestant interest'.[31] From the birth of the new regime, henceforth, a state of mutual suspicion bedevilled the relations between the new governors and their Catholic subjects: both turned instinctively to the language of conflict and conspiracy. The priest-holes, secret exits from mansions, and arrangements for safe passage to the continent – all the resources deployed by recusants in troubled times since the Reformation – appeared to be needed now as urgently as ever before.

The Revolution was thus as strongly *social* as political in its impact on the recusant community. The pre-eminent members of an articulate, cohesive and strikingly integrated lay-leadership had either left the shores, or had been made into subversives. Catholic responses accordingly drew upon images of cosmic disorder to summon up the mood of a society 'lost, astonished and aggrieved'. The poet and exile Jane Barker resolved to 'present the frenzie, mallice and madness of our present times', with a world rocked by the 'blazing meteors' of 'ruin and mischief'.

> I am compelled to leave my native shore
> In foreign lands my country's crimes deplore.[32]

Even retrospective writings were marked by a sense of incomprehension. In 1708, from his cell in the monastery of St Edmund's, Paris, the monk Benet

---

[29] Miller, *Popery and Politics*, p. 12; Beales, *Education under Penalty*, pp. 129–80.

[30] Arthur to Browne, 14 November 1690, AAW, Browne MSS, 55.

[31] Lord Gerard of Brandon to the earl of Shrewsbury, 15 June 1689, *CSPD 1689–90*, pp. 150–1.

[32] Jane Barker, 'A Collection of Poems Referring to the Times', 1700–1, BL, Add. MSS, 21,621, fols 5, 46, 58.

Weldon agonised at 'the wickedness, which, in the depths of God's judge-ment, was then permitted to prevail'. If such images seemed apocalyptic, this was because Barker and Weldon shared one important quality: they were converts, who had embraced Catholicism in the high noon of James II's reign, and felt that they lived out his fate in their own lives.[33] The form they chose was one of spiritual autobiography, with a narrative of zealotry and martyrdom.

A somewhat different tone was struck in a letter from Captain Stephen Tempest, a young Yorkshire gentleman of ancient recusant stock, to his brother, from the royal camp at Dublin in March 1689. Tempest abhorred the Revolution, and he advised his family to ensure that their 'loyalty be of the same standing as when I left you'. However, he expressed his response not in religious, but patriotic terms: 'Wee are borne Englishmen and nature seems to have inspired every one of us with the love of his country.' William of Orange was to be resisted from a sense of national honour: 'Can we then see him [James] banish't, heare him ill-spoke of, see him betrayed and see his throne filled with those water rats and frogs of Dutchmen, and not feel a generous heart urge us to revenge him?' When the religious theme *did* emerge, it was careful and discreet, though clear in its implications as to the direction of Catholic allegiance:

> I would not live so neare being an ill subject as to state need of self-interest to put you in minde of yr duty to yr Prince, but 'tis a happiness when both the motives meet, and I think they never did more so at this time.

Tempest's outlook was shaped by 'the natural allegiance we owe to our prince', when 'the aire we breathe ought to inspire us with devotion to him'.[34] He fought, he said, not as a Catholic but as a loyal English patriot, confronting a foreign conquest.

These two sentiments: the stark martyrology of the convert authors, offset by the bluff patriotism of the recusant squire, would echo through subsequent Catholic writings. The difference in emphasis was the product of a complex historical experience. The quality traceable in Stephen Tempest's letter was a Catholic mindset formed not in the conversion narrative of Barker or Weldon, but through a longer intellectual struggle. Over the course of a century, Catholics had sought to turn themselves from pariahs into patriots: 'His Majesty's most loyal subjects'. For a figure like Tempest, Jacobitism began not as a movement but as a *moment* in recusant history, when the

---

[33] Weldon, 'A Collection of Sundry things yt may contribute to ye History of Great Brittain's late Glorious Monarch', BL, Add. MSS, 10,118, p. 17; Barker, 'Poems', BL, Add. MSS, 21,621, fols 10, 25; Katherine King, *Jane Barker, Exile: A Literary Career 1675–1725* (Oxford, 2000), pp. 101–105.
[34] 'Letter of Mr Tempest to his brother', March 1689, Bodleian Library, Carte MSS, 181, fols 184–5.

loyalties and affections that comprised an English Catholic mentality were being tested, as never before.

The construction of a Catholic patriot

Traditional historiography, Whig and Catholic, professed that the recusant community in seventeenth-century England occupied a place akin to that of the Huguenots in Bourbon France, formally excluded from essential regions of public life, and denounced by their detractors as violently alien to the national *esprit de corps*. This perception was entrenched within Protestant confessional literature, and dramatised in the carnivals, processions and pope-burnings that marked the national commemorations on November 5th. Here, to a man, Catholics became idolaters, spies, debauchers and pyromaniacs, aligned with images of concealed daggers, psychotic monks and night riders.[35] In older scholarly narratives, the flight of the recusant elites in 1688 appeared the climax of a century of growing alienation; the English Catholic parallel to the revocation of the Edict of Nantes, when even *de facto* toleration seemed to have collapsed, and suppressed enmities finally burst into the open. The myth and memory of Elizabethan and Jacobean plots certainly left the Catholic community scarred with notions of sedition, subject to attacks from press and pulpit not dissimilar to the rhetoric levelled against Huguenots. However, even in the more volatile Tudor moments, most recusants had never envisaged themselves as an armed and vigorous opposition, advocating resistance to princes of another faith. In the words of one pamphleteer, 'We Abhor, we Renounce, we *Abominate* such principles. We protest against them and seal our Protestations with our Dying Breaths. What can we say? What can we do more?'[36] Such was their confidence in this argument that recusant visibility had been a growing phenomenon within the English polity. After 1603, when the succession of the son to Mary, Queen of Scots, appeared to herald more favourable prospects for religious liberty, Catholics had entered into a sustained interaction with the debates of the kingdom, linking their aspirations very closely to the welfare of the house of Stuart. The Glorious Revolution brought the unforeseen downfall of a century-long political strategy conceived to advance Catholic interests, raise their profile at court, and work towards the goal of a formal toleration.

In Catholic eyes, the most persuasive case to the nation came from the existence of the hundreds of recusant families of high social status, living peacefully and harmoniously with the Protestant majority, to undermine in

---

[35] John Kenyon, *The Popish Plot* (London, 1972), p. 4.
[36] James Maurus Corker, *Roman Catholick Principles, with reference to God and the King* (1680), p. 4.

their daily lives the public nightmare of 'popery'. Writing from Rome in 1681, Cardinal Philip Howard reminded his brother the duke of Norfolk that preserving 'the honour of your noble famely' represented the best way to safeguard the faith, 'in that part of the world wheare our Religion is judged of by our actions'.[37] Many of the émigrés of 1688 sustained kinship connections to the Protestant governing classes. The correspondence of Henry Browne included missives from his cousins Lady Danby and the duchess of Somerset, expressing concern for the family's welfare.[38] After the death of Lord Thomas Howard, his children were raised under their Anglican cousin, the earl of Carlisle.[39] The familiar depiction of a 'catacomb culture' behind English Catholicism evokes one dimension of the early modern experience, but it sums up only half of the recusant identity. Catholic writings took equal stimulus from the gentry traditions of public charity and paternalism: the preservation of the country house ideal that underpinned the life of the shires.[40] Contemplating his choice 'If Heaven the grateful ruling would give/ That I might choose my method, how I would live', the future Jacobite statesman John Caryll craved 'a little garden gratefull to the eye ... a study plaid/ With all the noble authors guid', stirred only in times of need to 'oblige my country, or to serve my King', with 'my tongue, my pen, my counsel, my sword.'[41] The recusant squires had imbibed a patriotic spirit similar to the 'country' principles animating the Protestant gentry, pressing in this case their sense of virtuous separation from the Holy See. The affirmation of the earl of Bristol that he belonged to the 'Church not the Court, of Rome' informed William Blundell's warm sentiment for 'my native and best beloved country' and invigorated the patriotic impulse behind Catholic writings such as Caryll's play The English Princess (1667).[42]

The defence of the Catholic interest intensified during the reign of Charles II. By 1660, the community could place a concrete demonstration of loyalty at the heart of their case, recalling the groundswell of royalist action throughout the years of Civil War that produced such iconic events as the defence of Chichester by Sussex recusants in 1643, the massacre of

[37] Cardinal Howard to the duke of Norfolk, 30 August 1681, Arundel Castle, Howard of Norfolk MSS, Autograph letters 1632–1723, 424.

[38] Arthur to Browne, 17 October 1692, AAW, Browne MSS, 130.

[39] Account book, papers of Thomas Howard, 8th duke of Norfolk, Arundel Castle, Howard of Norfolk MSS, family documents, 15.

[40] This theme gained an echo in Catholic devotional writing, exemplified by the Jesuit John Huddleston's The Phoenix, the Sepulchre and the Candle (1691), a eulogy to the marchioness of Winchester.

[41] 'Poems', BL, Add. MSS, 28,253, fols 116–17.

[42] William Cobbett, ed., The Parliamentary History of England, II, p. 564; Blundell, ed., Blundell Letters, p. 210; John Caryll, The English Princess (1667). See Howard Erskine-Hill, 'John, First Lord Caryll of Durford and the Caryll Papers', in Eveline Cruickshanks and Edward Corp, eds, The Stuart Court in Exile and the Jacobites (London, 1995), pp. 73–89, at pp. 76–7.

the mainly Catholic garrison at Basing House in 1645 and the sheltering of Charles II by Benedictine monks after the battle of Worcester.[43] The martyrologies composed by the Jesuit Ambrose Corbie identified Catholic deaths after 1641 as sacrifices to protect the throne of England against iconoclasts, just as they had suffered to preserve the altars of the 'King of Kings'.[44] Catholic squires framed the Civil War experience within their mental and physical worlds. Portraits of armour-clad family patriarchs lined the walls of Stonyhurst and Oxburgh Hall, the Throckmortons preserved the sword wielded for Charles I at Edgehill, and it was unsurprising that John Caryll, whose mind dwelt more on classical antiquity, chose to salute the soldier-statesman Fabius Maximus for his contribution to Dryden's rendering of *Plutarch's Lives*.[45] Catholic innocence of plots, dogma and foreign allegiances could be vindicated, it was claimed, when family traditions cast light on a mind attuned to the obligations of national loyalty. The Jesuit John Warner considered the humiliation of the Gunpowder Plot in relation to the Civil War, and concluded that: 'by their long fidelity through so many years ... by the way they shed their blood and sacrificed their lives to save the King's life, the Catholics have long since washed away that stain'.[46]

In pamphlet literature and private treatises, Catholics forged a shield for liberty and toleration out of Civil War memories, looking to address 'our perceived defect of loyalty' by redefining allegiance in terms of military virtue rather than simply adherence to the monarch's religion. A committee of the secular clergy posited in 1661 that it was not the Catholic faith in itself that roused animosity, but its association with 'Practises or of Principles destructive to Government'. They believed that the widened political possibilities of the Restoration presented an opportunity to show how 'meer religion' stood quite apart from such legends as the papal deposing power, or the belief that 'mental reservations' could override covenants sworn with men outside the faith.[47] Catholic loyalists built their case upon a dualist conception of human affairs, in which 'the wisdom of the divine providence' left papal authority caged behind the realm of 'matters spiritual', while civil

---

[43] Aveling, *Handle and the Axe*, pp. 162–7; P.R. Newman, 'Catholic Royalist Activities in the North, 1642–46', *Recusant History*, 14 (1977), pp. 26–38; Blundell, ed., *Blundell Letters*, pp. 10–17.

[44] Susannah Brietz Monta, *Martyrdom and Literature in Early Modern England* (Cambridge, 2005), pp. 220–4.

[45] John Caryll, 'Fabius Maximus', in *Plutarch's lives translated from the Greek by several hands; to which is prefixt the life of Plutarch* (5 vols, London, 1683), I, pp. 600–51.

[46] John Warner, *History of the Presbyterian Plot* (2 vols, Catholic Record Society, London, 1953), p. 145.

[47] *A Declaration of Allegiance to His Majesty, made by the Dean and Chapter of Catholic English Clergy* (1661). Private tracts included John Caryll, 'Not Guilty, or the Plea of Catholicks in England', BL, Add. MSS, 28,252, fols 141–50, a variant of which can also be found in the papers of the Belson family.

loyalties belonged exclusively to the temporal sovereign.[48] On this reasoning, Lord Henry Howard gave his word that: 'should the Pope himself come with an army to invade us, I dare swear that nere an understanding Papist in England but would upon that scoare shoot a Bullett in his head'.[49] Fidelity to a prince, according to John Caryll, was an imperative for 'all men indifferently and equally, be they Catholic or Protestant' leaving men 'bound with our lives to defend the sacred person of His Majesty'.[50] The truth of these maxims had, they added, been showcased across the two previous decades, when it was not 'popery' but Protestant parliamentary radicalism 'maskt under pretext of Religion' that had taken the life of Charles I.

Catholic authors aimed principally to engage an Anglican royalist tendency in the political nation, targeting their appeals to those Protestants who, in the words of John Caryll, 'pretend a good blood in their veins, & have any value for their ancestry'. Caryll served the reminder that by disavowing 'the ancient faith of the three kingdoms', Protestants would 'damne the souls of the whole race of their progenitors', in an act equating to 'Spirituall Parricide'.[51] In pressing to receive the same 'respect and understanding' that the Early Church Fathers offered towards Jews, they could manufacture a conservative case for the extension of Catholic liberty, and distinguish themselves from other Nonconformists. In the aftermath of the Civil War, Catholic literature was duly enlivened by converts from the Anglican faith, attracted by the historic laws, hierarchy and authority of 'the ancient mother church', at a time when the disputed Protestant institutions appeared no longer to be providing the glue for civil peace. The duchess of York attributed her epiphany to a reading of Peter Heylin's High Church *History of the Reformation*.[52] Another convert, the monk Hugh Serenus Cressy, sought to reclaim the Erasmian tradition in English religion, importing into the Catholic Church an idea of political moderation and religious toleration informed by his past membership of Viscount Falkland's Great Tew circle.[53] Cressy's *Exomologesis* (1647) pressed for the old faith to flower again, as the only way to heal 'these most unnatural bloody dissensions in Great Brittaine' and rekindle unity through the hand of divine providence rather than earthly coercion.[54]

---

[48] Appeal for toleration 'upon ye principles of the Declaration of Breda', Oxford, Oxfordshire CRO, Belson MSS, F/1/4/MS/7.

[49] Caryll, 'Not Guilty', BL, Add. MSS, 28,252, fol. 151; 'Letter in Defence of Catholicks', 1679, BL, Add. MSS, 28,252, fols 47–8.

[50] 'Not Guilty', BL, Add. MSS, 28,252, fols 147–8.

[51] CRS, 'Dominicana', pp. 198–9; John Caryll, 'Not Guilty', BL, Add. MSS, 28,252, fol. 146.

[52] Weldon, 'Collection', BL, Add. MSS, 10,118, fol. 332.

[53] David Lunn, *The English Benedictines, 154–1688* (London, 1980), pp. 130–3; Cressy, *Fanaticism Fanatically Imputed to the Catholick Church* (1672).

[54] Hugh Serenus Cressy, *Exomologesis* (1647), pp. 8, 17; Anthony Wood, *Athenae Oxoniensis* (3 vols, 3rd edn, London, 1817), III, p. 145.

Implicitly, Catholics also responded to the scent of religious sympathy growing within the Stuart court itself: an undertone in regal life before the Civil War that burgeoned in the wake of continental experiences during the Interregnum. Royal favour had kept converts such as the diplomat Sir Richard Bulstrode in employment and allowed former Civil War exiles such as Lord Arlington to return to court office with their religious sympathies at best somewhat ambiguous.[55] In Somerset House, the retinue of Queen Catherine of Braganza supported a Catholic printing press, provided places for members of the Scrope, Roper and Throckmorton families, and sheltered convert clergymen such as Cressy and Francis Nicholson.[56] Reopening dialogue between England the Holy See, the queen's entourage launched the career of Philip Howard of Norfolk, Catherine's former almoner, on his ascent to the Roman Cardinalate.[57] The public domain was being opened up to a Catholic circle far wider than the Europeanised networks usually associated with the court, and with recusant laymen maintaining a presence in the legal profession and sitting on the board of the Royal Africa Company, the expectations of the community were starting to amplify.[58] The Howard circle looked to the predilections of the monarchy to protect Catholics from 'the malitious dictates of the Rigid Presbiterians' who appeared whenever England was 'troubled with a Parliament'.[59] Emboldened by private exchanges at court in 1672, Serenus Cressy spelt out his dream of re-union between England and Rome, and appealed to Charles II to usher in a reformed Catholic church with clerical appointments under regal control, supporting vernacular services, clerical marriage, and toleration to those outside its fold.[60] The opportunities – and the dangers – were confirmed in 1673, when the smoking out of the duke of York as a secret papist ensured

---

[55] Sir Richard Bulstrode, Memoirs and reflections upon the reign and government of King Charles I and King Charles II (1721); V. Barbour, Henry Bennet, Earl of Arlington, Secretary of State to Charles II (Washington, 1914).

[56] Charles Dodd, The Church History of England ... chiefly with regard to Catholicks (4 vols, London, 1737–1742), III, p. 462; will of Dame Mary Scope, private collection, Tempest MSS, wills, 38; Commission of royal appointment, Warwickshire CRO, Throckmorton MSS, LCB 39; Edward Coleman to Sir Richard Bulstrode, 21 July 1676, Harry Ransom Humanities Research Center, University of Texas at Austin, Pforzheimer MS 103C, Box 7. I am grateful to Stephen Taylor for the latter reference.

[57] Philip Howard to Henry Howard, 21 September 1671, Arundel Castle, Howard of Norfolk MSS, Autograph letters, 409.

[58] Petition of the Royal Africa Company, 2 January 1665, National Archives, State Papers 29/110/13; Sir George Duckett, The Penal Laws and the Test Acts (2 vols, London, 1882–83), I, p. 240.

[59] Henry Howard to William Lesley, 30 August 1667, Arundel Castle, Howard of Norfolk MSS, Autograph Letters, 399; Philip Howard to Henry Howard, 21 September 1671, Howard of Norfolk MSS, Autograph letters, 409.

[60] Patricia Bruckmann, '"Paradice it selfe": Hugh Cressy and Church Unity', in Kevin L. Cope, ed., Ideas, Aesthetics and Inquiries in the Early Modern Era (New York, 1997), pp. 83–107.

that the controversy of Catholic life in a Protestant kingdom would now touch very closely on the affairs of the ruling dynasty.

The pursuit of court and Anglican alliances enabled Catholics to navigate the snares and pitfalls of the public sphere, when a period of greater exposure was also a time of renewed anxiety, and anti-popery, in the words of one private treatise, was once again 'ye spirit which walks ye nation'.[61] Already buffeted by suspicion following the Great Fire of 1666, and formally cast out of public offices by the Test Act in 1673, Catholic fears were crowned in 1678, when rumours of a 'Popish Plot' sparked the first parliamentary attempt to exclude the duke of York from the royal succession, and unleashed a national panic that brought the death of thirty-five prominent – and largely moderate-minded – recusants.[62] Throughout the storm, Catholics aimed to counter their detractors by promoting a discourse that kept memories of the Civil War alive, looking to reinvigorate the old Cavalier alliance and isolate the anti-court partisans in the Whig party as the real threat to the realm, the ghosts of Puritans past. Sir John Lytcott argued that the Catholic plight could be presented as the touchstone for a greater crisis in the kingdom, unleashed by the 'Faction that has made most of the Crowns in Europe totter'.[63] In newsletters sent to the diaspora communities in France, Lytcott and the Somerset House courtier George Throckmorton commented that a rediscovery of 'truth and unity' rested on the success of the emergent Anglican Tory party, represented in the writings of John Dryden and Roger L'Estrange, against 'the subtlety and insolence of the phanatic'.[64] Throckmorton embraced the label Tory – a name 'we accept, and intend by obedience to the Crowne to give credit to' – while Lord Thomas Howard participated in the campaigns to elect loyal sheriffs in the capital.[65]

The Exclusion Crisis appeared to show that for those Catholics who dared to foray into the public realm, the failure to articulate a compelling defence could result in fatal consequences. Yet, conversely, the very polarisation of the public realm unveiled a glimmer of political possibility. As Whig zealots started to overreach themselves, Catholic landowners found themselves fortified by sundry examples of support from Tory neighbours, while London juries began to return verdicts of 'not guilty' on the remaining 'plot' suspects, and the king proceeded to adopt a more assertive voice in

---

[61] 'Reflections upon ye Expediency of a War at present with France', BL, Add. MSS, 28,252, fol. 136.

[62] The outstanding account remains John Kenyon, *The Popish Plot* (London, 1972).

[63] Sir John Lytcott to Sir Robert Throckmorton, 20 April 1682, Warwickshire CRO, Throckmorton MSS, LCB/17.

[64] Thockmorton newsletters, 21 December 1681, 2 April 1683, Warwickshire CRO, Throckmorton MSS, LCB/17.

[65] Ibid.; Lord Thomas Howard to Cardinal Howard, 26 June 1682, Arundel Castle, Howard of Norfolk MSS, Miscellaneous Correspondence, 57.

defence of his brother's right to the throne.[66] In 1681, with the fall of the last Exclusionist Parliament, some recusants, according to Lytcott, had glimpsed a fresh opportunity and 'begin to send forth here and there expedients for a toleration'.[67] From Sussex to Northumberland, Catholics who had been thrown into the county gaols were released with honour, and returned to the heart of county society.[68] John Caryll's verse *Brisseis to Achilles* hinted that true loyalty could find a hearing in England, when 'Tyrants and Wolves can fight, Love is the test/ Distinguishing the hero from the Beast.'[69] By 1685, the principle of absolute allegiance had therefore given English Catholics the rhetorical armouring with which to approach the public arena. As the lawyer and Popish Plot martyr Richard Langhorne had put it prophetically: 'These are our known principles, by the strict professing of which we live and die with comfort, though poor and passing by our last home to the Gibbet.'[70] But the language of Catholic loyalty was not actuated simply by love of the irenic virtues: it conveyed a hard-headed calculation as to the best way to shape the Stuart realm, when the openings in Restoration London were providing a new terrain to support Catholic political projects. Four years after the securing of the royal succession, Charles II reportedly gave his soul to the Catholic faith.[71] After his death, the persistence of recusants appeared to bear fruit, when England enthroned a Catholic king.

James II and the problem of France

As James II ascended the throne, recusants dared to give words to the hope suppressed over thirteen decades of forbearance. John Warner heralded 'an end contrary to all expectation, preordained by God alone from eternity and brought about by the secret workings of his hand'.[72] As the penal laws went into suspension, James arguing wryly that he need have few doubts as to the loyalty of his Catholic subjects, members of the communion converged upon London to hear the sermons, attend services in the Chapel Royal, and soak up an atmosphere conducive to their liberty.[73] The Jesuit Edward Scarisbrick condemned the 'sacrilegious murder' of Charles I, and suggested

---

66 Kenyon, *Popish Plot*, pp. 123, 227.
67 Throckmorton Newsletters, 21 December 1681, Warwickshire CRO, Throckmorton MSS, LCB/17.
68 Swinburne Pedigree, 1712, Northumberland CRO, Swinburne MSS, 6/95; H.D. Gordon, *The History of Harting* (London, 1877), p. 93.
69 Caryll, *Brisseis to Achilles*, in Dryden, ed., *Ovid's Epistles, translated by several hands* (1684), p. 244.
70 Blundell, ed., *Blundell Letters*, p. 116; Kenyon, *Popish Plot*, pp. 185–8.
71 John Miller, *James II: A Study in Kingship* (London, 1978), p. 40; Weldon, 'Collection', BL, Add. MSS, 10,118, fols 61–4; Weldon, *Chronological Notes*, p. 192.
72 Warner, *Plot*, II, p. 184.
73 Miller, *Popery*, pp. 210, 218; Blundell, ed., *Blundell Letters*, pp. 244–7.

that, as recusants had stood faithfully by a non-communicant, so the Protestant majority must now repay the debt.[74] Three years later, as the queen, Mary of Modena, prepared to give birth, the midwife Elizabeth Cellier took from a 'learned Rabbi' the lesson of how Hebrew nursemaids defied Egyptian commands to protect the infants of ancient Israel: now she looked to the birth of 'another Moses ... a Mighty Captain for the Nation, [to] lead to Battle the Soldiers which the Hospital will preserve for him'.[75] News of the prince's birth rang out through the exiled Catholic world, with celebrations directed by James's diplomats. Lord Thomas Howard organised a public feast in Rome, distributing alms to the poor, while Sir Richard Bulstrode laid on lavish festivities from his embassy in Brussels, prophesying that, with 'this glorious starr now restored to our Hemispheer', history would see 'the three kingdoms restored to their ancient greatness and splendour'.[76] For English Catholics, a long lineage of virtue through trial appeared, finally, to find its providential reward.

Before the political implications had been explored, *religious* rebirth lay at the heart of Catholic considerations. Under the Vicar Apostolic, John Leyburne, the flock came into the open, and the gentry committed themselves with schools and chapels, underwritten by notables such as Lord Powis at Welshpool, and the Eystons of East Hendred.[77] The declarations of the priesthood carefully concentrated on a gentle prescription for 'planting the faith'.[78] John Warner voiced dreams of 'Judah and Israel living without fear, each man under his vine and his fig tree', having 'melted their swords into ploughshares and their spears into pruning hooks'.[79] The Benedictine Philip Ellis disavowed his order's claims over their old monastic lands: 'We desire nothing should be restored but our Reputation, and to be thought by our fellow Countrymen, neither Pernicious nor Useless members of our Country.'[80] John Leyburne's *Pastoral Letter* of January 1688 urged the flock to 'discharge of your duty in an edifying manner', concerned with 'spiritual

[74] Edward Scarisbrick, *Catholic Loyalty upon the subject of Government and Obedience* (London, 1686), p. 4; Geoffrey Holt, 'Edward Scarisbrick (1639–1709): A Royal Preacher', *Recusant History*, 23 (1996–97), pp. 159–65.

[75] Elizabeth Cellier, *An Answer to Queries, concerning the Colledg of Midwives* (1688), p. 7.

[76] Sir John Lytcott to Sir Richard Bulstrode, 9 October 1688, Bulstrode papers, British Library, Egerton MSS, 3683, fols 161–2; Sir Richard Bulstrode to Queen Mary, 16 July 1688, BL, Add. MSS, 28,225, fols 338–9.

[77] Miller, *Popery and Politics*, p. 11; Luttrell, *Brief Historical Relation*, I, pp. 391, 430, 433; Henry Foley, *Records of the English Province of the Society of Jesus* (7 vols, London, 1877–83), V, pp. 488, 943.

[78] Thomas Nicolson to William Leslie, 1 February 1690, SCA, Blairs, I, 132/2.

[79] Warner, *Plot*, p. 176; Blundell, *Letters*, p. 235.

[80] Douai Abbey, Woolhampton MSS, Weldon, 'Memorials' (5 vols), IV, p. 10, V, pp. 311–12; *The Ellis Correspondence*, ed. G.A. Ellis (2 vols, London, 1829), I, pp. 132, 133–4, 138.

improvements', not political or material hegemony. Their faith was to speak of 'liberty' and 'charity', even 'inoffensiveness', shot through with humility that 'A great part of the nation, whose persuasion in points of religion, doth differ from yours, is willing to enter into a friendly correspondence with you.' He directed a latent warning to the king's council: 'Take care to prevent and suppress all irregular motions ... if others do repine at being sharers in your liberty which themselves do enjoy to a much greater advantage, the most effective means to convince them of their error is to edify them by your good example.' As a purely English affair, recusant revival could be ascribed to 'the merciful Providence of God and the Piety of His Majesty', without acknowledgement of any debt to Rome, and the letter closed by saluting 'the God of Peace', the pastor of the sheep, risen from the dead 'in the Blood of the Eternal Testament'.[81] Such words captured the delicate paradox of recusant ambitions: a visionary project to be accomplished by quietist methods.

However, the attempt to re-order the kingdom took place in an extremely uneasy setting: a climate overshadowed by the alternative religious revolution pioneered by James II's cousin and putative ally Louis XIV in France, where the policy of coercion and inquisition against Protestant communities, together with the plan for military expansion on the continent, opened up a wellspring of suspicion towards the intentions of a Catholic monarch in England.[82] As early as 1683, with Huguenot refugees starting to seek shelter in England, George Throckmorton had warned that events on the continent were inspiring 'subscriptions towards the reprinting of Foxe's Book of Martyrs' in London.[83] By 1686, the apparent indifference of James II was rousing envenomed satire against a king with eyes 'fast closed with the enchanted slumbers of the French Delilah'.[84] For heightened Protestant consciences, the image of 'popery' was shifting away from Rome and Spain towards the new 'universal monarch' in Versailles, with serious implications for religious harmony in England. One anonymous philippic parodied a *Catholic Hymn* in a claim to unearth the true motivations of the emancipated recusants: 'Much may be done, by way of Dragoon/ As France has taught us to Fashion/ Religion to plant/ By true Church Militant/ Far better than convocation'.[85] For years after the Revolution had swept this fear away, Jacobites would be goaded that 'If the King had followed his own

---

[81] *Pastoral Letter from the four Catholic Bishops to the Lay Catholics of England* (1688).

[82] J.F. Bosher, 'The Franco-Catholic Danger, 1660–1715', *History*, 79 (1994), pp. 5–30; Steven Pincus, 'From Butterboxes to Wooden Shoes: The Shift in English Popular Sentiment from anti-Dutch to anti-French in the 1670s', *Historical Journal*, 38 (1996), pp. 333–61.

[83] George Throckmorton to Sir Robert Throckmorton 1 March 1682/3, Warwickshire CRO, Throckmorton MSS, LCB 17.

[84] *The Design of France against England and Holland* (1686), p. 2.

[85] Catholic hymn on the birth of the Prince of Wales ([London: s.n.], 1688).

Interest, he might have enjoyed his three Kingdoms ... professed his Religion, favoured his Catholick Subjects ... But instead of pursuing his own Interest, he blindly embraced that of France.'[86] If it was a disputed claim, it was enough to haunt the recusant imagination. As Bishop Nicolson lamented, the concern that 'the King of France intended the destruction of all protestantes, and that it was according to his religion to do so ... had a dismall influence to alienate the hearts of [James II's] subjects'.[87]

The problem posed for recusants by Louis XIV was just as pertinent to the international as the domestic agenda. French military expansion reawakened old enmities at the heart of Catholic Europe, when the crowns of Austria and Spain united their interests with William of Orange to enter the League of Augsburg in 1686, and, even before Louis's annexation of Avignon in September 1688, his designs over the French church had pushed Pope Innocent XI towards an equally strident opposition. In Rome, James II himself stood accused of being at best a vainglorious imitator, at worst a tool of the Sun King, averting his eyes from 'the common concerns of Europe': the estrangement from international coreligionists was affirmed when the Elector Palatine dissociated himself from the funds for London chapels raised by his own envoy.[88] To judge their public and private commentary, most English recusants were not immune to these concerns, and had no desire for James II to model himself on 'the Leviathan of France ... that powerful and jealous prince', in William Blundell's view.[89] Sources of Catholic opposition to France had risen at court, where the lords Arlington and Carlingford reactivated an older pro-Habsburg position, pressing for support for France's enemies in Austria and Spain with a view to preserving 'the balance of Europe'.[90] Similar assertions flowered among the Braganza retinue, where chapel clergy from the English and Irish Colleges of Lisbon framed their opposition to 'universal monarchy' in the language of Portuguese resistance to the Spanish crown.[91] John Caryll repudiated the persecuting tendencies of

[86] A view of the true interest of the several states of Europe (1689), p. 6.

[87] Thomas Nicolson to William Leslie, 1 February 1688, SCA, Blairs, I, 132/2.

[88] His Holyness the Pope of Rome's declaration against the French king, Louis the 14th (1689); Bishop Burnet's History of the Reign of James the Second; Notes by the earl of Dartmouth, Speaker Onslow and Dean Swift (Oxford, 1852), pp. 92–3; James Stanford, Account Book 1685–1688, in Tempest MSS (private collection); G.A. Ellis, ed., The Ellis Correspondence (2 vols, London, 1829), I, letters 23, 41.

[89] 'Letter in Defence of Catholicks', 1679, BL, Add. MSS, 28,252; Blundell, ed., Blundell Letters, p. 235.

[90] Carlingford to Ormonde, 2 July 1667, Bodleian Library, Carte MSS, 35, fol. 520; A free conference touching the present state of England both at home and abroad in order to the designs of France (1678); T. Barker, Army, Aristocracy, Monarchy: Essays on War, Society and Government in Austria, 1618–1780 (Boulder, Colorado, 1982), pp. 56–8.

[91] Edward Corp, 'Catherine of Braganza and Cultural Politics', in Clarissa Campbell Orr, ed., Queenship in Britain 1660–1837: Royal Patronage, Court Culture and Dynastic Politics (Manchester, 2004), pp. 53–73; Sharratt, ed., Lisbon College Register 1628–1813 (CRS,

'the Roman religion as it is practised in France', and concurred that England had a legitimate desire to 'secure ourselves from ye Danger of that over-grown power'.[92] George Throckmorton even doubted the Catholicity of the French realm, suggesting that vaulting ambition would turn the sovereign into 'another Henry 8th'.[93] However, such expressions were not sufficient to spare recusant leaders the ramifications of French policy. Since the royal marriage to Henrietta Maria six decades earlier, when Madrid's ambassador complained that recusants were deserting his chapel and 'going over to the French', the English Catholic leadership had been gravitating towards the political and religious example of Bourbon realm, in a shift that rendered it extremely difficult to achieve detachment from the 'Sun King'.[94]

By 1685, on a purely material level, the recusant gentry had amassed substantial interests in the French kingdom, ranging from Parisian residences to stocks in the Hotel de Ville corporation: in John Caryll words, 'the best security for English Catholics', should their domestic resources fail them.[95] However, the investment was as potently religious as commercial, with the Benedictine convent at Paris and the seminary of St Gregory's – affiliated to the Sorbonne – prominent among the new institutions opened since the Civil War, serving to draw Catholic pupils away from rival centres of education in Spain and leaving recusant libraries stocked with the pastoral and spiritual literature of the French Counter-Reformation.[96] However, recusants owed a deeper ideological debt to the Bourbon dominion. The Gallican rule of faith, enlarging the authority of national kingdoms over the Catholic Church, and shutting out the Holy See from the temporal domain, had given vital inspiration to Englishmen like Cressy who lamented the errors of Catholics 'zealously addicted to the Spaniards and [who] by their example exalted in Books the Power and Jurisdiction of the court of Rome'.[97] The secular clergy stood especially steeped in the Gallican world-view, in homage to the past friendship between Bishop Richard Smith and Cardinal Richelieu, and in 1661 their committee claimed ratification from

Southampton, 1991), pp. 88, 166–7, 173–6; Anthony Pagden, *Lords of all the World: Ideologies of Empire in Spain, Britain and France c.1500–c.1800* (New Haven, 1995), pp. 44–9.

92 Caryll, 'Not Guilty', BL, Add. MSS, 28,252, fol. 151; 'Edmund Bury Hutchinson' [alias Caryll], 'A Letter in Defence of Catholicks', 1679, BL, Add. MSS, 28,252, fols 43–56, at fols 47–8; 'Reflections upon ye Expediency of a War at present with France', 1687, BL, Add. MSS, 28,252, fol. 136.

93 George Throckmorton, newsletter, 6 April 1682, Warwickshire CRO, Throckmorton MSS, LCB/17.

94 Questier, *Catholicism and Community*, p. 415.

95 Diary of David Nairne, National Library of Scotland, 23 May 1697; John Caryll to Mary Caryll, 17 November 1706, BL, Add. MSS, 28,226, fols 125–6.

96 John Betham to James Gordon, 15 August 1693, AAW, St Gregory's Seminary MSS, 235; Lunn, *Benedictines*, pp. 197–217.

97 Serenus Cressy, 'On Reunion', 1671, BL, Add. MSS, 65,139, fol. 8

the Sorbonne for the case that recusants could, in conscience, take an oath to Charles II.[98] The importance of the link was reaffirmed in the Benedictine Henry Joseph Johnston's translations from Bishop Bossuet of Meaux, the apologist for the court of Versailles, whose rejection of 'ultramontane opinions' as 'the greatest obstacle to the conversion of heretical kings' spoke pointedly to an English sensibility.[99]

Most recusants had therefore invested in the hope that the French Catholic Church might provide an acceptable model to present to their compatriots: an ideal subject to continuing modification, but alluding more frequently to the *politique* tradition associated with Henri IV than the contemporary absolutism of Louis XIV.[100] The earl of Castlemaine had – fatally – cited the protections for Huguenots under the Edict of Nantes in 1673 as an example of the pragmatic toleration which, he claimed, flowed through the Gallican ideal.[101] Even Cardinal Howard, no admirer of Louis, agreed that the exiled houses on French territory offered recusant children a religion 'naturally more affected to our nation': the experience of Rome should wait for 'a more mature adge'.[102] The precedents of the Gallican Church offered Catholics grounds to address the claims of critics like John Evelyn that 'There were never any two doctrines more conformable' than the Council of Trent and the Rump Parliament.[103] Recusants had sought to engage the Tory tendency in English politics by outlining the monarchical religion endorsed in Paris as an acceptable *via media* between the twin perils of papal and Calvinist fanaticism, extracting ideas of commonality between the French Church and the Anglican establishment.[104] Before his conversion, John Dryden dedicated to Charles II a translation of Louis Maimbourg's history of the French wars of religion, with an approving nod to

[98] 'A Profession of Allegiance', 1661, in Oxfordshire CRO, Belson MSS, F/1/4/MS/30; 'Declaration by the doctors of theology at Paris', 1680, Belson MSS F/1/4/MS/32–33; Questier, *Catholicism and Community*, pp. 378–83, 415.

[99] Henry Joseph Johnston, *Vindication of the Bishop of Condom's Exposition of the Doctrine of the Catholic Church* (1680); John Betham to James Gordon, 15 August 1693, AAW, St Gregory's Seminary MSS, 235; François Gaquère, *Vers l'Unité chrétienne: James Drummond et Bossuet, leurs correspondance 1685–1704* (Paris, 1956), p. 111.

[100] Quentin Skinner, *The Foundations of Modern Political Thought*, II, *The Age of Reformation* (Cambridge, 1978), pp. 293–310.

[101] Roger Palmer, earl of Castlemaine, *A Full Answer and Confutation of a Scandalous Pamphlet* (1673), p. 134.

[102] Cardinal Howard to Henry, duke of Norfolk, 30 August 1681, Arundel Castle, Howard of Norfolk MSS, Autograph Letters, 424; Cardinal Howard to Mary, dowager duchess of Norfolk, 31 April 1684, Howard of Norfolk MSS, Autograph Letters, 428.

[103] John Evelyn, *The Pernicious Consequences of the New Heresie of the Jesuites against the King and the State* (1673), p. 4.

[104] J.H.M. Salmon, 'Catholic Resistance Theory and the Royalist Response', in J.H. Burns with M. Goldie, eds., *The Cambridge History of Political Thought, 1450–1700* (Cambridge, 1991).

its attacks upon 'the usurpations and encroachments of the papacy'.[105] But by 1685, when Louis XIV had destroyed that middle ground and Versailles had become not the corrective to 'Spanish Popery', but its reshaped incarnation in Protestant polemic, recusants had no ready answer. The stress of their discourse had fallen on rejecting papal power, teachings of resistance and republican sentiment, not the danger of absolute monarchy. France had provided spiritual, material and intellectual lifeblood for English Catholics: the problem was that by 1688 its model had been dangerously sapped of credibility.

Catholic writers were aware that the link to France left own fortunes caught in the wheels of international forces. However, support for the League of Augsburg appeared scarcely more palatable, when Cardinal Howard lamented that William of Orange remained the patron of an exiled Whig interest, harbouring many of the old Exclusionists of 1679, with all 'the ill influence which they have upon his M's three Kingdomes'.[106] Most recusant leaders leant their voice instead to the Atlanticist vision favoured by James II, Caryll contending that by exploiting her natural sea-wall, England might discover 'a free, undisturbed Trade and Commerce all ye Worlde over, with ye blessings and plenty of Peace'. Entry into the League would render her by contrast 'a lesser figure in ye Confederacy', which would surely be 'frail and short-lived, consisting of so many independent Bodies and Interests'.[107] John Leyburne and the earl of Powis encouraged James II to declare formally that 'he was in league with no prince whatsoever, nor would he come into any alliance, but to stand neuter, so as to be a mediator on occasion'.[108] But when, as Thomas Howard reported from Rome, 'the differences between this Court and France run high, every day producing something new, to widen old breaches', this ambition appeared increasingly stripped of credence.[109] Caught between two equally unattractive choices, the Stuarts and their English Catholic supporters risked moving not towards honourable neutrality, but international isolation. By December 1688, James II had incurred all the continental animosity but none of the benefits of a perceived Bourbon alliance, and was finding himself left with no option other than to 'trust his subjects'.[110]

---

105 Dryden translation of Maimbourg, *History of the League* (1684).
106 Cardinal Howard to Sir Richard Bulstrode, 24 February 1684/5, Arundel Castle, Howard of Norfolk MSS, Miscellaneous Correspondence, 72; Luttrell, *Brief Historical Relation*, I, p. 385.
107 [Caryll] 'Reflections upon ye Expediency of a War at present with France', 1677, BL, Add. MSS, 28,252, fol. 136; Miller, *James II*, pp. 43–4, 144–5.
108 Ailesbury, *Memoirs*, I, pp. 165–6; Van Citters to States General, 1 November 1687, BL, Add. MSS, 34,510, fol. 123; *Modern history, or, A monethly account of all considerable occurrences* (1688), p. 20.
109 'P. Ronchi' [Lord Thomas Howard to Cardinal Howard], 9 October 1688, Arundel Castle, Howard of Norfolk MSS, Miscellaneous Correspondence, 67.
110 Luttrell, *Brief Historical Relation*, I, p. 478.

Catholic divisions and the course of royal policy

In the light of political developments in France, it was not just Protestant minds that were agitated by the prospect of a radical pro-Catholic enterprise taking shape in England. Responses to the events after 1685 produced an unanticipated cleft in recusant opinion, when the warm enthusiasm for a revived Catholic kingship covered up a far more ambivalent and conflicting set of responses to James's reign. Politically, this divide was shaped between the minority who reacted rapturously to the prospect of 'confessionalisation' along the lines of the Bourbon monarchy, and those Catholics whose Gallican beliefs remained cast in a moderate, *politique* hue. The 'forward' party was composed chiefly of converted former Anglicans on the Privy Council, their political programme galvanised by admiration for Louis XIV. The zeal of the convert was displayed most notoriously by earl of Sunderland, and put forward with rather greater religious conviction by the Drummond brothers, the earls of Melfort and Perth, the latter of whom represented himself as 'one who does not desire to heare any Circumstances of his Life noticed except that of his Conversion from Heresie to Truth'.[111] The Drummond influence shaped the attempts to create an aggressively public face for the Catholic religion, with the overthrow of the Test Act and the office-holders who supported it, the intrusion of Catholic fellows into Oxford and Cambridge, and the dispatching of the earl of Tyrconnell to strike at the Protestant powerbase in Ireland. Before 10 June 1688, such policies could be justified by the need to rush through religious changes within the lifetime of a king without an heir of his own faith. However, after the birth of the Prince of Wales, this prospect was no longer at hand to reassure critics of the throne.

Against the converts stood the magnates of the older Catholic families, still attached to the more circumspect strategy of public engagement that had developed under Charles II.[112] Traditionalist voices stressed the need to set religious liberties on a solid platform before pursuing any project to reorient the state, from which 'the king's affairs will gain but little', as Lord Thomas Howard conceded.[113] The lords Powis and Belassis repudiated the attempts to pack parliament, appealed for clemency when the seven Anglican bishops were brought to trial for non-compliance, and strove to accentuate the protection of Protestant Nonconformists to offset the image

---

[111] Earl of Perth to Lewis Innes, 19 July 1687, SCA, Blairs, I, 106/16.

[112] Charles Whyteford to William Leslie, n.d. (1690), SCA, Blairs, I, 133/4; *The Memoirs of Sir John Reresby … written by himself*, ed. James J. Cartwright (London, 1875), p. 348; Henry Foley, ed., *Records of the English Province of the Society of Jesus* (8 vols, London, 1877), I, p. 33.

[113] Lord Thomas Howard to Charles Whyteford, 31 August 1688, SCA, Blairs, I, 106/9.

of the toleration policy as a narrowly Catholic design.[114] In Yorkshire, Lord Thomas liaised with Tory magnates, seeking to rebuild consensus on the bare issue of liberty of conscience, and therefore avoid any purge of office-holding Anglicans.[115] The Oxfordshire squire John Belson wrote to Lord Melfort, trying to prevent the dismissal of his friend Sir George Mackenzie as Lord Advocate in Scotland – to the latter he confided his fears about 'a spirit of party which, you know, I abhor'.[116] As the first royal envoy in Rome, John Caryll brought to a papal audience the need for a cautious strategy of revival, and later pursued reconciliation between the king and his own Sussex neighbour, the former Whig exile, Ford, Lord Grey.[117] In recognition of such efforts, he would be lionised by Alexander Pope, as an 'honest courtier and patriot' whose 'principle profes't' rendered him 'Fix'd to one side, but mod'rate to the rest'.[118] Yet court opinion ran against the moderate party. In December 1685, with the influence of the converts growing, Caryll was withdrawn from Rome, replaced by the stridently pro-Bourbon Lord Castlemaine, and Sunderland's faction began, in the words of Lord Ailesbury, 'to lay the axe to the tree ... so contrary to the sense of the old and landed Roman Catholics'. Foreseeing the shadow of future conflict with the dissolution of Parliament in November 1685, Lord Belassis announced: 'I date my ruin and that of all my persuasion from this day.'[119]

Yet the quietist reputation of the 'old Catholic' contingent sits oddly with the fact that most recusants who were offered the chance *did* enter into the political experiment.[120] The earl of Ailesbury reported 'to my wonder' that Lord Bellasis had chosen to place himself inside court and council: a wholly unexpected development when 'to my knowledge he desired nothing but to live at ease and quiet'.[121] From Rome, Cardinal Howard appealed to Caryll to remain close to the court, for which 'I know you will willingly sacrifice your own quiett, lest ye refusall might afterwards unquiett yr minde on the Sinne of Omission when you may be so great an instrument for the Reli-

---

114 Thomas Bruce, earl of Ailesbury, *Memoirs ... written by himself*, ed. W.J. Buckley (2 vols, Roxburgh Club, 1890), I, pp. 126, 152, 165; Sir John Reresby, *Memoirs*, ed. A. Browning (Glasgow, 1936), p. 561.

115 Reresby, *Memoirs*, pp. 393, 402.

116 John Belson to Sir George Mackenzie, n.d. September 1686, Oxfordshire CRO, Belson MSS, F/1/4/C1/13.

117 J.S. Clarke, ed., *The Life of James II* (2 vols, London, 1816), pp. 74, 76–8; Macaulay, *History of England*, II, p. 59; John Caryll to Ford, Lord Grey, 10 November 1688, BL, Add. MSS, 28,226, fol. 71.

118 Alexander Pope, *Epitaph on John, Lord Caryll* (1711). See also Howard Erskine-Hill, *The Social Milieu of Alexander Pope* (London and New Haven, 1975), p. 42.

119 Ailesbury, *Memoirs*, I, p. 85.

120 Luttrell, *Brief Historical Relation*, I, p. 428; 'Justices of the Peace yt are Catholics' in Worcestershire, 1688, Bodleian Library, Rawlinson MSS, A139a.

121 Ailesbury, *Memoirs*, I, p. 157.

gious good.'[122] In supporting the basic presumptions of royal policy, despite their disquiet over the pace of change, they levelled an explicit challenge to the concept of an Anglican ascendancy over the state. John Belson's amity with Sir George Mackenzie was rocked by clashes over the Test Act, repeal of which he insisted would leave 'all jars apt to rise upon differences in Religion cut up by ye roots, & things settled upon a lasting basis of quiet and security for ever'. Penal laws, Belson contended, could find warrant neither in the 'law of nature', nor that of human governance, when 'divers nations have excluded religious penaltys' and 'it would be no dishonour nor disadvantage to others to follow their good example'.[123] Much as they might baulk at the aggression of 'the hot party', the coronation of a Catholic king had released a stream of expectations among those who saw the Test Act stifling their natural position as a county governing class. These moderates trusted themselves to shape the course of royal policy against the will of their opponents, transferring recusant traditions of patriotism and toleration into the public realm to limit the zeal from the throne. The danger was that, just as French Gallican precedents had been undermined by the actions of Louis XIV, so the activity of recusant leaders now risked sacrificing the other core component of the Catholic Restoration strategy: a Tory Anglican alliance.

By daring to make their ambitions public, Catholic leaders had aligned their fates with that of the king, during a fragile period of supremacy. As Dryden put it, apprehensively, to James, in his *Britannia Rediviva*: 'Yourself, our Balance hold, the World's, our Isle.'[124] From Sir John Swinburne's preparations to raise a troop of horse against William of Orange from his Northumberland estate, to William Blundell's letters to friends at court, outlining a system of palisade fencing with which London might be secured from foreign attack, recusants declared themselves part of this new order, with no choice but to defend it.[125] At the eleventh hour, in December 1688, John Belson was called upon by the Tory lords Clarendon and Middleton, as a spokesman for 'the sober Roman Catholics', to help James draft an appeal to his subjects against the Williamite invasion. Belson rode through the night to Rochester, but missed by a matter of hours a king who was already embarking on his flight into France.[126] The fall of James II therefore brought a brutal end to a long Catholic foray into the public sphere. The vast majority of recusants

---

[122] Cardinal Howard to John Caryll, 22 December 1685, BL, Add. MSS, 28,226, fols 11–12.

[123] Belson to Mackenzie, 2 November 1686, Oxfordshire CRO, Belson MSS, F/1/4/C1/17.

[124] John Dryden, *Britannia Rediviva* (1688).

[125] Nicholas Thornton to Sir John Swinburne, 10 November 1688, Swinburne MSS, 27/4; Blundell, ed., *Blundell Letters*, p. 253.

[126] Samuel Weller Singer, ed., *Correspondence of Henry Hyde, earl of Clarendon, and of his brother, Laurence Hyde, earl of Rochester* (2 vols, London, 1828), II, pp. 232–3.

had not engaged in any vehemently confessional project, and the courtiers' programme, with its affinity to Bourbon absolutism, was alien to the traditions and aspirations of the community. But the effects of the Revolution made no distinction between moderates and extremists: all politically active Catholics were now branded potential enemies to the kingdom. Sunderland could renounce his *politique* conversion, and enter the Williamite fold, but Powis fled the country, John Leyburne was incarcerated, while Caryll, Lord Thomas Howard and Philip Ellis departed into exile.[127] They did so because it was not just the throne of the king, but their own political strategy, which had been comprehensively broken in December 1688.

The diagnosis of England in Catholic commentary

The mistake made by the architects of the Catholic loyalist tradition was a failure to recognise that their congregation would stand or fall not by an intellectual struggle, or even by the demonstration of exemplary lives, but through the public anxieties of high politics under the Stuart monarchy. In 1678, this alarm had been directed at the 'Popish Plotters'; ten years later, the casualty was the king himself. From Rome, the envoy Sir John Lytcott registered his shock: 'I cannot but drop still fresh teares ... the ways of God's Providence are incomprehensible'.[128] He comforted himself that 'what really is now acting in England seems so unnatural and horrid that 'tis much greater consolation to suffer than to triumph ... All the world now seems out of humour and disposed to Commotion.'[129] Catholics had trusted in the security of Stuart monarchy. They had spent a century asserting their belief that a prince of England was their prince, no matter what his religion, but now that whole skein of rhetoric had been rendered inoperative, because their compatriots had chosen not to abide by its terms. To commend a new king who owed his enthronement to the militant demonstration of the fact that he was not Catholic, to accept a principle of 'exclusion', hoisted into the sacred reaches of the English constitution, would require moral and intellectual leaps that even the most disciplined recusant conscience would deem unmanageable.

An ardent defence of James II was to become one of the distinguishing features of Catholic post-Revolutionary writing. To Weldon, 'King James came, Christ's living member, in ye name of ye Eternal Father, to ye comfort and profit of ye Nation ... which cast him off, to ye Decimation and ruine of

---

127 W.M. Brady, *Annals of the Catholic Hierarchy in England and Scotland A.D. 1585–1776* (London, 1877), pp. 142, 261–3.
128 Sir John Lytcott to Sir Richard Bulstrode, 29 January 1689, Hodgkin Papers, Vol. II, BL, Add. MSS, 38,847, fols 134–5.
129 Lytcott to Bulstrode, 27 November 1689, BL, Egerton MSS, 3683, fol. 163.

its spiritual and temporal advantages.'[130] In a paean to more earthly achievements, the king would be defended as Joseph among the Egyptians, 'England's admiral', who had calmed the rages of the Neptune to create the prospect of a 'British Empire gloried in ye fight of God and Man'.[131] Catholic writers harboured few doubts as to the pure intent of the Stuart toleration policy: to Weldon, a yearning to reward subjects for 'merit, loyalty and service', rather than just their private choice in worship. John Lytcott saluted the justice of a 'gracious patriot':

> To calm those minds disturbed for conscience sake
> He no less freedom gave than did he take
> To please all tastes, his Bounty upon all
> Without restriction did like Manna fall.

It was the cruelty and spite of anti-Catholic antagonists that confounded these hopes, assailing the king 'to take from him ye Liberty/ Yt he endeavoured should for all be free'.[132] Jane Barker's defence was conceived to be simple and poignant: 'This, sundry, as the thing itself declares/ He gave his people leave to say their prayers'. Her interpretation showed words and motives twisted, in a looking glass world where 'white was still made black and black made white', and in which 'The king, they say will arbitrary be/ Because he gave his people liberty'.[133]

At the highest level, a Catholic literary response to the Revolution might be located in Dryden's *Don Sebastian* (1689), with its depiction of a virtuous king assailed by malign conspiracy.[134] However, a cacophony of lesser-known voices wove a sense of the injustice done to the Stuarts into a spiritual diagnosis of a nation breaking the laws of God and man. For Barker and Lytcott, William III would appear as a highwayman or the new Richard III: a Lord of Misrule brought in by the 'machines' of the mob and the diabolical 'state magicians' in a time when 'rebels were sainted, foreigners did reign'.[135] Catholic commentary pinpointed the Revolution as the symptom of a habitual corruption in the English body politic: the hidden

---

[130] Ralph Benet Weldon, 'Collection', BL, Add. MSS, 10,118, fol. 206.

[131] Weldon, 'Collection', BL, Add. MSS, 10,118, fols 49, 103.

[132] Weldon, 'Collection', BL, Add. MSS, 10,118, fols 45, 49, 103, 157; John Lytcott, 'An Historical essay on the Life and Death of King James II of ever glorious Memory', in Weldon, 'Collection', BL, Add. MSS, 10,118, fols 444–9.

[133] Barker, 'Poems', BL, Add. MSS, 21,621, fol. 44.

[134] Francis Fenwick to Henry Browne, 'A few verses of Mr Dreyden on the times', 23 July 1691, BL, Add. MSS, 37,662, pp. 211–12; Steven Zwicker, 'Representing the Revolution: Politics and High Culture in 1688', in Eveline Cruickshanks and John Miller, eds, *By Force or by Default? The Revolution of 1688–9* (Edinburgh, 1989), pp. 109–35.

[135] Barker, 'Poems', fol. 37; Weldon, 'Collection', BL, Add. MSS, 10,118, fols 191, 256; 'Tarquin and Tullia', in Weldon, 'Collection', BL, Add. MSS, 10,118, fols 442–4; Lytcott, 'Historical Essay', in Weldon, 'Collection', BL, Add. MSS, 10,118, p. 799.

or 'perjured' plot, created by its conspirators under the smokescreen of bogus allegations against Catholic loyalty. 'Dr Oates is alive againe and at liberty', noted Charles Whyteford in January 1689, a comment expressed with literal and symbolic force.[136] At the exiled court, Jacobites reprinted 'Popish Plot' literature, such as John Caryll's *Naboth's Vineyard*: speaking to the deepest Catholic sensibilities, with its biblical retelling of a paragon of gentry virtue, 'his neighbour's safeguard and their peace', perjured by plotters who covet his vineyard.[137] The decay of the moral ethos, the loss of sober statesman-ship and the rise of demagogues had all been foreshadowed in the intrigues of the previous two decades. The difference in 1688 was that the real target of the conspirators had been revealed, and James II had become the victim of the most audacious hidden plot of all. In Barker's verdict of despair: 'it makes one think that all's a cheat/ And religion just a trick of state'.[138]

In works conceived for recusant consumption, the first reflex of Catholic commentary was to stress the public implications of differences in religion, as authors reflected on the spectacle of a Catholic king banished by Prot-estants, and concluded that England was reaping the whirlwind of her long descent into impiety. One Benedictine quatrain noted the presence of the two sons of the earl of Salisbury, descendants of Lord Burghley, at the exiled court, to reach a trenchant conclusion:

> Had ye Cecils foreknown either Father or Son
> What would happen in ye 3rd Generation
> They had stuck to ye Church and left in ye lurch
> That God of State, Reformation.[139]

Behind this satire lay a complex historical narrative, an investigation into the cyclical struggles of seventeenth-century England, which connected the Revolution to the Popish Plot and the Reformation before it. John Warn-er's *History of the Presbyterian Plot* exemplified this vision: written before the Revolution, its second edition became the first Jacobite text to roll off the printing press at St Omer. Warner argued that, since the Reformation, England had been imperilled by fanatics who thrived upon 'trying first to throw into turmoil, and then to overrun, the very constitution which they boast themselves determined to protect against the detestable contrivances of others'.[140] His interpretation gave the devoutly loyal recusant minority a critical function in the struggle – revolutionaries having to achieve first 'the

---

136 Charles Whyteford to William Leslie, January 1689, SCA, Blairs, I, 126/1.
137 John Caryll, *Naboth's Vineyard, or the Innocent Traytor* (1678); Diary of Sir David Nairne, National Library of Scotland, 4 February 1695. Both Barker and Weldon made use of the story of Naboth, Ahab and Jezebel: Barker, 'Poems', BL, Add. MSS, 21,621, fols 31–2; Weldon, 'Collection', BL, Add. MSS, 10,118, fol. 64.
138 Barker, 'Poems', BL, Add. MSS, 21,621, fol. 52.
139 Weldon, 'Collection', BL, Add. MSS, 10,118, fols 225–6.
140 Warner, *Plot*, I, pp. 156, 159.

removal of those citizens who protect the existing order'. Catholics would suffer by dint of the amazing mirage thrown up by their enemies, whereby the true faithful were turned into the incorrigible subversives of popular imagination. Thus, recurrently, England would see:

> The god-fearing summoned to court, imprisoned and dragged off to torment; religious men suffering at the hands of the sacrilegious; men loyal to the King at the hands of his most bitter enemies; the lovers of peace at the hands of men who detest peace.[141]

The kingdom had become the arena for an elemental struggle, in which 'the wolves rend the lambs'; the 'eagles fly upon the doves', as the national conflict played itself out. In this game, the Revolution would be simply one more stage.

Yet, if private analysis lamented, berated, and anathematised the English nation, a more public voice sought to keep alive the common royalist language, with its touchstones of 'innocence' and 'loyalty', sublimating Catholic partisanship into a call to arms to incorporate the wider political community. The first recusant pamphlet to appear after the Revolution, *An Humble Remonstrance* addressed to the Convention Parliament took a tone of measured reason, appealing to parliamentarians to calm a frenzy that had left them 'Armed, and in Consultation against your Sovereign, whom God hath set over you, and His Own Right by Succession'. The author offered a gentle mockery of Protestant fears that the simple bequest of toleration for Catholics would have led 'all your new Religions' to melt away 'like Snow against the Sun'. When recusants were outnumbered five hundred to one by members of the reformed churches, any rebirth for the old faith, no matter how zealously desired, could only come 'by the Finger of God, for the good of your Souls; for there was no Human probability of it'. However, the treatise was willing to concede that James had sufficiently alarmed and affronted his subjects that certain 'Conditions' could be viably laid down 'as he may, with Honour and Conscience, be able to accept of', before the act of 'humbly inviting His Majesty to return to His People'. If Anglicans genuinely feared for the security of their religion, then it was the duty of the king to provide solid grounds for reassurance, and so prevent 'the impoverishing and ruine of the Nation' by imaginary fears. On this premise, the author called upon the representatives at Westminster to devise a suitable 'treaty' that might save the realm from a new conflagration of 'Foreign and Civil Wars', and institute a 'Healing Convention', in the form of the parliament that restored Charles II: guided by 'the God of Peace and Mercy', for the future blessings of the realm.[142]

---

[141] Ibid., I, p. 156.
[142] *An Humble Remonstrance to the Lords and Commons in the present Convention Assembled* (1689), pp. 3–4, 6–7.

The search for rapprochement and reconciliation had not altogether departed from Catholic private commentaries. When Sir Richard Shire-burne of Stonyhurst died under guard in Manchester in 1689, his brother composed a simple epitaph: 'Departing this life in prison for loyalty to his sovereign'.[143] The 'loyalist' case raised Civil War memories, to protest that the motives through which recusants followed James II were as disinterested as those that had made them support his Anglican father. After the death of her son at the siege of Londonderry in 1691, Lady Gage of Firle located her plight in a tradition of suffering, royalist *virtu*: 'My father Sir Henry Gage, when Governor of Oxford was killed at Abingdon in the service of King Charles the First.'[144] Civil War memories would become lodged into the action, ritual and defence of the Jacobite cause. When Edward Tyld-esley unfurled the Jacobite standard at Preston in 1715, he chose the banner held aloft by his great-grandfather, a royalist colonel. This was emblazoned with his family's old motto: 'Love of King and Country is worth so much'.[145] Standing at the scaffold after the failure of the same rebellion, Richard Gascoigne would be at pains to assert that he fought *not* out of confessional zeal: 'My loyalty descended to me from my ancestors; my father and grandfather had the honour to be sacrificed doing their duty to their kings, Charles I and James II.'[146] Such thoughts expressed the contradictions of a topsy-turvy world. Now, in a spectacular turn in the course of an English century, Catholics would be punished not for their acts of subversion, but for the very good faith that they had sought to prove for so long. It was not without intent that Barker named the Catholic heroine of her poems 'Fidelia'.[147]

Invocation of the cavalier tradition was accompanied by direct addresses to the Tory Anglican communion; an attempt to shame the Church of England into returning to its duty. Here, Catholic responses were deeply ambivalent. Weldon's 'Collections' on the time were pointedly prefaced by a sermon on obedience given by Bishop Turner of Ely in 1685 in defence of royal power and privilege.[148] But moral suasion could easily slide into bitter asperity, exemplified by a manuscript in the papers of the English College, Douai:

[143] Shireburne family pedigree, 1689, Lancashire CRO, Shireburne of Stonyhurst MSS, DDST, 101/7.

[144] Lady Gage to Sir Henry Browne, 1 August 1691, BL, Add. MSS, 37,662, p. 228.

[145] John Lunn, *The Tyldesleys of Lancashire: The Rise and Fall of a Great Patrician Family* (Altrincham, 1966), pp. 73, 102; B.G. Blackwood, 'Lancashire Catholics, Protestants and Jacobites during the '15', *Recusant History*, 22 (1994), pp. 41–60.

[146] *A True Copy of the Paper Delivered to the Sheriffs of London by Richard Gascoigne* (1716).

[147] Barker, 'Poems', BL, Add. MSS, 21,621: 'I have made my Fidelia speak the common dialect of Catholicks.'

[148] Weldon, 'Collection', BL, Add. MSS, 10,118, fols 19–24; King, *Jane Barker*, pp. 10–20.

> Lost or stolen from the Ld Archbishop of Canterbury, a Cassock and Cloak made up of the Church of England, finely dyed with the Doctrine of Non-resistance ... that shined like Religion, lived quite through with Self-Interest, bound up with the oaths of Allegiance and Supremacy, and buttoned up with the Test.[149]

This strain in Jacobite literature inveighed against Anglicans for breaking with the loyalist consensus, and committing the very 'crime' that Catholics had been all-too-often accused of: choosing the interests of their church over their king. Jane Barker heaped opprobrium upon the false 'non-resistors', whose mouthing of divine right theology had been exposed as just a cover for vaulting ambition: 'you till a soyl in which you treasure find'. For her, Tory Anglicans had become England's 'Pharisees', the 'greatest hypocrites in town'. By contrast: 'who courts vertu for her sake alone? None, no such fools but we in [sixteen] forty-one.'[150] If nothing else, 1688 had shown the world in its true colours.

In refusing to recognise the destruction of James II, recusants kept alive the loyalist vocabulary, believing that a state of international flux and conflict would vindicate their choice. When they went to St Germain, they declared that they set sail as they would go to any English court, when, in the words of Edward Lutton, 'The iniquity of ye tymes makes it a thing not very easy to find Loyalty and Ability mett in ye same subject.'[151] After the death of the royal equerry Edward Perkins in September 1697, his son wrote from Berkshire to the English seminary in Paris, reflecting on the consequences of the Catholic exodus. He contended:

> we are something satisfied that he spent ye Remnants of his life in ye service of soe good a master and Lady, tho I cannot say his leaving us at such a time was a considerable loss to us young people, which nevertheless being a but a private one ought not to be putt in balance with ye publick.[152]

The affirmation of public duty allowed Catholics to claim a powerful imperative in entering exile, an attraction at least equal to the element of panic. In 1693, when Sir Henry Browne was experiencing disillusionment, his friend Daniel Arthur recalled how:

> ye circumstances of those times and ye example of soe many others then, was sufficient to justifie ye prudence of ye action. And wt ever his [Browne's] thoughts are now, I am apt to beleeve had things still continued to smile upon him, as once they did, he scarce would have repented his journey.[153]

149 AAW, Main Series, 36, 10.
150 Barker, 'Poems', BL, Add. MSS, 21,621, fols 32, 37.
151 Edward Lutton to Sir Henry Browne, 22 August 1696, AAW, Browne MSS, 42.
152 Edward Perkins to John Meynell, 7 September 1697, AAW, Main Series, 36, 151.
153 Arthur to Browne, 27 January 1693, AAW, Browne MSS, 143.

Catholics would rally to the defence of the king as resolutely in 1688 as in 1641, perceiving that their chance of success depended upon the ability to show that there was no overriding moral or political difference between the two occasions. They had invested too much intellectual capital in the English royalist tradition to abandon it now.

A vision for exile

Such comments addressed the Revolution as a public, religious and moral phenomenon. Away from the field of controversy, Catholics turned inwards, towards a visionary and introspective interpretation, straining to give sense to the unfathomable situation, in which God had given them a king, and taken him away again. After three decades of binding themselves to the greater national community, recusant writers now rediscovered the singularity of the English Catholic world, through the noble plight of a people compelled to 'wander, vagabonds alone' through 'this world's labyrinth', as Jane Barker phrased it.[154] It was through recourse to the poetic codes that recusants had expressed their sense of precariousness within a Protestant kingdom, communicating an idea of *spiritual* exile that was rooted in the basic facts of recusant life, with national colleges and convents on foreign soil.[155] John Caryll's eerily prescient translation of Virgil's *First Eclogue* (1684), lamented an 'eternal banishment' to 'strange lands in endless exile': the testimony to 'What dire effects from civil discord flow!' The theme of displacement was thus part of the texture of recusant literature, and Jacobite poetry revived the spiritual and aesthetic materials of the older Elizabethan canon, with its flaming hearts, lost lovers and motif of 'Weeping England'.[156] For English recusants, the impact of 1688 was to turn a figurative sense of exile into a physical reality.

Yet exile was treated with a touch of ambivalence: the experience could be prized as well as pitied, as a spur to heroic action, and an opportunity to nourish faith. Benet Weldon explored the possibility of Jacobitism as a spiritual trial, suffusing the struggles of the Stuarts into the personal search for redemption that flowed through his reawakening as a convert to the Catholic faith:

---

[154] Barker, 'A Dialogue between Fidelia and her little nephew Martius', in Shiner Wilson, ed., *Selected Poems*, pp. 317–18.
[155] Shell, *Catholicism*, pp. 194–9.
[156] John Caryll, *Virgil's First Eclogue*, in John Dryden, ed., *Miscellany Poems* (2 vols, London, 1684); 'Political Poems 1714–16', BL, Add. MSS, 29,981, fols 8, 15, 123; Shell, *Catholicism*, pp. 175–8.

Ye greatest saints do not always see what most imports them in regard of ye future life. We walk here in the dark and therefore easily stumble, but who has set his Guards over Israel interposes his hand yt our falls prove not mortal ...[157]

The birth of Catholic Jacobitism lent itself to epic themes of the fight sustained by the righteous few, as recusants snatched the language of the Elect from Calvinistic thought, and cast themselves as a new Israel, sent into Diaspora, and waiting, in John Caryll's words, for 'divine Providence to fix the time of our Redemption', so 'we may once more meet at home and praise him in our own Sion.'[158] A Capuchin monk, Raphael Noulan, wrote in 1690 to Captain Henry Staveley, comparing the Stuart army to the Hebrew children 'preserved in the furnace of Babilon whose flames consumed all those yt stood about it'.[159] Identification with ancient Israel was not new to recusant thought: it had appeared in Ralph Buckland's Jacobean renderings of the Hebrew psalmody, and his conflation of 'Hiersualem' with 'Albion'.[160] Now, it became the device for Jacobite exhortation. Father Noulan affirmed to Staveley: 'Dear Captain, you are sent to the wars to have more occasion to put in execution those holy resolutions ... more meritorious to yr self than whole days spent in meditation and contemplation and retreat.' He concluded: 'No profession has furnished more saints than ye Army. Endeavour you to be one of their number.'[161] It was up to English Catholics to fulfil their destiny, and fight their bloody way through to the Promised Land.

Jacobite partisans spoke with the conviction that virtue would be rewarded, after a final test of valour. From the events of the Popish Plot, Weldon drew the lesson of how 'mallice fell ... over-loaded with the blood of many martyrs', and divine justice had been successively re-affirmed in English history.[162] Now, he grasped the symbolism of the revolutionary moment, with the Prince of Wales smuggled out of England, as another infant king had been 'hurried in ye dark, out of miserable fury, into Egypt'.[163] The Jesuit Edward Scarisbrick dedicated his 'Life of Lady Warner' (1691), to Mary of Modena, and a study of patience under trial was charged with political expectancy:

---

[157] Douai Abbey, Weldon, Memorials, V, p. 496.

[158] John Caryll to Philip Ellis, 21 March 1695, HMC, *Stuart*, I, p. 101. See also Caryll to the earl of Perth, 3 October 1695, Bodleian Library, Carte MSS, 181, fol. 627.

[159] Raphael Noulan to Captain Henry Staveley, 27 December 1690, AAW, Browne MSS, 59.

[160] Josephine Evetts-Secker, 'Jerusalem and Albion: Ralph Buckland's "Seaven Sparkes of the Enkindled Soul"', *Recusant History*, 20 (1990–91), pp. 149–63.

[161] Noulan to Staveley, 27 December 1690, AAW, Browne MSS, 59.

[162] Douai Abbey, Weldon, Memorials, V, p. 433; Weldon, 'Collection', BL, Add. MSS, 10,118, fol. 61.

[163] Weldon, 'Collection', BL, Add. MSS, 10,118, fol. 191.

Methinks I hear the Angel Guardian of our Land whispering in our Soverain's Ear. As heretofore the Angel Guardian of Israel did in the ear of St Joseph, these joyful words 'Rise and take the child and his Mother, to your Country, for they are dead, who sought the Life of the Child'.[164]

Such works explain why Jacobitism was more than a formal recitation of divine right theory: it had become caught up in a heightened sense of Catholic identity, a providentialist narrative of trial and redemption. Catholic writers sought reassurance that God had not forsaken the community, that the vertiginous turn in 1688 was being worked towards a greater end. Thus inspired, they transposed their religious faith onto a dynastic cause. Chapels had been burnt, the mob unleashed and the king cast away, but God had preserved the lives of the royal family, had set his guards over Israel, and paved the way for a new Elect to attain deliverance.

Conclusion

In January 1689, Catholic leaders looked at the world, and saw a new dispossession. Lord Belassis, exhausted after his efforts to bring moderation to the council of James II, did not outlast the year: before his death, he told Sir John Reresby that 'he had been very averse (though a papist) to the measures used in that reign for promoting that religion' and now believed that it would be 'almost impossible' to get the house of Stuart restored.[165] Lord Arundell of Wardour withdrew to Wiltshire, to find solace in tending his gardens.[166] Viscount Montagu retreated to Sussex, where, it was reported, 'he leads a dull life, and is become very mellancholly and heavy'.[167] Such men were old: they nurtured memories of the Civil War, Interregnum and Restoration, and they had now seen their world turned upside down once more. Yet many of those who made the choice to enter exile were equally aged: John Caryll had been born in 1625, and the earl of Powis in 1626. The baptism of English Catholic Jacobitism must be studied through the longer life experiences of this generation. Recusants had found an equilibrium between faith and nation in the principle of service to an hereditary dynasty. But in 1688, the expulsion of a Catholic king seemed to prove that Protestantism was a stronger bond than monarchy within the English nation, and it stripped them of their last barrier of defence. Figures like Caryll had spent thirty years enunciating the language of loyalty – 'Fix'd to one side, mod'rate to the rest' – but now this 'principle profes't' had turned them into reluctant rebels: the climactic failure of a political, rhetorical and

---

164 Edward Scarisbrick, *The Life of Lady Warner* (1691), p. 6.
165 Reresby, *Memoirs*, p. 445.
166 G.E. Cokayne, *The Complete Peerage*, II, pp. 90, 126.
167 Arthur to Browne, 12 August 1692, AAW, Browne MSS, 125.

intellectual struggle. The 'loyalist' centre had not held, and individuals who had committed their lives to reconciliation had been driven further from the heart of the nation than ever before.

The study of eighteenth-century recusancy can ill-afford to neglect the political heritage of the years before 1688. The response to the Revolution shows how the Catholic gentry saw themselves as neither 'survivalists' nor outcasts, but harboured a political consciousness that would not simply vanish with the loss of their king. They desired a public space within their nation, and saw 1688 as a decisive test of ambition and integrity: as Stephen Tempest reminded his brother, never had duty and self-interest appeared in such happy conjunction. The consequence was a curious paradox. As Jacobites, recusants were invited to become part of a cause that lived through the promise of plots and insurrection. Yet this was the political offspring of a movement that had renounced religious conquest and conversion, in favour of royalism and toleration. Seventeen years before the reign of James II, John Caryll's tract 'Not Guilty' had brought home the principle of Catholic loyalty: 'it may be in the power of our enemies to make us suffer, but they can never make us guilty'.[168] Now, the same articles of faith that had made Catholics 'innocent' of any plot against Stuart England would make them complicit in sustained action against the post-Revolution settlement. The royalist rhetoric that sought to demolish the myth of the 'Popish Plot' was preserved within the Jacobite movement, and used to justify more conspiracies in the following sixty years than in the whole sweep of post-Reformation history. If this was something of an irony, it was, to Jacobite recusants, entirely consistent with a world in which the 'non-resistors' had resisted, in which the royal bearer of 'liberty' had been cast as an intolerant bigot, and in which a Dutch invasion had been hailed as a national deliverance. England, in the coldly sardonic words of a Benedictine poet, had sacrificed 'our Holy Religion', had 'beggared and perjured the Nation all O're ... For an Orange'.[169] This was no place for any true, loyal Catholic to linger long.

---

[168] 'Not Guilty', BL, Add. MSS, 28,252, fol. 150.
[169] 'A Song of an Orange', in Weldon, 'Collection', BL, Add. MSS, 10,118, fol. 479.

2

The making of the Catholic gentry
in England and in exile

By 1691, when James II's forces withdrew from Ireland back to the continent, the Glorious Revolution had been established as a disruptive and traumatic moment for the Catholic community: a blow struck against the hope of peaceful integration into England. Despite the bursts of patriotic defiance with which they rallied around the Stuart banner, recusant leaders were forced to confront the creation of a new order far harder to negotiate, in which the utility of old political and intellectual resources appeared fatally undermined. Catholic religious and political writings after 1688 were not conceived in abstraction: they articulated the high stakes faced wherever the recusant world was strong enough to exert an identity, in a time when national allegiances had been overturned and the welfare of the flock cast into doubt. This chapter will look at how the social institutions of recusant England responded to the challenge, concentrating on the laymen who had assumed public leadership within the Catholic community, but had now become vulnerable to exile or imprisonment, after their reluctance to acknowledge the transference of the English crown. Outside the ranks of the clergy, the dominant voice in eighteenth-century Catholic writing remained that of the gentleman lay leader. Tracing the social fortunes of the recusant elites therefore lays a foundation to explore the way in which Catholics mediated between the contested national, political and religious identities that impinged upon their place in England after 1688.

Until the failure of the 1715 rising at least, the lives of the English recusant gentry remained caught in the fragments of the fallen political and dynastic order. By 1689, the Catholic communities of the south and the midlands had surrendered a constituency of magnates into exile with James II; in subsequent years the militant Jacobitism of Lancashire and Northumberland was unveiled as an overwhelmingly patrician phenomenon, mobilised in a fashion to parallel the Elizabethan Rising of the Northern Earls. Beyond the moment of defeat, a generation of more ostensibly tranquil Catholic gentlemen ruminated upon the wounded dynasty in their households, dispensing moral and material support to feed the dream of a second Stuart restoration. It is therefore not entirely coincidental with their Jacobite politics that the recusant gentry of eighteenth-century England have attracted an extremely negative historical verdict. Social historians, clericalist 'Second Spring' scholars and later Catholic revisionists unite in judging the patrician leaders an etiolated caste, their 'sleepy, dust-laden laden kind of Catholicism' pounded by feudal pessimism, political isolation, and punitive legislation.[1] Devotion to a failed dynasty was the outward symptom of cultural decline for a community faced with the stark choice: 'change or decay'.[2] However, in revisiting the lives of the laity, this chapter will contest the common perspective. Rebellions, religious apostasy and bouts of economic hardship certainly enhanced fears over the safety of the flock, but scholarly opinion has received too readily the narrative of 'degeneration', and formed too hasty a premise that the later transformation of English Catholicism in the nineteenth-century was built upon the collapse of the older edifice of gentry life.

Beyond the common Augustan propensity to berate the apparent turpitude of an age of 'new money', Catholic gentlemen after 1688 evinced surprisingly few signs of living in a broken world, and if the practice of religion was necessarily recondite, their habits of sociability remained open to the public gaze. Once the immediate crisis of the Revolution had been absorbed, a pattern of shrewd estate management, economic innovation and family alliances preserved the ideal of English recusancy as an independent moral community under gentry rule. In their marriages, their connections to the local governing elites and the architecture of their manor houses, recusant landowners shadowed the construction of a county ruling order; their chosen models of devotion and spirituality sought to reconcile inward piety with a practical re-engagement in the Protestant nation. These experiences generated a didactic vision, inscribed in recusant commonplace books and private reflections, which captured the 'little commonwealth' of the Catholic landed estate as an alternative model for the governance of a divided country. But if recusant society reconfigured itself in a form more cohesive, more prosperous and more ambitious than existing accounts have allowed, inhabitants still operated within the shadow of the Jacobite cause. Increasingly, they began to brush against the brimming diaspora of exiles on the continent, and even recusants not formally outlawed from the Hanoverian state started to participate in the construction of a Jacobite world. By integrating the activities of English Catholics overseas into the picture of the community, this chapter will suggest that, far from just a utopian yearning for a 'prince over the water' the Stuart cause remained an immanent feature of elite recusant life. The Jacobite movement – more than any other force

---

[1] Angus McInnes, 'The Revolution and the People', in Geoffrey Holmes, ed., *Britain after the Glorious Revolution 1689–1714* (London, 1969), pp. 80–95, at p. 82; R.C. Wilton, 'Early Eighteenth Century Catholics in England', *Catholic Historical Review*, n.s., 4 (1924), pp. 367–87.

[2] J.A. Williams, 'Change or Decay? The Provincial Laity 1691–1781', in Duffy, ed., *Challoner and his Church*, pp. 27–54.

in eighteenth-century society – exposed the unstable position of a recusant elite existing with one foot inside the mainstream patrician world, and one placed firmly outside. As the community itself did not decay, neither did its interest in the public realm. The flight of James II did *not* mean the end of the political designs linked to Stuart claims upon the English throne.

Inside the 'Iron Age'

The landed gentry represented by no means the only solid sector within eighteenth-century recusant society, but they were the group who provided it with the means of survival, through the preservation of tenaciously guarded privileges. In the recusant strongholds of the north, 210 'persons of quality' kept a chaplain in 1720, with the English Dominicans recording the existence of one hundred gentry families loyal to the faith in Yorkshire alone.[3] In pockets of Sussex and Hampshire, Norfolk and the Welsh borders especially, the Catholic population possessed a similar density and a comparable level of religious activism. With the constraints of the statute book placed upon clerical activity, co-religionists across the social spectrum tended to cluster around the households of local notables, who provided the space of worship in their manor chapels, sheltered the clergymen and vicars apostolic, and funded the nascent mission stations even in urban centres such as London and York.[4] John Gother and Richard Challoner, the clerical writers most affiliated with the growth of a new London Catholic environment, both owed their patronage to the older gentry world; the one serving as chaplain, the other nurtured as a child in the household of the Holmans of Warkworth.[5] As a 'riding missioner' to the poor in East Anglia, the Benedictine Alban Dawnay gained his funding from the seigniorial houses of Southcott and Bedingfield, having served as tutor to their sons on the grand tour in Florence and Tuscany.[6] In such settings, the absence of the episcopal or parochial structure produced the sort of lay activism normally associated with a presbytery. It was the squire, not the priest, who embodied the religious conscience of his locality.

As a faith heavily dependent on lay guardianship, the decades following the Revolution ushered in an extremely unpromising period for the English Catholic community. In 1688, the fluctuations in national politics had shaken this private world; thereafter, the military challenge of a Catholic

---

3   Aveling, *Handle and the Axe*, pp. 248–53; Visitation and Confirmations by Bishop Dominic Williams, 1728–9, CRS, *Dominicana* (London, 1926), pp. 108–115.

4   Bossy, *Community*, pp. 70, 100–110.

5   E.H. Burton, *The Life and Times of Bishop Challoner* (2 vols, London, 1909), pp. 1–30; Marion Norman, 'John Gother and the English Way of Spirituality', *Recusant History*, 11 (1972), pp. 306–19.

6   Letter-book of Alban Dawnay, 1710, BL, Add. MSS, 28,254, fol. 47.

court with foreign allies meant that the eye of the state remained closely fixed on any potentially disaffected country gentlemen. For those who knew where to look, evidence of subversive recusant activity could be adduced in abundance. The Manchester trials of seven Catholic gentlemen in 1694 brought the 'popish plot' back into public discourse: two years later, the Assassination Plot contrived by Jacobite fanatics in London confirmed the image of terror as a trusty weapon in the papist arsenal. In 1715, it was seemingly easier for Catholics than Protestants to ride out in the service of the Stuart cause, and to justify it afterwards.[7] Recusants constituted 1,500 of the rebels taken at the siege of Preston.[8] By 1716, the Tower housed such notables as the earl of Derwentwater, the duke of Norfolk's brother Edward Howard, the lord Widdrington, and members of such illustrious northern families as Towneley, Standish, Hesketh, Tyldesley, Swinburne and Collingwood. The life of the talismanic Derwentwater ended by public execution on Tower Hill; in the north, 27 executions and a wave of imprisonments and transportations made the administration of justice conspicuously harsher than in the capital.[9] 'Misfortunes, I think, crowd around in upon us, but for god's sake, lett us bear up against them, with the Christian patience to suffer not nature's tenderness to goe too farr beyond its bounds, as to be forgetting of our duty', wrote James Swinburne to his sister-in-law. Yet, he confessed to tears, as he signed his letter 'yr fellow sufferer'.[10]

A dynastic contest shot through with the language of religious conflict posed a source of anxiety even for recusants who played no part in Jacobite conspiracies. The exposure of Jacobite activity in London and Lancashire provided the grounds for arrests and threatened estate confiscations over a wider area: the lords Stourton and Brudenell were immured without judicial process in 1692, while the 1696 Assassination Plot prompted the imprisonment of Sir Philip Constable of Everingham, Colonel Bernard Howard of Norfolk and the younger John Caryll of West Harting, none of whom had any connections to the London conspirators.[11] John Dear, the Chichester

---

[7] W.M. Beaumont, ed., *The Jacobite Trials at Manchester in 1694* (Chetham Society, 1853); T.C. Porteous, 'New Light on the Lancashire Jacobite Plot, 1692–4', *Transactions of the Lancashire and Cheshire Antiquarian Society*, 50 (1934–5), pp. 1–60.

[8] Peter Clark, 'Journal of Several Occurrences from 2d November 1715', Northumberland CRO, Radcliffe MSS, 5828/5; Monod, *Jacobitism*, pp. 317–26.

[9] Lord Acton, ed., *An Account of the VICTORY obtain'd at Preston over the REBELS by the King's forces under the command of General WILLS* (1716); Robert Pattern, *History of the Late Rebellion* (1717), pp. 107–20; Hibbert Ware, ed., *Lancashire Memorials of the Rebellion*, pp. 159, 186–7, 191–5; B.G. Blackwood, 'Lancashire Catholics, Protestants and Jacobites during the '15', *Recusant History*, 22 (1994), pp. 41–60.

[10] James Swinburne to Lady Mary Swinburne, 8 April 1716, Northumberland CRO, Swinburne MSS, Box 5.

[11] John Dear to Richard Caryll, 20 August 1696, BL, Add. MSS, 28,227, fol. 20;

lawyer, forecast that Catholic households would experience the 'Inquisition' of 'this prying, jealous age', and the most serious alarm stemmed from a belief that the prejudices of the mob and the underhand tyranny of the executive were becoming indistinguishable, to leave a polity directed by arbitrary actions and perjured evidence, in which their community stood outside the protection of the laws.[12] The 1694 trials at Manchester cast light on the use of false informers – former highwaymen and ex-Jacobites – by local Whig agents seeking to seize the lands of recusant squires that included that improbable conspirator, the 82-year-old William Blundell.[13] At a popular level, it was true that antipathy was not always realised in particular and personal anti-Catholicism: Daniel Defoe might reasonably express disdain that an enraged mob could rarely identify the target of popery 'whether it be a man or a horse'.[14] However, the attacks on Lancashire chapels in 1715 and the continuing liability of priests to arrest by private individuals showed how pope-burnings and pulpit addresses might create a durable framework for local conflict, played out in the actions of the crowd.[15]

The immediate Catholic concern arose from the recriminatory legislation that enshrined, codified and legitimised the anti-popish tendency in English government. The penal laws had returned with a vengeance under William III, with an additional bill of 1692 leaving Catholics liable to a double land tax, to be levied in times of war.[16] In 1700, the government systematised the ramshackle corpus of legislation with *An Act for the further preventing the growth of Popery*.[17] The laws reiterated restrictions on Catholic mobility, forbade a continental education, and reinforced the old proscription of priests and the ban on the purchasing of land and the inheritance of property. An *Order of Council concerning Papists*, submitted in 1706, enjoined Anglican clergymen to compile a national list, with a view to eradicating any 'rights of presentation, donation of churches, benefits or schools in the

---

Constantine Phipps to John Caryll, 16 January 1699, BL, Add. MSS, 28,227, fol. 22; Bernard Howard to William III, April 1696, Bodleian Library, Carte MSS, 181, fols 734–7.

12 Dear to Caryll, 11 June 1696, BL, Add. MSS, 28,227, fol. 17.

13 Weldon, 'Collection', BL, Add. MSS, 10,118, fols 280, 311; 'Taft's narrative of the Lancashire Plot', 1695, Bodleian Library, Carte MSS, 228, fols 237–44; HMC, *Kenyon*, pp. 293–7, 324, 348; P.A. Hopkins, 'The Commission for Superstitious Lands of the 1690s', *Recusant History*, 15 (1979–81), pp. 265–82.

14 Duffy, 'Poor Protestant Flies', p. 290.

15 Plowden to Eberson, 1 August 1718, EPSJ, Notes and Fragments, 106; Robert Witham to Lawrence Mayes, 20 July 1718, AAW, Epistolae Variorum, VI/92; Haydon, *Anti-Catholicism*, p. 55.

16 Bossy, *Community*, pp. 280–90; Duffy, ed., *Challoner and his Church*, pp. 7–14; Aveling, *Handle and the Axe*, pp. 284–307.

17 Aveling, *Handle and the Axe*, p. 246; W.R. Ward, *The English Land Tax in the Eighteenth Century* (1953), pp. 69–70.

disposition of any Papists, or reputed Papists, or in trust for them'.[18] After the 1715 rebellion, the Commissioners for Forfeited Estates were sent into the provinces to note the possessions of those whose consciences did not permit them to accept the Protestant vocabulary of the state oath, raising the prospect of a two-thirds confiscation of recusant lands. The Catholic gentry, as the Devon squire Sir Edward Southcott lamented, lived trapped in an 'Iron Age' of taxes, restrictions and prohibitions; the Covent Garden merchant Henry Jerningham, bewailed the state of 'the Poor Roman Catholicks whose condition is like that of the Israelites in Egypt'. Recusants reeled under 'such inhuman laws as all Nations blush to Read', he informed the Jacobite court, while wicked statesmen, 'make laws to stop our mouths, and judge it high treason to speak in our own defence … have layd us under the power of every lackey and beggar in the streets to put the laws into execution against us, whenever their Malice or the Devil shall promote them'.[19] Even without such apocalyptic fears, the systematic pursuit of property put to 'superstitious uses' appeared confirmation of a political establishment setting out to expunge all trace of recusancy from the land.[20]

After the rebellion, the temper of state affairs presented proof enough for a rare Catholic Whig, the vicar apostolic John Talbot Stonor, to predict that the suspicion of Jacobitism would lead to 'the ruin or Apostasy of our friends'.[21] Correspondingly, the most serious indication of a seigniorial crisis was manifested in a succession of high-profile Protestant conversions. In the reign of George I, the lordships of Montagu, Powis, Waldegrave and Teynham brought striking incidences of sons reneging on their Jacobite fathers' religious convictions as well as their dynastic allegiances. In Maryland, the lords Baltimore changed their religion to confirm the end of the iconic experiment in Catholic colonial governance, while a triumvirate of Sussex baronetcies fell away with the entry of Sir John Shelley, Sir Henry Goring and Sir William Gage into the Anglican communion.[22] 'O folie! O extravagance! O visible and abominable Ambition!' the monk Benet Weldon inveighed against the tendency, but, as the Douai priest Edward

[18] *Order of Council concerning Papists* (1706), copy in Lambeth Palace Library, MS 930/83.

[19] 'Hugh Thomas' [Henry Jerningham] to James Edward, n.d. 1720, Royal Archives (Windsor), Stuart papers, 47/48.

[20] Bodleian Library, Rawlinson MSS, D/387; P. Purcell, 'The Jacobite Rising of 1715 and the English Papists', *English Historical Review*, 44 (1929), pp. 418–32; Williams, 'Change or Decay?', pp. 31–2; M. Rowlands, 'The Iron Age of Double Taxes', in *Staffordshire Catholic History*, III (1963), p. 45.

[21] John Talbot Stonor to Lawrence Mayes, 3 March 1722, AAW, Epistolae Variorum, VII/97.

[22] Philip Caryll to John Caryll, 21 September 1726, BL, Add. MSS, 28,228, fol. 209; George Flint, *Robin's Last Shift, or Weekly Remarks* (London, 1717), pp. 102, 145; Anne Fortescue to Lady Mary Fortescue, 26 February 1717, Cambridgeshire CRO, Huddleston MSS, MF/4.

Dicconson acknowledged, the lure of 'so great an estate and so high a place in the House of Lords' was 'too inticing not to be resisted but by good solid principles'.[23] Some apostates undeniably prospered. Sir William Gage began a career in parliament in 1723, James Brudenell, brother to the earl of Cardigan, was made Master of the Jewel Office in 1716, and the first Earl Waldegrave incurred Jacobite fury as he capitalised on childhood experiences at the court in exile to serve as British ambassador to Paris.[24] Worldly prosperity did not seemingly put an end to all spiritual anguish: Waldegrave died reputedly crying out for a priest, Goring left a bequest to the English Jesuit colleges, and Teynham committed suicide in 1723.[25] Nonetheless, whatever the state of the converts' souls, the drift into the Protestant fold brought explicit rejection of a recusant identity now interwoven with the taint of treason, the sparks of political controversy and the threat of material ruin.

The conditions of Catholic revival

Against the doom-laden prophecies of Stonor and Weldon, the penal laws of Hanoverian England were not all that they seemed. Despite the intent of some legislators in Westminster, the summoning of Catholics to take the oath was confined to moments of national emergency, the application of the laws by magistrates was sporadic enough to be ineffective, and, as the earl of Hardwicke commented, the wording of the legislation was sufficiently cruel and coercive to render its imposition quite impractical.[26] In Lancashire, the Scarisbricks and Dicconsons were able to exploit kinship ties with local office-holders to press for leniency, even in the wake of the 1700 legislation: the Tory sheriff Sir Charles Stanley recommended that a quiet sojourn outside the county would be a sufficient strategy to avoid judicial action.[27] While this reality was not sufficient to reassure recusant minds, the ultimate *failure* of the state to ruin those who refused to pledge allegiance was more perceptible than the rate of persecution. In consequence, predictions of the imminent destruction of Catholic England obscured the greater line of continuity. With exceptions such as Goring, Gage and Shelley, the trend towards apostasy should be seen more precisely as feature of the *aristocracy*,

---

[23] Edward Dicconson to Mayes, 7 April 1713, AAW, Epistolae Variorum V/11; Weldon, 'Collection', BL, Add. MSS, 10,118, fol. 208.
[24] Flint, *Weekly Remarks*, p. 102; Brian Foley, *Some People of the Penal Times: Aspects of a Unique Social and Religious Phenomenon* (Lancaster, 1991), pp. 60–2.
[25] Edward Gage to Thomas Eberson, 17 May 1723, EPSJ, Notes and Fragments, 111; Gage to Levinius Browne, n.d. June 1724, EPSJ, Notes and Fragments, 114.
[26] Aveling, *Handle and the Axe*, p. 254.
[27] Sir Charles Stanley to Robert Scarisbrick, 4 May 1701, Lancashire CRO, Scarisbrick MSS, 44/5.

whose ties to the religion had, since before the reign of James II, been of a somewhat fragile nature.[28] Even among this class, the two decades after 1688 saw the return of the dukes of Norfolk and the earls of Shrewsbury, after several decades of Anglican flirtation, to the old family faith.[29] Below them, supported by shrewd management of family and estate affairs, most of the recusant baronets and lesser landowners were distinguished by tenacity in their inherited religion.

On the eve of the 1715 rebellion, after over twenty-five years of punitive legislation, there was scant evidence to affirm the myth that English Catholics had dwindled into an impoverished 'desperate faction'. Among the Jacobite militants, the Widdringtons and Radcliffes could raise £6,000 from their estates, the Thorntons valued their land at £1,585, while the Shaftoes and Collingwoods fell just below £1,000.[30] Some of their Northumberland neighbours – the Charltons, Riddells and Claverings – sent younger sons alone into the Jacobite army: a tacit acknowledgement that more than just family reputation lay at stake.[31] Even after 1715, very few Catholic estates left the hands of their owners, and many of the rebellious families, such as the Radcliffes and the Collingwoods, made a partial recovery of their possessions, thanks to relatives who had eschewed military action.[32] Most of the recusant gentry did not leave their survival to fortune, but opted to resist the Hanoverian state by a series of overtures outside their community, placing hope in the camaraderie of provincial gentry life to shield them after a fall from grace. The most widely exploited legal loophole permitted recusant landlords to relinquish their estates nominally into the hands of Anglican friends, with the intention, as the Lancashire Tory Sir John Statham assured the Shireburne family, 'to returne 'em if the times mend'.[33] Catholic squires would reduce their own position to that of tenants for life, with a private agreement that the status would be inherited by the family heir. In sympathetic counties, the method bore fruit, with the more prosperous magnates assembling formidable networks of Protestant protectors. In 1714, the Whig Lord Tankerville pledged to save the property of

---

[28] Kenyon, *Popish Plot*, pp. 34–5.

[29] Mathew, *Catholicism*, p. 124.

[30] 'Estates forfeited by the late rebellion', Northumberland CRO, Radcliffe MSS, M15/A49a.

[31] Leo Gooch, *The Desperate Faction? The Jacobites of North East England 1688–1745* (Hull, 1995), pp. 55–8.

[32] Thomas Errington to the countess of Derwentwater, 16 September 1722, Nathaniel Piggott to the countess of Derwentwater, n.d. 1724, both in Northumberland CRO, Radcliffe MSS, M17.104; Catherine Collingwood to Lady Throckmorton, 14 October 1743, Warwickshire CRO, Throckmorton MSS, Folder 49/6; Collingwood estate titles, Throckmorton MSS, LWB/1.

[33] Sir John Statham to George Errington, 18 January 1720, Lancashire CRO, Shireburne MSS, 97/10. See also Dorothy Witham to Lawrence Mayes, 17 September 1714, AAW, Epistolae Variorum, V/65.

the Swinburnes of Capheaton from any hostile attentions on the part of George I's new government.[34] After 'the misfortunes' of 1715, the family employed the Tory attorney Sir Constantine Phipps to 'make all the friends we can in the Parliament' with a view to resisting the Commissioners for Forfeited Estates.[35] In 1742, the Swinburnes placed their lands successfully under the trusteeship of the MP William Shippen.[36] The ability of northern Jacobites to contain the damage of political ostracism set a precedent for the wider recusant community.

The more pioneering recusant landowners sought to place the tools of survival in their own hands, modernising their estates to exploit new sources of revenue, as a bulwark against double taxation. The Radcliffes and Swinburnes pursued programmes of field enclosure, accompanied by investments in the Tynedale lead mining industry, while the Viscounts Molyneux founded the Torbock colliery.[37] Nicholas Blundell of Little Crosby voraciously studied the new agricultural techniques – the first northern landowner to exploit the potential of the six-sail windmill – while Sir Nicholas Shireburne of Stonyhurst committed himself to proto-industrial experimentation, introducing the jersey spinning wheel as a source of employment into his locality.[38] The economy of the recusant gentry exposed the Janus-faced character of English Catholicism: allegiance to an old order had to be sustained by touches of enterprise and innovation, protecting landed wealth often founded on the back of dissolved monastic lands.[39] 'Get learning and knowledge', counselled Sir Thomas Strickland of Sizergh, from Jacobite exile, to his sons in 1698, 'and I particularly recommend the study of Law, for men of that Science not only raise great fortunes but are adapted for all the great employment of this kingdom'.[40] In deference to this advice, recusant gentlemen showed no visceral attraction to the ties of land, and a small

---

34 To Earl of Tankerville to Lady Mary Swinburne, 13 March 1714, Northumberland CRO, Swinburne MSS, 7/95.

35 William Radcliffe to Lady Mary Swinburne, 26 January 1720, Northumberland CRO, Swinburne MSS, 178/5; Denis Maloney to Lady Swinburne, 27 February 1720, Swinburne MSS 178/7; Lady Swinburne to Maloney, February 1720, Swinburne MSS, 178/19.

36 Will of Sir John Swinburne, 26 March 1742, Northumberland CRO, Swinburne MSS, 12/4.

37 Account book, Northumberland CRO, Swinburne MSS, 43/1; Thomas Errington to Lady Derwentwater, 14 June 1722, Northumberland CRO, Radcliffe MSS, M15/A49a; Title deeds, Lancashire CRO, Molyneux MSS, 4/1–3.

38 Viscount Molyneux to Sir Nicholas Shireburne, 1707, Northumberland CRO, Shireburne MSS, 114/56; Shireburne title deeds to mines and quarries at Clitherhoe, Shireburne MSS, 1/26; Sir Nicholas Shireburne, 'Use of Lancashire lands', Shireburne MSS, 87/17; F. Tyrer and J.J. Bagley, eds, *The Great Diurnall of Nicholas Blundell of Little Crosby, Lancashire* (3 vols, 1958–62), I, p. 237.

39 Tempest, 'Religio Laici', 1739, Tempest MSS (private collection).

40 'Sir Thomas Strickland to his sons', in Foley, ed., *People of the Penal Times*, p. 105.

number flourished in the legal profession, with Nathaniel Pigott, Henry Eyre and Strickland's grandson Mannock pushing Catholic interests at the Inns of Court by persuading Anglican colleagues to represent their clients at the bar.[41] A contingent of younger sons seized mercantile opportunities, with Thomas Mannock prospering in the wine trade, Thomas Huddleston of Sawston trading in cloth in Leghorn, and Henry Jerningham enriching his Norwich family as a Covent Garden banker.[42] Building up knowledge of the financial world, the Huddlestons placed over £2,000 in the East India Company and the London lottery.[43] Alexander Pope's admiration for the 'country house' idyll of bucolic retirement was belied by the efforts of landowners who entered into the commercial world with all the energy of the most ruthless plutocrats.[44]

For family patriarchs such as Thomas Strickland, 'good housekeeping' became synonymous with spiritual self-discipline. Nonetheless, as affirmed by account books, diaries and commonplace notes preoccupied with bonds, loans and all the mechanisms of modern credit, Catholic squires felt obliged to prove their capacity for consumption, throwing themselves into the market for architects, merchants, designers and musicians. The priest Lewis Innes reminded the Carylls of the need to present a robust face to the world, lest 'it might frighten people and make them suspect your affairs in worse condition than really they are, and would certainly hinder your finding any tolerable match for your son'.[45] The pressures of marital advancement served especially to embolden recusant gentlemen towards displays of social ostentation. The Mannocks adorned Gifford's Hall with cloth from India and Persia, while private concerts showcased the Tempest and Towneley households, with instruments acquired from priests in Italy.[46] At Scarisbrick Hall, 'five Lords' attended a ball of 1705 to court the heiress Catherine Walmesley.[47] The resultant conjugal ties underscored the cohesion of recusant society. At

[41] Nathaniel Pigott to Thomas Errington, 27 June 1719, Northumberland CRO, Shireburne MSS, 97/10; Henry Eyre to John Caryll, 14 January 1717, BL, Add. MSS, 28,227, fols 420–1; Mannock Strickland to Lady Mary Radcliffe, 10 July 1732, Northumberland CRO, Swinburne and Radcliffe papers, 322/20.

[42] Thomas Huddleston to Mary Huddleston, 3 November 1720, Cambridgeshire CRO, Huddleston MSS, TH/1; Suffolk CRO, Mannock accounts, H5/1; Thomas Sayes to Sir Francis Mannock, 5 May 1733, Suffolk CRO, Mannock MSS, G/4; Mary of Modena to William Dicconson, 7 October 1717, HMC, *Stuart*, V, p. 104; Dicconson, Accounts, 31 January 1718, HMC, *Stuart*, V, p. 426.

[43] Edward Webbe to Mary Fortescue, 12 April 1730, Cambridgeshire CRO, Huddleston MSS, MF/32; Webbe to Fortescue, 20 September 1731, Huddleston MSS, MF/36.

[44] Erskine-Hill, *Social Milieu*, pp. 42–68.

[45] Lewis Innes to John Caryll, 12 June 1710, BL, Add. MSS 28,227, fol. 84.

[46] Richard Towneley to Lawrence Mayes, January 1714, AAW, Epistolae Variorum, V/43.

[47] Account books, 1724, Downside Abbey, Mannock MSS, H3/14, 18; Miscellaneous Accounts, 1710, Lancashire CRO, Walmesley MSS; Stephen Tempest to Lady Petre,

a local level, the betrothals in Lancashire and Northumberland fostered the loyalties of Jacobite houses such as Dicconson and Walmesley, Towneley and Widdrington.[48]. Elsewhere, endogamous confessional behaviour promoted geographical *exogamy*, with kinship patterns highlighting the larger national consciousness of the Catholic community. A list of godparents to the Swinburne children reached into Derbyshire, Gloucestershire, Sussex, Berkshire and Essex.[49] The house of Norfolk entered into two marriages with Jacobite Lancashire, with Ralph Standish bound to Lady Philippa Howard, and the eighth duke wedded to Maria Shireburne of Stonyhurst.[50] This elision of gentry and aristocratic houses prevented northern notables from fossilising into the 'Squire Western' caricature of the lesser rural landowner. To William Fenwick of Meldon, congratulating his kinsman Sir William Swinburne on marriage into the Berkshire Englefields, family alliances allowed recusants to prove their vigour to the world. Fenwick believed that 'a frutefull offspring' for the match, 'heires as well to your bravery and education as your estate' would allow the Swinburnes to 'equal any gentleman in the land'.[51]

Recusant squires could therefore gain a lease of life in post-Revolution England if they rejected devotional seclusion, to discharge the patrician duties of sociability and hospitality. In the circuit of race and hunt meetings, seasons in York and Bath, and ventures to the London opera, Catholics shaded into the larger hinterland of a gentry that, it has been argued, was becoming more homogenous and hegemonic, sustained by shared tastes, ambitions and anxieties over the national status of landed property.[52] In Sussex, the Carylls belonged to the shooting circle of the Whig duke of Richmond, in Suffolk the Mannocks served as masters of the county foxhounds, while the enduring friendship of the Throckmortons

---

10 April 1734, Walmesley MSS, Correspondence; John Gillibrand's Accounts, 24 June 1712, Walmesley MSS, 171.

[48] Robert, Lord Petre, to Sir Nicholas Shireburne, n.d. 1712, Northumberland CRO, Shireburne MSS, 88/3; Family pedigrees, Lancashire CRO, Walmesley MSS, DDpt/24; Juliana Dicconson to Roger Dicconson, 2 April 1743, Lancashire CRO, Scarisbrick MSS, 44/9.

[49] 'The children's godfathers and godmothers', n.d., Northumberland CRO, Swinburne MSS, 517/1.

[50] Anna Maria Webb to Lady Mary Swinburne, 17 August 1710, Northumberland CRO, Swinburne MSS, Box 5; Derwentwater to Lady Swinburne, 18 March 1714, Swinburne MSS, Box 5; Account book, Lancashire CRO, Shireburne MSS 94/1.

[51] William Fenwick to William Swinburne, n.d. 1693, Northumberland CRO, Swinburne MSS, 508/18.

[52] Elizabeth Marsh to Mary Huddleston, 1 August 1727, Cambridgeshire CRO, Huddleston MSS, MH/9; Inventory, 1705, Lancashire CRO, Shireburn MSS, fols 193–203; J.A. Williams, *Catholicism in Bath* (2 vols, CRS, 1974–75), I, pp. 45–8; Leo Gooch, '"The Religion for a Gentleman": The North Country Catholics in the Eighteenth Century', *Recusant History*, 23 (1997), pp. 543–68; J.M. Rosenheim, *The Emergence of a Ruling Order: English Landed Society 1650–1750* (London and New York, 1998), pp. 2–8, 91–7.

with the Pakington family in Warwickshire offered a reminder that many Tory gentlemen possessed a recusant lineage.[53] *Noblesse oblige*, as much as high fashion, shaped the virtues of the recusant gentleman. Entering the recusant strongholds in Essex, Daniel Defoe acclaimed 'the noble family of Petre ... by a constant series of beneficent actions to the poor and bounty on all occasions, having gained an affectionate esteem through all that part of the country such as no prejudice of religion should wear out'.[54] Stephen Tempest and Sir Robert Throckmorton both established free schools and almshouses under Anglican auspices, while helping to select the church-wardens who served on their estates. In Oxfordshire, the overlapping social and religious identities of the Eystons were displayed when the family dead received public burial in a Catholic chapel inside the walls of East Hendred parish church.[55] The result was that in 1715, when the Jacobite contagion appeared to run through Catholic society, observers were faced with the troubling spectacle of suspects whose lives had long diverged from the hoary caricature of the delinquent papist. Before he took rebel command, Lord Derwentwater's conduct in public life had earned him the affection of Whig business partners, Nonconformist tenants, and peers such as the Hanoverian general, the duke of Argyll, who stopped to pay a parting gesture of respect before the hearse as he made his victorious journey back along the Great North Road.[56] Rebel politics entered the worlds of men who had otherwise laboured to draw the confessional sting from the reputation of the Catholic faith in England.

Recusant religion

If public pressures stamped a mark on Catholic life, the religious conscience placed a rival set of images and ideas at their disposal. When Lewis Innes informed the Carylls of 'the reall worth of Ladyholt', he meant not the value of the land, but the character of the estate as a lynchpin of the faith.[57] In the absence of an institutional church, the spirituality of English Catholi-

[53] Nathaniel Pigott to Sir Robert Throckmorton, 8 March 1711/12, Warwickshire CRO, Throckmorton MSS, Box 65, Folder 2/2; Mannock account books, 1724, Suffolk CRO, Mannock MSS, H3/14, 18; Duke of Richmond to John Caryll, 10 November 1731, BL, Add. MSS, 28,228, fol. 449.

[54] Daniel Defoe, *A Tour through the Whole Island of Great Britain*, ed. G.D.H. Cole and D.C. Browning (2 vols, London, 1902), I, p. 173, II, p. 249.

[55] Account book 1735–1754, Tempest MSS (private collection); Agreement for foundation of Free School at Coughton, 12 April 1709, Warwickshire CRO, Throckmorton MSS, EB/17; Henry Bell to Sir Robert Throckmorton, 4 May 1692, Throckmorton MSS, 55/6.

[56] Robert Patten, *History of the Late Rebellion* (1717), pp. 42–3; F.J.A. Skeet, *The Life of the Rt. Hon. James Radcliffe, Third Earl of Derwentwater* (London, 1929), pp. 119–120.

[57] Lewis Innes to Caryll, 12 June 1710, BL, Add. MSS, 28,227, fol. 84.

cism was centred on a cult of the devout family, evidenced in the art of Oxburgh Hall, where the Bedingfields were pictured, enfolded in the arms of the Virgin, and dramatised inside the private chapel at Harvington Hall, where the Throckmortons worshipped within walls decorated with red and white drops symbolising the blood and water of the Passion. Against the vicissitudes of the period, there were few signs of exhaustion in recusant religious practise. Drawing up his will, Sir William Mannock was concerned to pass down 'my Cross of Gold which hath continued in the family for several generations (and for which I very much desire it may not go out of the family but go to the heir)'.[58] Under gentry funding, the old sites of pilgrimage, notably St Winifred's Well in North Wales, provided rallying points for families from across the country.[59] It was in the devotional sphere that recusant gentlewomen came into their own, with William Blundell hailing his wife, Anne, as 'the Ark who has saved our little cockboat at Crosby from sinking in many a storm'.[60] Noblewomen such as Lady Catherine Petre were vaunted by the clergy as exemplars 'to propagate God's glory upon Earth' through their acts of neighbourhood charity, and religious life was nourished by the convents discreetly established at York and Hammersmith by the Institute of the Blessed Virgin Mary.[61] Sponsored by the squires for their own daughters, and 'poor distressed orphans' on their estates, these houses were lauded by the vicar apostolic, James Smith, as 'standing out amongst all schools, the most considerably and flourishing of all in England'.[62]

Against the prosperous bustle of gentry life, a skein of spiritual literature reminded Catholic squires of the need to observe 'the heroical way of the Cross', as described by the Jesuit Francis Mannock, to see earthly suffering for the faith as 'desirable above gold and pretious stones and sweeter than honey'.[63] The Caryll and Paston households were replete with handwritten catechetical instructions, bibles and lives of the saints, with the traditions of English sainthood and martyrology disseminated in Richard Challon-

---

58 Will of Sir William Mannock, 1711, Suffolk CRO, Mannock MSS, C/129.
59 Mary Griffith to Lady Petre, n.d. c. 1735, Lancashire CRO, Walmesley MSS, Correspondence; William Fleetwood, *The Life and Miracles of St Wenefrede* (1713); Mary Caryll to John Caryll, 13 July 1708, BL, Add. MSS, 28,226, fol. 135.
60 Blundell, ed., *Blundell Letters*, p. 51.
61 John Gillibrand to Lady Petre, 22 April 1716, Lancashire CRO, Walmesley MSS, Correspondence; S. O'Brien, 'Women of the English Catholic Community: Nuns and Pupils at the Bar Convent, York 1690–1790', in J. Loades, ed., *Monastic Studies* (London, 1990), pp. 270–2.
62 'Account book', Suffolk CRO, Mannock MSS, H5/1; Bishop Smith to Mrs Bedingfield, 3 May 1693, AAW, Main Series, 36/33; Dorothy Paston to Lady Petre, 22 March 1714.
63 Francis Mannock to Lady Petre, 24 March 1727, Lancashire CRO, Walmesley MSS, Correspondence.

er's *Britannia Sancta* and *Memoirs of Missionary Priests*.[64] Yet the question of how far to embrace these social and confessional rigours aroused perceptible tension for the laity. James Smith was anxious to refine the Medieval Kalendar, limiting the feast days that strained financial resources on the landed estates, and in 1693 a set of 'Reflections concerning the English College at Rome', sent to Cardinal Howard, cited widespread lay hostility to the intrusion of foreign devotional pressures on the mission.[65] Privately, recusant squires sought to strip away the separatist instincts of their religion, and their ethos was encouraged by the selection of chaplains such as the Benedictine Alban Dawnay, who considered 'that zeal for faith not much to be commended that destroys charity, and that affection which we ought to bear not only to all Christians of other denominations but to mankind in general'.[66] At Ugbrooke House in Devon, where Lord Thomas Clifford had meditated on the prospect of reconciliation between the Roman and Anglican Churches, the family chapel was consecrated to St Cyprian, the apostle of Christian unity.[67] The Erasmian sensibility of Sir Robert Throckmorton was embodied in a library stocked with Anglican and even Calvinist titles.[68] Stephen Tempest believed that any educated discussion of religion among Catholics and Protestants 'not resolved to eavil' would see theological conflicts reduced to 'the splitting of a hair', aroused by nothing more than speculative notions of church authority. He castigated 'ecclesiasticks on both sides' who, 'instead of charitably healing, endeavour to widen differences'.[69] Preserving the honour of a spiritual tradition did not mean taking a stand outside the larger society to which Catholic squires wished to belong.

The devotional literature disseminated from Catholic printing presses in London, Douai and St Omer proved sensitive to the conflicts of lay life in the post-Revolution realm. English authors imported into recusant discourse a model of piety inspired by the writings of St Francis de Sales, whose *Introduction to the Devout Life* had showed the way in which a Catholic bishop

[64] Paston Inventory, 1751, Gloucestershire CRO, D5563/11; Caryll inventory, listed in Alexander Gordon to John Caryll, 29 July 1716, BL, Add. MSS, 28,227, fols 320–1; Richard Challoner, *Memoirs of missionary priests, as well secular as regular* (1741); Challoner, *Britannia sancta, or, The lives of the most celebrated British, English, Scottish and Irish saints* (1745).

[65] George Witham to John Betham, 15 March 1701, AAW, St Gregory's Seminary MSS, 149; 'Reflections concerning the English College, Rome', 1695, AAW, Main Series, 36/95.

[66] Dawnay letter-book, n.d. 1710, BL, Add. MSS, 28,254, fols 190–1.

[67] Lady Anne Clifford, *Collectanea Cliffordiana* (Paris, 1817), pp. 104–5; Cyril Hughes Hartmann, *Clifford of the Cabal* (London, 1937), pp. 203–4.

[68] Commonplace book, n.d., Warwickshire CRO, Throckmorton MSS, LCB/72.

[69] Tempest, 'Religio Laici', Tempest MSS (private collection).

navigated the challenges of the Calvinist majority in the diocese of Geneva.[70] Received by devotees such as John Belson in Oxfordshire, the works of De Sales promoted 'active judgement', moral rigour and patient virtue as 'the true manly way' to God, against the 'mournful apprehensions and tragicall expressions' that coloured continental baroque devotion.[71] The *Introduction* aimed to reassure the believing Christian that, just as a firefly flitted through the flames, so 'a vigorous and constant soul' could move through the temptations and corruptions of earthly existence, tapping into 'the springs of sweet piety in the midst of the brackish waters of the world'.[72] De Sales's English disciples anchored their model of worship in reading, family prayer and private meditation.[73] The homespun imagery of John Gother's handbooks was especially hewn to suit the experiences of Catholics compelled to enter into the public and commercial arena: 'If the hours of necessary business give little opportunity for prayer or recollection, yet they may find Christ present within them, even in their business. The Tradesman may find Him in his shop, the labourer in his work ... the Afflicted in all their Distress.'[74] In its literary and liturgical efforts, the church therefore aimed to help its flock carve out a distinction between the confessional and the civic realms, shifting the environment of devotion into the domestic inner sanctum, while seeking to incarnate charity through an active Christian life within the world. The Douai editors of one Salesian translation hoped for 'our friends in England' that 'on a journey when the wayes are dangerous', the richest writings of the faith would 'pass through the eye to the heart ... and enflame them with the love of God'.[75]

Honour and aspiration

The devotional stress on finding redemptive conditions *within* the world allowed recusant squires to harness their thoughts on private religion to the veneration of their own ancestors as guardians of the faith. In 1712, Sir William Swinburne drew up the pedigree of his 'illustrious house': a monument to 'the continuance of our family, with relation to the steadiness of principalls for consciences sake, by wandering through ye adversity of

---

[70] Francis de Sales, *An Introduction to the Devout Life* (1695), Preface; Viviane Mellinghoff-Bourgerie, *François de Sales (1567–1662): un homme de lettres spirituelles* (Geneva, 1999).

[71] John Belson, religious discourses, n.d., Oxfordshire CRO, Belson MSS, F/1/4/MS/59.

[72] De Sales, *Introduction*, pp. 3, 5.

[73] Evidenced in Richard Challoner, *The Garden of the Soul* (1740); Richard Luckett, 'Bishop Challoner: The Devotionary Writer', in Duffy ed., *Challoner and his Church*, pp. 71–89.

[74] Gother, *Works*, I, p. 108.

[75] De Sales, *Introduction*, Preface.

difficult times'.[76] In the 'Religio Laici' put before his son in 1739, Stephen Tempest of Broughton insisted that only the 'truly loyal and indigent party', in politics and in faith, could maintain 'honour' and 'Christianity' against the 'little artifices' of those 'not long out of the dirt'.[77] Reflections on Christian nobility were accordingly framed within a squirearchical culture of public virtue, grounded in principles of lineage and patriotism. Sir Nicholas Shireburne saw his family's tenacity in matters of religion springing from the same root as their military achievements, to leave 'Marks of Honour derived from so many Ages and Generations to these times'. Feats of courage in the Civil War were connected in a golden thread with the triumphs of England in 'Catholick tymes', made manifest in the deeds of Shireburne knights at Crecy and Agincourt, to pinpoint an unchanging patriotic principle on either side of the Reformation.[78] The re-modelled Shireburne monument in Great Mitton chapel, revered by Sir Nicholas as 'the buriall place of my ancestors', brought Catholic piety into contact with chivalric romance, with cross-legged, recumbent effigies of past family members surrounded by lit candles.[79] Valorising the past allowed recusants to write themselves back into English history without disguising their religious convictions, while offering more than a broad hint as to the location of their dynastic loyalties. The Swinburnes assisted Arthur Collins, the author of a new history of the *Baronetage*, with information on the military achievements of their family less than a year before riding out into the 1715 rebellion: instructing their correspondent to accentuate their suffering at the hands of the Cromwellian state, in testimony to a consistent principle of allegiance.[80]

The converging influences of family honour, private religion and public aspiration gained freest expression inside the houses and gardens of the Catholic squirearchy. Marching in step with the gentry fashion, when Sir John Vanbrugh judged that 'all the World are running mad after building', the decades following the Revolution bore witness to a great process of rebuilding, redesigning and renovation on recusant estates.[81] In a pithy symbol of the collision between fashionable wealth and the consciousness

---

[76] Sir William Swinburne, family pedigree, 1712, Northumberland CRO, Swinburne MSS 6/95; Sir William Swinburne to Arthur Collins, 12 March 1712, Northumberland CRO, Swinburne MSS, 6/94.

[77] Tempest, 'Religio Laici', Tempest MSS (private collection).

[78] Sir Nicholas Shireburne to the earl of Bindon, 21 December 1708, Lancashire CRO, Shireburne MSS, 97/4; Robert Dale to Sir Nicholas Shireburne, 25 September 1694, Shireburne MSS. DDST 97/4.

[79] 'Will of Sir Nicholas Shireburne', Lancashire CRO, Shireburne MSS, 115/7; John Callow, 'The Last of the Shireburnes: The Art of Death and Life in Recusant Lancashire 1660–1754', *Recusant History*, 26 (2002–3), pp. 589–615.

[80] Arthur Collins to Edward Swinburne, 24 March 1715, Northumberland CRO, Swinburne MSS, 6/98; Sir William Swinburne to Arthur Collins, 12 March 1712, Swinburne MSS, 6/94.

[81] Sir John Vanbrugh, *Complete Works*, ed. Dobree and Webb (1928), IV, p. 25.

of religious strife, the Swinburnes built seven priest-holes into their recon-structed mansion at Capheaton, which otherwise conformed to the designs of Robert Trollope, with 'courts, gardens and a bowling green' laid down 'in a very moderne fashion'.[82] The Tempests transformed Broughton Hall into the picture of Georgian neo-classical splendour, while Sir Nicholas Shire-burne sought to create a gentry paradise beneath the walls of Stonyhurst Hall, adding marbled hall-ways, flanking towers, ornamental gardens, and lead-eagles imported from Antwerp.[83] Such extravagance met a macabre end in 1702 with the death of Shireburne's only son, reputedly occasioned by eating poisoned berries, while lost in the maze that wound through his father's Arcadia.[84] Yet, Sir Nicholas's passions represented more than genteel eccentricity. In their estates, the gentry could construct imaginative, ordered realms, and revel in the chance of governance over a small part of the nation. Alexander Pope lionised the Caryll family's 'little commonwealth' at West Harting; Stephen Tempest saw 'every man possessed of a great landed estate as a kind of petty princeling', holding dominion over the moral and material welfare 'of those who live under him'.[85] Here, he was a figure to reconcile religious divisions, helping to rescue the local parson from the debtors' gaol and clashing with Anglican authorities only when he insisted on his right to lease farms to Quakers from within the locality.[86] Tempest was adamant that 'tho a Gentleman's calling is said by some to be an idle one', such a man 'ought to be in theory a lawyer, a tradesman, mechanick, husbandman, every thing with which he must be frequently concernd'.[87]

The process of beautifying, improving and competing on their estates showed that confessional retreat was not part of the plan for recusant life. Through the organisation of their 'little commonwealths' and 'petty prin-cipalities', the Catholic gentry declared their fitness for public office, and laid down a vision for the greater commonwealth that they wished to see established over the English nation. In line with the pastoral tradition from Marvell to Pope, they perceived their estates not as realms for retreat, but places to rekindle the virtuous sparks in the human mind, and so equip themselves for service to their realm.[88] Tempest mused that ''tis unpardon-

---

[82] Notes in family pedigree, 1712, Northumberland CRO, Swinburne MSS, 2/95.
[83] Broughton Hall Deeds, nos 150, 160 (Surtees Society, 11, 115); Pevsner, Buildings of England, Lancashire, II, pp. 220–2, 239–42.
[84] Epitaph to Richard Francis Shireburne, 8 July 1702, Lancashire CRO, Shireburne MSS, 101/35; Will of Sir Nicholas Shireburne, 1717, Shireburne MSS 115/7.
[85] Tempest, 'Religio Laici', Tempest MSS (private collection); Pope, Correspondence, I, p. 457; Erskine-Hill, Social Milieu, pp. 75–96.
[86] Account book 1735–1754, Tempest MSS (private collection); M.E. Lancaster, The Tempests of Broughton (Skipton, 1987), pp. 83–6.
[87] Tempest, 'Religio Laici', Tempest MSS (private collection).
[88] D. Hirst and S. Zwicker, 'High Summer at Nun Appleton, 1651: Andrew Marvell and Lord Fairfax's Occasions', Historical Journal (1993), pp. 247–69; Erskine-Hill, Social Milieu, pp. 74–98.

able to see a man of parts so indolent as to sit at home, enjoying himself in a small fortune, whilst he might be doing eminent service to his King, Country and Family'.[89] Moreover, for squires versed in recent history, the notion of recovering a lost birthright appeared far from inconceivable. Elevated to baronetcies under James I, raised to officer rank in the Civil War, and swept into public office as deputy lieutenants, sheriffs and magistrates under James II, the openings of the Stuart polity had released waves of ambition in Catholic families such as Swinburne, Shireburne, Mannock and Throckmorton that would not be readily forgotten beyond the Revolution.[90] The re-fashioning of Catholic households in England ran as one with the refiguring of an active spirituality, and the emphasis placed upon kinship networks, family history and material wealth, to create an alternative vision of the national order outside the confines of the post-Revolution state.

English Catholics and the exiled court

The dreams of power and restoration among the Catholic gentry were inflamed by the fact that, just across the Channel, they enjoyed access to an alternative political world. Between 1689 and 1718, England possessed a 'shadow court' in France, a Jacobite 'capital' sustained by pensions and subsidies from the treasury of Louis XIV.[91] The exiled Stuart milieu has been subject to renewed scholarly attention in recent years, with a slew of works by Edward Corp accentuating its vigorous literary, devotional and artistic life. Though the household was projected further south in 1718, taking up residence in Rome, it remained the centre of a diaspora of literary and aristocratic talent, and a locus for recusants from across the three kingdoms. After the arrival of the main body of émigrés in 1689, a trickle joined at regular intervals, making recourse to the continent in a time when 'the air of England [is] too hot to live in'.[92] Between 1692 and 1713, English Catholic families featured among the 1,000 British names appearing yearly in the parochial registers of St Germain. In the same period, they helped to make

---

[89] Tempest, 'Religio Laici', Tempest MSS (private collection).
[90] Lancashire appointments, 1687, Lancashire CRO, Molyneux MSS, 3/19, 26, 27; J.O. Payne, *English Catholics of 1715* (London, 1889), pp. 145–7; Jacobite Commissions, 1693, Bodleian Library, Carte MSS, 181, fols 9–19, 558–62.
[91] Edward Corp, ed., *A Court in Exile: The Stuarts in France 1688–1718* (Cambridge, 2003); Corp, ed., *The Stuart Court in Rome: The Legacy of Exile* (Aldershot, 2003); Corp and Eveline Cruickshanks, *The Stuart Court in Exile and the Jacobites* (London, 1995).
[92] Edward Dicconson to Mayes, 5 May 1715, AAW, Epistolae Variorum, V/93; Thomas Southcott to James III, 30 August 1728, Royal Archives (Windsor), Stuart papers, 119/134; Wilton, 'Early Eighteenth-Century Catholics', pp. 371–2.

up 1,250 Jacobite baptisms, 814 burials, and 318 marriages.[93] The second significant wave appeared after the failure of the 1715 rising. It was, initially at least, considered in the interests of the Stuarts to encourage the development of a large courtly society, and the Jacobite officer Sir William Jennings recorded his efforts to 'relieve severall of his Matie's subjects that hath been in distress', by attracting them 'over to St Germain'.[94] Bemoaning 'the experience of a banished man out of all employment in a foreign country', the recusant Francis Stafford saw the chance for promotion 'after soe many yeares faithful service', and the court surveyed the diaspora with an eye to recruitment.[95]

The Jacobite royal palaces were staffed by a body of 220 court families, drawn mainly from the ranks of the English and Irish Catholic squirearchy.[96] They occupied rooms in the royal household, worshipped in the Chapel Royal and enrolled their children at the Scots College, the English Augustinian convent and the Jesuit academies of La Fleche and Louis le Grand in Paris.[97] Their elevation was attested by gifts in the royal wills, generous pensions and the distribution of positions in the court administration.[98] In the highest political echelons of St Germain, the recusant manors of Sussex supplied two secretaries of state, John Caryll of West Harting and Henry Browne of Cowdray Park.[99] As ladies in waiting to the queen, Lady Winifred Strickland and the Countess of Stafford helped to nurse the infant royal heirs.[100] However, the English Catholic influence was especially marked in the education of successive Stuart princes. The young James Edward Stuart lived under the regime of three recusant under-governors – Francis Plowden, Edward Perkins and later William Dicconson – gained spiritual instruction from his preceptors Dr John Betham and Dr John Ingleton, and received training in the art of warfare from Captain Charles Booth and Lieutenant

93   Natalie Genet-Rouffiac, 'Jacobites in Paris and St Germain-en-Laye', in Cruickshanks and Corp, eds, *The Stuart Court in Exile*, pp. 19, 24.
94   Sir William Jennings to Henry Browne, 23 February 1691, BL, Add. MSS, 37,662, p. 36.
95   Francis Stafford to Henry Browne, 7 August 1693, AAW, Browne MSS, 222.
96   Lewis Innes to John Caryll, 3 December 1711, BL, Add. MSS, 28,227, fol. 122; Lart, *Parish Registers*; 'The Establishment of Salaries, Pensions & c. Commencing in the month of January 1709', BL, Egerton MSS, 2517.
97   John Caryll to Mary Caryll, 17 November 1706, BL, Add. MSS, 28,226, fols 125–6; Thomas Marwood, Diary, 29 December 1700 – 24 January 1701, *Bedingfield papers* (CRS, 6, London, 1909), pp. 71–92; Ralph Arnold, *Northern Lights: The Story of Lord Derwentwater* (London, 1959) pp. 45–50.
98   Will of Queen Mary of Modena, HMC, *Stuart*, pp. 201, 700; Charles Leyburne to James Edward, 7 December 1720, Royal Archives (Windsor), Stuart papers, 47/151.
99   C.E. Lart, *Jacobite Extracts from the Parish Registers of St Germain-en-Laye* (2 vols, 1910–12); Edward Corp, *A Court in Exile: The Stuarts in France, 1689–1718* (Cambridge, 2003), p .139.
100 Rooms in the palace of St Germain, BL, Egerton MSS, 1671, 181/23.

Dominic Sheldon.[101] The experience evidently left a favourable impression: two decades later, when he appealed for an under-governor for the infant Prince Henry, James III stated his preference for 'a Catholick, a good Gentleman, but no Lord, and twere to be wished, an Englishman'.[102]

With St Germain observed by the watchful eyes of William III's agents, a family's decision to throw themselves into court life invariably meant formal severance from England. Lady Anne Lytcott, the daughter of James II's barrister, Robert Brent, reminded the Pretender that her family had sacrificed a Gloucestershire estate of £2,500, and as early as 1691, the court hierarchy was advising its supporters to place their estates in the hands of friends: the gesture of recognition that this was to be a prolonged spell away from their native country.[103] Neither was there to be a life of permanent luxury at St Germain. Social and economic hardship peaked after the death of Mary of Modena in 1718, when the French ministers chose the moment to affirm their alliance with George I, and curtailed the payment of subsidies and pensions for the Jacobite community left in Paris.[104] 'Since the Queen's death this place has become the den of all you can imagine most dismal in nature', announced the household officer Roger Strickland, and moments of material discomfort exacerbated national and religious tensions among the émigré community: Irish co-religionists and Scottish Protestants were subject to varying forms of social and moral distrust from the English Catholic grandees.[105] Yet at its grandiloquent height, the espousal of a life among the exiled Stuarts opened new horizons to recusant squires, which frequently outstripped their prospects before 1688. The Carylls enhanced family prestige with the acceptance of a Jacobite peerage, and the portraits, masques and concerts turned gentry families into courtiers, with the poet Anthony Hamilton heaping panegyrics upon the Stafford and Strickland girls as 'nymphs of St Germain'.[106] Colonel Robert Fielding recalled how:

---

[101] Henry Browne, Letter-book, 1691, AAW, Browne MSS, 208; Marquis de Ruvigny and Raineval, *The Jacobite Peerage* (London, 1904), pp. 214–15; James II, warrant, 2 August 1700, HMC, *Stuart*, I, p. 151; Earl of Perth to John Caryll, 29 July 1695, Bodleian Library, Carte MSS, 209, fol. 313; Charles Booth to Charles, earl of Middleton, 14 June 1709, Carte MSS, 210, fol. 152.

[102] James Edward to Lewis Innes, 28 April 1727, Royal Archives (Windsor), Stuart papers, 106/70.

[103] Browne to Arthur, 7 August 1692, AAW, Browne MSS, 208; Sir Richard Bulstrode to Browne, 22 February 1691, BL, Add. MSS, 39,662, pp. 33–4.

[104] George Hinde, 9 May 1718, AAW, Epistolae Variorum, VI/87; JI, 19 September 1718, 6/97; William Dicconson to the earl of Mar, 20 February 1719, Royal Archives (Windsor), Stuart papers, 42/46.

[105] Roger Strickland to John Paterson, 28 August 1718, HMC, *Stuart*, VII, p. 244; Philip Caryll to John Caryll, 19 November 1726, BL, Add. MSS, 28,228, fols. 213–14; Robert Witham to Mayes, 24 April 1718, AAW, Epistolae Variorum, VI/83.

[106] John Caryll to Mary Caryll, 15 July 1695, BL, Add. MSS, 28,226, fols 103–4; Comte

The ladies like soe many stars attended our brighter planet, the Queen ... from hence they went to hunt the wild boar, and whereas Mr Richard Biddulph had two horses carried under him like a true knight errant ... wee had an entertainment of musick from thence to cards and other playes and soe to bed ...[107]

His report came tinctured with a curious ambivalence, as a group enchanted by their experience came close to forgetting the essential political mission: 'all this time not a word of England or anything that looked like thinking wee deserved to go back, and if I might be free with you ... I doe not find other folks be over-pressing for that matter'.

Association with St Germain worked to revivify the British Catholic communities after the body-blow dealt in 1688. The loss of apostate houses was partially compensated by conversions in the Jacobite entourage, including the diplomat Bevil Skelton, the Oglethorpe family and the secretaries of state Charles Middleton and John Hay.[108] Families who had previously gained only a glimpse of Stuart royalty now had an intense experience of its magic, and for the wealthier émigrés maintained in the royal household, the endurance of exile could be understood as a magnificent trial of virtue. 'Though our estate is now in the hands of a professed enemy to your Majesty in particular and Monarchy in general, our Loyalty is still the same', professed Charles Widdrington, in October 1721.[109] From this sense of intimacy came the incentive for recusants to throw themselves into Jacobite designs: the chance to shape the political character of a restored Stuart kingdom. As Daniel Arthur said to Henry Browne, on the latter's assumption of the secretaryship: 'Sir, let me heartily congratulate with you not so much for wt it is, as in respect of what it may be ... soe now my love and concern for you will make me long for it, with much more eager desires.'[110] John Caryll compared his nurturing of the young Prince of Wales to the tending of English oaks on his Sussex estates. He confided to his brother that though 'I can entertain no reasonable hopes of outliving ye bad times and consequently seeing my friends again at home ... all joy here is in our nursery which is as thriving and promising as can be wisht' with effects that 'your sonne and grandchildren may see come to perfection'.[111] Behind

Antoine Hamilton, Oeuvres, 4 vols (Paris, 1762), II, p. 263; Corp, Court in Exile, pp. 181–214.

[107] Colonel Robert Fielding to Henry Browne (from Paris), 19 October 1690, BL, Add. MSS, 37,662, fol. 4.

[108] Sheridan, 'Political Reflexions', Royal Archives (Windsor), Stuart papers, Miscellany, VII, p. 117; George Hilton Jones, The Main Stream of Jacobitism (Harvard, 1954), pp. 181–2.

[109] Charles Widdrington to James III, 1 October 1721, Royal Archives (Windsor), Stuart papers, 55/14.

[110] Daniel Arthur to Henry Browne, 10 October 1690, AAW, Browne MSS, 52.

[111] John Caryll to Richard Caryll, 17 September 1694, BL, Add. MSS, 28,226, fols 99–101.

courtly self-fashioning was a greater hope still: the expectation of a return to England, and the re-capture of power.

The exiled colleges

Such was the sheer volume of the Jacobite presence in Europe that the refugee world could not be confined within the walls of St Germain. By the end of the first decade in exile, international Jacobitism had fragmented into a genuine diaspora, with inhabitants settling in France, Spain, Italy, the Low Countries, the German states and even moving as far a field as Russia. However, the first point of sanctuary emerged from the national colleges, monasteries and convents exiled on European soil. In 1689, the family of Sir Richard Bulstrode, James II's envoy in Brussels, were totally dependent on the charity of the English Dominican convent.[112] By 1695, 300 émigrés were taking refuge in the Benedictine abbey at Lambspring in Hanover, with wanderers in the Low Counties finding shelter from the nuns of Dunkirk, where the abbess Mary Caryll, was sister to the Jacobite court secretary.[113] In the decade after the Revolution, the colleges consolidated their provision of essential resources to the widening exiled world, safeguarding the finances of refugees, and finding tutors and governesses for those families who had become separated.[114] 'I foresaw that so many persons in England as well as on this side of ye seas would apply to ye Seminary to take care of their accounts in this Country', William Dicconson reflected to the superiors of St Gregory's, Paris. Servants of the Jacobite cause would, he added, be sure to 'stand in need of some persons in ye seminary on many occasions both spiritual and temporal'.[115]

With some exceptions – Cardinal Howard in Rome and Richard Russell, bishop of Visieu in Portugal, promoted through the Braganza entourage – the English clergy were less absorbed into European ecclesiastical structures

112 Sir Richard Bulstrode to Browne, 22 February 1691, BL, Add. MSS, 39,662, pp. 33–4; Sir Richard Bulstrode to Browne, 12 June 1691, BL, Add. MSS, 39,662, p. 156; Mary Knatchbull of Ghent to Browne, 10 July 1691, BL, Add. MSS, 39,662 p. 154; Robert Witham to Mayes, 12 April, 1716, AAW, Epistolae Variorum, VI/9.

113 Weldon, *Chronological Notes*, pp. 232–3; CRS, *Dominicana*, p.211; Raymond Greene to Sir Henry Browne, October 1689, AAW, Browne MSS, 14. Mary Knatchbull to Sir Henry Browne, 21 June 1691, BL, Add. MSS, 37,662, p. 169.

114 Benedicta Fleetwood to John Caryll, 8 August 1720, BL, Add. MSS, 28,227, fol. 48; Thomas Brockholes, Accounts, 20 September 1719, AAW, St Gregory's Seminary MSS, 449; Richard Arundell to John Ingleton, 1 November 1718, St Gregory's Seminary MSS, 413.

115 William Dicconson to Dr Holden, 31 June 1732, AAW, St Gregory's Seminary MSS, 585.

than their Irish counterparts.[116] But the colleges in Paris and Douai had grown in affiliation with the city universities, from which the monks and clergy received their doctorates, while local courts and cathedrals helped to sustain over 50 English foundations across Europe.[117] Stocked with the children of refugees, the exiled institutions flourished visibly through the Jacobite period. By 1725, the secular clergy college at Douai and the Augustinian canonesses at Bruges boasted of reaching their highest number of pupils.[118] Many of the college superiors were themselves children of Jacobite courtiers, with the two sons of the Pretender's *aide-de-campe* Charles Booth resident inside the Jesuit seminary at St Omer, and Lady Lucy Herbert, daughter of the earl of Powis, made abbess of the Bruges convent.[119] In reconstituting old alumni families with the offspring of the exiled world, they left a vital legacy. According to the *Gentleman's Magazine* of May 1766, 350 boys and 300 girls aged between eight and fifteen, from the English recusant families, could be found receiving education in the Low Countries alone.[120] With foreign education officially proscribed, children had to travel under aliases: an early induction into the cloak and dagger dimension to papist life. However, while England stood 'soe drained by these warrs, and still Catholicks go by the worst', as Abbess Mary Caryll put it in 1706, continental teaching was deemed an urgent resource to secure them in their social and religious identity.[121] At its best, it could present what one Northumberland squire called 'the best education England and France could bestow upon you'.[122] Students at Douai received a humanist regimen, centred on the apparatus of Grammar, Poetry, Rhetoric and Philosophy, but also encompassing the works of Grotius, Malebranche and Newton. At St Omer, the Jesuit curriculum was re-crafted by the Hebrew scholar, Thomas Fairfax, while the Benedictines at Douai offered the pedagogical talents of Obadiah Walker, former Master of University College, Oxford.[123]

---

[116] J.J. Crowley, 'Dr Richard Russell (1630–1693), Bishop of Vizeu', *The Lisbonian*, 18/1 (1935), pp. 12–16; 18/2 (1935), pp. 17–22.

[117] For English Benedictine doctoral theses at the University of Paris, see Douai Abbey, Woolhampton MSS, Weldon, 'Memorials', IV, p. 51.

[118] Witham to Mayes, AAW, Epistolae Variorum, VI/4, August 1718; Witham to Mayes, 10 September 1724, AAW, Epistolae Variorum, VIII/69. Lady Lucy Herbert to Mary Fortescue, 11 January 1724, Cambridgeshire CRO, Huddleston MSS, MF/8.

[119] Lady Lucy Herbert to Mary Fortescue, 11 January 1724, Cambridgeshire CRO, Huddleston MSS, MF/8; Elizabeth Huddleston to Mary Fortescue, 23 May 1723, Huddleston MSS, MF/21; Account book, 1735–154, Tempest MSS (private collection).

[120] *Gentleman's Magazine* (May 1766), p. 206; Leo Gooch, 'Religion for a Gentleman', pp. 547–9.

[121] Mary Caryll to John Caryll, 14 November 1706, BL, Add. MSS, 28,226, fol. 127.

[122] William Fenwick to Sir William Swinburne, 10 March 1714, Northumberland CRO, Swinburne MSS, 510/12.

[123] Lunn, *English Benedictines*, pp. 180–1; Michael Sharratt, '"Excellent Professors and an Exact Discipline": Aspects of Challoner's Douai', in Duffy, ed., *Challoner and his*

The vitality of the colleges and convents was evidenced in generous bequests. The Huddlestons of Sawston endowed a foundation for scholars at Lambspring in 1729, on condition that the family would enjoy burial rights in the abbey church; the Throckmortons gave a yearly gift of £100 to the Benedictines in Paris.[124] The Scots College, Paris held masses in the memory of their benefactor, Secretary Caryll, and the director of studies Thomas Innes described the disposal of such gifts as 'a means for Parents to entail a blessing on their Children as Heirs, that is, to serve Christ, to whom all belongs, one of them by leaving a share to Him in their poor and pious uses'.[125] Foreign schooling would become a natural extension of family life, a formative 'rite of separation' building up the character of the Catholic child.[126] William Blundell imparted to his children that time spent away from Little Crosby must be viewed as a chance to 'sweeten their memories with a taste of spiritual joy against those times of greater trial' – though it is perhaps unlikely that many boys under the austere tutelage at Douai would have felt moved to agree.[127] The journey abroad was a liminal moment, a voyage not just into a different place but to a different time, in centres that preserved much of the paraphernalia of pre-Reformation religion. The colleges fostered a sense of national community by creating the first ties that took recusant youths out of their counties of birth, and the armorial bearings embossed onto the chapel of the Benedictine monks in Paris offered a potent reminder of the inheritance of noble alumni within the English realm.[128] Loyalty to one's institution would be the first thread to bind a Catholic to a sense of nationhood, in a world constructed as much to keep recusants thoroughly *English* when they moved through Europe, as it was to keep them Catholic when they returned across the Channel.

The Catholic Jacobite diaspora

The principal reason why the Catholic element in the Jacobite diaspora did not descend into poverty and dispossession was, therefore, because the refugees of 1688 found the architecture of an expatriate world already waiting for them. Neither was this represented solely in the colleges and convents. Partly through the fear of persecution, partly as a stimulant to the religious

Church, pp. 112–25; Robert Witham to Mayes, 19 February 1728, AAW, Epistolae Variorum, 9/66; Geoffrey Holt, 'Two Seventeenth-Century Hebrew Scholars: Thomas Fairfax and Edward Slaughter', *Recusant History*, 22 (1994–5), pp. 482–90.

124 Huddleston bequest, Downside Abbey, Birt Box, A/332; Accounts, 1711, Warwickshire CRO, Throckmorton MSS, 44/19.

125 Thomas Innes to John Caryll, 18 November 1711, BL, Add. MSS, 28,227, fol. 120.

126 Shell, *Catholicism*, pp. 169–93.

127 Blundell, ed., *Blundell Letters*, p. 76.

128 Scott, 'Benedictine Conspirator', p. 69; Weldon, *Chronological Notes*, p. 188.

conscience, generations of recusants had ventured freely across what Lady Henrietta Herbert casually described as 'the herring pond', in a way of life that left national borders distinctly porous.[129] Entering St Germain in 1688 John Caryll moved back into a familiar Catholic, aristocratic culture, having served as page to the duke of Parma during the first period of Stuart exile.[130] Affluent enough to have acquired residences in the metropolis, his fellow émigrés the Waldegraves and Staffords ventured with ease among the Parisian *beau monde*; the Throckmortons maintained a full household in Brussels, where they revelled in trips to the 'opera and comedies'.[131] Religious commonality did not guarantee emotional bonds. When Margaret and Jane Blundell had arrived at Rouen in 1657 to commence their education with the Poor Clares, they stared in astonishment at the great images on the walls of the cathedral, wholly foreign to their own devotional experience.[132] But by the time of the Revolution, the diaspora was sufficiently mature to have developed a tenacious national character. Fleeing to the Low Countries in 1716, Nicholas Blundell listed encounters with over 200 English laymen and women on his journeys to galleries, castles and cathedrals. He could call upon English priests, English landowners, English apothecaries, and tradesmen such as 'Fodergills the Yorkshire halters' in Bruges, sustaining remarkably little contact with the native population.[133] Blundell captured the emergence of an alternative Catholic nation, disarmingly similar to the recusant heartlands of the English provinces.

Foreign education and property-ownership imprinted the experiences of Catholic exile on the character of life at home. With lay leaders such as Sir Marmaduke Constable of Everingham spending up to three months of the year abroad, English recusants became early exponents of the Grand Tour, and adolescents enlarged their cultural horizons in the company of cultivated tutors, such as James Dodd, who took care of Lord Teynham's orphaned sons after 1691, or Thomas Marwood, who found employment with the Bedingfields in Norfolk and Paris.[134] The experience fostered a cosmopolitan spirit in recusant life: Sir Edward Gascoigne traversed Italy in the hope of building

129 Henrietta Herbert to George Wakeman, 27 August 1735, AAW, St Gregory's Seminary MSS, 609.

130 The duchess of Parma to Lady Catherine Caryll, February 1648, BL, Add. MSS, 28,226, fols 2–4.

131 Marwood's diary, 24 January – 25 May 1700, *Bedingfield Papers*, pp. 57–64; Thomas Southcott to James Edward, 30 August 1728, Royal Archives (Windsor), Stuart papers, 119/134; Ann Fortescue to Lady Mary Fortescue, 26 February 1717, Cambridgeshire CRO, Huddleston MSS, MF/4; Accounts, 1712, Warwickshire CRO, Throckmorton MSS, 44/1–2.

132 Blundell, ed., *Blundell Letters*, p. 75.

133 Blundell, *Great Diurnall*, II, pp. 101–206.

134 Alban Dawnay, Letter-book, BL, Add. MSS, 28,254, fols 46, 48, 69; James Dodd to Henry Browne, 1 September 1692, AAW, Browne MSS, 128; Sir Marmaduke Constable to Bede Potts, 27 February 1739, Hull University, Brynmor Jones Library, Constable

up his art collection in 1726, while Sir Thomas Haggerston imbibed from Parisian academies the architectural styles later introduced into his Northumberland estates.[135] European encounters could even bring rapprochement between recusants and Protestant compatriots: the priest George Thomson requested that fellow clergymen in Rome show the city to the touring son of the Tory MP, Sir Thomas Hanmer, since 'it may tender service hereafter to the Catholicks in this neighbourhood'.[136] Throughout the eighteenth century, British government officials warned of 'shoals of priests and papists regularly crossing the seas', and the Jacobite court sought to make use of those already acclimatised to foreign nations: the merchant John Aylward was put in charge of contracts for soldiers enlisting in 1692 for the first of the abortive expeditions into England.[137] The relative comfort with which recusants moved through the continent rendered it hard to tell who was or was not an avowed supporter of James II.

Initially, the outgrowth of the Jacobite diaspora was controlled by the court. The certificates of naturalisation, dispensed by the court secretariat for noblemen, soldiers and even artisans, offered the recommendation: 'a good Catholick, and a loyal subject of the king ... he has left his country for his religion and takes refuge in France'.[138] The precocious language of suffering and sacrifice was crafted to make these documents serve as tickets into the heart of the *ancien régime*. Members of the retinue were sent out on diplomatic service, with the Norfolk squire George Jerningham of Costessy, paid 4,000 livres a year to serve the interests of James III from a base in The Hague.[139] In the French army, Marshal Dillon's regiment of naturalised Frenchmen was founded on the remit of an armed Jacobite restoration, offering commissions to the children of Tempests and Dicconsons.[140] The Stuarts also laboured to obtain places for their client families over a larger area of Europe, acquiring the post of page to the duke of Lorraine for

MSS, DDEV/56/30, fols 147–8; Jeremy Black, *The British Abroad: The Grand Tour in the Eighteenth Century* (2nd edn, Stroud, 2003), pp. 51–2, 234–48.

135 Sir Edward Gascoigne to Mayes, 13 May 1726, AAW, Epistolae Variorum, 9/19; Sir Marmaduke Constable to Sir Carnaby Haggerston, 14 March 1743, Hull University, Brynmor Jones Library, Constable MSS, 60/85, II, 30.

136 George Thomson to Mayes, 24 September 1725, AAW, Epistolae Variorum, 8/114.

137 HMC 15th Report, Appendix, pt IV, p. 470; Petition of Henry Arundell, BL, Add. MSS, 61,620, fol. 184; Henry Browne, warrant, 6 February 1691, Arundel Castle, Howard of Norfolk MSS, Howard Letters and Papers 1636–1822, vol. I.

138 John Betham, warrant, 14 June 1700, HMC, *Stuart*, I, p. 140.

139 George Jerningham to the earl of Mar, 20 December 1718, HMC, *Stuart*, VII, pp. 659–60; William Dicconson, List of payments, November 1720, Royal Archives (Windsor), Stuart papers, 47/150.

140 Juliana Dicconson to Roger Dicconson, 13 April 1743, Lancashire CRO, Scarisbrick MSS, 44/11. Corp, *Court in Exile*, pp. 201–14; P.K. Hill, *The Oglethorpe Ladies and the Jacobite Conspiracies* (Atlanta, 1977), pp. 20–3.

Henry Browne's son, Anthony, in 1705, and later the young Henry Caryll in 1717.[141]

However the more enterprising Jacobites increasingly started to shape their own worlds outside the sphere of the exiled court, entering into the life of the European Catholic domain as tutors and soldiers, merchants and musicians, and wives to the indigenous aristocracy. Individuals could take more unusual routes towards integration: when the Catholic Jacobite Sir Charles Carteret looked for military postings for his sons, he invoked the assistance of his cousin, the Whig minister who had helped to forge the new Anglo-French alliance, at deep cost to the house of Stuart.[142] Émigré communities could spring up through private philanthropic initiative: after her marriage to the Marquis de Meziere in 1696 Lady Eleanor Oglethorpe devoted herself to establishing a refuge for displaced recusant ladies.[143] The social and economic complexion of recusant life was also redrawn by immersion into the French commercial world, where expatriate families had 'made most money in stock-jobbing', according to the procurator of the Scots College, Paris.[144] Few émigrés proved more industrious in exploiting the riches of the continent than Mary Herbert, grand-daughter of the earl of Powis, who entered into partnership with the Sussex recusant and financier Joseph Gage, to mine the hills of southern Spain, and prevailed upon the government to allow the import a non-Catholic workforce from England and Wales. Alexander Pope spoke satirically of 'Maria's Dream', alleging that she and her coevals had betrayed her family lineage by embracing the values of lucre.[145] Such critics could gain a certain decree of vindication when the collapse of one Jacobite brainchild, John Law's Mississippi Company, ensured that exiled Catholic gentlemen anticipated by four years the troubles of their compatriots following the bursting of the South Sea Bubble.[146] But, through the more successful ventures, recusant patricians came into their element in a climate where their religion was no longer a disability, replacing the quiet gentility of the rural manor with the trappings of state employment and commercial success.

[141] Lewis Innes to John Caryll, 2 April 1718, BL, Add. MSS, 28,227, fol. 442; Petition from Henry Browne, Viscount Montague to the Queen's Most Excellent Majesty, 1708, BL, Add. MSS, 61,620, fols 216–17.
[142] Eveline Cruickshanks and Howard Erskine-Hill, The Atterbury Plot (Basingstoke, 2004), pp. 63, 270.
[143] Pittock, Jacobitism, p. 52.
[144] Lewis Innes to Lady Caryll, 9 September 1719, BL, Add. MSS, 28,228, fol. 22; Robert Witham to John Ingleton, 28 April 1722, AAW, St. Gregory's Seminary MSS 505.
[145] Alexander Smith to Lady Mary Caryll, BL, Add. MSS, 28,228; Henrietta Tayler, Lady Nithsdale and her Family (London, 1939), pp. 247–8; Pope, Epistle to Bathurst, lines 129–34.
[146] Alexander Smith to Lady Caryll, 14 January 1724, BL, Add. MSS, 28,227, fol. 130. See also John Caryll to Mary Caryll, 22 May 1707, BL, Add. MSS, 28,226, fols 130–1.

Although it relieved the financial burden, total assimilation could be as great a danger to the Jacobite court as apostasy, when the cause had to be lived out largely in the imagination, enduring leagues of separation and periods when the political possibilities appeared distinctly fallow. The Stuarts needed to come up with the method to bind a community lacking territorial or institutional boundaries, and George Jerningham implored James Edward to summon the exiled nobility to attend the birth of his first child in 1720, to mark the occasion as an authentically British affair. Court edicts extolled the Jacobite 'family', inverting the language of royal authority to speak of 'the Obligation of a *King towards his subjects*'. As 'Our Saviour in the Gospel owns none for his relations but such as do the will of his Divine Father', so the same was true of the Stuarts, 'there being few there who have not lost for his Majesty'.[147] A Jacobite consciousness was amplified by applying across the exiled world the rituals affirming legitimate monarchy, with James Edward ministering the 'royal touch' to émigrés afflicted with disease in France and Rome. The English colleges at Liege and Lisbon sent stricken pupils to seek a cure from the mythic regal healing cult, and the practice was accentuated in the Jacobite press as a sign that God's blessing still resided in the Stuart line.[148] The cohesion of the émigré world was deepened when the court clergy established themselves as the architects of marital alliances between households of the faithful, with Lewis Innes arranging the betrothal of his pupil the young John Caryll of West Harting, to Mary MacKenzie, daughter of the earl of Seaforth, in 1710.[149] This match between a Sussex gentleman and a scion of the Scottish aristocracy pointed to the origins of an authentically 'British' Catholic experience in Europe, when the common pull of the exiled Jacobite court worked at least to lower the barriers that had originally positioned English, Scottish and Irish refugees in separate émigré communities.

To the relief of Stuart diplomats, most of the Catholic exiles did not surrender their allegiances. Jerningham reported that in Ghent 'I found many persons of note zealously engaged for yr Majestie's service ... which has left such an impression on their mindes and hearts yt yr Person and yr Cause are equally dear to them.[150] Jacobite loyalties were enshrined by

147 Orders to William Dicconson, 22 June 1719, Royal Archives (Windsor), Stuart papers, 44/13.

148 Eberson to Richard Plowden, 15 February 1721, EPSJ, LPC, fol. 76; M. Sharratt, ed., *Lisbon College Register 1628–1813* (CRS, Southampton, 1991), p. 196; 'M.T.', A *Letter from a Gentleman at Rome to his Friend in London, Giving an Account of some very Surprising cures of the King's Evil by the Touch, lately Effected in the Neighbourhood of that City* (London, 1721); Marc Bloch, *The Royal Touch: Sacred Monarchy and Scrofula in England and France*, trans. J. Anderson (London, 1973).

149 Lewis Innes to John Caryll, 2 June 1709, 24 July 1710, 12 October 1709, 18 December 1710, BL, Add. MSS, 28,227, fols 76, 86, 94, 97.

150 George Jerningham to James Edward, 1 May 1720, Royal Archives (Windsor), Stuart papers, 46/95; George Jerningham to David Nairne, 4 April 1720, Stuart papers, 46/39.

sacrifice in the exiled world, with the earl of Carlingford among the émigrés who lost their lives at the battle of the Boyne, and the lord Hunsdon killed in the naval assault on La Hogue in May 1692.[151] Promotion in a foreign court could be defined as the spur to Jacobite service: Sir Timon Connock's acquisition of a lieutenancy in Spanish forces in 1732, would, his mother assured James Edward, make him 'a zealous imitator of his father's loyalty'.[152] Nonetheless, the conflicts between a legitimist Jacobite conscience and the demands of host nations with fluctuating diplomatic interests would become a recurring source of tension for the English Catholics constructing new worlds after 1688.

The growth of Jacobite culture in England

The traffic between the English counties and the realm of Catholic exile moved in both directions. When it was assured that the post-Revolution settlement did *not* mean the rise of an unstoppable persecution, refugees began to drift back to their estates, with Henry Browne and the new earls of Stafford and Powis securing passes from the government of Queen Anne.[153] Retreat from the Jacobite world did not necessarily mean the renunciation of Jacobite loyalties, however, and when most of the returning exiles left with fulsome pledges of support, the lives of their families might interweave with the diaspora for over a century. John Caryll's great-great nephew, John Baptist, would also adopt the position of secretary of state, after a journey from Sussex into Rome in 1768.[154] It was in the links between England and the continent that an apparatus of domestic Jacobite loyalty was created, strong enough to endure in its varying forms for at least half a century after the Revolution, as the officers of St Germain imitated the methods applied within the diaspora to extend their influence over recusant activity at home. If it could not be nourished by personal contact with the exiled court, English Catholic Jacobitism was built upon the dissemination of the royal image, manifest in the Stuart portraits brought into Stonyhurst Hall, and the medallions, caparisoned with Jacobite images, which were believed to possess healing properties.[155] The transmission of written texts could serve

[151] Cokayne, *The Complete Peerage*, XI, pp. 682–3, XII, p. 396; Aveling, *Handle and the Axe*, pp. 241–2; J. Gillow and R. Trappes-Lomax, eds, *The Diary of the 'Blue Nuns', or Order of the Immaculate Conception at Paris, 1658–1810* (CRS, 8, London, 1920), pp. 413–14.

[152] Mary Connock to James Edward, 21 March 1732, 152/81.

[153] Petition from Henry Browne, Viscount Montague to the Queen's Most Excellent Majesty, 1708, BL, Add. MSS, 61,620, fols 216–17; Petition of Henry, earl of Stafford, 1704, BL, Add. MSS, 61,620, fol. 226.

[154] Ruvigny, *Jacobite Peerage*, p. 214.

[155] Edmund Perkins to Dr Meynell, 7 September 1697, AAW, 36/603; Shireburne Inventory, 12 December 1706, Lancashire CRO, Shireburne MSS; F.J.A. Skeet, *Catalogue*

the same purpose, with the exiled Dicconsons sending laudatory accounts of the Stuart princes to their Scarisbrick cousins and even the more politically non-committal Throckmortons preserving heroic narratives of the 'miracle of providence' witnessed in Charles Edward's 1746 escape through the Western Isles.[156] The grip of Jacobite ideology in the most fervent loyal households was affirmed when Sir Nicholas Shireburne and Francis Jerningham sent children afflicted with scrofula from England to the exiled court.[157]

The Jacobite cause opened up a new conspiratorial undercurrent in sections of recusant life, threatening to disturb the fragile equilibrium that had revived the faith in post-Revolution England. A culture of treason could start with 'seditious words', punishable by death, and move outwards through forms of social protest: the Carylls of Harting and the Racketts of Wingham sheltered smugglers and poachers defying not just the excise and forest laws, but reputedly used to pass on messages and ciphers in the Jacobite interest.[158] However, the Jacobite endgame was the prospect of a militant insurrection, and the years between 1689 and 1715 saw the passing of the Stuart torch into a region less susceptible to the reach of the state, where the interplay between salaried agents and local notables served to develop a 'secret army' of active conspirators.[159] Papers uncovered from the brickwork at Standish Hall, Lancashire and weapons unearthed behind a fireplace in the Scrope household at Danby correspond with the records of the exiled court and stray hints and whispers in recusant correspondence to confirm that, by 1693, an independent conspiratorial apparatus had been brought into the north of England.[160] Returning to Yorkshire from Ireland in 1689, Colonel Stephen Tempest was entrusted with twenty-two commissions to raise a troop of horse for King James: 'tho his Regiment for good

of Jacobite Medals and Touchpieces in the Collection of Miss Maria Widdrington (London, 1929).

156 William Dicconson to Robert Scarisbrick, 'Excerpts of letters from ye Camp at Gaeta', 7 August 1734, Lancashire CRO, Scarisbrick MSS, 78/2; 'An account on wch you may rely concerning His R H', 16 December 1746, Warwickshire CRO, Throckmorton MSS, Box 61, Folder 2/2.

157 F.J.A. Skeet, 'The Eighth Duchess of Norfolk', Stonyhurst Magazine, 257 (1925), pp. 73–4; C.S. Durant, A Link between Flemish Mystics and English Martyrs (London, 1925), p. 317.

158 Philip Caryll to John Caryll, 5 March 1730, BL, Add. MSS, 28,228, fol. 308; Eveline Cruickshanks and Howard Erskine-Hill, 'The Waltham Black Act and Jacobitism', Journal of British Studies, 24 (1985), pp. 358–65; E.P. Thompson, Whigs and Hunters: The Origins of the Black Act (London, 1975), pp. 92–3, 278–94.

159 P.A. Hopkins, 'Aspects of Jacobite Conspiracy in the Reign of William III', unpublished PhD thesis, Cambridge University (1981), pp. 410–45. Monod, Jacobitism, pp. 271–99.

160 James Ogle to Sir John Swinburne, 11 August 1692, Northumberland CRO, Swinburne MSS, Box 5; Lord Widdrington to Sir William Swinburne, 14 April 1712, Swinburne MSS, Box 5; T.C. Porteous, 'New Light on the Lancashire Jacobite Plot, 1692–4', Transactions of the Lancashire and Cheshire Antiquarian Society, 50 (1934–5).

reasons never took the field, yet it was compleat in number and well armed and horsd, all by his own interest and at his own proper charge', as his son recalled.[161] From London, the earl of Shrewsbury cited 'dark discoveries', with horse fairs, markets and bowling matches used to convey Jacobite weapons along the highways.[162] Later, Lord Lovat witnessed Durham recusants solemnising their allegiance through a heavily ritualised emotion: kissing commissions and kneeling before portraits of the Pretender.[163] At St Germain, the secretary of state, Lord Melfort viewed the Catholic secret army as 'the best feather in his wing'.[164] It was the peculiar misfortune of the government that the 1694 trials at Manchester, blown apart by the exposure of perjured witnesses, targeted some of the few local landowners *not* complicit in mobilisation for the Stuart cause.[165]

A striking continuity of northern recusant names persisted at the forefront of Jacobite conspiracy between 1689 and 1715, with the Catholic dynasties of Lancashire and Northumberland comprising the core of partisans. The military formations of the 'secret army', presented to the exiled court in 1693, were closely mimetic of the regimental line-up raised for Charles I in the north under the earl of Derby in 1644.[166] The scholarship of recent decades has drawn attention to the social structures that kept northern families closely bound to Jacobite activity into the reign of George I, with subversive exchanges embedded into the rituals of local gentry confraternities such as the mock-corporation of Walton-le-Dale.[167] Nonetheless, the agents of the exiled court could draw upon a wide geographical field of Catholic society. The concealed Standish papers named co-religionists from Staffordshire, Lincolnshire, Suffolk and Berkshire, while William Dicconson's St Germain account book testifies that £3,000 was received from the widowed Lady Petre in support of the '15, with the duke of Norfolk lending £2,000, and comparable sums sent from notables such Anne Holman in Northamptonshire, Anthony Kemp in Sussex and Thomas Eyre of Hassop in Derbyshire. Even those who did not rise up in arms were prepared to

---

161 Tempest, 'Religio Laici', Tempest MSS (private collection).

162 The earl of Shrewsbury to Lord Lumley, 16 January 1690, *CSPD 1689–90*, 412; Sir John Morgan to Shrewsbury, 26 March 1690, *CSPD 1689–90*, 527.

163 'A Memorial to the Queen of Lovat's dealings in England and Scotland', 1704, in James MacPherson, *Original Papers, Containing the Secret History of Great Britain* (2 vols, London, 1775), II, p. 641.

164 Melfort to Perth, 18 February 1701, printed in *Commons Journal*, 13, p. 336.

165 Beaumont, ed., *Jacobite Trials*, pp. 92–105.

166 Commissions signed by James II, 1692, Tempest MSS (private collection); Jacobite commissions, Bodleian Library, Carte MSS, 181, fols 9–19, 559.

167 Blundell, 'Great Diurnall', I, p. 174; J. Gillow and A. Hewitson, eds, *The Tyldesley Diary* (Preston, 1872), pp. 25, 52; Frank Coupe, *Walton-le-Dale: A History of the Village* (Preston, 1954), pp. 142–3; Gooch, *Desperate Faction?* pp. 39–40, 51–4.

make personal investments in the house of Stuart.[168] Supported from across the kingdom, an element of northern Catholic society was turned into a tinderbox, with two generations of squires keeping their weapons oiled to await the moment of command. If the rebel entry into Preston in November 1715 was serenaded with a waving of banners, a flourish of music and celebrations by the ladies of the town, this was because the arrival of the Jacobite regiments was a moment that had been intimated for years, in the club meetings, hunts and the horse races that offered the hint of a Catholic order reclaiming its rightful state of governance in the northern counties.[169]

The simultaneous strength and weakness of the Jacobite movement rose from its ability to stimulate a culture of private devotion and emotional perseverance away the battlefield: hardly a blessing for a cause that relied more upon armed action than the stoical virtues, but a means of withstanding a worsening political fortune. In the wake of the recriminations that followed the 1715 rebellion, the younger Stephen Tempest could claim sound justification in advising his sons not to 'run headlong into a rash scheme of a projecting statesman, which … seldom fails to utterly destroy the person engaged'. But he qualified his sentiment with the instruction 'Don't refuse to serve yr King and Country when a proper occasion offers.'[170] Even after the imprisonments, transportations and executions, a significant proportion of recusants strove to adhere to the identifying codes and motifs of dynastic loyalty. The Stuart cause could be a motivating principle in family life, with the marriages of Anne Mannock in Suffolk to the Stuart banker in Paris, Sir Daniel Arthur, and the court lady-in-waiting, Mary Skelton, to Viscount Molyneux in Lancashire, forging kinship networks between court and country.[171] A demilitarised Jacobitism could still function at a defiantly festive level: Maria, duchess of Norfolk emblazoned the houses of her Worksop estate with sprigs of oak on 10 June 1717, 'to celebrate this Holy Day' – the anniversary of James Edward's birth, while the Royal Oak Society established by John Baptist Caryll in 1743 brought Stuart medals into the households of Towneley, Anderton, Mostyn and Molyneux.[172] Its elite culture altered the topography of recusant estates, when the young earl of Powis chose to rebuild his castle in imitation of the terraced gardens,

168 Bodleian Library, Carte MSS, 181, fol. 559; Porteous, 'New Light', pp. 12, 23, 55–60; William Dicconson, 'Accounts', 1715–1719, Royal Archives (Windsor), Stuart Papers, 44/82.

169 Samuel Hibbert Ware, ed., Lancashire Memorials of the Rebellion, 1715 (Chetham Society, 1843), pp. 89–97.

170 Tempest, 'Religio Laici', Tempest MSS (private collection).

171 Henry Foley, Records of the Society of Jesus, V, pp. 546–52; Mary Skelton to the earl of Mar, 28 October 1718, HMC, Stuart, VII, p. 448.

172 'Phillis Balguy' [Maria, duchess of Norfolk) To 'Mr Heaton Junior at Sheffield', 10 June 1717, Arundel Castle, Howard of Norfolk MSS, Miscellaneous correspondence, 114. For Caryll see BL, Add. MSS, 28,249, fols 208–97.

fountains and statues at St Germain.[173] But allegiance was also affirmed in the homeliest of personal gestures, exemplified when William Turville wrote from Leicestershire to offer a family cure against miscarriage to Queen Maria Clementina, 'out of a pure love', and care for the welfare of 'our lovely young king'.[174] For at least three decades beyond the 1715 rebellion, therefore, the proponents of the exiled court sought to bind the mental landscape of English recusants into an alternative Stuart kingdom, animating a culture of estrangement from the prevailing power of state. Against, the prosaic reality of military defeat, its participants imbibed the hope declared in the poetry of the Scarisbrick family, that 'Peace and Plenty then entering/ Halcyon Days shall come again', and dreamed of the lost order returning once more.[175]

Conclusion

The culture of English Catholicism had long been shaped by a set of arrangements that expressed physical and spiritual distance from the post-Reformation kingdom, conferring the resources for a time of exile, but nonetheless giving recusants the ability to participate in the life of a Protestant realm. After 1688, the institutions of Catholic life rallied to prevent diaspora turning to disintegration, and the recusant gentry consolidated their position within a social mosaic centred on the manorial estate, the chapel and the cloisters in exile, with their connections to a county world outside the faith providing a platform of cultural support. Seventeen years after the rebellion in the north, the Jesuit, John Thornton, put it to Sir Marmaduke Constable that 'the old castle, far from drooping, looks like a rather venerably governed one'.[176] On these foundations, the community could foster certain temporal as well as religious virtues, considered essential to the integrity of English Catholic life. Writing to her brother, Abbess Mary Caryll enunciated her hope 'that our family may propagate religion, and be servisable to their King, as their ancestors have been, witness yourself that has spent these eighteen years in banishment for their service'.[177] In the recusant counties, a shadow ruling order was reconstructing itself, with memories of public service in the Civil War and the reign of James II revitalised by the lifeblood injected from Jacobite Europe. In their most ambi-

[173] 'Herbertiana', *Montgomeryshire Collections*, 2 (1873), pp. 368–9; 19 (1886) pp. 83–4.

[174] William Turville to Mayes, 25 July 1722, AAW, Epistolae Variorum, VII/130.

[175] 'Jacobite poetry', Lancashire CRO, Scarisbrick MSS, 19/33.

[176] John Thornton to Sir Marmaduke Constable, 31 January 1733, Hull University, Brynmor Jones Library, Constable MSS, 60/84a.

[177] Mary Caryll to John Caryll, November 1706, BL, Add. MSS, 28,226, fol. 127.

tious private moments, they prepared for a glorious return to authority in the public sphere.

In recent years, sociological studies have linked the rise of nations to a sense of 'imagined community', a consciousness uniting individuals and communities who would never actually meet.[178] A similar affinity can be traced in the Catholic and Jacobite world: an alternative conception of the English nation, entertained in the interior lives of men and women resting their feet on French, Flemish or Italian soil. It was imperative for the court to make itself the capital of this imaginary kingdom, to dispense privilege and position, create rituals, and levy obligations so that it never became remote from the men and women who sustained it in their faith. Their efforts left an imprint across the Channel, among a host of recusant gentlemen who strove to embody the virtues of patriotism and tranquillity in the conduct of their social and religious lives, but had bound their *political* allegiance to a different order. In 1715, the convergence of public and private realms came with violent and – for the Catholics – calamitous consequences. But by defining itself just as potently as a political culture, the Jacobite movement was robust enough to linger in the recusant imagination beyond the siege of Preston. Its fortunes would be dictated not simply by force of arms but in the political and intellectual struggles, debates and controversies raised within the British Isles and across Catholic Europe, in which the recusant community played out the tensions locked within its own conflicted identity.

[178] Benedict Anderson, *Imagined Communities: Reflections on the Origins and Spread of Nationalism* (London, 1991).

1. The English College, Douai c. 1790, showing the results of the rebuilding programme commenced under President Witham in 1715 and completed in 1758. Printed by kind permission of the Headmaster, St Edmund's College, Ware.

2. Harvington Hall, Warwickshire. Photograph reproduced by kind permission of the Harvington Hall estate.

3. Broughton Hall, Yorkshire, by W.D. Fryerdel c. 1700. Reproduced by kind permission of Henry Tempest.

3

Conscience, politics and the exiled court: the creation of the Catholic Jacobite manifesto 1689–1718

The grip of the diaspora on recusant lives, the instability of their place in England, and an impassioned sense that the laws of God and man preserved the right of the exiled Stuarts had all established Jacobitism as an overwhelming presence in the political imagination of the English Catholic community. By 1716, recusant leaders were proclaiming these convictions at the public scaffold, exhorting their countrymen to work towards 'Uniting and Reconciling all their Interests ... in the only Measure that can render them happy'.[1] However, Jacobite ideology could not be frozen in a state of such exalted self-certainty. Its advocates were soon forced to convert private zeal into a voice that could speak outside the sanctuary of the loyal household, enter into the less comforting arena of national controversy and confront the taunt that 'You labour more than ever to estrange them from King James with such authentique wrighting ... to declare he will not reign but to signify his publique zeal for the Catholique religion.'[2] The political thought of Catholic Jacobitism was fashioned out of successive exchanges between the court, the diaspora and its following in England: fixed on the terms of a restoration settlement, but ranging across wider horizons, to contemplate the moral image of a Catholic king, the place for Stuart piety in a Protestant realm, and the status of recusants beyond the point of an imagined second Restoration. This chapter will reveal how the absolutist and pietistic vision of Jacobite kingship was undermined by the political challenge after 1688, forcing its adherents to offer new responses, reassess the public role of the Stuarts' religion, and recuperate a patriotic narrative to pursue Catholic revival across the three kingdoms.

Some of the most potent and formative debates about the direction of English Catholicism after 1688 took place among the community of émigrés

---

[1] A True Copy of the Paper Delivered to the Sheriffs of London by Richard Gascoigne (1716).
[2] 'The Answer in Dutch to the King's Manifesto', 1693, Bodleian Library, Carte MSS, 209, fols 381–4.

clustered close to the exiled Stuart court. Jacobite attitudes towards matters political, confessional and devotional were originally configured by a wide circle of Catholics who had flocked overseas in the wake of the Revolution. The networks of political decision-making incorporated veteran courtiers, converts, gentry from the shires, and priests drawn from the exiled clerical institutions. In their hands, the Jacobite base embodied more than just a cultural 'event': its prime function was to serve as the cockpit of a counter-revolutionary project, seeking, as one statesman put it, to 'turn ye scales of Europe'.[3] At it disposal was a network of diplomats posted in the power-bases of the continent, a chain of agents operating in secret across England, and a diaspora of loyal soldiers. In a succession of declarations, memorials and manifestos, the Jacobites announced their imaginary settlement for the governance of the English nation.

The political character of exiled Jacobite Catholicism has not emerged with credit from historical scrutiny. John Miller has summed up an environment overhung with 'devotion, disappointment and death'. Daniel Szechi has characterised the drafting of 'a blueprint for tyranny', synonymous with the military ambitions of Louis XIV.[4] Such judgements could call upon a wealth of testimony from Whig observers of the scene at St Germain. Anti-Jacobite pamphleteers republished the strident commands of Robert Persons's *Memoriall for the intended reformation of England*, alerting their countrymen to the designs of Catholic émigrés, and the high stakes therefore upheld in the 1689 Revolution settlement.[5] Writing in December 1694, Matthew Prior identified a 'blind bigotry for the Catholic religion' taking over the exiled entourage, while John Macky's *View of the Court of St Germain*, offered a devastating exposure of the reality beneath James II's 'specious pretence of liberty of conscience':

> Once he went to France, he has taken all the Pains imaginable to let the World know his inveterate Aversion to all those of the Reformed Religion ... has given us the most authentick Demonstrations of his firm Design never to allow any there of his Favour, nor owe his Restoration to any but Roman Catholicks.[6]

[3] The earl of Perth to John Caryll, 29 June 1695, Bodleian Library, Carte MSS, 209, fol. 313.
[4] Daniel Szechi, 'A Blueprint for Tyranny? Sir Edward Hales and the Catholic Jacobite Response to the Revolution of 1688', *English Historical Review*, 116 (2001), pp. 343–67; Miller, *James II*, p. 224.
[5] *The Jesuit's memorial for the intended reformation of England under their first popish prince* (1690).
[6] Matthew Prior to the earl of Jersey, 14 February 1698, HMC, *Bath*, III, p. 198; John Macky, A *View of the Court of St Germain and an account of the Entertainment Protestants meet there, Addressed to Malcontent Protestants in England* (London, 1695), p. 4.

If much of this was naked propaganda, such reports nonetheless laid bare the chasm that stood between the exiled court and its political objective: the need to convince the nation that a Catholic king could be entrusted with the welfare of the English constitution. To Viscount Bolingbroke:

> Can anything be thought more absurd than for those of one persuasion to trust the supreme power ... to another? Must it not be reputed madness in those of our religion to trust themselves to the hands of Roman Catholicks? Must it not be reputed impudence in a Roman Catholick to expect that we should?[7]

As its enemies strove to impress this contradiction upon the subjects of the three kingdoms, the exiled court became the repository of all the oldest motifs of the Catholic 'black legend' in English Protestant discourse. Its very presence across the seas conjured up a nightmare of 'popery', raised to send shivers down the national spine.

Did St Germain, then, nurture a clique who schemed to send the last shockwaves of the Counter-Reformation through English government and society? In most existing models of study for the exiled court, historians have endorsed the notion of division between the party of moderate, Protestant 'Compounders' under the earl of Middleton and the revanchist, Catholic 'Noncompounders', personified by the Drummond brothers, the earls of Melfort and Perth.[8] Prior called these rival partisans the 'Whigs and Tories' of the expatriate milieu.[9] However, I will suggest that this dichotomy presents a caricature, drawn from Whig literature, which artificially raises the significance of debates in 1693–4, over the larger context of political thought in the Stuart polity. The perceived divide of Protestants against Catholics was itself largely an illusion generated by the personality clash between Melfort and Middleton, 'those two demons for intrigue' as dubbed by the Duc de Saint-Simon, belied by the fact that Middleton's greatest influence emerged *after* his Catholic conversion in 1702.[10] Investigating a larger period, I will show that it is false to treat the Catholic Jacobite position as a commitment to religious intolerance and political absolutism, fended off by Protestant moderates. Rather, the Catholics were themselves riven, and the 'absolutist' case sidelined after vigorous debate among co-religionists. Even before the death of James II, the proposal for a Stuart

---

[7]   Henry St John, Viscount Bolingbroke, *A Letter to Sir William Wyndham* (1717), pp. 298–9.
[8]   George Hilton Jones, *Charles Middleton: The Life and Times of a Restoration Statesman* (London, 1967), pp. 255–66; Daniel Szechi, 'The Jacobite Revolution Settlement, 1689–1696', *English Historical Review*, 108 (1993), pp. 610–28.
[9]   Prior to Jersey, 15 October 1698, HMC, *Bath*, III, pp. 271–2; G.H. Jones, *The Main Stream of Jacobitism* (Harvard, 1954), p. 20; Szechi, 'Jacobite Revolution Settlement', pp. 621–6.
[10] Duc de St Simon, *Memoirs*, ed. F. Arkwright (6 vols, London, 1918), III, pp. 51–2.

restoration centred on a programme of militant Catholic uniformity had been scattered to the winds.

In looking outside the traditional analytical models, the chapter will begin by uncovering the worldview of the Catholic 'hard-liners', showing how the providentialist and martyrological vision of Stuart monarchy fired their political and religious ambitions, and their rise to power at the exiled court. Then, I will consider how the backlash was rejected; arguing that the change of direction was actually foreshadowed while Catholics occupied the dominant positions at court: the revenge of the party of 'old recusants' marginalised while James II sat on the throne, against the *devot* converts who had displaced them. The political tilt at St Germain marked therefore the revival of an older English Catholic vocabulary, quarried from native religious traditions, and rediscovered when the desire to promote James II as a 'Catholick in religion, but a Protestant in government' changed the relationship between the private and public spheres in royal life. Moreover, the turn was driven not merely by strategic calculation, but a profoundly religious debate over the collision of the Stuarts' Catholic conscience with the need to recapture and preserve the crown of the three kingdoms. The final part of the chapter will show how a new Jacobite manifesto was built in models of education, polemical self-representation and an alternative image of kingship, offered by courtiers in correspondence with the clergy of the Catholic religious houses. In their hands, the restoration movement was not just the centre of diplomatic, military and conspiratorial machinations, but the forum for a battle of ideas, to be examined in the higher context of Catholic political and religious thought.

The exiled court and the confessional idea of Catholic kingship

'We have at Court a Protestant and a Catholique faction' declared the Scottish clergyman Charles Whyteford in his observations on the politics of St Germain in 1694.[11] It is a judgement seemingly corroborated by the details of rank and privilege within the Jacobite retinue, highlighting in particular the strength of the latter party. Before the arrival of the earl of Middleton, St Germain was in almost exclusively Catholic hands, run between 1689 and November 1691 by a cabinet council comprising the former Sussex recusants John Caryll and Henry Browne, the diplomat John Stafford, and the secular clergyman Lewis Innes, president of the Scots College, Paris.[12] The earl of Melfort thenceforth monopolised the position of secretary of state until his dismissal in August 1694, serving for the last year jointly

---

[11] Charles Whyteford to Lewis Innes, 19 July 1694, SCA, Blairs, I, 186/2.

[12] Henry Browne, Letter-book, 1691, AAW, Browne MSS, 208; Marquis de Ruvigny and Raineval, *The Jacobite Peerage* (London, 1904), pp. 214–15.

with Lord Middleton. Thereafter, the promotion of Caryll was engineered to balance the Catholic and Protestant interests, with a system of two serving secretaries drawn from the different denominations.[13] This careful counterpoise appeared to have collapsed after the death of James II in 1701, when Middleton converted to the Catholic faith, and a new generation of statesmen ascended onto the court council. The earl of Perth, the duke of Berwick, the Lancashire recusant and royal treasurer, William Dicconson, and the convert Sir David Nairne ensured that the political education of 'James III' was advanced on a firmly Catholic footing: a hold that endured until the arrival of a wave of Scottish Episcopalian émigrés, in the wake of the 1715 rising.[14]

That there was a strong revanchist instinct in Catholic Jacobite circles is indisputable, and it marched hand-in-hand with the rise of a faction that wished to resolve the dynastic question in political and religious forms familiar to observers of Louis XIV's France. This position was originally synonymous with the rise of the Drummond brothers, James, earl of Perth and John, earl of Melfort. The latter had left a mark in England as 'a bigot Papist, so generally ill-behoved', according to the earl of Nottingham, and his *Declaration of King James*, penned in March 1689, promised condign punishment to subjects who did not return to their duty of obedience.[15] Perth's Catholicism, charged by a close relationship with Bishop Bossuet, bore all the lesions of his imprisonment as Lord Chancellor of Scotland in 1689, an incident that led to his comparison with St Thomas More by Jesuit admirers, and elicited his own view of the British Isles as 'an asylum full of madness' in a 'a country once called the land of saints'.[16] From the tenets of Gallican Catholicism, Perth extracted an Augustinian justification for his belief in the duty of kings to put pressure on subjects adhering to erroneous beliefs, discoursing on the needs of a polity, where, in the words of Bossuet, 'he who does not groan like a pilgrim cannot rejoice as a citizen'.[17] However, a certain unforgiving stance towards the English nation was by no means confined to the Drummonds. 'All morality is banisht' declared Edward Hales in June 1692:

[13] Philip Michael Ellis to John Caryll, 13 July 1694, Bodleian Library, Carte MSS, 209, fol. 118.

[14] Ruvigny, *Jacobite Peerage*, p. 215; Jones, *Charles Middleton*, pp. 269–78.

[15] The earl of Nottingham to the earl of Portland, 4 September 1692, HMC, *Finch*, III, p. 431; *Declaration of King James* (1689).

[16] William Aloysius Leslie, *Vita di Sancta Margherita* (1693 edn); Gaquére, *Vers l'Unité Chrétienne*, pp. 81–2.

[17] Jacques-Benigne Bossuet, *Oeuvres* (20 vols, Paris, 1841), XVII, p. 172; M.A. Goldie, 'The Theory of Religious Intolerance in Restoration England', in Grell et al., *From Persecution to Toleration*, pp. 331–68.

Friendship, generosity, honour, our very English courage has forsaken this effeminate land. If good liquor can wind us up to a drunken squabble, we are heroes, but if the King and our native country implore our aid, we hide our thick-skulled heads and to sleep in a whole skin turn traitorously to the invader.[18]

From this diagnosis emerged the classic Non-compounding position, expressed by Melfort in 1691, when he predicted to Henry Browne that the loss of dynastic stability 'cannot but end in the destruction of the Church of England, the Privileges of the House of Peers ... confusion and Civil War', to be resolved by the services of a French army.[19] In a time of international conflict, restoration was a far from improbable prospect, and in England, the optimism of exiled Jacobites could generate expectant hopes within the ranks of Catholic society. The London lawyer Daniel Arthur reproached Henry Browne in 1692 that 'our fancies in these parts were grounded upon ye stories heard from you'.[20]

The crux of this stance was a defence of indefeasible Stuart legitimacy. John Caryll's satire 'The Duumvirate' unveiled a dystopian picture of the rudderless 'floating Isle', left 'Lost in the Wilderness of Anarky', after a slide into blasphemy and barbarism that began with the death of Charles I. Having thrown away the moral compass of legitimate monarchy, the land was haunted by 'phantoms', 'strange monsters' and 'many-headed beasts'; its statesmen, 'hunt and fish for Kings like Aesop's Logs/ In German forests and in Holland bogs'.[21] However, the origins of Jacobite Noncompounding drew upon a distinctive and uncompromising vision of Catholic monarchy, fostered in the magnificent artistic setting of the Chapel Royal, in retreats at the Cistercian abbey at La Trappe, and the devotional culture of confession, submission and earthly disengagement, sensitive to the influence of European texts as Nicholas Caussin's *The Holy Court*.[22] The conviction 'All Catholick good consists in Unity', was the opening gambit in a collection of notes in the writing of Lord Perth.[23] 'All diabolical Art tends to violate Unity', he continued: 'Of all evils Heresy is ye greatest and ye most dangerous'; 'He that hates not heresy is not a fitt instrument to sett up ye Catholick religion.' Confessional fervour was sanctioned through a cyclical

---

[18] Hales to Melfort, 'Treatise on Government', July 1692, AAW, Old Brotherhood MSS, III, p. 258.

[19] Melfort to Browne, 2 July 1691, BL, Add. MSS, 37,662, p. 183.

[20] Daniel Arthur to Henry Browne, 17 October 1692, AAW, Browne MSS, 130.

[21] John Caryll, 'The Duumvirate', Bodleian Library, Carte MSS, 208, fols 397–8. A copy also appears in the Caryll papers, BL, Add. MSS, 28,253, fols 56–60. See also Erskine-Hill, 'Poetry at the Exiled Court', pp. 231–3.

[22] John Caryll, St Germain inventory, listed in Alexander Gordon to John Caryll, 29 July 1716, BL, Add. MSS, 28,227, fols 32–3; Clancy, *Literary History of the English Jesuits*, pp. 11–13; Geoffrey Scott, 'The Court as a Centre of Catholicism', in Corp, ed., *A Court in Exile*, pp. 233–50.

[23] 'Grounds of a true Catholick', n.d., Bodleian Library, Carte MSS, 208, fol. 204.

reading of the divine will in human affairs, when the extraordinary events of recent history – not least the precedent of the 1660 Restoration – could only hint at an unseen hand steering them through the 'labyrinth' of life in banishment. 'His Majesty has bin so often preserved by Miracles, and pass'd through so many Wildernesses, that I cannot infine believe but he will return Triumphant to his own land of Canaan' proclaimed Sir John Lytcott.[24] Sir Richard Bulstrode believed that, though the judgement exercised upon a private individual would only be realised in eternity, the greatest powers must live by a different rule. The temporal stature of kingdoms meant that God's justice fell upon them publicly and visibly, within the world:

> The great crying sins of a nation cannot hope to escape publick Judgements ... sooner or later they have reason to expect His Vengeance. God hath Leaden feet, but Iron hands, he is long e're he punishes, but strikes home at last, and usually the longer punishment is delayed, the heavier when it comes.[25]

At court, providential convictions worked together with sense of pietistic obligation to strengthen the case against concessions to Protestant England.

Readings of the divine will imported into court Catholic thought a narrative of sanctity and martyrdom for the life of the fallen king, used to bind Jacobite consciences with a promise of redemption for the suffering of 1688. Richard Bulstrode believed that an 'eternal Crown in Heaven' vindicated a blameless monarch 'villainously' treated 'by ye most abominable treachery of a powerfull Faction'.[26] After the death of James II, the conviction reified into a literature of royal sainthood, mimetic of the cults of Henry VI and Charles I, and conceived to underpin the pilgrimages, reliquary exchanges and miraculous claims that informed an official campaign for canonisation.[27] The idea was developed in the monk Benet Weldon's manuscript 'Collection' towards the life of the king, drawn up at the command of Prior Henry Joseph Johnston, at the monastery of St Edmund's, Paris.[28] Its evolution as a literary campaign was evidenced in the *Life* by James's Jesuit confessor Francis Sanders, and enhanced by eye-witness accounts of miracles at the

[24] Sir John Lytcott to Sir Richard Bulstrode, 2 April 1689, Bulstrode papers, BL, Egerton MSS, 3683, fol. 169.

[25] Sir Richard Bulstrode, *Miscellaneous Essays*, ed. Whitlocke Bulstrode (1724), VII, 'Of Religion', p. 318.

[26] 'A Discourse of Monarchy & of ye Kings Prerogative In dispensing with Penal Laws', by Sr R. B., University of Texas at Austin, Harry Ransom Research Center, Pforzheimer MS 2d, p. 33. I am grateful to Stephen Taylor for drawing my attention to this document.

[27] J.M.W. McKenna, 'Popular Canonisation as Political Propaganda', *Speculum*, 45 (1978), pp. 608–23; Andrew Lacey, *The Cult of King Charles the Martyr* (Woodbridge, 2003).

[28] Weldon, 'Collection', BL, Add. MSS, 10,118, pp. 712–15.

royal tomb, with the release of a flow of poems and extracts from royal conversations, meditations and public speeches.[29] Its impact was made evident in the correspondence of Jacobite émigrés. To Charles Radcliffe, the fallen king had left his son 'a Crown of the Thorns given him by Allmighty God in place of those Crowns He took from him to punish us unworthy of so good a Prince. Your Majesty has worn it long and soon I hope to see you wear th' imperial crown of England.'[30]

Confessional Jacobite writers aimed to surpass even Charles I's *Eikon Basilike* by transmuting the battered reputation of James II into the mould of 'A King, a Martyr, Confessor and Saint', who governed 'his lawfull inheritance with Justice and Piety', before the act of 'losing all to win a glorious day'.[31] The literature of Jacobite sainthood had three key components. Firstly: the biblical-classical typology for suffering royalty, the parallel of James II with David 'in all his afflictions'.[32] For the medievalist Benedictine scholars, James would gain historic authenticity as heir to St Edward the Confessor, the Saxon royal martyrs Sigebert and Edmund and 30 other kings and queens from the 'land of saints' who had embraced 'the humility of a monastic habit and the obscurity of a cell'.[33] Yet Jacobites also targeted a continental audience, melding the idealised concept of Christian kingship with the Counter-Reformation spirituality of the Cross to turn the 'banished pilgrime' into a 'new Josiah ... beloved of God, seeking the Lord with all his heart'.[34] Under the direction of Paris Jesuits such as Francois Bretonneau, with the patronage of Bishop Bossuet and a Sorbonne committee, parallels would be pressed between the performance of James II and icons such as St Carlo Borromeo.[35] This literature shadowed the Tridentine canonisation process, which demanded that the life and death of a martyr conform to the

[29] Douai Abbey, Woolhampton MSS, Weldon, 'Memorials', V, p. 51; Francis Sanders, *Short Relation of the Life and Death of James II* (1703); *Imago Regis, or the Sacred Image of His Majesty* (1692).

[30] Charles Radcliffe to James Edward, 23 November 1723, Royal Archives (Windsor), Stuart papers, 70/29.

[31] Weldon, 'Collection', BL, Add. MSS, 10,118, p. 727; Elizabeth Skerpan Wheeler, 'Eikon Basilike and the Rhetoric of Self-representation', in Thomas N. Corns, ed., *The Royal Image: Representations of Charles I* (Cambridge, 1999), pp. 122–40, and Laura Lunger Knoppers, 'Reviving the Martyr King: Charles I as Jacobite Icon', in Corns, *Royal Image*, pp. 263–87.

[32] *Imago Regis*, pp. 75–7; Lacey, *Charles the Martyr*, pp. 213–16.

[33] Weldon, 'Collection', BL, Add. MSS, 10,118, pp. 82–3; Weldon, *Chronological Notes*, p. 229.

[34] 'A coppie of a letter giving an account of the late change of state and Revolution of the Government in England (1689)', Bodleian Library, Rawlinson MSS, D 91.

[35] Weldon, 'Collection', BL, Add. MSS, 10,118, pp. 711–13; François Bretonneau, *Life of James II*, trans. R. Wilson (1704); Jean Delumeau, *Catholicism between Luther and Voltaire: A New View of the Counter-Reformation* (London, 1977), pp. 43–7.

Passion of Christ, enduring agony and humiliation with preternatural stoicism. Since James had not perished in the flames, or at the sword-strokes of his enemies, the experience of 1688 must instead be represented as the death of his worldly persona, the sacrifice of a temporal estate.[36] The arc of his life, traced by Lewis Innes from 'perfectly accomplished prince' to 'Christian hero', to 'Penitent penetrated with the deepest sense of his own failings', would be crowned by *subversion* of the trappings of kingship, when the consequence of retaining them would be to concede ground on sacred principle.[37] 'Let other Kings of Conquered Kingdoms boast/ Thy Glories are ye Kingdoms thou hast lost' saluted Weldon.[38]

The sanctification of James II created a form of confessional politics to bind the Jacobite court to the English recusant country. Printed material found its way from London booksellers like Thomas Metcalfe into Catholic households such as Broughton Hall; the same manuscript verses and prose entered the possession of the Scarisbricks in Lancashire and the commonplace book of the Warwickshire monk John Anselm Mannock.[39] The idea was vocalised among the rebels of 1715, when Northumbrian gentry leaders chose for their banner the tableau of a pelican feeding her young with her own blood, as an evocation of Christ's Passion.[40] After the collapse of the rising, it was reinvigorated in native, more demotic form, in the strain of martyrology that commemorated the executed Lord Derwentwater, accentuating his refusal to renounce his religion, as the purported condition for George I's offer to spare his life. In recusant households, the treatment of Derwentwater's memory mirrored the veneration of James II. Yearly masses were held in the Swinburne chapel at Capheaton, while the red velvet cloth that shrouded his head found its way to the Eyres of Warkworth in Northamptonshire, and even the politically quietist Throckmortons preserved a handwritten copy of the last instructions to Derwentwater by his confessor Benjamin Petre.[41] But Derwentwater was also a maternal grandchild of Charles II, and his relics were believed to possess the mythic regal power

---

[36] Dillon, *Construction of Martyrdom*, pp. 81–92.

[37] Lewis Innes to James Edward, 20 May 1737, Royal Archives (Windsor), Stuart papers, 197/96.

[38] Weldon, 'Collection', BL, Add. MSS, 10,118, p. 716; Wheeler, 'Eikon Basilike', pp. 125–8.

[39] Tempest of Broughton library; Political poems, Lancashire CRO, Scarisbrick MSS, 19/33; Richard Howard of Norfolk to James Gordon, 18 April 1703, AAW, Epistolae Variorum I/ 9; Downside Abbey, Mannock miscellany, p. 391.

[40] Hibbert Ware, *Lancashire Memorials of the Rebellion*, pp. 97–8.

[41] List of anniversaries, Northumberland CRO, Swinburne MSS, 6/103; Emma Agnes Petre to Philip Petre (undated, early nineteenth century), Northumberland CRO, Radcliffe MSS, 5828; *Catholic Miscellany*, August 1824; F.J.A. Skeet, *The Life of the Rt. Hon. James Radcliffe, Third Earl of Derwentwater, and Charles Radcliffe* (London, 1929), p. 119; Devotional papers, Warwickshire CRO, Throckmorton MSS, Box 84.

of curing scrofula, 'the King's Evil'.[42] To Jacobite poets, these 'poor bleeding wounds' attested to the death of a royal martyr, who had laid his own neck on the scaffold 'to set three nations and their head together'. One writer appropriated the narrative of the 1649 regicide, and incorporated the earl into a lineage stretching back to Mary, Queen of Scots, which had seen generations of Stuarts 'lay down their heads and bless ye parting blow':

> No wonder veins filled with martyr's blood
> So unconcern'd pour'd out ye sacred Flood
> A God-like spirit does attend ye Race
> Souls well assur'd with heavenly Grace.

The land could be seen scarred with antecedents to 'this bloody day', and the execution at Tyburn brought a physical reality to the sacrifice of power made by James II in 1688.[43]

Reflections on Christian heroism aimed to produce not simply a monument to dead martyrs, but a spirit of active piety to reanimate the Jacobite conscience. Francis Sanders prayed that the greatest intercession of the 'Holy King' would be upon the hearts of his subjects, to make Englishmen 'a little consider what they rejected, *and what they chose*'.[44] Declarations of this nature invited the 'heroick band' whom 'all but faith and loyalty have lost' to 'move Heaven's batteries', as John Lytcott exhorted, and live out the sacrifice of James II by making the recovery of the three kingdoms the supreme expression of Christian piety.[45] Lord Derwentwater's death would lift English eyes to a prospect of 'another James ... exil'd, innocent and young', the prince who would 'purge the enemies of a guilty land'.[46] Through the prism of this devotional worldview, the earthly goods provided in the English nation were not deemed worthy of a major political concession. For the court statesmen who had disseminated the claim, the idea of 'holy sacrifice' meant that debates over a speculative Jacobite settlement could never be conducted outside the framework of the religious conscience.

The theory of Jacobite absolutism

The political convictions of the 'Noncompounders' may have been nurtured by their confessional reading of English royal affairs, but the vindication

---

[42] Robert Carnaby to Lady Catherine Radcliffe, 20 October 1724, Northumberland CRO, Radcliffe MSS, M.17.104; Skeet, *Life of Derwentwater*, p. 122.

[43] 'On the Death of James, Earl of Derwentwater, Who was beheaded on Tower Hill, February ye 24th 1716', in 'A Collection of Loyal Poems', BL, Add. MSS, 29,981, fols 108–9.

[44] Sanders, *Short Relation*, p. 12.

[45] Lytcott, 'Historical Essay', in Weldon, 'Collection', BL, Add. MSS, 10,118, p. 804.

[46] 'On the Death of James, Earl of Derwentwater', BL, Add. MSS, 29,981, fols 108–9.

of dynastic sanctity was matched by a hard-headed, Bodinian programme of absolute monarchy, preoccupied with matters of sovereignty, jurisdiction and principles of statecraft.[47] As Richard Bulstrode conceded: 'ye soldier like spirit in ye Prince hath ever been much more fortunate, & more esteemed than ye Pious'.[48] Penning his 'Discourse of Monarchy & of ye Kings Prerogative In dispensing with Penal Laws', Bulstrode accepted that the maladroit actions of past princes had left core tenets of the constitution contested: the financial profligacy of James I exemplified a failing 'wch alwayes breeds ill humors in the people, & soon lessens their duty to their Sovereign', while 'ye sad catastrophe of Charles ye First' emerged when that 'Prince made unhappy denials to what was required from Him, & at other times more unhappy condescensions'. Yet Bulstrode was adamant that the greater sin of Charles I lay not in his abuses, but his *surrender* of powers to parliament, a move that presented 'one great (if not ye only cause) of all our sad intestine troubles'.[49] Turning even to the writings of Sir Edward Coke to study 'the Imperial Monarchy of England', Bulstrode traced from Elizabeth I to the Saxon King Edgar the prerogative powers of the hereditary ruler as 'Vicarius Dei ... free in all times, & in no earthly Subjection but imediately to God'. In this state, 'supposing any sharers in ye Supream Power is a Contradiction' for 'Souereignty lyes radically in the King'.[50]

Bulstrode's 'absolute' monarchy was far from unconstrained. He concurred that 'the liberty of the Subject is a precious thing' and posited a sharp difference 'betwixt absolute Power under ye cloak of a Dispensation, or absolute Power barefaced, that is exercis'd at Will & Pleasure'. He affirmed that 'the fundamentall Laws of Gouernment are imutable', being 'to mankind what ye Sun is to plants, which it cherishes & preserves', when 'without ye Laws ye world would become a Wilderness'. The king could never override laws that went against things 'euill in themselues', such as treason or murder, when 'such a permission would be contrary to original Justice, moral honesty & common equity'.[51] Nonetheless, Bulstrode believed that in the governance of the realm, 'the Laws are called ye Kings Laws, the Parliament his Parliament', in homage to 'the Prerogatiue, which first gave, & euer since supported that liberty'. Therefore 'to set Laws above ye Maker of them ... above ye fountain of that first Power, is to usurp upon ye Original Founder & to ... remove ye unchangeable foundations of Power itself'.[52]

---

47 Julian H. Franklin, 'Sovereignty and the Mixed Constitution: Bodin and his Critics', in Burns and Goldie, eds, *History of Political Thought*, pp. 298–328; Mark Goldie, 'Restoration Political Thought', in Lionel K. Glassey, ed., *The Reigns of Charles II and James VII and II* (1997), pp. 13–35.
48 Bulstrode, 'Discourse', p. 7.
49 Ibid., pp. 3–4, 6–8.
50 Ibid., pp. 18–19
51 Ibid., pp. 2, 12–13, 15–16.
52 Ibid., p. 2.

The common law, Bulstrode argued, must be judged according to higher principles of justice and equity, and a prince would find himself forced to grant exemptions, temper or dispense with legislation in order to support 'ye common weal & safety of his people ... as for example a loyal Subject leavies Soldiers without a Comission to rescue his Prince out of ye hands of his Enemies'.[53] Therefore, although 'there is undoubtedly more honor & authority in a resolution of State than there is in a particular & personal Declaration', the dispensing power had to remain lodged inside the constitution, as it was in every government the world over: a 'remedy' against 'errors & contingencies' in a universe beset by 'ye chances, ye vicissitudes & ye emergencies of humane affaires'.[54]

Bulstrode highlighted a vein of thought inside St Germain that saw the precedents set in 1689 as a strictly contested notion of the English constitution. Declaring his thoughts in a 'Treatise on Government', Sir Edward Hales dreamed of triumph and revenge, in a Jacobite settlement buttressed by a vast Catholic standing army, with a purge of Protestants from the great offices of state and a programme of royal centralisation.[55] 'The King of Britain's Case' (1690) and later 'Political Reflexions' (1709) by the Irish courtier Thomas Sheridan damned a Revolution 'more suitable to the extravagances of Bedlam, than the gravity of the Nation's representatives', assailed mixed monarchy as 'an empty, false republican notion, invented and set on foot by rebels', and sought a return to the Norman-Plantagenet 'absolute monarchy', where civil power derived from the king 'as light from the sun or stream from the fountain'.[56] Religious affairs were to be similarly monopolised. Sheridan argued that the ecclesiastical institutions created through the Reformation had been made redundant in 1688, by their acquiescence in the fall of their Supreme Governor: the overthrow of James II proved that 'the King of England's interest is so interwoven and blended with the Catholic religion that they cannot possibly be separated or divided'.[57] In stumbling towards their 'new devis'd church', the Tudors had fatally unleashed 'schism, irreligion, sedition and rebellion, the 'unavoidable consequence of Protestant principles'.[58] By contrast, 'all men of sense must conclude that nothing can be more impolitic than to suffer varieties of religion'. It was not simply that Sheridan wished to suppress delinquent ideas; he denied the very integrity of private conscience, as a self-deluding instinct, masking the Hobbesian realities of a world in which men act

---

[53] Ibid., pp. 13–14.

[54] Ibid., pp. 15–18.

[55] Hales to Melfort, 27 May 1692, AAW, Old Brotherhood MSS, III, p. 253; Szechi, 'Blueprint for Tyranny?' pp. 343–67.

[56] Thomas Sheridan, 'Political Reflections', Royal Archives, Windsor, Stuart Papers, Miscellaneous Volumes, 7, p. 169.

[57] Ibid., p. 175.

[58] Ibid., pp. 136–40, 188–90.

according to 'their passions, more than reason'. To impress this point, he was prepared to cite with approval the programme of Lutheran intolerance used to safeguard the principalities of Sweden and Denmark, and, provocatively, the Roman policy of 'exterminating by death and banishment' the Empire's Christian dissenters. This was the temporal theory of intolerance, re-legitimising Catholicism in the body politic through the conviction that 'the effect of contrary opinions will soon appear in Rebellion, blood, rape and plunder'.[59]

Outlining a restored settlement in which oppressed voices should content themselves with the virtues of stoicism and resignation, it was lucky for the Jacobite entourage that the thoughts of Hales and Sheridan, and even the more nuanced commentaries of Bulstrode, were not disseminated publicly across England. However, it was harder to characterise such writings as uniquely or emphatically Catholic. Indeed this apparent, ready confirmation of Protestant fears had intellectual origins separate from the traditions of the English recusant community, when Sheridan, Hales, Melfort and Perth were all converts to the faith who had crossed the religious divide in the reign of James II – Bulstrode having preceded them in 1667.[60] In the political philosophy of these leading Noncompounders, there was continuity on either side of the conversion moment: a natural convergence between the Gallican spirit of Bourbon France and the more high-flown reaches of the Tory Anglican programme that had held dominion in the last years of the reign of Charles II. Melfort and Perth transferred their original, uncompromising opinions as to how to deal with English Nonconformists and Scottish Presbyterians into a new faith, enlarging their list of Dissenters to include recalcitrant members of the Church of England.[61] Sheridan still believed that 'passive obedience and non-resistance are two of the principles of Christianity', and the potentially conflicting allegiance levied by the papacy was absent from his writings. The historical commentary was redolent of the Tory scholarship of Robert Brady, the main assailant of Whig myths surrounding the ancient constitution, and the inspiration behind Sheridan's belief that the Magna Carta represented nothing more than a transient concession, since princes as 'but usufracturies, tenants for life' left their successors 'at Liberty to regaine what his predecessor suffered to be lopt off'.[62] This rule of faith therefore brought a revival of an older royalist doctrine, taken over the bridge of the Revolution, and acculturated to the discourse of *ancien régime* Europe, when the experience of conversion completed a vision of the world

[59] Ibid., pp. 153–4; Goldie, 'Theory of Religious Intolerance', pp. 364–8.

[60] Szechi, 'Blueprint for Tyranny?' pp. 345–7; Whyteford to Leslie, n.d. 1690, SCA, Blairs, I, 133/4; Burnet, *Reign of James II*, p. 77.

[61] Clare Jackson, *Restoration Scotland, 1660–1690* (Woodbridge, 2003), pp. 155–7.

[62] Royal Archives (Windsor), Sheridan, 'Political Reflexions', pp. 129–35, 151; J.P. Somerville, 'Absolutism and Royalism', in Burns and Goldie, eds, *History of Political Thought*, pp. 347–73.

split between the moral order and the spirit of anarchy and deception. This was not the time for Anglican ambiguity, and in the Catholic Church, the absolutists found the comfort of infallible authority.

The *Gracious Declaration* and the defeat of absolutism

For all the force of their opinions, the backlash against the Revolution by former Tory Anglicans speaking through a Catholic mouthpiece did not achieve lasting momentum. By the middle of the first decade in exile, the Noncompounding ideology had been comprehensively banished from Jacobite memorials, and a decisive change of course heralded by the release of a new manifesto on 11 April 1693. Marked by its forgiving tone, its spirit of concord and reconciliation, the King's *Gracious Declaration to His Loving Subjects* amounted to a striking political change, promising a free parliament, an act of indemnity and oblivion for all but a small number of miscreants, and a pledge to 'protect and defend the Church of England as it is established by law', constrained only by freedom of religious worship for Catholics and Dissenters.[63] Under its terms, the emphasis at St Germain had shifted from conquest to conciliation, hoping to overthrow the Williamite regime by articulating popular, patriotic Stuart credentials, as counterweights to principles of divine right and hereditary legitimacy. Symbolically, this new trajectory was fronted by the earl of Middleton, the moderate Tory now in residence as secretary of state at the exiled court. However, the ideological change had in reality flowed from other sources. The original moves towards the Gracious Declaration had been undertaken over a year before Middleton's arrival, in the commentaries of a circle of former recusant gentry leaders present at the exiled court. Moreover, their deliberations were conducted within an intensely Catholic framework of debate.

Noncompounding proposals had been galvanised by a military possibility: steeped in confidence that 'a day of reckoning will come', to dispose of that 'hereticall, unnatural, usurping tyrant' by the swords of a French-led coalition.[64] Concurrently, it was the military situation that did most to undermine absolutist remedies. If Jacobite statesmen had steeled themselves for the failure of the Irish wars by 1691, they were confronted with a more serious setback in May 1692, with the crushing of the Franco-Jacobite naval expedition at La Hogue and the intervention of the English army in Europe, driving Louis XIV back towards his natural frontiers.[65] Thereafter, the failure of Versailles to back up support for the Jacobites with force of arms impelled

---

[63] *His Majesty's Gracious Declaration to His Loving Subjects* (London, 1693).

[64] The earl of Perth to John Caryll, 9 May 1695, in James MacPherson, ed., *Original Papers: Containing the Secret history of Great Britain from the Restoration to the Accession of the House of Hanover* (2 vols, London, 1776), I, p. 518; Caryll to Perth, 4 July 1695, *Original Papers*, p. 532.

[65] P.A. Hopkins, 'Aspects of Jacobite Conspiracy in the Reign of William III', unpub-

the Benedictine Joseph Kennedy to voice the thinking of many in the exiled retinue: 'A man can assure himself of nothing from the French until he be in possession of it (because they make no conscience of what they promise).'[66] Faced, as a subsequent chapter will show, with similar pusillanimity from Rome, more inquiring members of the court began to question, or at least temper their zeal. John Caryll argued that the Stuarts should anticipate a longer process of 'much purging and blooding', to work against 'the nature of the disease', concerned that militant policies had risked a 'want of submission to our supreme physician', whose will worked just as powerfully through the aid of 'benign medicines'.[67] In framing this conclusion, Caryll pushed at an open door. Similar thoughts had been implicit in the exchanges of a cohort present at the exiled court, since the failure of the Irish campaign.

The principles behind the Gracious Declaration were adumbrated in 1691, whilst Melfort was in Rome, in discussions at the cabinet council spearheaded by Caryll, Henry Browne, Lewis Innes and John Stafford: remnants of the party of Catholic moderates who had resisted the antagonising pace of royal policy before the Revolution. Long discomforted by the prospect of sending men against the Royal Navy – in which his own Protestant cousins held office – Browne pressed that the court must consider new methods, to allow their monarch to 'returne as much on his own interest as he can' without the devastation of war ... and ye hazard of being at last a Property and Tributary to the Power that aids him'. The king could not be restored without winning the affections of subjects, he argued, and 'it will be well to consider that fear, whether reall, Imaginary, or artificiall, of ye prevalency of Popery, and despotick Rule, is that wch holds them yet so fast together'.[68] Backed up by Browne's correspondents, the reaction against 'despotick' manifestos came with veiled critiques of the model of Catholic rule found in the kingdom of Louis XIV, which had exercised such an influence over the conversions of Melfort and Perth. Caryll suggested pointedly that a kingdom whose glory rested on military power and perpetual conflict had thrown herself upon the mercy of fortune, and could all too easily be 'humbled' in 'a true Christian sense' by the will of God.[69] From Rome, the Scottish clergyman William Leslie went further, in recuperating

lished PhD thesis, University of Cambridge, 1981, pp. 287–8; John Childs, *The Nine Years War and the British Army 1688–97* (Manchester, 1991), pp. 175–6, 240–59.

66 Daniel Arthur to Browne, 17 April 1691, AAW, Browne MSS, 80; Browne to James II, 29 September 1691, Browne MSS, 103; Joseph Kennedy to William Leslie, 1 December 1693, SCA, Blairs, II, 38/15.

67 John Caryll to Philip Ellis, 2 August 1693, HMC, *Stuart*, I, pp.78–81.

68 Sheridan, 'Historical Narrative', HMC, *Stuart*, VI, pp. 72–4; Browne to James II, December 1690, AAW, Browne MSS, fol. 244.

69 'The Duumvirate', Bodleian Library, Carte MSS, 208, fol. 398; Caryll to Browne, February 1691, AAW, Browne MSS, fol. 156.

the distaste for Bourbon religious absolutism voiced within the circle of Cardinal Howard before the Revolution. He insisted to Caryll that James must liberate himself from the Jesuit rule over public consciences that had corrupted the French realm: the sovereign must foreground instead 'the rules of good government and policy' against the pressure of 'men nourished in schools, convents, monasteries, colledges ... as ignorant of state affairs as they are to be pilots of a shippe'.[70]

The logic of this discourse impelled the cabinet council to re-engage opinion in the three kingdoms, making overtures to a collection of British notables who had betrayed qualms at the consequences of the Revolution. They concentrated first upon a section of dissident opinion in the Whig and Nonconformist community, aiming to revive the alliances forged by James II's policy of 'indulgence' before the Revolution. The councillors resumed contact with the Quaker leader William Penn, the Presbyterian Sir James Montgomerie, the Baptist ex-Cromwellian Edward Roberts, and the pamphleteer- barrister Charlwood Lawton.[71] The architect of these exchanges was the recusant lawyer Robert Brent, who had helped to draft James II's 1687 Declaration of Indulgence, and established a network of Catholics and Dissenters as electoral 'regulators' designed to enter local public office in support of the king.[72] The settlement proposal that emerged after 1692, prioritising religious liberty before any plan to dislodge the Anglican grip on the public realm, was true to the agenda of those who had resisted Melfort and Sunderland in Whitehall before 1688. Caryll and Browne remained alive to the hope of elevating the recusant community in national politics, but they insisted that any systemic change must be left to a later day. Before then, the court must accept 'the breaking of the laws' by James II's counsellors as a signal cause of the Revolution, and show itself willing to retreat from past excesses, by confining itself to advocacy of religious toleration.[73] The discussions bore fruit. Confronted with the political shift on his return in November 1691, Lord Melfort found himself ill-equipped to return the court to hard-line solutions, and Lawton believed that Caryll, Browne and Brent could prevail upon him to arrest any drive towards reaction: 'His char-

---

[70] William Leslie to Caryll, 26 November 1692, SCA, Blairs, I, 152/11.

[71] Monod, *Jacobitism*, pp. 49–52; Mary K. Geiter, 'William Penn and Jacobitism: A Smoking Gun?', *Historical Research*, 73 (2000), pp. 213–17; Caryll to James II, 11 September 1691, AAW, Browne MSS, B7, fol. 260; William Penn to Henry Browne, 10 March 1691, Browne MSS, 85; 'Mr Lawton' to Innes, 10 November 1691, SCA, Blairs, I, 138/3.

[72] Daniel Arthur to Browne, 14 March 1693, AAW, Browne MSS, 143; James Coriton to Browne, 9 August 1691, BL, Add. MSS, 37,662, p. 234; Sir George Duckett, *The Penal Laws and the Test Acts* (2 vols, London, 1882–83), I, p. 240; J.R. Jones, 'James II's Whig Collaborators', *Historical Journal*, 3 (1966), pp. 65–73; M.A. Goldie, 'James II and the Dissenters' Revenge', *Historical Research*, 66 (1993), pp.141–63.

[73] Sheridan, 'Historical Narrative', HMC, *Stuart*, VI, pp. 72–4; Ailesbury, *Memoirs*, I, pp. 126, 152, 165.

acter is softened amongst the 3 and were I with you I could make him in some measure their Darling.'[74] Outnumbered in council and urged forward by Brent, Melfort was pressed to reassure his critics that 'I love to know my faults, and to mend them', and 'though my education has been at court, yet I come of ye country and know both'.[75]

By 1693, according to the recusant commentator Charles Dodd, the 'old Catholic' leaders had been successful enough to leave the Noncompounding party in 'some kind of disgrace' for its opposition to political change.[76] But in making approaches outside the Jacobite community, the council leaders had sparked a debate with serious ideological implications. In order to have 'the Crown established upon ye Love and affections of the subjects', they had to convince both their Catholic king and his Protestant realm to accept an alternative to the tenets of religious 'unity through uniformity': the idea that a monarch and his subjects must uphold the same faith in order to secure the safety of the realm.[77] As Melfort now concurred, the way had to be found for 'King and People to be united in a National *Civill* interest', creating temporal bonds that rose above the differences in religious belief.[78] Writing to an unnamed Protestant nobleman, Browne said that the court no longer deemed the union of the king with *any* single church to be capable of supplying the glue for civil allegiance. While he declared personal pride in Catholic loyalty to a Protestant monarch in the Civil War, he acknowledged that 'if ye difference of our Carriage in ye like occasions were all yt our Religions differ'd in, I should not think mine worth suffering much for', since 'ye Reigns of ye 2 last Harrys of France' proved that his own communion had not always been scrupulous for the hereditary principle.[79] Politics should instead be constructed in a sphere separate from debates of religion. It could be accepted that 'as ye Protestants are the most numerous their 'Place in the Government will be by far the greatest' and by reconciling himself to English laws, James II must 'resolve to be a Protestant King though a Catholick Man, and submit his personal and privat passions in Government to the publick interest of himself and Royal Prosperity'.[80] But this agreement was reached on grounds of public safety, not as a moral endorsement of Anglican claims over the state.

[74] Charlwood Lawton to James II, 13 July 1691, AAW, Browne MSS, 93.

[75] Melfort to 'Laty' (Lawton): 4 July 1692, BL, Add. MSS, 37,661, p. 8; 29 August 1692, pp. 244–8; 29 August 1692, p. 48; 26 December 1692, pp. 374–5.

[76] Charles Dodd, *The Church History of England … chiefly with regard to Catholicks* (3 vols, London, 1737–42), III, pp. 421–2; Melfort to Ailesbury, 7 September 1692, Melfort letter-book, BL, Add. MSS, 37,661, pp. 67–8.

[77] Melfort to 'Laty' (Lawton), 4 July 1692, BL, Add. MSS, 37,661, p. 8.

[78] Melfort to Lawton, 8 September 1692, BL, Add. MSS, 37,661, p. 82.

[79] [Browne] Letter from St Germain, n.d., Arundel Castle, Howard of Norfolk MSS, Autograph letters, 441.

[80] Browne to James II, December 1690, AAW, Browne MSS, 244.

On this principle, Browne and his allies began the audacious print campaign to re-establish a Catholic king as the guardian of 'our Ancient, Legal, Limited and Hereditary Monarchy'.[81] David Nairne and John Caryll deployed Machiavellian logic to contend that religious difference between sovereign and subjects represented the *deterrent* towards absolutist rule, embedding into the constitution the dynamic tension that would leave each side 'jealous of their liberties' and keeping a watch over the other:

> ... if I were to choose ye Government I would live under, it would be that of a King whose religion is different from that of the rest of ye Nation ... the more I shall think myself secure, for thereby he will be more obliged to be careful in preserving ye rights of the subject, and even of the Church established by law.[82]

The 1689 Revolution settlement, Jacobite authors argued, had not secured the liberty of the subject – it had merely exchanged one king for another. Moreover, a monarch seated by 'ancient laws', purged of 'evil counsellors' and weak enough in exile to submit to the terms of his subjects, could be better trusted to preside with a 'gentle hand' over constitutional freedoms than a conqueror installed by military descent, who would be pushed towards coercion and arbitrary rule by the instability of his title.[83] Endorsed by Caryll and Melfort, Lawton's pamphlets exploited the political change at St Germain to introduce a transformation in Jacobite ideology, fit to engage with the 'Country' opposition to the governments of William III in parliament.[84] The defences of James II berated the Williamite regime for its standing armies, Dutch placemen and treatment of Jacobite suspects, in the attempt to show how a Protestant prince was guilty of the sins so widely held against his Catholic predecessor.[85] Lawton drew attention to the reappearance of past stewards of 'arbitrary government', the lords Danby and Sunderland, in Williamite counsels, to argue that the crisis of English liberties remained unresolved.[86] Caryll complained of administrations draining the 'blood and treasure' of a nation, loading 'tax on tax, not thinking/

---

[81] 'Account of a politick conversation between a Catholick and a Whig', Bodleian Library, Carte MSS, 210, fols 411–14.

[82] 'Letter to a Friend in Amsterdam', Bodleian Library, Carte MSS, 181, fol. 641.

[83] Ibid., fol. 6421; Caryll, 'The Duumvirate', Bodleian Library, Carte MSS, 208, fol. 398.

[84] Paul Monod, 'Jacobitism and Country Principles in the Reign of William III', *Historical Journal*, 30 (1987), pp. 289–310.

[85] [Charlwood Lawton], *A Reply to the answer Doctor Welwood has made to King James's declaration* (1694); Lawton, *A French Conquest neither practicable nor desirable* (1692), p. 24; Lawton, *The Jacobite Principles Vindicated* (1693); Sheridan, 'Historical Narrative', pp. 46, 65–6; Mark Goldie and Clare Jackson, 'Williamite Tyranny and the Whig Jacobites', in Esther Mijers and David Onnekink, eds, *Redefining William III: The Impact of the King-Stadtholder in International Context* (Aldershot, 2007), pp. 177–200.

[86] *A Reply to the Answer*, pp. 8, 17.

Under the burden how the nation's sinking'.[87] Melfort's letters to England discussed the virtues of trade, fiscal retrenchment, the 'true constitution of government' and the 'mastery of the sea', all identifiable 'country' themes, to forge a case at once monarchic and moralistic, patriotic and libertarian, for a Stuart restoration.[88]

The political change at the exiled court was sealed in early 1693, when the Catholic priest Edward Cary was sent to liaise with Middleton, the son-in-law of his patron Lord Brudenell.[89] Latterly, it was Anglicans such as the Earl of Clarendon and the Marquis of Worcester who expressed the most outspoken reservations about the shift, urging James to make no 'further engagements to the republicans' who schemed to render him no more than a 'Doge of Venice'.[90] It was a doubt that haunted James II in his memoirs, and aroused similar anxiety in Melfort, who was cast out of the court circle in 1694.[91] Yet the architects of the change – Caryll, Browne and Innes – issued a more cast-iron commitment, because they were aware that in crafting the Jacobite blueprint, they were defending not just the reputation of James II but their own position as Catholic subjects of a Protestant realm. If they could not find a way to make their religion acceptable, there could be no chance of an exiled Stuart coming close to his dynastic goal. Henceforth, court policy would be developed, in the words of David Nairne, to voice the aspirations of 'the poor Catholics, who desire only to live in peace and ... love old England so well that [they wil] do anything to please her that an honest man can do'.[92] Melfort himself had insisted that recusants stood: 'as truly Englishmen in all their Nationall maxims as any Whig in England, and would as little desire to see their titles, fortunes, or liberties in the hands of any depraved minister or court favourite'.[93] If Catholics had not hitherto been the most vocal in the defence of the ancient constitution, the government must grant them toleration: 'and they will love liberty and property as well as your state Whigs ... They that talk foolishly let us come to direct in the right way. And I shall answer for the rest.[94] Charlwood Lawton was apt to concur, for 'I believe in my conscience Catholicks may be made Englishmen.'[95] The move towards 'Compounding' at St Germain is therefore best understood as an expression not just of recusant thought but

[87] 'The Duumvirate', Bodleian Library, Carte MSS, 208, fols 397–8.
[88] Melfort to Lawton, 4 August 1692, 19 September 1692, 20 November 1692, BL, Add. MSS, 37,661, pp. 41, 97, 242.
[89] Clarke, ed., *Life of James the Second*, II, p. 498.
[90] Clarke, ed., *Life of James the Second*, II, pp. 502–5.
[91] Ibid., pp. 504–5; Melfort to Perth, 18 February 1701, printed in *Commons Journal*, XIII, p. 336.
[92] David Nairne to Berry, 6 April 1713, MacPherson, ed., *Original Papers*, I, p. 397.
[93] The earl of Melfort to 'Laty', 19 September 1692, BL, Add. MSS, 37,661, fol. 49.
[94] Melfort to Lawton, 20 November 1692, BL, Add. MSS, 37,661, pp. 243–5; see also David Nairne to Agent Berry, 6 April 1713, MacPherson, ed., *Original Papers*, I, p. 397.
[95] Lawton to James II, 1691, AAW, Browne MSS, 256.

of English recusant lives. In overturning the blueprint of the absolutists, the political world of St Germain would be made to resemble the Catholicism familiar to Caryll, Browne and Brent, remote from dreams of the Counter-Reformation and earthed within the solid reality of English provincial life.

The *Gracious Declaration* and the conscience of the king

For confessional Jacobites, the most troubling implication of the change in policy at St Germain lay in the question of how to accommodate temporal compromises with the fiery assemblage of martyrdom, pilgrimage and devotion that had shaped the imagination of the Stuarts in exile. The Gracious Declaration represented a revolutionary step for a Catholic king. In committing James II to the protection of Anglican institutions, the court not merely reversed pre-Revolution policy but repudiated the very vocabulary of the Counter-Reformation: the idea that the conversion of heretical kings would re-constitute the realm of universal Christendom.[96] There was no erosion of the Catholic character of the court; no lessening of *spiritual* zeal. But the courtiers sought to shift the religion of the Stuarts out of the theatre of politics, diplomacy and constitutional decision-making, and into the private sphere of family piety, culture and devotion. In defining the territory of debate at St Germain as earthly, not eschatological, they had sidelined any lingering influence of 'cuius regio, eius religio' and dealt a deathblow to the Non-compounding notion that a king could only be secure if he embodied the conscience of his subjects. Accordingly, the document drew a denunciation from the *devot* faction at court, with Perth raging against his colleagues: 'Religion is gone and a wicked policy set up in its place.'[97] Even the staunch 'Compounder' William Leslie agreed that its passage had been a salient moment for that realm of court life where 'the consciences of princes are to be framed and formed'.[98]

In Jacobite circles, the new manifesto was duly treated as an affair of religious gravity. A committee comprising the secular clergymen John Betham and Lewis Innes, the Benedictine Francis Fenwick and the Jesuit Francis Sanders was convened to present a formal endorsement.[99] James II wrote to his confessor at La Trappe, and the clerics prevailed upon Bishop Bossuet to

---

[96] The only writer to explore this theme is Susan Rosa in her discussion of the political thought of James, earl of Perth: 'Bossuet, James II and the Crisis of Catholic Universalism', in James G. Buickerood, ed., *Eighteenth-Century Thought*, I (2003), pp. 37–122.

[97] Dodd, *Church History*, III, pp. 421–2; Royal Archives (Windsor), Sheridan, 'Political Reflexions', pp. 100–103.

[98] William Leslie to the earl of Melfort, 26 November 1692, SCA, Blairs, I, 152/11.

[99] John Betham, petition to Bishop Bossuet, n.d. April 1693, AAW, Main Series, 36, pp. 87–8; Royal Archives (Windsor), Sheridan, 'Political Reflexions', pp. 98–9, 103.

defend the document before the Holy See.[100] Court spokesmen contended that, once the freedom of the Catholic faith had been restored, the precise civic arrangement conceived to support the recusant community in a Protestant nation was not a matter for the religious conscience. James II had been true to the obligations of his Church by entering exile for his faith: in finding grounds for him to return, the needs of private piety did not demand religious and political absolutism. James himself agonised over the concessions, agreeing that a true Christian should not 'hazard his own salvation for the saving of the whole world', but arguing that the chance of a Catholic king would serve a public advantage and do much to diminish the suffering of the embattled flock.[101] Francis Sanders insisted that it was no violation of the religious conscience 'to make a great difference between governing a Kingdom that was not of his religion generally, and that of a kingdom where the King's subjects are of the same communion'.[102] Most daringly, the committee of priests persuaded Bossuet to invoke the provisions previously outlined for Huguenots under the Edict of Nantes as a precedent for the status now proposed for English Catholics – justifying by 'the needs of public peace' the law he had striven so successfully to overthrow.[103] This distinction between civic and spiritual obligations informed reflections from the court priesthood into the following century. Lewis Innes insisted that James had not been obliged to protect the Anglican *church* as a spiritual institution, but rather 'finding all her rights and privileges already settled by such lawes as he could not abrogate, he might promise to protect the members of the Church of England in the quiet possession of all their rights and privileges'.[104] The Gracious Declaration was not a matter of defining true and false churches, but accepting worldly conditions as they stood.

In Rome, France and England, the need to justify the compromises of 1693 heightened the importance of religious toleration as a tenet of the Jacobite manifesto: the step deemed 'most agreeable to the laws and the spirit of the Christian religion' and a better foundation for the security of the state than a web of penal laws and constrictions.[105] The official 'Life of James II', edited by John Caryll and William Dicconson, instructed the Jacobite prince of Wales that the greatest precedent lay with 'our blessed Saviour' who 'whipt people out of the Temple, but I never heard he commanded

---

[100] Graquére, *Vers l'Unité Chrétienne*, pp. 118–120; Clarke, ed., *Life of James the Second*, II, pp. 508–9.

[101] *Letters of James to the Abbot of La Trappe*, ed. Lord Acton (Miscellany of the Philobiblon Society, 14, 1872–76), pp. 21–3.

[102] Ailesbury, *Memoirs*, II, p. 490.

[103] Betham, petition to Bossuet, AAW, Main Series, 36, pp. 87–8.

[104] Lewis Innes to James Edward, 23 August 1728, Royal Archives (Windsor), Stuart papers, 119/84.

[105] 'Gracious Declaration', September 1692, in Clarke, ed., *Life of James the Second*, I, pp. 283–6.

any should be forced into it'.[106] In adopting this strategy, the court was not wholly out of step with the times. A *de facto* toleration was starting to take root across some German and Italian dominions, in regions where princes were obliged to rule over mixed populations.[107] In these principalities, the widening of religious liberty did not entail support for permitting multiple opinions as a positive good in itself. Toleration was characteristically advocated as an act of Christ-like forbearance on the part of an authority that still retained the power to coerce: in a context familiar to English Catholics, the Douai-Rheims New Testament of 1582 declared the remission of sins wrought by the Crucifixion to be 'the toleration of God'.[108] The stance was most commonly construed as a means to the end of civic harmony: Richard Bulstrode argued that toleration, like clemency and pardon, should be in the gift of a strong monarchy, for 'Mens mindes have been then most disunited when there was the greatest need of union & concord amongst them' and without grounds to rally religious dissenters, 'the service of these his faithfull Subjects would be lost'.[109] The 'Life of James II' also invoked earthly benefits, citing the expansion of commercial life bequeathed by liberating subjects from penal constraint.[110] Acknowledging these examples, the monk Benet Nelson attacked the 'vain and frivolous apprehensions' of 'half-witted weak Catholics' who 'grow strangely disturbed and alarmed' by the altered policy. He insisted that James was under no obligation to offer Catholics dominion over English politics, since the spirit of the Gospels demanded that true faith be sustained for more than temporal reasons.[111]

However, the Jacobite case also harked back to an earlier recusant literature of engagement and accommodation, present in scholarly reflections that had sought to redress the Foxean caricature of Catholicism as a persecuting religion. Anthony Copley's *A Fig for Fortune* (1596) had promised that stoical adherence to conscience would serve better than martyrdom or violent resistance to open the gates of 'Sionrie' and permit a glimpse of Jerusalem.[112] The monk Serenus Cressy, whose work was described by Anthony Wood as 'the Golden Calf which the English papists fell down and worshipped', had turned to the Erasmian distinction between essential faith and *adiaphora* ('things indifferent'), to argue that Christ's 'law of peace and

---

[106] Clarke, ed., *Life of James the Second*, II, p. 621; E. Gregg, 'New Light on the Authorship of the Life of James II', *English Historical Review*, 108 (1993), pp. 947–62.

[107] Joachim Whaley, 'Tolerant Society? Religion and Toleration in the Holy Roman Empire, 1648–1806', in Grell and Porter, *Toleration*, pp. 175–195; T.C.W. Blanning, 'The Enlightenment in Catholic Germany', in Porter and Teich, *Enlightenment*, pp. 118–26.

[108] Alexandra Walsham, *Charitable Hatred: Tolerance and Intolerance in England, 1500–1700* (Manchester, 2006), p. 4.

[109] Bulstrode, 'Discourse', p. 4.

[110] Clarke, ed., *Life of James the Second*, I, p. 170.

[111] Weldon, 'Collection', BL, Add. MSS, 10,118, pp. 525–6.

[112] Anthony Copley, *A Fig for Fortune* (1596).

charity' could never be found in that 'troublesome pretended zeal for the Catholick faith' present in 'the tribunalls of the Inquisition'.[113] Cressy had located the condition for free conscience in a Gallican, 'dualist' construction of the state, when providence had distributed 'those powers by wch ye whole man is to be govern'd' into two separate realms, the spiritual and the temporal, 'that they may no way clash one wth ye other'. If Catholics could pledge to shield civil affairs from the spiritual authority of the Papacy, fair reciprocity demanded that temporal powers did not impinge upon the private space 'which properly belongs to God'.[114] These ideas echoed among the thoughts of the court Jacobites. John Caryll, who had taken Cressy as chaplain in his Sussex estates in 1673, lamented privately in his commonplace book how state forces of 'Passion and self-interest' had 'turned Religion, whose end is charity, into an Engine of Cruelty'.[115] Benet Nelson turned to the imagery of St Cyprian, contending that through toleration God winnowed his flock, granted the chance to separate visible manifestations of 'the wheat from the tares' as the harvest flowered. Catholicism, if set free, would find its providential pathway in England, undermining the strictures of the Test Act far more effectively than any revolution led from the throne.[116]

By the death of James II, the defeat of the Noncompounding argument had generated a new court orthodoxy in matters of religion. John Betham, the secular clergyman and royal chaplain at St Germain, claimed to have extracted from 'my experience in England' the lesson that 'treating hereticks with bitterness is not ye way to convert them'.[117] The idea that royal piety should be driven away from the scene of worldly politics, was made manifest in a series of redescriptions of the life and reign of James II, which confined his spiritual achievements, in John Lytcott's words, to 'the conquest of himself and his sufferings', and offered a hint of criticism of events following his succession. An *Ode upon the Death of the late King James*, printed at St Germain, paid tribute to a 'sacred memory', but lamented the 'tragick fall' brought about when 'Christian zeal' collided with 'the troubles of the state' and Jesuit dogma turned the monarch into an ingénue, trapped by 'fanaticks' and 'evil counsellors' of both creeds, before he 'saw too late/

---

113 Hugh Serenus Cressy, *Exomologesis* (1647), pp. 528–34; Cressy to Thomas Clifford, n.d. 1671, BL, Add. MSS, 65,139, fol. 17; Bruckmann, '"Paradice It Selfe"', pp. 105–6.
114 Cressy to Clifford, n.d. 1672, BL, Add. MSS, 65,119, fol. 7; Anthony J. Brown, 'Anglo-Irish Gallicanism 1635–1685', unpublished PhD thesis, Cambridge University, 2004, pp. 123–7; Appeal for toleration 'upon ye principles of the Declaration of Breda', Oxfordshire CRO, Belson MSS, F/1/4/MS/7.
115 Caryll commonplace book, BL, Add. MSS, 28,252, fol. 291.
116 Weldon, 'Collection', BL, Add. MSS, 10,118, pp. 524–9.
117 John Betham, 'Ruff Draught of the Reasons Given and the Methods Taken for Removing from St Germain John Betham, Preceptor to King James ye 3rd', January 1705, AAW, St Gregory's Seminary MSS, fols 231–45, at fol. 237.

Th' unhappy signs of his approaching Fate'.[118] Even the 'Life of James II' hinted at the same conclusion, lamenting how the king's confessors had been seduced by the 'false' convert Lord Sunderland into proposing reckless measures: 'dazzled with the dust that this cunning statesman threw in their eyes' against the greater caution of country recusants.[119] These writings helped to shift the balance between royal piety and public virtue in the Jacobite imagination. Two decades later, the Capuchin monk Archangel Graeme was at pains to inform 'hot-brained churchmen' that the Stuart claimant was 'obliged in conscience to observe his coronation oath', just as tenaciously as he should observe his own faith – the corollary was to 'maintain the Protestant religion as it is established by law'.[120]

The king's 'wise men' and the image of the court 1701–1715

The ideology of the court in exile came to maturity after the death of James II, crystallised in the hands of the close-knit circle of friends who sat on the Council of Regency, before the Pretender came of age. Middleton re-affirmed that 'natural-born Englishmen', those 'best acquainted with the constitution' who 'have an affection for it', must dominate the Jacobite court, and the principle was shared by his allies who staffed the council: Caryll, Nairne, Dicconson and Innes, and the prince's preceptors, the secular clergymen John Betham and John Ingleton.[121] According to Betham, individuals charged with the 'breeding' of a king 'are yet more guilty than he, if they do not procure him the best, and most worthy a prince, that possibly they can'.[122] Charles Booth, the prince's *aide-de-camp*, concurred: 'his Reputation was as much to be taken care of as his person'.[123] In purely social terms, the composition of the council marked a re-assertion of the power of old English Catholic families at St Germain, a shift that left residual Noncompounders voicing their frustration. The court, suggested a disgruntled Sheridan, was succumbing to a recusant old boys' network of 'Doway and Lancashire', adopting methods quite unsuited to the raising of

---

[118] *An Ode upon the Death of the late King James ... Dedicated to his son the Prince* (St Germain, 1701); Lytcott, 'Historical Essay', in Weldon, 'Collection', BL, Add. MSS, 10,118, p. 803.

[119] Clarke, ed., *Life of James the Second*, II, pp. 74–8.

[120] Archangel Graeme to the earl of Mar, 7 October 1717, HMC, *Stuart*, V, p. 105.

[121] Royal Archives (Windsor), Sheridan, 'Political Reflexions', pp. 91–2, 204; National Library of Scotland, Nairne Diary, 19, 21, 24 September 1701; Browne letter-book, 1691, AAW, Browne MSS, p. 208; the earl of Perth to John Caryll, 29 July 1695, Bodleian Library, Carte MSS, 209, fol. 313.

[122] John Betham, *A Brief Treatise of Education* (Paris, 1693), p. 3.

[123] Charles Booth to Middleton, 28 June 1709, Bodleian Library, Carte MSS, 210, fols 186–7.

a prince.[124] Yet the solutions proposed by this coterie would stamp a deep impression on the youthful James Edward Stuart. 'I desire your company' he wrote to Middleton from Flanders in 1710, 'to have at least one wise man with me, yet I think you are more necessary there than you are here, so I must prefer my interest to my private intuition'.[125] Unlike his father, James Edward was not a convert – a fact that rendered him culturally closer to the 'old Catholics' in his entourage – and the courtiers hoped to make a political asset of the condition. In Middleton's judgement, 'Those who hate the Catholique religion do not hate those who were bred up in it, and the resentment may be much abated by time.'[126] Schooled in the ways of a land he had never seen, James was duly moulded according to the interests of his 'wise men', and cast as an exemplar for the English Catholic country.

The need to promote a different idea of the relationship between the prince's Catholic faith and his duty to the state was brought home in the reports sent from allies operating outside the court. Edward Dicconson, the Douai vice-president and sibling to the Jacobite royal treasurer, voiced his belief that James Edward had the chance to embody 'a great turn of providence' towards Catholic rebirth. He maintained that since 'often ye Parsons do preach to ye people that Rome is better than Geneva, there seems to be dispositions, which, if artfully improved upon a restoration, give once more hopes of a re-union of yt great Kingdom with the See of Rome'.[127] However, Dicconson warned that the path remained perilous when 'Some to this day talk with a lively sense of their great deliverance from that danger by the Revolution', and would readily 'ring the Tocksin' against clerical minds 'disposed to act over again the improvidences of the late K. James's reign'.[128] In commentaries submitted to the exiled court over twenty years, he interpreted England through a Harringtonian lens, suggesting that the structure of land-holding placed a range of socio-political obstacles before any Catholic king, even if the nation possessed no strident 'zeal for the Protestant religion'. Englishmen were principally animated by anxieties over the possession of dissolved monastic lands, when lay encroachments had constructed 'a political system formed by men of interest and great power', and 'the credit of those concerned has all along … managed the Deliberations in both Houses of Parliament'. Property interests had drawn 'the nobility and gentry headlong into the extravagant and inconsistent measures of Hen: 8th', the same impulse had sounded the death knell for 'the Innocent Queen of Scotland' and even catalysed the Civil War in resist-

---

124 Royal Archives (Windsor), Sheridan 'Political Reflexions', pp. 92–4.
125 James Edward to Middleton, 4 June 1710, Bodleian Library, Carte MSS, 210, fols 344–9.
126 Royal Archives (Windsor), Sheridan, 'Political Reflexions', pp. 114–15.
127 Edward Dicconson to Lawrence Mayes, 5 May 1715, AAW, Epistolae Variorum, V/93.
128 Dicconson to Mayes, 17 March 1714, AAW, Epistolae Variorum, V/48.

ance to Laudian ambitions. Now, 'it seems almost impossible for any Popish Prince to sit on the English throne unless he hath first ... made the Possessors of those Lands intirely easy'. In alleviating these anxieties, the exiled court had to accept that religious revival could not override worldly politics. Jacobites should look into English opinion and engage instead 'the discors of the gentry'.[129]

In line with Dicconson's concerns, the attempt to show that the religion of the royal family brought no disturbance to earthly state and society was reflected in the shifting patterns of the court's culture of devotion. When a change of faith *did* occur -notably for Middleton in 1703 – it would increasingly be presented as an affair of the 'private soule', without political ramification. The earl informed the royal council that 'though he had renounced his religion, he had not changed his principle of policy. He still thought the Restoration of a Popish King impossible to be affected but by Protestant hands.'[130] This mood informed the development of the devotional libraries at St Germain with chaplains and tutors from the secular clergy – who had displaced their Jesuit predecessors – introducing a set of rigorist texts, stressing the cultivation of the religious interior over injunctions towards the purging of heresy. In an ode to *A Contrite and Humble Heart*, republished from St Germain and dedicated to the memory of James II, the Paris priest Sylvester Jenks urged his co-religionists to reject the 'Self-Love' of those confessional zealots who 'violently accuse their Neighbours in the Sight of Men', insisting that 'nothing but the Grace of God can calm the Spirits of Men' out of false doctrine, 'else one might as well pretend to chide the Winds and the Waves in a Storm'.[131] The alternative tone was set by the practical, 'state of life' Christianity animated in the writings of St Francis de Sales and cited as an inspiration to James II just as it was being hewn to English tastes in the works of Betham's friend John Gother.[132] John Caryll's translation of the *Psalms of David* was endorsed as a vernacular work to show a cross-confessional audience 'the language they are to use in addressing themselves to God'.[133] Caryll recommended the Anglican writer John Norris, who had gleaned from translations of Malebranche the view of Christian faith as 'an universall key' to 'purify and refine your minds, brighten, and enlarge your

[129] Edward Dicconson to William Dicconson, 29 July 1736, Dicconson letter-book, Lancashire CRO, RCWB/5, pp. 501–12.

[130] Royal Archives (Windsor), Sheridan, 'Political Reflexions', p. 117.

[131] Sylvester Jenks, *A Contrite and Humble Heart. With Motives and Considerations to Prepare it* (St Germain edn, 1705), Preface.

[132] John Betham to George Witham, 16 March 1704, AAW, Epistolae Variorum, I/2; Geoffrey Scott, 'The Court as a Centre of Catholicism', in Corp, ed., *A Court in Exile*, pp. 235–56.

[133] Caryll, *The Psalms of David, Translated from the Vulgate*, with a preface by Betham and Ingleton (St Germain, 1701).

thoughts', to 'rid you of your prejudices'.[134] In St Germain, as in England, the ecumenicist undertones of this 'religion of the heart' served a pastoral purpose interwoven with social and political needs. A creed centred on the idea of charity, simplicity and moral perfection was conceived in part to redress some of the worst canards clinging to the Catholic name.

The link between rigorist religion and a form of purified, non-absolutist monarchy was spelt out in the pedagogical instructions for the Stuart Pretender contained within John Betham's *Brief Treatise of Education* (1693). This work placed strict emphasis on psalms, catechisms and pastoral practices, as the keystone of a 'Christian education', but it also renewed the Salesian vision of Catholicism stripped to its practical essence, tempering the excesses of the confessional vision. Betham warned that intense personal piety brought no inevitable blessing for the realm, when 'the life of a Saint may be as dangerous as that of a wicked Man'; moreover the career of a prince could not feasibly be modelled on the habits of the monastic cell, since it 'passes in almost continual commerce with men'.[135] At its worst, confessional zeal fostered a false self-certainty driven by the 'passions'. Instead, the seeds of an 'heroick and elevated' form of 'Christian vertue' could be found just as richly scattered in civic humanist reflections on the purpose of royal power: the works of Lipsius would serve as a superior form of political instruction to anything generated in the cloisters.[136] The true exertion of Christian piety, Betham argued, would be to discipline the mind, fend off 'debauchery and disorder' and resist the sinful 'intoxications of the world' that led to tyranny and false presumption.[137] Prone to corruption like any other mortal man, the monarch must therefore learn to guard himself: 'A Prince is not his own; he is the State's. God gives him to the people in making him Prince. To them he is accountable for all his time.' Finding the balance between action and devotion would unlock the key to successful kingship, when 'the love and affection of men are necessary to the employment to which Princes are call'd'. The purpose of royal education was to alert the pupil to the 'secret springs' in 'what purchases or loses them, in what gains or shocks men's minds and in what pleases or displeases the World'.[138]

Betham's prescription aimed to recast the Stuart prince as a monarch fit for 'ye methods and constitution of England'. His writings brought the first inkling of an ideological alliance between the Jacobite community and the

---

134 'A Character of Father Malebranche's Search after Truth', BL, Add. MSS, 28,252, fols 56–7.
135 Betham, *Brief Treatise of Education*, pp. 6–15. For the spiritual influences on Betham, see Geoffrey Scott, 'The Education of James III', in Corp, ed., *A Court in Exile*, pp. 256–77, at 275–6.
136 Betham, *Brief Treatise*, p. 20.
137 Ibid., p. 16.
138 Ibid., pp. 10–12.

Catholic moral and political opposition in the kingdom of Louis XIV. The tract took inspiration from the Jansenist Pierre Nicole, whose own description of *The Education of a Prince* (1671), had been composed as a frugal, patriotic counterblast to the luxury and excess of Versailles.[139] The work also disclosed the wider Jansenist influences that would later drive Betham into conflict with the Holy See. He alluded to Pascal's *Treatise of Grandeur* and drew from the writings of Antoine Arnauld the conclusion that, in a world cast far from God, 'full of continual illusions, and fed with dreams and chimeras', the Church would be better rebuilt not by confrontation with Protestants, but an inward recovery of pure doctrine and discipline.[140] Rather than tilting into a pure form of Jansenism, however, the Pretender's curriculum incorporated a larger corpus of sources. In 1710, the courtiers brought James Edward an audience with Archbishop Francois Fénelon of Cambrai, critic of the Huguenot persecutions and assailant of Bourbon absolutism, who had veiled his attacks in a celebrated text of royal education, *The Adventures of Telemachus*.[141] In four days of conversation assiduously promoted by Jacobite authors, the archbishop offered implicit rebukes to Louis XIV as he set before James the advantages of a parliamentary constitution: 'every wise king … should wish for such a body to consult with him'. He also 'recommended to him above all Things, never to compel his subjects to change their Religion', to view liberty of conscience as 'an impregnable Fortress, which no human Power can force'.[142]

The impact of the encounter with Fénelon, and the doctrines absorbed from John Betham, was made increasingly evident in James Edward's correspondence:

> I am a Catholic, but I am a king and subjects of whatever religion have an equal right to be protected … I am not an apostle, I am not bound to convert my people other than by my example nor to show apparent partiality to Catholics, which would only injure them later.[143]

The mosaic of reformist influences left a lingering afterglow over court affairs. In 1723, as a later chapter will show, James drew animosity from the court of Rome with the appointment of Andrew Michael Ramsay, the

---

[139] Ibid., p. 10; Pierre Nicole, *De l'education d'un prince, divisée en trois parties, dont la dernieere contient divers traittez utiles a tout le monde* (Paris, 1671).

[140] Betham, *Brief Treatise*, p. 10; O'Connor, *Irish Jansenists*, p. 19.

[141] Frank E. Manuel and Fritzie P. Manuel, *Utopian Thought in the Western World* (Oxford, 1979), pp. 381–6. See Chapter 7 for a full discussion of the English Catholic link to Fénelon.

[142] Andrew Michael Ramsay, *Life of François de Salignac de la Motte Fénelon, Archbishop and Duke of Cambray* (1723); Booth to Middleton, 26 May 1709, Bodleian Library, Carte MSS, 210, fol. 124.

[143] James Edward to Father Gaillard, 28 February 1718, HMC, *Stuart*, V, pp. 513–15.

radical Masonic Catholic and disciple of Fénelon, as tutor to his son. By 1732, when Lewis Innes and David Nairne announced the second wave of the campaign to canonise James II, the narrative of the fallen king had been shot through with quietist religious forms. Nairne's eulogy recalled that 'this pious prince so divided his time, between the duties of his station, and those of religion, that the one never interfered with the other'. Above all, 'he never sought to force the conscience of his subjects, believing himself obliged to be a common father to all, independent of religion'.[144] This was a more complicated kind of Christian hero: a divergence from the Counter-Reformation template. The exiled court had introduced the example of a king whose only absolute quality was not his power but his virtue, and whose only crusade was in the conquest of his innermost soul.

Conclusion

Judged by its own political goals, the experiment undertaken at St Germain was a failure. Having defeated the *devot* Catholic faction in their own court, the ruling council became increasingly vulnerable to confessional pressures raised in England, where domestic anxiety over a 'Church in danger' stiffened the sinews of the Tory leadership as defenders of the Anglican order and reduced the chance of a sympathetic audience for a Catholic claimant.[145] From 1710 onwards, as Edward Dicconson lamented, 'all imaginable efforts have been made on the King's religion' by Tory stipulation, and Lord Middleton was hounded out of his post, a despised apostate to the Anglican party.[146] James's preceptor John Ingleton counselled him to stay away from religious controversy – the fatal trap which had lured his father, and the refusal to undertake Protestant re-education was not without justification.[147] Montesquieu averred that a change to a prince's religion was likely to result in a loss of credibility; later, Samuel Johnson voiced the common perception that, for a man to abjure Catholic beliefs, 'there is so much laceration of mind … that it can hardly be sincere and lasting'.[148] But if it was

---

144 David Nairne, 'Concerning what he knew of the life and virtues of the late King of Great Britain, James II' (1734), in MacPherson, ed., *Original Papers*, II, pp. 593–9.

145 Kenyon, *Revolution Principles*, pp. 69–80.

146 Jones, *Charles Middleton*, p. 295; Lewis Innes to Middleton, 2 January 1713, MacPherson, ed., *Original Papers*, II, pp. 365–6; Duke of Berwick to James Edward, 24 April 1715, HMC, *Stuart*, I, p. 359; Dicconson to Lawrence Mayes, 17 April 1714, AAW, Epistolae Variorum, V/50.

147 Ingleton to Mayes, 1 August 1714, AAW, Epistolae Variorum, V/61; Dicconson to Mayes, 17 April 1714, AAW, Epistolae Variorum, V/50.

148 Sylvana Tomaselli, 'Intolerance, the Virtue of Princes and Radicals', in Grell and Porter, eds, *Toleration in Enlightenment*, pp. 86–101, at p. 92; Eamon Duffy, '"Over the Wall": Converts from Popery in Eighteenth-Century England', *Downside Review*, 94 (1976), pp. 1–25, at p. 1.

an article of faith at St Germain, the principle of religious toleration – even without the radical separation of spiritual and temporal powers – remained a matter of suspicion in many European courts, and Bolingbroke ridiculed the way in which James 'made the principal motive for the confidence we ought to have in him to consist in his firm resolution to popery'. In Tory eyes, it left him 'the simplest man of his time'.[149] In the face of such antagonism, the prince could fill his household with as many Anglicans and Dissenters as he wished – attempting 'all that was possible for me towards the quieting of men's minds' – but the central problem that had bedevilled the reign of James II remained. As the Pretender remarked: 'The whole of the question must come to this dilemma, either they will have and will receive me as a Catholic or they will not.'[150] When negotiations with the Tories ground to a halt, James at least had the satisfaction of receiving an answer.

By the end of the following decade, after the 1715 rising brought an influx of Protestant émigrés into the Jacobite diaspora, the influence of the English Catholic families over the exiled court was set for steady diminution. In the political arguments disseminated into Britain, the Stuart cause appeared increasingly 'Protestantised'. Yet it was the political realignment initiated by the circle of 'old Catholic' allies in 1692–93 that had given the court of St Germain its ideological lease of life, fostering the belief that the Stuarts' religion was no longer an insuperable barrier to the governance of the three kingdoms, and presenting Catholic communities with a language to reconcile consciences with the *politique* needs of a dynastic cause. The revived image of Stuart kingship was accordingly taken into England in the scaffold speeches that followed the 1715 rising, when Lord Derwentwater, Henry Oxburgh and Richard Gascoigne spelt out expositions of Jacobite belief so similar that Whig observers were convinced that they must have been written by the same Jesuitical hand.[151] The position of the exiled court allowed the rebels to attack 'the calumny' that 'the Catholicks taken at Preston engaged in that affair in view only of setting a Catholick King on the throne', to invoke instead ancestral loyalties to Charles I, and so refigure their deaths as a stand for 'the ancient and fundamental constitution of these Kingdoms', when in Oxburgh's judgement, 'I never could find that … Difference of Religion in the Prince made any Change in the Allegiance of the Subject'.[152] After two decades of political evolution, the idea forged at St Germain could be pitched to the sensibilities of the crowd, in a patriotic appeal to revive 'the British genius', and let 'the Stuart laurels reflourish

---

[149] Bolingbroke, *Letter to Wyndham*, pp. 264, 291.
[150] James Edward, 'Reasons for not assisting at *Te Deum* at Perth, January 1716', HMC, *Stuart*, V, pp. 11–13.
[151] Arnold, *Northern Lights*, p. 170.
[152] T.B. Howell, *State Trials* (34 vols, 1809–28), XV, p. 802.

once more'.[153] The public realm, even in the eyes of a condemned Jacobite prisoner, was there for the capture.

According to J.R. Jones, 'only very old-fashioned Catholics now share the values and principles which James II held'.[154] This chapter has attempted to exhume the reality behind the myth of the Jacobite court, and so re-examine the idea that political failings wrote the epitaph for an ancient and dogmatic strain of the English Catholic faith. I have sought to show how the approach adopted by sundry historians of St Germain has been limited by a concentration on diplomatic and conspiratorial machinations, at the expense of the greater contextual framework of Catholic politics, culture and spirituality. The courtiers at St Germain were faced with an unusual situation. Recusant arguments for liberty of conscience had usually been conceived as an address from Catholic subjects to a Protestant king; the conditions after 1688 brought an inversion of circumstances, with the advisers of a Catholic sovereign now required to convince a Protestant people of his benign intent. In seeking to overthrow the diabolical images that clung to the Stuart reputation, the royal councils probed totemic questions of national and religious identity. Could a king do his private duty to one faith, whilst preserving the public liberties and privileges of another? Could religious truths be held separate from reason of state? Could a Catholic bound to the needs of spiritual unity still be a loyal Englishman? These were old questions, and old conflicts, but they carried stark implications for a displaced community, who would not gain the chance to return home until they could provide a compelling answer. The result of this peculiar dynastic conundrum was the wresting apart of the 'two bodies', public and private, of the man Jacobites saw as God's earthly vicegerent. They may not have been aware of the radical implications of the enterprise they had embarked upon, nor the controversy they were set to arouse with the counsels of the Holy See.

---

[153] Howell, *State Trials*, XV, p. 804.
[154] Jones, *Revolution*, p. 8.

4

Catholic politics in England 1688–1745

If the ideology of Catholics in exile grew within a relatively free and prosperous political space, recusant discourse in England was framed in an environment far more threatening and claustrophobic. Though the Catholic lay leaders demonstrated notable resilience in the face of social pressure, their prospects for the future still appeared, in contemporary judgements, to be distinctly parlous. Memories of 1688 entrenched a state of estrangement from the body politic: a starkly ironic end to the great loyalist turn in Catholic thought, when older Jesuit theories of resistance had been surmounted by a patriotic commitment to the Stuart throne. Now, in a kingdom vigorously asserting its Protestant identity, Whig pamphlets could assert that 'Foreign jurisdiction in the Pope, and a Foreign Pretender to our Crown, are inseparable', in a manner that mocked the very appellation of the loyal recusant.[1] The situation was paradoxical, when private correspondence revealed the continuing regard in which Catholics held the patriotic virtues. The Lancashire landowner Caryll, Lord Molyneux reserved admiration for those who 'will serve their own country as is duty bound, who will … act like men of honour and integrity … . This is my intention and only design [to be] steadie to my principles and to act like a man of Honour.'[2] However, in the wake of the Glorious Revolution, it was far harder to articulate national feeling – or, at least, far harder to be heard. With suspicions of treason cast over Catholic leaders, and the penal laws returned, the political odds were stacked more heavily against the recusant community than at any time since the Gunpowder Plot.

Catholic politics in England, no less than abroad, were shaped in the shadow of the Jacobite cause: both as a genuine source of commitment and as a spectre exploited by their opponents to raise the national tradition of anti-popery. Scholarly consensus has accordingly, in the words of John Bossy, seen the 'devout patriotism' of English recusants 'held back by loyalty to the Stuarts'.[3] In reappraising this judgement, this chapter will show how the

---

[1] Arthur Ashley Sykes, *The reasonableness of mending and executing the laws against papists* (1746), pp. 31–2.
[2] Caryll, Lord Molyneux to John Caryll, 20 January 1738, BL, Add. MSS, 28,229, fol. 300.
[3] Bossy, 'English Catholics after 1688', p. 386.

political state of the Catholic community certainly encouraged a Jacobite challenge to the Revolution settlement, initially in a recondite or defiantly partisan form. However, I will suggest that the unquestioning and obscurantist Jacobitism of Whig caricature was never the dominant impulse within the recusant community. Moreover, the complexity of Catholic political attitudes was brought emphatically into the open by the minority movement that sought to make a formal renunciation of their old dynastic loyalties. The attempt marshalled between 1716 and 1721 by the clergymen John Stonor and Thomas Strickland, to formulate a Catholic oath of allegiance to George I, has been well-sketched by Eamon Duffy, who detected the thwarted cry of the Catholic gentry – 'Englishmen in Vaine' – to discard what Stonor called the 'the fetters of an erroneous conscience'.[4] However, I will argue that the Catholic oath debate should actually be assessed within a longer time-frame, and a far wider context of political debate, when the issue was originally created in the 1690s by questions of British foreign policy, with rival party lines shaped by the divided continental allegiances of the recusant community. Catholic support for the Revolution settlement should be seen not as a purely insular or pragmatic cast of mind, but the product of a pro-Austrian persuasion, stimulated by exiles operating within the territory of the Holy Roman Empire. The diplomatic alliances of William III and later George I contrived to draw a section of recusant society away from the Jacobite cause, in the hope that the European Catholic affiliations of the new monarchs might provide an alternative route towards toleration. The debate within the community therefore incorporated concerns over the position of the papacy, the larger world of Catholic Christendom and the linkage between dynastic allegiance and true doctrine, to raise the most overt conflict of recusant political theology since the reign of James I.

The Catholic oath project ultimately ran to ground because most of the lay leaders caught up in the affair expressed far greater ambivalence than Stonor and Strickland, and sought to make a fragile distinction between their broad desires for integration and toleration on the one hand, and the precise issue of Hanoverian legitimacy on the other. However, just as importantly, the Catholic Jacobite ideology – in England as in St Germain – was itself moving away from its early militant and doctrinaire image, towards a platform that aimed to reconcile the pious iconography of Stuart kingship with a 'patriot' discourse of laws, liberty and constitutional virtue, to level a stronger critique against the post-Revolution state. By abandoning their appeals to unreceptive Whig governments and engaging instead the 'Country' opposition in parliament and the press, English Catholics were able to work their way back into national politics, and pronounce their case

---

[4] Eamon Duffy, '"Englishmen in Vaine": Catholic Allegiance to George I', in S. Mews, ed., *Religion and National Identity*, Studies in Church History, 18, (Oxford, 1982), pp. 345–67.

against penal laws and prosecution, while keeping dynastic commitments opaque. The final part of the chapter will suggest therefore that Jacobitism was retained within the community because it represented more than simply the 'fetters of an erroneous conscience', and had become compatible with a culture of 'patriotism', sensitive to the Protestant mood, and crafted through a body of Catholic pamphlets and journals. The case against the 1689 settlement had become more than just the recitation of old Divine Right injunctions. Moreover, the variety, ubiquity and self-confidence of Catholic 'patriot' arguments calls into question the exclusively Protestant conception of British national identity in this period. Despite the unpromising public circumstances, there was sufficient political and rhetorical space for Catholic writers to declare their position against the will of the executive, not by rejecting but by appropriating the definitive language of eighteenth-century nationhood.

The political threat and the discovery of a Jacobite voice

The turn of political discourse after 1688 certainly appeared to show a deep, growing and highly mutual state of alienation between English Catholics and their compatriots. After 1688, papists were believed to be engaged in 'Horrid and Bloody Conspiracies' to uproot the liberties of the constitution, the security of the throne and the tenets of the Protestant Reformation.[5] A 1715 declaration from the Anglican bishops invoked the memory of Mary I to allege that the restoration of James III, 'Together with the long train of Papists in the Succession, can bode nothing but fatal and Irrecoverable Ruin'; a 'new yoke of bondage', and, conversely, 'a spirit of libertinism and infidelity'.[6] The confessional argument drew upon a resurgent strain of European Protestant solidarity.[7] Jesuit missioners warned in 1725 that the execution of a contingent of Polish Protestants after religious riots at Thorn 'makes a noise in England' and had aroused fresh calls 'to drain it of Jesuits, as if they were appeared witness in *causa sanguina*'.[8] High ideals melded with low politics to make the prosecution of the Catholic community the surest way for governments to pin down the slippery phantom of Jacobite support – not least in a manner that was financially remunerative. The belief that

---

[5] A Full and True Account of the Horrid and Bloody Conspiracies of the Papists ... In the North of England (London, 1689); Sir Richard Blackmore, A True and Impartial History of the conspiracy against the person and government of King William III of Glorious Memory in the year 1696 (London, 1723), pp. 1–30.

[6] Declaration of the Archbishop of Canterbury, and the Bishops in and near London, Testifieing their Abhorrence of the Present Rebellion (1716).

[7] Andrew C. Thompson, Britain, Hanover and the Protestant Interest, 1688–1756 (Woodbridge, 2006).

[8] John Gage to Levinius Browne, May 1725, EPSJ, Notes and Fragments, 114.

the papists of England were returning to delinquent ways created an ideo-logical context ripe for the revival and expansion of the penal laws, and left the community pitted against the concerns of 'his Majesty and the Pious and Godly Informers' as the Hampshire squire John Matthews sarcastically put it.[9] The possibility of Jacobitism within the recusant community and the rise of anti-popery within the English nation therefore grew together, when national discourse appeared weighted against Catholic subjects, when it materialised so readily into punitive legislation, and when the chance of Catholic survival appeared inseparable from a great turn in political and constitutional fortunes. To the Paris priest John Ingleton in January 1716, 'the prisons are full, especially of Catholicks and nothing but a restauration can rescue religion in this nation from ruin'.[10]

The evidence of their political commentaries suggests that most English recusants still wished to harbour, nurture and disseminate the traditions of royalist action that had shaped the identity of their community. In 1716, members of the Giffard, Yate and Pendrell families petitioned George I, seeking relief from the penal laws 'as Catholics whose ancestors have been of service to the Crown', sheltering Charles II 'in his afflictions' after the battle of Worcester.[11] A handwritten copy of the Civil War tract *The Royal Martyrs* entered into the papers of the Vicar Apostolic Richard Challoner, as he prepared his treatises on British Catholic sainthood in 1735, 'faith-fully transcribed from a Catholic almanack for the year 1686'.[12] But the old memories and motifs of Catholic patriotism remained so intensely bound to the experiences of the previous dynasty that their very expression appeared – however unintentionally – to carry the hint of Jacobite protest. Less obliquely, in personal reflections and pious prophecies, Catholic partisans looked to a cosmic turn that would bring about deliverance of the house of Stuart. Verses possessed by William Haydock of Cottam Hall, Lancashire foresaw a time of trial and 'usurpation', before a rousing climax brought an end to the days of conflict: 'When the Pentecost shall be/ The nearest to St Barnaby/ Then ere a Spring or two be o're/ Expect this prince to his native shore'.[13] These fugitive moments of hope emboldened recusants towards at least a passive rejection of the prevailing powers. Under pressure to sell his family collieries to government contractors, Lord Charles Howard of Grey-

---

9   Richard Chandler, *The History and Proceedings of the House of Commons from the Restoration to the Present Time* (7 vols, 1742), VI, p. 292; P.S. Fritz, *The English Ministers and Jacobitism between the Rebellions of 1715 and 1745* (Toronto, 1975), pp. 84, 105; John Matthews to John Caryll, 13 May 1716, BL, Add. MSS, 28,227, fols 308–9.

10 John Ingleton to Lawrence Mayes, 17 January 1716, AAW, Epistolae Variorum, VII/1.

11 'Copy of an order of council', 6 April 1716, Warwickshire CRO, Throckmorton MSS, Folder 52/3b.

12 AAW, B series, 28, no. 15.

13 CRS, *Miscellanea*, 4 (London, 1707), pp. 439–40.

stroke rejoined that 'as the Government did stand upon the Revolution, and hath continued ever since, it was not fitt to work such rich mines, nor advance Treasures out of the Earth'.[14]

However, the growth of a public dimension to these sympathies was inhibited by the antennae of the state. The impounding of Sir Rowland Stanley in Chester for 'laying wages about King James's return' in 1692 exposed the dangers inherent in any expression of Stuart loyalties, however ingenuous.[15] Writing to his son, John Dryden considered that 'dissembling, though lawfull in some cases, is not in my talent', yet 'I will struggle with the plain open-ness of my nature and keep in my just resentments against that degenerate order'.[16] The result was a division between the rare examples of 'free Jacobitism', realised most startlingly in the death speeches of rebels, and a series of meditations, delivered with varying degrees of obliquity, but leaving Catholic high literature penetrated by hidden Jacobite motifs. Dryden's opera-masque *King Arthur* called upon the traditional 'Britannic' imagery of the house of Stuart to rebuild the apparatus of Catholic royalist thought, with a female embodiment of the realm forced to choose between the counterfeit seductions of a usurper, and the forbearing chivalry of a legitimate prince, her faithful lover.[17] Two decades later, disturbing images of conquest and violation brought a seditious whisper into the sunlit landscape of Pope's *Windsor Forest*, offset by glimpses of redemption in the future of patriotic promise when 'a Stuart reigns'.[18] The novels of Jane Barker centred upon characters 'greatly embarrassed between Love, Religion and Loyalty', confronted with broken vows and moral choices. She advanced that 'whilst each Pretender thinks himself alone/ ... Nay, well it is, as such will grant/ That there is one elsewhere Triumphant'.[19] Allusively and enigmatically, Catholic poets chronicled the drama of the dynastic contest in their own interior lives.

The choice of dynastic loyalty was not however, left to Catholics to make at their leisure. The old oath of allegiance, revived with the Revolution, aimed to bring the political alignments of the community into the open, by presenting individuals with their only chance of avoiding liability to the penal laws. The extensive list of Catholic non-jurors, either absenting

[14] J. Jones to R. Pinckard, attorney, 15 October 1711, Arundel Castle, Howard of Norfolk MSS, miscellaneous letters, 100.

[15] Luttrell, *Brief Historical Relation*, III, p. 140, IV, p. 52.

[16] John Dryden to Charles Dryden, undated copy in Lambeth Palace Archives, Main Series, 933/56.

[17] John Dryden, *King Arthur: The British Worthy* (1691).

[18] Alexander Pope, *Windsor Forest* (1712); Howard Erskine-Hill, *Poetry of Opposition and Revolution* (Oxford, 1996), pp. 71–84.

[19] Jane Barker, *A Patchwork Screen for the Ladies, or Love and Virtue Recommended* (1723), in Shiner Wilson, ed., *Selected Poems*, pp. 80, 151; *The Lining of the Patchwork Screen* (1726), in Shiner Wilson, ed., *Selected Poems*, pp. 193, 218, 222; Katherine King, *Jane Barker*, pp. 162–7.

themselves from their counties, or bluntly refusing to appear before the magistrates, gave the government its readiest demonstration that to be a recusant implied at least passive disloyalty to the new line of succession.[20] After the Convention Parliament debates of 1689, a formidable body of Anglican oath literature showed that a wider section of the nation was similarly absorbed by controversy over the way to approach the Revolution settlement.[21] However, for Catholics, the biggest stumbling block was the explicitly confessional nature of the required oath. Declaring loyalty to William III, Anne and George I required a recitation of the old Jacobean declaration of allegiance, which enjoined the signatory to disavow transubstantiation, ridicule the 'adoration' of saints and the Virgin, and damn the Catholic doctrine as 'superstitious and idolatrous'.[22] For recusants, post-revolutionary doubt was therefore set in the context of a century-old debate over the meaning and possibility of temporal obedience, when the state itself appeared to possess an anti-Catholic architecture.[23] While the oath stood in this way, the choice between compromise and resistance could be defined in black and white terms.

The Catholic Jacobite response to the oaths was brought home with an assault on the legitimacy of the post-Revolution state, in writings dwelling less on the constitutional mechanics of 'sovereignty', than its moral and spiritual dimensions. One of the most frequently re-printed recusant books of the 1690s was the *Treatise of Policy and Religion* (1624), an anti-oath tract penned by the Jacobean Jesuit, Thomas Fitzherbert. This work had advocated pious resistance to 'Machiavellian maxims', and 'Atheistical Politicians', pressing for Christian forbearance against the transient threats of a worldly power. Its re-emergence, printed for the first time since 1663, possessed timely intent, and the Jesuit publishers declared their hand by dedicating five editions to James II or his son. A preface exalted the fallen king as one who 'preferred true Religion to all human policy ... with such a constant submission to Providence that you pass through all the different turns and Labyrinths thereof'.[24] Statements of spiritual resistance moved in step with deconstructions of the post-Revolution state that denounced a fissile polity, born of force, prejudice and self-interest, where affirmations of allegiance could represent no more than 'villainous perjury' from those

---

[20] Bodleian Library, Rawlinson MSS, D/387; J.E. Estcourt and J.O. Payne, *The English Catholic Nonjurors of 1715* (London, 1885), p. 8; Hodgkin papers, vol. III, BL, Add. MSS, 38,851, fol. 47.
[21] See especially M.A. Goldie, 'The Revolution of 1689 and the Structure of Political Argument', *Bulletin of Research into the Humanities*, 83 (1980), p. 514, and J.P. Kenyon, *Revolution Principles: The Politics of Party, 1689–1720* (2nd edn, Cambridge, 1990).
[22] Printed in R.C. Jarvis, *The Jacobite Risings of 1715 and 1745* (Carlisle, 1954), p. 223.
[23] Campbell, *Intellectual Struggle*, pp. 3–25, 44–68.
[24] Thomas Fitzherbert, A *Treatise of Policy and Religion* (1696 edn), Preface, pp. 4–19.

who had already sworn oaths to James II.[25] An anonymous Benedictine poet sought to show that, as two negatives make for an affirmative, so 'two Affirmations (in their turn) make Negations'. Henceforth:

> He to 2 Kings takes an Oath
> Is by ye last absolv'd from both.
> Thus, Scientifically, you may seem
> The more we're bound, the more free.[26]

Intellectually, it was possible for some recusants, like most Tories, to acknowledge the prince 'in possession' as a ruler established by right of conquest. Imprisoned in the Tower in April 1696, Colonel Bernard Howard, former Master of the Horse to James II wrote to William III, envisaging a bleakly pragmatic submission to making 'use of your name in writs, and ye like', if this was required 'to recover and preserve our just Rights'. However, Howard drew back from crediting this *de facto* kingship with the level of authority implicit in an oath. He was painfully adamant that 'ye new Protestant and Commonwealth principle' could never equate to a moral and spiritual right to the succession, and his missive would become a solemn and regretful account of 'why I cannot swear allegiance to your Majesty ... nor never can while my old Master lives', though 'I must now dye or starve here, if following ye Oaths in fashion are ye price of my life, liberty or relief'. In the event, Howard was unable to maintain this delicate balance. In 1699, he left England for St Germain, to return to the service of 'my ever honor'd and almost ever unfortunate old master'.[27]

The most notorious example of resistance to the governing powers was provided by the band of ex-officers from the army of James II, who undertook to slaughter William III as he rode hunting through Turnham Green in 1696.[28] 'The nation cries loudly for deliverance' proclaimed Colonel John Parker, at the head of the conspiracy, 'and I have not omitted to fill up the chorus.'[29] The defence proffered by one of their number, the former fellow of Magdalen College, Oxford, Robert Charnock, was closely aligned with contemporary discourse over the question of allegiance to a disputed throne. In a paper written before his execution, Charnock returned to Tertullian's

[25] Colonel Bernard Howard to William III, 11 April 1696, Bodleian Library, Carte MSS, 181, fols 733–7.

[26] Weldon, 'Collection', BL, Add. MSS, 10,118, fol. 200.

[27] Howard to William III, 11 April 1696, Bodleian Library, Carte MSS, 181, fols 733–7.

[28] *A True Account of the Horrid Conspiracies against the Life of His Sacred Majesty William III, King of England, Scotland, France and Ireland* (London, 1696); Jane Garrett, *The Triumphs of Providence* (Cambridge 1980).

[29] John Parker to the earl of Melfort, n.d. 1692, in Porteous, 'The Lancashire Jacobite Plot', pp. 30–1.

maxim that 'against a public enemy, every man is a soldier'. He invoked Grotius, selected Roman and Hebrew authorities 'applauded by all Antiquity', and appealed to English laws and liberties to invoke the venerable principle of *tyrannicide*.[30] William would be dehumanised as 'a wolf or wild beast' who had 'corrupted and debauched the King's sworn subjects' to pull apart 'all the ties of Nature and Consanguinity'. Defining usurpation as a breach of the covenant, human and divine, Charnock insisted that William's snatching of the throne left him 'the greatest and worst of Robbers, exceeding them in guilt as much as a Kingdome exceeds in value a private family'. As the law empowered a man to punish a common thief, so every subject bound to James II became a 'warrantable minister of justice', even if they must operate 'outside All Regular forms of a Judiciall Proceeding'. Otherwise, 'you must grant that the greater the crime is, the greater would be the impunity'.[31] Charnock had defined the limits of the Jacobite anti-oath argument. The attempt at political murder would be positioned within a rich humanist lineage, to depict the author as an everyman figure, engaged in 'the best piece of service that could be done for my King and Country'.

Recusant objections to the oath, violent or passive, carried grave political consequences. There was nothing therefore quintessentially Catholic about Charnock's declaration. To his fellow conspirators, he offered less the zeal of the Counter-Reformation than a neo-Roman language of patriotic martyrdom, made conducive to the cavalier underworld of taverns and gambling-houses, into which the officers had slipped. Alexander Knightley confessed to 'a mistaken notion of Honour', from which 'I thought I would not retreat without infamy and cowardice'.[32] However, the Assassination Plot sent shockwaves through political opinion, and in laying the ground for a new Oath of Association, to be taken by all office-holders to William III, the reaction to its exposure made dissent far harder to articulate without suspicion.[33] In Whig pamphlet literature, the enterprise revived memories of the Jesuit murder of Henri IV of France, and it was gleefully attributed to the designs of the exiled court.[34] In turn, the assassination attempt was publicly reviled by most English Catholic commentators. To the monk Benet Weldon, 'ye undoing of tyrants is ye hand-work of God alone ... they that dare be so impiously bold as to be for taking this work out of his dread hands

---

[30] 'Charnock's paper', Bodleian Library, Carte MSS, 181, fols 652–3; Quentin Skinner, *The Foundations of Modern Political Thought*, II, *The Age of Reformation* (Cambridge, 1978), pp. 284–6.

[31] T.B. Howell, ed., *State Trials* (23 vols, London, 1809–26), XII, pp. 1462–4.

[32] 'Mr Knightley's paper, read out in court', May 1696, Lambeth Palace, Main Series, 942/123.

[33] Hoppitt, *Land of Liberty?* pp. 153–4.

[34] Blackmore, *A True and Impartial History*, pp. 30, 73, 80; MacPherson, ed., *Original Papers*, I, pp. 252–7; Ailesbury, *Memoirs*, I, p. 352.

come to untimely ends'.[35] Faced with such public blows to their reputation, Catholic Jacobites came to awareness that they must defend themselves more decisively, to retain the faith of their own co-religionists, and proffer an explanation to their countrymen, for their state of opposition. Supporters of the house of Stuart were soon obliged to find a new expression, because the convictions of English recusants were about to be forced into the open, in a series of rancorous debates, and an attempt, from within and outside the community, to pin down the elusive principles of Catholic allegiance.

The plan for a Catholic oath

It was the melancholy grievance of Catholic Jacobite zealots that, against their own standard of political purity, large numbers of their brethren might often be found wanting. While the oath as it stood was rejected, an important minority of recusants nonetheless looked to explore forms of accommodation with the post-Revolution state, and encourage a debate to 'answer definitely what is lawful, or unlawful in conscience'.[36] The original move to step down from the pure heights of resistance came from an uncomplicated impulse among Catholic leaders to 'live peaceably', in a time of duress. Laymen with estates close to London were the first to press for a legal agreement that could protect them against harassment from the state, private informers and the mob. In 1696, John Caryll, nephew of the Jacobite secretary of state, contemplated 'how farr a man goe with honour and conscience and how farr not'; thirty years later, his neighbour Edward Thurland reflected that 'Wee have been a long time contending for the balance of power between our Religion and our Liberties.'[37] The bid was founded on Catholic acknowledgement of the alliances and engagements with Anglican notables at a local level, and the solidarity of a gentry society that had, in practice, prevented the outbreak of any full-scale persecution. With the authority to influence votes, sway the sentiments of corporations, and activate networks in support of a parliamentary candidate, the more prosperous recusants commanded a certain political purchase in the shires even after the Revolution. In 1696, the earl of Carlisle pledged to act favourably for Sir John Swinburne, by dint of 'the considerable interest you have in the county of Northumberland, as also the good character I have received of your personal worth'. In return for electoral backing, Carlisle assured his neighbour, 'you may depend upon the best services I may be capable to render you'.[38] Not least because of the need to keep sympathetic county

---

[35] Weldon, 'Collection', BL, Add. MSS, 10,118, pp. 652–3.

[36] John Stonor to Mayes, 25 November 1716, AAW, Epistolae Variorum, VI/31.

[37] Edward Thurland to Caryll, 26 April 1727, BL, Add. MSS, 28,228, fol. 231.

[38] The earl of Carlisle to Sir John Swinburne, 14 January 1696, Northumberland CRO, Swinburne MSS, 322/ Box 5.

office-holders in place, recusant landowners could be found engaging in forms of conventional politics across the post-Revolution period: from Edward Thurland initiating parliamentary petitions over the state of the public highways in Sussex, to the Norfolk recusants reported 'pushing their interest' to such an extent in the 1734 election that they were courted by the duke of Newcastle.[39]

In the reign of Queen Anne, efforts towards engagement were strengthened by the influential pen of Sir Robert Throckmorton, whose descent from Gunpowder Plotters left him well apprised of the peril that stemmed from extreme resistance, and who lived with an uneasy sense that 'the miracle of God's providence' would not necessarily 'continue to preserve us if we are not wanting to ourselves'. Founding his stance 'on the principles of the gospel and practices of the primitive Xtians', Throckmorton hired the Catholic lawyer Nathaniel Pigott, to establish an appropriate wording that would commit Catholics to 'behave ourselves as becomes good subjects' in case the Government encourages either an address or a declaration by word of mouth from us'.[40] Pushing for accommodation with the 'possessing power' was not spelt out as an anti-Jacobite gesture. Throckmorton's backers included members of the Sheldon, Radcliffe and Conquest families, all of whom had kinship connections to the exiled court.[41] The monk John Anselm Mannock devoted one section of his commonplace book to the issue of 'how subjects ought to behave towards an usurper', and inferred that the utility of oaths would inevitably weaken in a time of disputed right: 'Where a person is threatened with violence from a stronger hand, he may be compelled to do those things which he hates and abhors. But if he afterwards finds an opportunity, no man will censure him for breaking his way thro' these unjust impositions.'[42] John Matthews sought simply to provide affirmation that he could abide by the laws of a Protestant country, like his co-religionists in Holland and Germany: 'although they are under ye direction of ye Pope in matters Spirituall, yet they live undisturbed so long as they pay a due obedience to ye Government'.[43] Pigott took a more trenchant line, insisting that 'protection and subjection are correlatives', so that 'he cannot bee presumed to bee a subject who refuses submission to

---

[39] Thurland to Caryll, 12 September 1727, BL, Add. MSS, 28,228, fol. 246; W.C. Lukis, ed., *The Family Memoirs of the Rev. William Stukeley, M.D. and other Correspondence* (Surtees Society, 73, 1882), p. 274; Richard Chandler, *The History and Proceedings of the House of Commons* (14 vols, 1742–44), VIII, p. 177.

[40] Sir Robert Throckmorton to Nathaniel Pigott, 5 May 1706; Throckmorton to Pigott, 15 December 1706; Pigott to Throckmorton, 30 December 1706, all Warwickshire CRO, Throckmorton MSS, Box 65, Folder 2/5.

[41] Robert Throckmorton to Nathaniel Pigott, 8 December, 1706, Warwickshire CRO, Throckmorton MSS, Box 65, Folder 2/5.

[42] Downside Abbey, Mannock Miscellany, p. 384.

[43] John Matthews to John Caryll, n.d., BL, Add. MSS, 28,227, fols 96–7.

those powers by which he possesses his life, liberty and estate'. However, he agreed that the affair should not be coloured by conscience, when English history proved that a measure of obedience was 'lawful even in the case of a notorious usurper'. Pigott concluded: 'I would have the Catholiques of England ... look back and survey all the revolutions in England, of King Stephen, Henry ye 4th &c.'[44]

Despite support received from the duke of Devonshire at court, the first plan for accommodation floundered on recusant divisions over the appropriate wording, bringing Throckmorton's rueful acceptance that the relatively benign conditions of Anne's polity rendered it feasible to suspend the campaign until Catholics were faced with the tangible danger of 'a persecution'.[45] However, the recriminations after the 1715 rebellion left fewer options. The Catholic lawyer Henry Eyre despaired that 'every week brings new Alarums from Westminster of bills being brought in against Recusants'.[46] In the prognosis of Bishop John Stonor, the belief that 'Catholick families and by consequence Catholick religion are in such eminent danger of being ruined' meant that it was more than just the most devoutly Hanoverian minds who accepted that 'we ought to lay hold of any occasion of trying even a doubtful remedy'.[47] The renewed push for an oath of allegiance was coordinated by Stonor, a kinsman of the Whig earl of Shrewsbury who served as one of the four Catholic Vicars Apostolic in England, and pursued with the aid of Dr Thomas Strickland, the clergyman son of Jacobite courtiers, and Edward Blount of Blagdon, a Devon squire and literary connoisseur.[48] The plan was forged in consultations with members of the Whig ministry – the secretary of state James Craggs, the earl of Stanhope, and Viscount Townshend, and Stonor aimed to rally a large constituency of Catholic lay and clerical opinion. A meeting of London priests drew support from the Benedictine Lawrence Fenwick, with the Jesuit George Blake concurring: 'It would be a sad thing to see all the Catholics of England set down on Gravelines sands.'[49] Copies of the scheme were sent into recusant households, and the bishop forced the initiative onto a committee of magnates, drafting in the duke of Norfolk, Lord Charles Howard of Greystroke, the

---

44 Pigott to Throckmorton, 9 May 1706, Warwickshire CRO, Throckmorton MSS, Box 65, Folder 2/5.
45 Throckmorton to Pigott, 11 January 1706/7, Warwickshire CRO, Throckmorton MSS, Box 65, Folder 2/5.
46 Henry Eyre to John Caryll, 24 April 1716, BL, Add. MSS, 28,227, fol. 304.
47 Stonor to Mayes, 25 November 1716, AAW, Epistolae Variorum, VI/31.
48 James Edward to William Dicconson, 4 November 1718, HMC, *Stuart*, VII; Robert Witham, 6 May 1721, Epistolae Variorum, VII/54; Monod, *Jacobitism*, p. 122.
49 George Blake to Thomas Lawson, 24 December 1716, HMC, *Stuart*, III, pp. 405–6; Thomas Parker to Thomas Eberson, March 1716, EPSJ, Notes and Fragments.

marquis of Powis, the lords Waldegrave and Montagu and the landowners Sir John Webb and William Giffard.[50]

Stonor's design rested on the establishment of a new oath, to assert: 'I am, by the grace of God, an English Catholic, and believe that it is my duty to be actively obedient where I can ... and passively where I cannot, to whatever Government God permits to come over me ... I would willingly take an oath of fidelity to King George.'[51] It was contrived to expunge 'that inveterate prejudice against Papists, where they are thought not to deserve the same consideration as other Englishmen'.[52] The bishop declared that Catholics stood 'at the beginning of a political conversion', into men 'as zealous for the government as any other subjects', despite 'prejudices' spawned by 'the nature of their education'.[53] He delivered a bitter judgement on a Jacobite party that harboured little regard for 'the thoughts and views of the RCs and would sooner be for the venturing their destruction a thousand times over than wink at their taking means for their preservation'.[54] The rebels would be damned as 'mostly women, younger brothers, people of desperate fortune', whose 'exalted notions of prophecy and futurity' must be 'broke' and 'exploded' before they might embrace the future.[55] Stonor propounded a changed conception of English Catholic identity, positing his flock as a group who might follow 'their duty and interest ... *as well as other dissenters*'.[56] The label 'dissent' would negate the precocious elements within the recusant imagination – the internationalism and antiquity of the faith – and fix the community within the same spectrum as Protestant Nonconformists. The extension of civil rights could therefore be pursued within a broader strategy for toleration, as the ministry explored ways to undo Tory measures against the Dissenting community.[57] By assuring the government that any 'tergiversation' could 'never be coloured with any pretence of Religion or conscience', Stonor implied that any non-compliant recusant could be ruthlessly and rigorously punished.[58]

[50] Eyre to Caryll, 5 January 1716, BL, Add. MSS, 28,227, fols 279–80; Eyre to Caryll, 14 January, fols 427–7; 'Paper put into the hands of Catholicks', BL, Add. MSS, 28,252, fols 94–5; Stonor to Mayes, 6 December 1719, AAW, Epistolae Variorum, VI/133; Stonor to Mayes, 6 December 1719, AAW, Epistolae Variorum, VI/133.

[51] 'Papers relating to a scheme for inducing the English Catholicks in general to become, by degrees, truly and heartily well-affected to His Majesty's Government', 1719, BL, Stowe MSS, 121.

[52] Stonor to Mayes, 13 May 1717, AAW, Epistolae Variorum, VI/47.

[53] 'A form of an oath proposed expressing the submission of Catholics to his Majesty King George', Warwickshire CRO, Throckmorton MSS, Box 86/16.

[54] Stonor to Mayes, 9 November 1720, AAW, Epistolae Variorum, VII/26.

[55] Stonor to Mayes, 13 May 1717, AAW, Epistolae Variorum, VI/47.

[56] Stonor to Mayes, 25 November 1716, AAW, Epistolae Variorum, VI/31; 'Papers relating to a scheme', BL, Stowe MSS, 121, fol. 2.

[57] Hatton, *George I*, p. 202.

[58] 'Papers relating to a scheme', BL, Stowe MSS, 121, fols 1–8.

If the case for accommodation was politically potent in 1716, it was ideo-logically far less stable. Two decades later, out of favour with the court of George II, Stonor would insist to fellow clergymen that he took his inspira-tion from Pufendorf, stressing the duty of subjects to a 'prince in possession' who could safeguard their lives and liberties, when the 'laws of nature and nations' tend 'to regard indifferently all established governments, whatever title they may subsist upon.[59] But in originally committing his flock to an oath abjuring the Stuart Pretender and offering 'fidelity' to George I, he had founded his argument on the specific legitimacy of the Hanoverian succes-sion.[60] The uncertainty at the heart of the Catholic case was illustrated in the works of one of Stonor's most trenchant supporters, Hugh Tootell, chap-lain to Sir Robert Throckmorton, who wrote under the pseudonym, 'Charles Dodd'. This polemical historian was haunted by events of 1715, and he 'stept a little out of his calling, the perplexed Circumstances of Friends and Acquaintances [having] awak'd me to his understanding', to promote a new *Roman Catholick System of Allegiance* (1716).[61] Dodd ventured into sacred history and the laws of nature and nations to show that any continuing adherence to the Stuarts was not merely politically suicidal, but doctrinally errant. Jacobitism had compelled recusants 'to press a private conceit for a Dogma of Faith, and left them so 'Inebriated' that they had become 'Martyrs to Titles and Notions'.[62] The belief that English Catholics had a moral obligation to adhere to a monarch of their own faith represented a woeful misreading of the political scene, he said, when the Jacobite movement was increasingly giving way before confessional interests not from the Catholic royal family, but the 'high flying' Tory Anglicans: 'Is not their whole cry *The Church! The Church!* And which Church, I pray, but their own, which they truly pretend to be in Danger.'[63] Rejecting these men would allow Catholics to prove the integrity of those claims they had protested for over a century; their willingness to recognise a king outside their own religion, to posit 'two Independent powers of Church and State', and 'let each be Umpire in their own Sphere', building a political theology upon the premise that 'The Almighty' does not desire 'that Heaven and Earth be mingled'.[64]

So far, these assertions were true to the traditions of Catholic loyalist thought. But Dodd's arguments were not designed to appeal to the reigning dynasty. Instead, he revelled in the 'Revolutionary' character of 1688, calling upon the rhetorical devices of a radical Whig to declare that the

[59] Stonor to Dicconson, n.d., Dicconson letter-book, Lancashire CRO, RCWB/5.
[60] [Stonor], 'Of the first monarch unjustly deposed', n.d., AAW, Main Series, A, 38, 101.
[61] Duffy, '"Rubb-up for old soares"', pp. 291–2, 315–17.
[62] P.R. [Charles Dodd], *A Roman Catholick System of Allegiance in Favour of the Present Establishment* (1716), pp. 4, 77.
[63] Ibid., p. 83.
[64] Ibid., pp. 58, 87–90.

king had 'violated the contract, by virtue whereof he wore the Sceptre', and 'the Community claimed their Original Right'.[65] From Magna Carta to the rise of parliamentary power, 'mixed' constitutions reflected the true origins of government, before royal sovereignty was augmented by the seventeenth-century innovation of indefeasible hereditary right. 'No man is born with a scepter in his hand' Dodd declared, and in too many instances, 'Hereditary Right has introduced Hereditary Miseries.' Beneath the illusions spun from throne and altar, the lineal principle remained purely 'an arbitrary form of Government, embraced or laid aside by the Supream Legislative Power, according to the Publick Good'.[66] Furthermore, no nation had 'afforded so many Instances of this kind as England', where only thirteen of the twenty individuals who held the crown between William I and William III inherited through direct descent.[67] The Hanoverian ascendancy would thus be sanctioned, not by virtue of any supreme righteous foundation, but the very opposite: an assertion of the *limits* of earthly monarchy. The dynastic contest could be divested of any cosmic significance, reduced dispassionately to a 'civil schism', between 'Hanover and Barleduc'; a struggle of 'two Pretenders', neither of whom would be 'qualified to put an end to this Controversy', without the consent of the 'Community'.[68]

The attempt to separate Catholics from a single 'contending power' led Dodd into territory that many recusants found discomforting. He unburdened himself of the pieties surrounding Catholic service in the Civil War, acknowledging that 'they suffered very much and I suppose upon a good motive', but denying that an action undertaken in a time of 'National Delirium' was part of any deep historical continuum.[69] He invoked instead the precedents that recusants had been most concerned to eclipse from public discourse: the Catholic League's theory of resistance to Henri IV of France, and the writings of Cardinal Allen and William Reynolds *against* Elizabeth I, adding that 'if our present English missioners think it fit to forsake such Noble Ancestors, 'tis no Injustice to pronounce them Inferior to these Great Men'.[70] Dodd was no friend of the Society of Jesus, and, despite the convergence of rhetoric, his ideas harked back less to the 'resistance' treatises of Robert Persons or Juan de Mariana than the minority 'Blacklowist' party within the English secular clergy, formed when the clergyman Thomas White voiced a rationalising, Hobbesian argument for submission to civil powers to press for Catholic rapprochement with Oliver Cromwell.[71] Dodd redefined the concept of allegiance as a wholly profane

---

[65] Ibid., pp. 70–1.
[66] Ibid., pp. 4–8, 28–32, 39.
[67] Ibid., p. 53.
[68] Ibid., pp. 91–2.
[69] Ibid., pp. 48, 62.
[70] Ibid., p. 64.
[71] Stefania Tutino, 'The Catholic Church and the English Civil War: The Case of

matter of submission to civil powers, when 'the Gospel looks not into Titles' and 'there has been no wardrobe of Laurels to crown Politick Notions'.[72] Dodd's objective was not itself dissimilar to that of the earlier Stuart loyalists whose ideals he had been so keen to disavow, searching to demonstrate that his community might be made tolerant, pacific and obedient. But he operated by a radical inversion of the trends in English Catholic thought, and it was partly for this reason that the 'system of allegiance' was an object of suspicion to Stonor, who believed it was written without sincere principle.[73] Though subsequent publications would confirm the belief that his support for George I rested on weak foundations, Dodd had dramatised the crisis of Catholic loyalty in 1716, and exposed the impact of the rebellion on larger questions of political theology.[74] In one section of the community at least, the location of allegiance had not just shifted, but its very function had been daringly re-defined.

Europe and the 'Catholic oath'

As a campaign in the English public sphere alone, the bid for formal Catholic toleration had little chance of gathering momentum: there was slight political capital to be gained in either Whig or Tory ranks from backing any expansion of recusant liberties. However, the oath design derived both its prospect of success and much of its Catholic support base from the primacy of foreign policy on ministerial considerations in London. A paper released by Strickland informed recusants that unjust reprisals against Catholics in England 'could not but be very disagreeable to the King's RC allies abroad, and very much weaken his interest in em', giving 'the Pretender who has all along made it his business to represent his own case to be the same as that of Catholick religion' the chance to add 'fresh colours and more weight to his insinuations', and therefore threatening the safety of European Protestant minorities.[75] George I, as the treatise recalled, had to preserve a balance between Protestant pressures at home and the interests of his continental partners of a different religion, notably the Austrian Emperor and

---

Thomas White', *Journal of Ecclesiastical History*, 58 (2007), pp. 232–55; Jeffrey R. Collins, 'Thomas Hobbes and the Blackloist Conspiracy of 1649', *Historical Journal*, 45 (2002), pp. 303–31.

[72] *Catholick System*, pp. 4, 34.

[73] Stonor to Mayes, 23 October 1721, AAW, Epistolae Variorum, VII/82.

[74] The 'Catholick System', as will be seen in Chapter 6, was extremely discordant with the message of the *Church History*, which was royalist and implicitly Jacobite in sympathy.

[75] 'Considerations upon the most proper method of raising £100,000 on the estates of the English Roman Catholicks', Warwickshire CRO, Throckmorton MSS, Box 86/12.

the Regent of France.[76] Hence, the Hanoverian crown had a positive incentive towards separating loyal from Jacobite recusants and defining penal laws exclusively as a matter of state security. Catholic hopes for relief therefore rested somewhat ironically on the post-Revolution monarchs being guilty of the precise charge levelled in Jacobite tracts – a dependence on foreign interests. From the same standpoint, the original plan to shrug off Jacobite affiliations had risen over twenty years before the coronation of George I. Far from being a narrowly English design, it was actually marshalled by Catholics operating abroad.

The possibility of accommodation after 1688 had been made viable for the more optimistic recusants by the division cutting through 'the Catholic interest' in Europe, when hostility to French expansion had locked Spain and Austria into the League of Augsburg alongside William of Orange, and the king of Spain had celebrated William's coronation publicly at Messina as a crushing defeat for Louis XIV.[77] The fear of French incursions had also driven Pope Innocent XI onto the stage of European politics to lacerate the pretensions of the Gallican church, and before 1688 French diplomats had bitterly asserted that the pontiff 'hopes almost openly that this Catholic monarch will be thrown out of his rightful throne'.[78] Before the Revolution, the Prince de Vaudemont had pre-empted Stuart emissaries by venturing to Rome on behalf of the Emperor, offering the assurance that William of Orange represented no enemy of the Catholic faith in Europe, and adjuring papal counsels to 'favour and promote this attempt upon England'.[79] James II, too Catholic for his British subjects, was seemingly not Catholic enough for his co-religionists in Europe, and after 1688, the anti-Bourbon arc stretched into the Holy See to grant the League of Augsburg a steady supply of Roman funding up to the Treaty of Ryswick in 1697.[80] These developments did not go unrecorded in English political discourse. It was one of the quirks of pamphlet literature during the reign of William III that some Jacobite treatises appropriated touches of anti-papal rhetoric, with both the radical Robert Ferguson and the High Tory Bevill Higgons describing the 1688 Revolution as the only 'popish plot' truly to descend upon the English realm.[81] The developments on the continent provoked the clerics of the

---

76 Hatton, George I, pp. 180–92.
77 Walter Lorenzo Leslie to Whyteford, 16 July 1689, SCA, Blairs, 1/123/14; Carswell, Descent, pp. 155–6, 215–16.
78 E. Michaud, Louis XIV et Louis XI (3 vols, Paris, 1883), II, p. 129; The Life and Reign of Innocent XI late Pope of Rome (1690), pp. 1–3, 25–8.
79 'The Prince de Vaudemont in Rome', Bodleian Library, Carte MSS, 231, fol. 31.
80 His Holyness the Pope of Rome's declaration against the French king, Louis the 14th ... written by a person that is lately arrived from Germany (1689); Israel, Anglo-Dutch Moment, pp. 32–3, 131–6, 381–3.
81 Robert Ferguson, Whether the Preserving the Protestant Religion was the motive unto or the end that was designed in the late Revolution (1695).

Scots College, Paris, to warn of 'an advantageous design in England carry'd on by the Spanish Embassador, wch is to bring the Catholiques to acknowledge the Usurper to be King, providing he grant them ease and liberty'. Charles Whyteford predicted that 'this will certainly produce a schisme and will give great scandal to all loyall hearts'.[82]

In the immediate years after the Revolution, the confessional tendencies in the new regime had been mitigated by William's need to offer assurances to his allies that 'he would undertake to procure a toleration for the R. Catholiks' and govern England 'sans distinction de Religion'.[83] Though this pledge failed to materialise, it had nonetheless positioned the recusant community for possible dialogue with the reigning power. John Dryden believed that pressures towards 'persecution' sprung not from William himself, but the Archbishop of Canterbury.[84] In Ireland, the earl of Carlingford's service in Austrian forces saved his family estates from the confiscation threatened by his brother's death in Jacobite arms at the Boyne.[85] Accordingly, a small body of pamphlet literature, written to mobilise opinion in support of the campaign against Louis XIV, claimed that 'King William's toleration' extended to 'the private and peaceable recusant' and argued that the conflict was not an exclusively Protestant war of religion.[86] A number of these tracts adopted a Catholic voice to contend that if Louis XIV was infamous for his aggression against Huguenots, 'all men do not sufficiently know him to be an enemy to the Roman Religion, and the Catholick Princes'.[87] In allying with the Turks against the sovereign rights of Austria and Poland, the French king had proved 'an enemy to the progress and enlargement of the Church', a man who 'rather chuses that Constantinople should be subject to Mahomet, than Jesus Christ'. The attempts to wrest Avignon from Rome marked the ignoble climax for a reign scarred by 'bloody outrages against the Holy See', from a king 'sitting like an Anti-Pope in his Cathedral'.[88]

Catholics gained a potential avenue into state affairs when the war in Europe could be captured outside the standard forms of Protestant polemic,

---

[82] Richard Bulstrode to Henry Browne, 25 June 1691, BL, Add. MSS, 37,662, fols 174–5; Whyteford to Leslie, 16 April 1689, SCA, Blairs 1/123/7; Whyteford to Leslie, 1690, Blairs, I, 133.

[83] 'Copie de la response de l'Empereur a' son Addresse monsr le Prince de'Orange', 10 January 1689, Arundel Castle, Howard of Norfolk MSS, Miscellaneous letters, 69.

[84] C.E. Ward, ed., *The Letters of John Dryden* (Durham, NC, 1942), p. 112.

[85] Francis Taaffe, earl of Carlingford, to Mary of Modena, 6 December 1701, *Memoirs of the family of Taaffe* (Vienna, 1856), pp. 246–7.

[86] *King William's toleration being an explanation of that liberty of religion, which may be expected from His Majesty's declaration* (1689); *A view of the true interest of the several states of Europe* (1689), p. 1; *Some reflections on the oaths ... in reference to the Roman Catholicks of England* (1695).

[87] *The Present King of France demonstrated an enemy to Catholick as well as Protestant religion* (1691), pp. 1, 23.

[88] Ibid., pp. iii, 14.

redefined as a defence of the 'law of nations' against 'universal monarchy', but also lauded in more visionary terms, as a moment for religious reunion. The coalition of 'Christian princes' against Louis XIV encouraged some pamphleteers towards a reinvention of the crusading ideal, as a syncretistic vocabulary used to justify alliances across the religious divide.[89] Even Colonel Bernard Howard could approach a form of loyalty to William as a warrior-prince, the 'Belgick Lyon' rising to unite Europe on the mission of 'planting Christ's Cross in Constantinople'.[90] The result of the 'war tracts' was to release the first English government defence of papal rights in over a century (writings of this nature had not emerged under James II) – written, with sublime paradox, to justify the dethroning of a Catholic king. Rome, like Austria and England, was identified as a state in need of defence: the Pope threatened with a power that would 'deprive him of his Infallibility, subject him to the power of a General Council, imprison his Nuncios … hang in effigie his Vicar Generals and streighten the Papal power in such a manner, that it will become no more than an Airy Name, without any reality'.[91]

While it was uncertain whether these works represented a hidden seam of recusant opinion, it was no coincidence that the first spasms of Catholic loyalty to the Revolution appeared from the continent, in religious houses situated on the territory of William's allies. In 1691, Jacobite diplomats warned of 'disloyal' addresses from the Irish rector Dr Thomas Stapleton, at the University of Louvain, celebrating the 'heroick virtues' of the new king.[92] At the English College, Lisbon – birthplace of the Blacklowist tradition – the president Edward Jones proffered acceptance of the Hanoverian succession in deference to the Anglo-Portuguese alliance, and expressed relief that few of his alumni were ensnared in the 1715 rising.[93] Across Europe, the politics of the exiled clergy were imprinted by the persuasions of host nations: considerations that could serve at least to downplay Stuart allegiances. The Jesuit superiors in Liege were warned by the 'German Fathers' not to imperil their patronage from the house of Bavaria, when Jacobite activity would, 'highly displease' the duke, who 'is so great with the Emperour', and therefore 'still stands fast to George'.[94] Benedictine support

[89] A view of the true interest, pp. 1–4, 13; Tony Claydon, Europe and the Making of England 1660–1760 (Cambridge, 2007), pp. 170–73.

[90] Bernard Howard to William III, April 1696, Bodleian Library, Carte MSS, 181, fol. 736.

[91] The Present King of France, p. 13.

[92] Sir Richard Bulstrode to Henry Browne, 25 June 1691, BL, Add. MSS, 37,662, fols 174–5.

[93] Edward Jones to John Vane, 5 July 1715, UCA, Durham, LC, Book Archive 89, Letterbook Edward Jones; Sharratt, Annals, p. 104.

[94] John Eberson to Richard Plowden, 26 March 1723, EPSJ, LPC, no. 147; Eberson to Plowden, 3 April 1723, LPC, no. 150; Lewis Sabran to Levinius Browne, July 1727, EPSJ, Notes and Fragments, 120.

for the oath project sprung from the Hanoverian monastery of Lambspring, where the president Lawrence Fenwick had been in residence.[95] The needs of an international church did not always sit easily with a dynastic cause, and continental engagements could provide the wellspring for a serious division within the English Catholic community.

If Stonor rallied recusants in England, Strickland's enterprise within the oath design was by contrast thoroughly European. By 1717, he had established contact with members of the Regency in Paris, and it was reported that he 'relies on an interest by means of Prince Eugene at ye Court of Vienna to advance his design and request the Emperor to ask K. George to grant us liberty'.[96] The Jacobites at Douai commented acerbically that 'He is so full of the Emperor and Empress & co. yt you would imagin him a bosome friend of theirs.'[97] Strickland promised the Austrians a permanent influence in England as advocates for the Catholic community, strengthening the Hanoverian alliance 'for the good of the Empire', but also allowing Vienna to present itself in Europe as 'the saviour of the ancient and illustrious church, to the great good of the souls of many numbers of Catholics'.[98] To George I he offered to represent the voice of Hanover inside the Empire.[99] Most audaciously, he presented the oath to Rome as a precedent to help ensure the safety of all Catholics who lived under Protestant princes.[100] Through Strickland's efforts, the proposals came sealed with the support of Vincenzo Santini, the Brussels internuncio and Cardinal Michael Althan, the principal imperial voice at the papal court, and freighted with promises of a new international system driven towards the destruction of the house of Stuart.[101] The move also commanded some initial sympathy from the Jesuits at the English College, Rome, where John Turberville recorded papal opinion that a struggling dynastic movement represented no safe institution for English Catholics to 'preserve themselves & religion if may be'.[102] Strickland's full strategy enjoined a letter to the Pope, requesting acquies-

---

95   Kennett to Eberson, n.d. 1718, EPSJ, Notes and Fragments, 106; Scott, *Gothic Rage*, pp. 65–7.
96   Gage to Eberson, 19 January 1720, EPSJ, Notes and Fragments, 108; H. Hornyold, *Genealogical Memoirs of the Family of Strickland of Sizergh* (1928), p. 152.
97   George Hinde to Mayes, 8 May 1719, AAW, Epistolae Variorum, VI/114.
98   Ibid., fols 203–5.
99   Thomas Strickland, 'Memoire presente a' sa Majeste', June 1719, BL, Add. MSS, 61,547, fols 213–14; Plowden to Eberson, 17 January 1720, EPSJ, Notes and Fragments, 107.
100   Thomas Strickland, 'Memoire', 1717, BL, Add. MSS, 61,612, fols 199–205; Parker to Eberson, January 1717, EPSJ, Notes and Fragments, 100.
101   'Informazione alla Persona del Sig l'Abbate Strickland', n.d. 1716, BL, Add. MSS, 20,311, fol. 291.
102   John Turberville to Levinius Brown, n.d. 1728, EPSJ, Notes and Fragments, 122.

cence to four conditions 'evidently consistent with R. Cath. principles'.[103] The pontiff was to confer the office of Cardinal-Protector of the British Isles upon an ecclesiastic 'no ways engaged in any factions or obnoxious to this Government'. The authority of James Edward over Vicars Apostolic in the three kingdoms would be dissolved, and vested in the Emperor, who would 'govern these Missions without any communication direct or indirect with ye Pretender'. Finally, Rome would affirm the legitimacy of an oath that would oblige recusants to acknowledge George I as lawful king and abjure the Pretender.[104]

The 'accommodationists' therefore sought to be recognised not merely as better Englishmen, but as better Catholics than their opponents. For all the rhetoric of separation between temporal and spiritual separation, the priests sought to have 'the rules of our conduct' enshrined with the religious authority of the Catholic world order, portraying themselves before an audience in the Holy See as pillars of true doctrine.[105] 'My non-Hereditary system of Allegiance is Supreamly Catholick and Orthodox', claimed Dodd, and he raised the memory of the anti-Jacobite popes, Innocent XI and Innocent XII, to show how the authorities of Christendom 'rather pity our Folly, than our Sufferings'.[106] Stonor reminded Rome that scriptural laws of obedience 'seem to regard indifferently all established government', and that while the status of pope and bishops was 'divine' because it 'regards the goods of another life', it was 'impudent' for kings to wield such an authority, let alone claim recognition from subjects in this light.[107] Quite swiftly, the course of events appeared to be running their way. From the English College, Rome Thomas Parker, reported that 'the decree of the Pope says that we not only may but ought to use the words fidelity and entire obedience. By this we may please our Masters & give them their own words.'[108] In 1717, the Holy See assented verbally to Strickland and the English College, Rome that an oath of submission to George I lay within the bounds of Catholic conscience, and Jesuits in England argued that the instruction offered a legitimate guide, 'consistent with conscience', to 'give the Government a proof that we are willing to oblige it'.[109] The missioner William Kennett insisted that whether

103 Richard Plowden to Cardinal Gualterio, n.d. 1719, BL, Add. MSS, 20,310, fol. 258; John Stonor to Gualterio, 10 September 1719, BL, Add. MSS, 20,310, fols 280–81.

104 'Papers relating to a scheme', BL, Stowe MSS, 121, fols 3–5.

105 Stonor to Mayes, 13 May 1717, AAW, Epistolae Variorum, VI/47; Witham to Ingleton, 2 May 1717, AAW, St Gregory's Seminary MSS, 379.

106 P.R. [Dodd], Catholick System, pp. 55, 84–6.

107 Stonor to Gualterio, 10 September 1719, BL, Add. MSS, 20,310, fols 253–4. Stonor to Mayes, 23 August 1736, in Dicconson letter-book, Lancashire CRO, RCWB/5, p. 61.

108 Thomas Parker to John Eberson, March 1720, EPSJ, Notes and Fragments, 107.

109 Stonor to Mayes, 13 May 1717, AAW, Epistolae Variorum, VI/47; Kennett to Eberson, 17 February 1720, EPSJ, Notes and Fragments, 107.

the resultant pledge was a matter of outright allegiance or not: 'We must not then boggle at forms of words, and thereby lose all.'[110]

The 1716 oath design was therefore conceived as an international project. For all its claims to represent the suppressed feelings of 'Englishmen in vaine', Strickland's design was weighted down with attempts to come up with a definitive statement of English Catholic conscience. Recusants would, he admitted, 'owe their liberty to Rome and Vienna', should the plan come to fruition.[111] However, Strickland's conviction that the battle over recusant allegiance would be won in Europe ensured that the political thought behind the oath movement pulled in different directions. By styling itself variously more patriotic *and* more orthodox than its Jacobite opponents, the campaign masterminded by the Catholic Hanoverians harboured a seam of tension in its midst, which, in the end, led to its unravelling.

The fall of the Catholic oath design

With Jacobite efforts raised to counter the campaigns of Strickland, the battle over the Catholic oath was played out before a gallery of international opinion. If Austrian interests dictated the composition of the Hanoverian camp, supporters of the exiled dynasty continued to dominate the religious houses on French territory, retaining their faith in the Stuarts despite the diplomatic shifts of the Bourbon crown after the death of Louis XIV. The conflict entered into France, where the clergymen of Paris and Douai developed a vigorous Jacobite lobby, backed by émigrés such as Secretary Caryll's great nephew Philip and the English Benedictine Thomas Southcott.[112] The party was fortified by the switch in Spanish policy, when the French-born Philip V swung his domain into line with the Stuarts against his Bourbon cousin.[113] Michael Connell, the rector at the English College, Valladolid was assured that the new king 'being no Spaniard', and therefore 'not being byassed' by the 'naturall affections' of his predecessors, would prove 'a more impartial judge' of world affairs.[114] The controversy also simmered in Vienna, where the English Jesuit provincial Richard Plowden informed

---

[110] Kennett to Eberson, n.d. 1720; Kennett to Eberson, 17 February 1720, EPSJ, Notes and Fragments 107.

[111] Strickland, 'Memoire', 1717, BL, Add. MSS, 61,612, fol. 204.

[112] Philip Caryll to John Caryll, 5 December 1726, Caryll papers, BL, Add. MSS, 28,228, fol. 216; Philip Caryll to John Caryll, 9 January 1730, Add. MSS, 28,228, fols 381–2. Thomas Southcott to James Edward, 30 November 1722, Royal Archives (Windsor), Stuart papers, 63/83; Southcott to James Edward, 9 December 1722, Stuart papers, 63/41.

[113] L.B. Smith, 'Spain and Jacobites 1715–16', in Cruickshanks, ed., *Ideology and Conspiracy*, pp. 159–78.

[114] Michael Connell to Thomas Eberson, 8 March 1719, EPSJ, LPC, 73; Connell to the General of the Jesuits, 15 May 1720, EPSJ, LPC, 74.

the Emperor that 'Catholic gentlemen are much obliged and gratefull to the Court ... but desire that Strickland be not employed, he has many ends that they dare not confide in him.'[115] With the vacillating superiors of the English College, Rome eventually tilting in their favour, Jacobite opinion had gained a machinery of support in the Holy See, to propound the case that the oath plan ran 'against the honour of the Catholics of England, who have a regard for hereditary right and a sovereign exiled for religion'.[116]

Nonetheless, the battle over the Catholic oath to George I would ultimately be decided in the centre ground of English recusant opinion. The Jacobite rejoinder to Stonor and Strickland was pitched to this audience, centred on an appeal to the community's political conscience against 'the greatest scandall to our Religion that ever happened in England', as it occurred to Lewis Innes: the rejection by Catholics of a legitimate king for whom 'honest Protestants' had fought and died.[117] The Benedictine John Anselm Mannock recorded in his private commentaries that it was not the notion of oaths that was in doubt, but the legitimacy of those who now demanded them: 'Our allegiance is certainly due to the Stuarts, who have ye right of blood on their side, as well as an act for recognising their title.'[118] Robert Witham, the president of the English College, Douai weighted his defence of the Stuarts in 'the studie of ye laws and ye history of England', and cited 'ye laws enacted at K. James ye First coming to ye Throne, and ye Restauration of K. Charles ye 2nd'. It was not the mark of 'good subjects', but of rebels, to make Catholics abjure 'their lawfull, rightful sovereign ... against the fundamental laws of the constitution of the Kingdom', and Catholic fidelity to the English nation would be better demonstrated by sticking to a legitimate prince, against the temptations of the time.[119]

Writing to Rome in 1717, Witham had predicted that the practical effect of the oath would be a 'great confusion if not a sort of schisme', when 'Catholick religion will in all appearance be extirpated partly by the temporal ruine of those that are strong in faith, and more by the spirituall ruine of

---

[115] Gage to Eberson, 19 January 1720, EPSJ, Notes and Fragments, 108.
[116] Plowden to Eberson, 10 April 1718, EPSJ, Notes and Fragments, 106; Richard Plowden to Gualterio, December 1719, Gualterio papers, BL, Add. MSS, 20,309, fols 258–9.
[117] Lewis Innes to James Edward, 1 January 1720, Royal Archives (Windsor), Stuart papers, 45/125; 'Traduction de la preface d'un livre Latin compose depuis peu a Rome', 1719, Warwickshire CRO, Throckmorton MSS, Box 86/12; 'Answer to the aforesaid proposals', c. 1719, BL, Add. MSS, 28,252, fols 96–7.
[118] Downside Abbey, Mannock Miscellany, p. 201.
[119] Witham to Ingleton, 26 February 1717, AAW, St Gregory's Seminary MSS, 389; Witham, 27 February 1717, AAW, Epistolae Variorum, VI/41; 'Traduction', Warwickshire CRO, Throckmorton MSS, Box 86/12.

those that are weak'.[120] Recusant society was indeed virulently politicised by the discord forming on the continent, with consequences that ran for over a decade.[121] The fiery Jacobitism of Maria, duchess of Norfolk (imbibed from her father Sir Nicholas Shireburne), drove her towards a breach with her husband, eloping with her kinsman, Peregrine Widdrington, a former rebel of 1715.[122] The new Viscount Molyneux succeeded to his father's title in 1721, and followed his Whiggish tastes by securing a position for his step-mother, Lady Mary, as Lady of the Bedchamber to the royal household. A child of the Jacobite court, the daughter of the diplomat Bevil Skelton, she demurred, and was cast out of her estates, fleeing across the channel with her daughter.[123] Among the Benedictines, the Hanoverian stance of President Fenwick opened up a vehement conflict that led to his overthrow by the Jacobite Thomas Southcott in the election of 1722.[124] It was partly in response to these divisions that the oath design began to lose momentum, with a slackening of the pace evident from 1719 when some of the original architects began to retreat from a full declaration of allegiance towards a position that would command wider consensus among their co-religionists. According to Craggs, Lord Greystroke was the first to enter an 'insurmountable opposition' to Stonor's proposals, alleging that the bishop wished to coerce recusants into going further than most had desired. This stand, according to the secretary of state, went some way towards breaking down the resolve of Greystroke's cousin Norfolk.[125] The complaint, attested in Jesuit reports, concentrated on the belief that Strickland 'clogs the petition with so many plans of his own ... they get more than they can bear'.[126] Behind this concern was the fear of a design proceeding just 'to gratify Strickland's private revenge ... and to expel out of the mission all such as

[120] William Dicconson to James Edward, 1 January 1720, Royal Archives (Windsor), Stuart papers, 45/125; Witham to Ingleton, 2 May 1717, AAW, St Gregory's Seminary MSS, 379.

[121] Witham to Mayes, 2 June 1721, AAW, Epistolae Variorum, VII/59; Thomas Southcott to James Edward, 30 August 1728, Royal Archives (Windsor), Stuart papers, 119/134.; Thomas Lawson to James Edward, 23 January 1717, HMC, *Stuart*, III, pp. 466–7; Richard Plowden to Gualterio, December 1719, BL, Add. MSS, 20,309, fols 258–9.

[122] 'Abstract of the Duchess of Norfolk's case', December 1729, Lancashire CRO, Shireburne MSS, DDST 98/19; J.O. Payne, *Records of the English Catholics of 1715* (London, 1889), pp. 144–7.

[123] Mary Molyneux to James Edward, 28 January 1725, Royal Archives (Windsor), Stuart papers, 79/103; Mary Skelton to James Edward, 26 June 1724, Stuart papers, 75/29.

[124] Mayes to Ingleton, 10 March 1722, AAW, St Gregory's Seminary MSS, 485; Southcott to James Edward, 17 January 1722, Royal Archives (Windsor), Stuart papers, 55/116; Scott, *Gothic Rage*, pp. 50–6.

[125] Parker to Eberson, 22 February 1718; the duke of Norfolk to Craggs, 1 July 1719, Craggs to Stanhope, 7 July 1719, 'Papers relating to a scheme', BL, Stowe MSS, 121, fols 6, 8.

[126] Plowden to Eberson, 17 January 1720, EPSJ, Notes and Fragments, 107.

Bp Stonor dislikes': a conviction strengthened after the two clerics encouraged the government to make a series of arrests of intransigent recusants in 1719.[127]

Lay leaders were especially alarmed by the way in which a civil arrangement had been recast as an international affair of conscience. John Matthews declared himself 'Reddy cheerfully to submitt so long as tis ye permissive will of God it should be so'. However, he argued that presenting the case to Rome breached the wall between spiritual and temporal concerns; it coloured political decisions with matters of doctrine, and risked stripping away the freedom of the communion to make its own domestic arrangements. Far from falling into dependence on the Holy See, he added that gentry leaders wanted their declaration to entail an explicit renunciation of the 'abominable notion' of the Pope's deposing power – a move thoroughly supported by the government in London, but to which Rome could never assent.[128] The second constraint on lay opinion concerned the issue of how far an oath entailed political service to the dynasty. In Brussels, the Jacobite diplomatic George Jerningham insisted that his brethren made a sharp distinction between 'simple acquiescence' to the reigning power, and stronger concepts of 'fidelity and service' about which they were chary. That 'these words come to be synonymous in ye opinion of some amongst us appears surprising and makes me confident no good will ever be produc'd upon such false principles'.[129] The Jesuit James Blake protested that he had simply desired a 'bare oath of living peacefully and quietly', set alongside the assurance that he would not 'make use of any papal dispensation to free me from the foresaid oath I have taken'.[130] Strickland had seemingly over-reached himself by pushing for a grand commitment of conscience that would proclaim the legitimacy of George I, abjure James III and get the whole statute sealed as a point of orthodox religion.

Far from seeking to resolve the issue of the dynastic choice, Catholics therefore experimented with a number of rhetorical permutations, offering the pledge of 'peaceable behaviour', but giving themselves as much space as possible to avoid committing to active support for George I. Sir Robert Throckmorton's design under Queen Anne was increasingly recalled as a more favourable precedent: its stress on 'passive' acceptance limiting the degree to which recusants should bind themselves to the state.[131] In his 1718 treatise, *The Freeman, or Loyall Papist*, Charles Dodd signalled a retreat from

---

[127] Gage to Eberson, 19 January 1720, EPSJ, Notes and Fragments, 108.

[128] John Matthews to John Caryll, n.d., BL, Add. MSS, 28,227, fols 96–7; Parker to Eberson, n.d. November 1716, EPSJ, Notes and Fragments, 102; Duffy, 'Englishmen in Vaine', p. 359.

[129] George Jerningham to James Edward, 1 May 1720, Royal Archives (Windsor), Stuart papers, 46/95.

[130] James Blake to Thomas Lawson, 24 December 1716, HMC, *Stuart*, III, pp. 348–9.

[131] Parker to Eberson, 21 May 1716, EPSJ, Notes and Fragments, 101; Plowden to

the anti-Jacobite invective of his earlier pamphlet and contended that he based his own willingness to sign the oath on the principle of an 'entire Submission to Providence': by sticking to this basic precept, he argued, Catholics might have 'purchased their ease on very moderate terms'. Dodd was tremulous about Stonor's plan for abjuration of the Stuarts, and implied that if '*Present* Allegiance to King George is Absolute', the same criteria could apply to another prevailing power, if God so willed it.[132] Twenty years later, the Irish priest, Cornelius Nary appealed against persecution in his *Case of the Roman Catholics in Ireland* (1737): on the principle that 'all Peoples in a Society whose Principles *in Religion* have no Tendency to hurt the Public, have a Right to Toleration'. The claim that *religious* principles would not lead to rebellion was very different from pinning down Catholic *dynastic* loyalties, while the notion of 'hurting the public' – as opposed to the reigning royal family – was consciously enigmatic.[133] The problem for Catholics was that this reticence obliged them to push for an extremely narrow conception of an oath, with little currency in the political nation. A Williamite document had asserted that allegiance had to be more than a passive force: an oath 'properly signifies ye whole duty of a subject to his Soveraign', which extended far beyond willingness to 'sit still and be quiet'.[134] Robert Witham espoused the same opinion: 'I consider Oaths so sacred that one ought to perform exactly what is ... intended by those that propose the said oaths, otherwise ... this is to deceive them by mentall reservations and such like pitifull unchristian tricks', precisely one of the canards held against Catholics by their detractors.[135]

Jacobite resistance was compounded by events beyond the control of the recusant community, as Strickland's fragile coalition started to disintegrate. In 1718, the movement of the Jacobite court into Rome had brought the Stuarts a powerful bulwark against Austrian enterprises; in the same year, the failure of the Emperor to prevent the marriage between James Edward and the Polish princess Maria Clementina elicited protests from the English government, bringing a sharp loss of confidence in the Whigs' capacity to shape the Catholic world.[136] Moreover, the proposed renunciation of the papal 'deposing power' offered by Stonor's lay acolytes to the British

Eberson, 8 February 1717/18, Notes and Fragments, 105; Kennett to Eberson, n.d. 1720, Notes and Fragments, 107.

[132] P.R. [Charles Dodd], *The Freeman, or Loyall Papist* (1718), pp. 21, 24, 37.

[133] Cornelius Nary, *Case of the Roman Catholics in Ireland* (Dublin, 1746); C.D.A. Leighton, *Catholicism in a Protestant Kingdom: A Study of the Irish Ancien Régime* (Basingstoke, 1994), p. 7.

[134] Anon., Discourse on the oaths, Lambeth Palace Archives, Main Series, 941/76.

[135] Witham to Ingleton, 9 October 1716, AAW, St Gregory's Seminary MSS, 365.

[136] The earl of Stanhope to Emperor Charles VI, 7 November 1718, Bodleian Library, Clarendon MSS, 90; Strickland to Sunderland, 5 June 1721, BL, Add. MSS, 61,547, fol. 211.

government presented 'several substantial difficulties' to Rome, as a slight, however theoretical, on papal authority.[137] The fracturing of papal, recusant and Whig interests disrupted the momentum of the design, and ensured that Strickland received no reaffirmation of the 1717 decree of support from the cardinals on his venture back to Rome in 1720, though the Holy See did not formally reject the oath.[138] Political developments in England were equally unwelcome. In 1722, the Catholic spokesmen were confronted by the fall of the administration, the deaths of Stanhope and Craggs, and the rise of Sir Robert Walpole.[139] The appearance of a new executive 'much more concerned for our spoils, than our submission', in the words of Stonor, appeared to support the old objection that, regardless of the sympathies of the court, the mood of the nation's representatives was ill-disposed towards Catholic liberty.[140] 'Whosoever imagines he can effect this is but little acquainted with the genius of our Parliament', Bonaventure Giffard put it – few MPs would dare to make the recusant case for fear of 'an imputation of being popishly affected'.[141] Under Walpole's administration, this adage appeared to hold true. However energetically they might try to revive the project in England and Rome, the change at Westminster brought Strickland and Stonor's plan to a decisive halt.

Hanoverian politics beyond the oath scheme

As his design lay in tatters, John Stonor professed himself beaten and bewildered by co-religionists who craved no more than to be 'left alone to hobble on their old way ... without troubling them with engagements about bettering their condition'.[142] The bishop continued to present himself to England and Rome as a thwarted herald of social and religious progress, against a gentry class shrouded in Jacobitism and apostasy. When 'ye powerful grace of Christ has triumphed in great numbers of ye inferior or middling sort of people, who have embrac'd His faith', there remained 'hopes of Religion continuing in this Kingdom', and a future beyond 'this time of misery'.[143] His English aspirations defeated, Thomas Strickland embraced a

---

137 Parker to Eberson, n.d. November 1718, EPSJ, Notes and Fragments, 102.
138 Plowden to Eberson, 17 January 1720, Kennett to Eberson, 17 February 1720, both in EPSJ, Notes and Fragments, 107.
139 Stonor to Mayes, 3 March 1722, AAW, Epistolae Variorum, VII/97; Duffy, '"Englishmen in Vaine"', pp. 362–3; Basil Williams, *The Whig Supremacy* (2nd edn, Oxford, 1962), pp. 72–3.
140 Stonor to Mayes, 3 March 1722, AAW, Epistolae Variorum, VII/97.
141 Giffard to Mayes, 26 September 1720, AAW, Epistolae Variorum, VII/23.
142 Stonor to Mayes, 6 December 1719, AAW, Epistolae Variorum, VI/133.
143 Stonor to Mayes, 5 August 1717, AAW, Epistolae Variorum, VI/55; Stonor to Ingleton, n.d. 1719, AAW, St Gregory's Seminary MSS, 427.

fully international career, appointed bishop of Namur on the nomination of the emperor in 1728.[144] He was next to appear in England in 1734, lobbying opposition Whigs against Walpole to promote a bellicose anti-French policy, driven towards restoring the 'balance of Europe' to Austrian advantage.[145] The earl of Marchmont recorded that 'the bishop of Namur, who had been in England last summer ... was to make a proposal that his Imperial Majesty should make over the Austrian Netherlands to England and Holland, in order to have the barrier maintained against France; and that England should keep 25,000 men there'. He added that 'the bishop had dined where they had drunk freely, and was very open'.[146] European horizons had turned Strickland from supporter to critic of British government policy, but the Catholic anti-Jacobite case remained firmly rooted in foreign affairs. A later, anonymous foray into print, the 1735 *Sketch of French Politicks*, appealed for a common alliance of true Catholics and Protestants across Europe against the irreligious 'universal monarch' seated in the court of Versailles.[147]

From the Jacobite side of English Catholic society, William Dicconson expressed relief in 1720 that 'Providence seems to have warded ye blow' of the Hanoverian oath, and returned to the visionary cadence that had guided generations of his brethren through the post-Reformation wilderness: 'by wch we see that tho Almighty God suffers the Catholicks of England to be exposed to frequent troubles and persecutions, yet in his goodness he still preserves them from utter ruin'.[148] Recusants remaining in England could not afford to be so sanguine. In December 1722, the lords Stafford, Montagu and Fauconberg met Robert Walpole, and put to him the issue of the penal laws. Reported by the Benedictine Thomas Southcott, 'His answer was that when they were brought low enough they would influence their papist interests abroad not to give protection to the Pretender ... he found fault with their religion which procured interest abroad, and it was fitt they should suffer for it'.[149] In the same year, the exposure of the Atterbury Plot was exploited by the administration, and, despite minimal recusant involvement, Catholic leaders found themselves the principal targets of state action. The arrest of the duke of Norfolk appeared sweet revenge for his withdrawal of support from Stonor, while recusant landowners were summoned to take the oaths, and Walpole raised the threat of a confiscation

---

144 Turberville to Browne, 12 December 1725, EPSJ, Notes and Fragments, 114.

145 J. Hervey, *Memoirs of the reign of George the Second*, ed. J.W. Croker (2 vols, 1848), II, p. 51.

146 Sir George Henry Rose, *A Selection from the Papers of the Earl of Marchmont* (3 vols, London, 1831), II, p. 15.

147 *A sketch of French politicks deduced from history and modern facts* (1735).

148 William Dicconson to David Nairne, 22 April, 1720, Royal Archives (Windsor), Stuart papers, 46/75.

149 Thomas Southcott, 10 December 1722, Royal Archives (Windsor), Stuart papers, 63/128.

of estates for those who refused to commit themselves.[150] This punishment was eventually reduced to a one-off levy of £100,000, but it accentuated the extent of Catholic vulnerability in the kingdom, with Thomas Southcott predicting further misery from 'An old Whig method made much use of to great effect in the Popish Plot'.[151]

Yet the best efforts of Walpole could not prevent opportunities arising within the precinct of Hanoverian politics, when an undertone of support for the Catholic position persisted in court and parliament, even if it was excluded from government circles. The royal entourage itself displayed inklings of sympathy, evidenced when Princess Caroline invited the former Douai clergyman Edward Hawarden to enter into conference with the Protestant theologian Samuel Clarke in 1722.[152] In the Lords, the earl Cowper damned the government's move against the duke of Norfolk as an assault on 'the ancient and undoubted rights of the House, that no member ... be imprisoned or detained' without the consent of his peers.[153] Norfolk's kinsman the Earl of Carlisle pledged a campaign against the imprisonment, and helped to marshal an alliance that included the bishops of York and Chester and the peers Lichfield, Bathurst, Oxford, Strafford, Bristol and Exeter.[154] Cowper renewed his critique in opposition to the proposed new taxation after the Atterbury Plot, recalling that the Huguenot persecution in France 'drove away the wealthiest of their merchants and most industrious artificers', and suggesting that the loss of the recusant community would 'carry eight or nine hundreds thousand pounds into foreign countries'.[155] More surprisingly, a restive spirit was intensified in the House of Commons, where animus against the prospect of new Catholic taxes, surpassed, according to the Yorkshire squire Cuthbert Constable, all 'that we could have imagined'.[156] By 1723, even the Jacobite priest John Ingleton

---

[150] Maria, duchess of Norfolk, to the earl of Carlisle, 2 November 1722, Lancashire CRO, Shireburne MSS, DDST 97/15; Cobbett, ed., *Parliamentary History*, III, pp. 47, 51; Howard Erskine-Hill and Eveline Cruickshanks, *The Atterbury Plot* (Basingstoke, 2004), pp. 166–7.

[151] Southcott to James Edward, December 1722, Royal Archives (Windsor), Stuart papers, 63/124; Southcott to Gualterio, 31 May 1723, 14 June 1723, BL, Add. MSS, 20,309, fols 31–2, 34–5.

[152] G. Anstruther, *The Seminary Priests*, III (London, 1976), pp. 94–5; J. Kirk, *Biographies of English Catholics in the Eighteenth Century*, ed. J.H. Pollen and E. Burton (London, 1909), pp. 113–16.

[153] Cobbett, ed., *Parliamentary History*, III, p. 44.

[154] Lady Mary Howard to Maria, duchess of Norfolk, 31 October 1722, Lancashire CRO, Shireburne MSS, DDST 97/15; the earl of Carlisle to the duchess of Norfolk, 3 November 1722, Shireburne MSS, DDST 97/15; 'List of peers who voted against the Duke of Norfolk going to the Tower', 1722, Shireburne MSS, DDST 97/15.

[155] Cobbett, ed., *Parliamentary History*, III, pp. 362–3.

[156] Cuthbert Constable to Sir Marmaduke Constable, 3 December 1722, Hull University, Brynmor Jones Library, Constable MSS, DDEV 68/101b.

expressed his relief that 'we now have very great hopes of escaping this storm, for it pleased God to rayse us many zealous friends ... who spoke against the bill with that force and efficacy as seemed astonishing'.[157] The motion to increase tax obligations on Catholics passed by sixteen votes, but one Tory MP was adamant that 'had not many of our friends been gone into ye Country ... we had rejected it'.[158]

The defeat of the oath scheme was therefore unable to arrest a drift towards Hanoverian loyalty within a section of Catholic society. The ninth duke, brother to the man imprisoned in 1723, had stood in rebel ranks at the siege of Preston and spent time in the Tower in consequence, and as late as 1737 he was still attending Jacobite assemblies in London, judged 'full of true zeal', by his cousin Lord John Drummond.[159] But a marital union with the Blount family, the chief lay sponsors of Stonor's scheme, exerted a domestic pressure that brought him within the pale of the constitution: an ironic reversal of the split that had driven his brother's marriage into crisis.[160] In 1733, Norfolk's Anglican cousin Lady Anne Irwin wrote that the family were 'received with great distinction' at court. 'The Duchess assured the Queen that though they were of a different religion, they had as much duty and regard for the King as any of his subjects.' Lady Irwin admitted: 'it was not expected they would give this open declaration of quitting the interest of the Pretender'.[161] Other defections, she anticipated, would be set to follow.

It was no coincidence that by the time of Norfolk's appearance at court, the international affiliations of his family had tilted towards the Austrian interest. In 1734, the duke secured a position as page to the Elector Palatine for his cousin Thomas Howard of Winchester – the boy was to be 'design'd for ye German service afterwards', in the judgement of the family lawyer.[162] Thomas sent regular reports to England hailing the success of Austrian army on the Rhine, when the imperial powers encountered once more the 'imaginary presumptions' of the French, who were renewing their sympathy for the Jacobite claimant in Rome.[163] Family affinities with the house of Stuart had diminished logically with the growth of links to the Holy Roman Empire, and the shift proved that the continental conditions for Catholic

---

157 Ingleton to Mayes, 4 January 1723, AAW, Epistolae Variorum, VIII/3.
158 Linda Colley, In Defiance of Oligarchy: The Tory Party 1714–60 (1982), pp. 200–1.
159 Lord John Drummond to James Edward, March 1737, transcript in Arundel Castle, Howard of Norfolk MSS, Howard letters 1687–1735.
160 J.M. Robinson, The Dukes of Norfolk (Oxford, 1982), pp. 145–7.
161 Lady Anne Irwin to the earl of Carlisle, 16 January 1733, HMC, Carlisle, p. 96.
162 Charles Jerningham to Bernard Howard, 9 December 1732, Arundel Castle, Howard of Norfolk MSS, Howard Letters, 1687–1735, 26.
163 Thomas Howard to Bernard Howard, 26 April 1733, Arundel Castle, Howard MSS, Howard Letters, 29; Thomas Howard to Bernard Howard, 9 October 1734, Howard MSS, Howard Letters, 48.

loyalty to the house of Hanover had not collapsed. It was not without a certain logic that, as late as 1750, the duke of Newcastle could suggest to his brother Henry Pelham that brigading British Catholics into the service of Maria Theresa would provide the best method to 'prevent such numbers of the King's subjects being engaged in the French service, enlisted and incorporated into the Rebel Regiments, and quartered just on the other side of the water'.[164] Government influence over the recusant community rested on more resources than simply coercion.

Catholics and Country politics

While the accommodationists had done enough to loosen the inevitability of the recusant link with the Stuart cause, Jacobitism itself had not disappeared from the English Catholic consciousness. If the disaster of the 1715 rising forced them to reconsider the benefits of armed resistance, the dynastic sympathy itself possessed greater endurance. Its advocates sought to counter the Catholic Hanoverians by offering an alternative form of political engagement, tempering legitimist pieties and introducing the Stuart appeal as a corrective to more tangible ills. For two decades before the 1715 rising, an undertone in recusant writing had sought to locate the plight of Catholics within the wider experience of groups estranged from the Revolution state. If Stonor and Strickland based their strategy on an appeal to the court and the ministry, Jacobites looked instead to find an ideological shield from the 'Country' opposition developing in parliament and the pamphlet press. Their commentaries increasingly denounced government policy as degenerate not so much for the subversion of divine rules but a contempt for human laws and institutions that betrayed 'ye Liberty and Property once boasted in ye Revolution', as a correspondent of Lady Mary Huddleston remarked.[165] As early as 1691, the recusant printers Francis Dormer and William Canning had published *The Case of Henry Neville Paine*, to expose the imprisonment and torture of a Catholic author by agents of the state in Scotland. Paine's treatment was attacked as an 'unpresidented and unparallel'd instance of illegal and arbitrary power', signifying 'the despotick power of a conqueror', and confirming an unpalatable truth that the success at the Boyne 'sett the Prince of Orange above all the laws ... above all the contracts he had made with his people'.[166] However, in pursuing this complaint, recusants had to discard the censorious voice that had surfaced towards compatriots in 1688. The author of *The Case* insisted that he wrote as 'an enemy' to 'civill as well as religious inquisition'. As for Paine: 'Tho'

---

[164] Newcastle to Henry Pelham, 7/18 May 1750, BL, Add. MSS, 32,720, fols 277–87.
[165] Anon. to Lady Huddleston, 4 April 1697, Cambridgeshire CRO, Huddleston MSS, MF/60.
[166] 'The Case of Henry Neville Paine', 1691, in HMC, *Finch*, III, pp. 368–8.

a Roman Catholick, I have heard toleration is innate to his constitution, that all his politicks are consistent with the English, that he despises those fooles of all sects who dreame of conquest.'[167] The bloodshed of invasion or assassination could have no place within this reconstructed vision of the Jacobite cause.

The armoury of Country politics was stocked with a rich corpus of 'Patriot' literature that had developed through the civil disharmony of the seventeenth century: constitutional histories, law-books and dissections of the limits of government presented a set of propositions over the safeguards for an Englishman's ancient liberty.[168] Within the recusant community, John Matthews kept by his side the legal texts of Sir Edward Coke, to inform 'the methods Catholicks design to pursue in these unhappy times' and when Sir Robert Throckmorton planned his appeal to the court in 1706, he suggested that since 'our enemies accuse us of favouring arbitrary power, I think we ought to have a good parragraff whereing wee declare our selves for the English constitution wch undoubtedly is the best in the world'.[169] Nathaniel Pigott contended that recusants could turn to the tenets of 'Magna Charta and those excellent statutes yt secure our liberties', including petitions presented against the Personal Rule of Charles I when subject rights possessed 'a liberall and large construction' to transcend religious allegiance.[170] In calling upon these precedents, most Catholics still identified the Tory party as their natural supporters: Jesuit missioners applauded arguments from Swift's *Examiner* that identified Whigs as 'the true papists', who would 'rise and cut the throat' of the nation's civil institutions out of a false confessional zeal.[171] Moreover, the Jacobite suspicion that periodically fell upon Tory magnates served to deepen the affinity: after the 1694 trials at Manchester, the north-west MPs Roger Kenyon and William Hayhurst confessed to fears that they too could suffer from the revolutionary spirit of a time when 'it is judged a crime to have a good estate', and Tories were depicted glued to the Catholic interest 'as clay at the feet of Nebuchadnezzar's image'.[172] However, 'Country' politics offered a potentially broader alliance. By the accession of George I, Edward Dicconson was looking opti-

---

[167] Ibid., p. 368.

[168] J.G.A. Pocock, *The Ancient Constitution and the Feudal Law* (1957); Corinne C. Weston, 'England: The Ancient Constitution and Common Law', in J.H. Burns and Mark Goldie, eds, *The Cambridge History of Political Thought 1450–1700* (Cambridge, 1991), pp. 374–411.

[169] Throckmorton to Pigott, 15 December 1706, Warwickshire CRO, Throckmorton MSS, Box 65, Folder 2/5; John Matthews to John Caryll, 13 May 1716, BL, Add. MSS, 28,227, fols 358–9.

[170] Pigott to Throckmorton, 20 January 1704/5, Warwickshire CRO, Throckmorton MSS, Box 65, Folder 2/5.

[171] Kennett to Plowden, March 1714, EPSJ, Notes and Fragments, 94.

[172] Roger Kenyon, Draft speech, 1694, HMC, *Kenyon*, p. 370; William Hayhurst to Roger Kenyon, 2 January 1695, HMC, *Kenyon*, p. 375.

mistically for shifts in opinion in 'ye most Whiggish counties', contending that those regions most hostile 'at ye time of ye Revolution are ye most passionate and bold Jacobites now'.[173]

The 'Country' strain in Georgian political life drew together Tories and dissident Whig 'Patriots' into a civic humanist-inspired attack on the quickening encroachment of the state and the perceived threat to the spirit of liberty within the British kingdom. Dramatised in the writings of Lord Bolingbroke, this diagnosis connected corruption in the Commons with the growth of the standing army, swelling levels of taxation and a foreign policy based upon Hanoverian interests to weld an opposition centred on the ideal of virtuous independence in public life.[174] As avowed Protestants and champions of the Revolution of 1688, the disaffected Country notables offered ostensibly slight appeal to Catholics.[175] However, in the parliament of 1723, Country arguments were used to attack Walpole's methods against recusants: the threat of arrests and new taxation would, it was warned, would create a precedent to aid the oppressive ministerial tendencies. The Somerset MP Sir Thomas Lutwyche argued that William III would have been far warier of raising anti-papist prejudice, because he 'knew that no free state could long subsist, but in doing equal and impartial justice'. Lutwyche believed that since the evidence for Catholic plotting had offered little more than 'hearsay, conjecture and forced constructions' – with the most recent Jacobite conspiracy designed by high Tories – the recusant community was being punished on speculative grounds, out of the belief that 'their religion maintains principles inconsistent with the welfare of the subject'. This, he said, was a confessional motive getting close to 'persecution', a result 'highly reflecting upon the honour of Parliament, and greatly infringing upon the freedom of the subject'.[176]

For cultural as much as political reasons, the opposition fashioned an environment sympathetic to Catholic lay leaders. Country arguments rested on a defence of the landed gentry as dispossessed guardians of civic liberty, bringing the concerns of recusant squires into contact with the jeremiads of MPs from a similar social background. Moreover, opposition literature was underpinned by an Augustinian consciousness of political life as a theatre for human sin, and an emphasis on the cultivation of private, pastoral virtue that paralleled the ruminations of recusant squires.[177] Stephen Tempest's 'Religio Laici' laid bare a similar yearning for moral reform, lamenting

---

[173] Dicconson to Mayes, 25 November 1714, AAW, Epistolae Variorum, V, 78.

[174] Quentin Skinner, 'The Principles and Practice of Opposition: The Case of Bolingbroke versus Walpole', in Neil McKendrick, ed., *Historical Perspectives: Studies in English Thought and Society in honour of J.H. Plumb* (London, 1974), pp. 93–128.

[175] Christine Gerrard, *The Patriot Opposition to Walpole: Politics, Poetry and National Myth 1725–42* (Oxford, 1994), pp. 151, 212.

[176] Cobbett, ed., *Parliamentary History*, III, pp. 355–61.

[177] W.A. Speck, *Stability and Strife: England 1714–1760* (London, 1977), pp. 4–7.

the spread of gambling, alcohol and sexual licence, and inculcating that the gentleman should practise 'Resolution and self-denial' in public affairs 'as the Religious man does in his convent'.[178] Catholic landowners could be captured as models of the Country ethos, excluded from elections, set outside factional alignment and therefore immune to the bribery and patronage that cut across the public domain. The link was made explicit in the writings of Alexander Pope, who idealised the rural households of the Carylls and Blounts as templates for a future moral renewal. If Pope's warning against 'Universal Darkness' under the corrupted parliament, his dread of the state's 'Great Anarch' and his desire to draw 'the last Pen for freedom' inspired the Whig Lord Cobham to immortalise his image in sculpture in the gardens at Stowe, the poet also spoke to the deepest convictions of his co-religionists.[179] The Scarisbricks took subscription to Bolingbroke's journal *The Craftsman*, while Edward Thurland linked his political education to 'Mr Pope and all his fraternity', whose works informed his attacks on 'stockjobbers' and supine parliaments: 'I am sorry to say that the virtue and honour of this nation is so sunk downe.'[180]

The Country movement therefore induced a shift in recusant political culture. Having adapted to the needs of the seventeenth-century by flaunting their royalist credentials, Catholics increasingly rewrote their own history to promote themselves as the keenest *patriots*, and set the struggle for recusant liberties within a search to reclaim *all* ancient freedoms from an overmighty executive. In his defence of the policy of Catholic toleration, the Jacobite pamphleteer Charlwood Lawton had recalled the 'old Papists who have transmitted to us our *Magna Charta, Charta de Forresta*, &c', and recusants snatched eagerly upon the idea, looking to repossess the lost heritage of the gothic constitution on behalf of their community.[181] The commentaries of John Anselm Mannock invoked Becket and More to infer that, far from being a popish invention, arbitrary government was a 'trick of state' that Catholics would sacrifice their lives to overthrow.[182] From Paris, the monk Benet Weldon invoked the last resistance of the kingdom of Kent to William of Normandy as an example to subjects faced with a new 'Norman yoke'; in England, Pope's *Windsor Forest* also hinted that the heroic imagery of Saxon freedoms struggling under conquest could be turned to a Jacobite purpose.[183]

---

178 Tempest, 'Religio Laici', Tempest MSS (private collection).
179 Erskine-Hill, *Social Milieu*, pp. 90–8; Gerrard, *Patriot Opposition*, pp. 68–95.
180 Edward Thurland to John Caryll, 3 September 1730, BL, Add. MSS, 28,228, fol. 413; Edward Thurland to John Caryll, 25 November 1727, BL, Add. MSS, 28,227, fol. 254.
181 Lawton, *French Conquest*, p. 93.
182 Downside Abbey, Mannock Miscellany, pp. 47–8, 84–7.
183 Douai Abbey, Woolhampton MSS, Weldon, 'Memorials', V, p. 496; Alexander Pope, *Windsor Forest* (1712); Erskine-Hill, *Poetry of Opposition and Revolution*, pp. 71–84.

The new trajectory was exemplified by the talented, but shambolic figure of George Flint, a Jacobite pamphleteer who had conceived a near-mystical belief in 'the power of the pen in England', to turn the scales of dynastic politics. By 1716 his literary activities had aroused sufficient notoriety for Lord Townshend to offer employment in government service if he defected.[184] Instead, Flint published his first Jacobite journal, *Robin's Last Shift, or Weekly Remarks* in 1716; it was followed by *The Shift Shifted*, a euphemistic reference to Newgate gaol, to which he had been summarily dispatched by the secretary of state. Smuggling compositions into the London print market with the aid of his wife, Flint sought to revive the genius of true political discourse, as the route to national virtue. Anticipating Pope's *Dunciad*, he suggested that literary decline ran parallel with a descent into political corruption: 'Since a Man must either write Nonsense, such as no Man cares to read, or if he ventures upon a poignant Truth or two he must perish for it in Prison. How sad, how Calamitous is this!'[185]

Weekly Remarks fortified Country broadsides with an older ideology of Stuart kingship in its depiction of a nation sliding into tyranny, over fallacies of contractual rule. A usurper could oblige a parliament with contracts, but 'that very knot which the Senator ties, the Soldier makes no scruple of cutting away'. Flint demanded to know 'Who can read the writings of Sir Richard Steel, Mr Addison and others, without being stirr'd with the Love of Liberty and without being ready to draw his Sword against Arbitrary Power?'[186] He appealed to Englishmen to 'shed generous Blood for dying Laws', and hoped that the duke of Argyll – a Patriot icon – might play the role of a new General Monck and bring back the dispossessed dynasty.[187] Flint's vision of Jacobitism was struck from images of the Jews under captivity, drawing upon Josephus, Philo and the 'Martyrdom of the Maccabees' to claim: 'It is a point of Duty the most eminently meritorious, next to that of Dying a Martyr for the Faith, to suffer and expire for your King and Country.'[188] In yearning to 'rouze the British Lions', and revive the 'Sweet and Royal Roses', he predicted that the loss of the Stuarts would unleash a civil conflict to outmatch even the clash of York and Lancaster, when the consequences of usurpation, from Henry IV to William III, 'drain'd the Oceans of the best blood in the Nation'.[189] The call for Stuart restoration

---

184 'Account of George Flint, from Rome', 5 July 1718, HMC, *Stuart*, VII, p. 19; George Flint to the earl of Mar, 18 June 1718, HMC, *Stuart*, VI, p. 551.Thomas Witham to James Gordon, 19 December 1705, AAW, Epistolae Variorum, I/36; Gooch, *Desperate Faction*, pp. 144–7.

185 George Flint, *Robin's Last Shift, or Weekly Remarks and Political Reflections* (London, 1717), p. 107.

186 Ibid., pp. 85, 96.

187 Ibid., pp. 185, 262.

188 George Flint, *The Shift Shifted* (18 August 1716).

189 Ibid. (12 March 1716, 7 July 1716).

could thus be held compatible with the recovery of ancient freedoms, when the loss of England's hereditary line haemorrhaged the only safe shield for liberty and social order. If it was 'very strange' to find 'a Pretender express more Tenderness for us than the King', this was because a rightful prince was naturally conditioned to serve the people.[190]

Absorption into the Country movement therefore kept a whisper of Jacobite politics alive in English Catholic commentaries, preserving at least an elusive attitude towards dynastic allegiance. In the build-up to the 1745 rising, John Baptist Caryll was one of the hands behind a series of Jacobite manifestos that appealed to the memory of free institutions and lost national honour.[191] Subsequently, he campaigned with the radical Independent Electors of Westminster, and worked with his recusant neighbours Edward Matthews and Ralph Sheldon to establish the *True Briton*, a journal that aimed to unite the concerns of the City and the colonial community with the House of Stuart, against 'the ruin of our Constitution'.[192] However, the Country platform also created space for reconciliation between rival strands of Catholic opinion. The Anglo-Irish historian Nathaniel Hooke, born into a Jacobite family, drew his patronage from opposition Whigs: the earl of Marchmont, Lord Chesterfield and Sarah Churchill, the dowager duchess of Marlborough, who commissioned him in 1741 as editor of her memoirs.[193] Through Hooke's voice, the duchess proffered a litany of attacks on the polity of William III, confiding regret that the Revolution had not 'been compassed by some other man who had more Honour and Justice than he, who could depose his Father-in-Law and Uncle, to maintain Liberty and Laws, and then act the Tyrant himself in many instances'.[194] As a later chapter will show, Hooke proceeded to play an important role in establishing cultural connections between Whig dissidents in England and political and religious critics of the Bourbon state in France.

For Catholics less inclined to the Stuart cause, the Country opposition created an alternative royal allegiance, in the person of Frederick, Prince of Wales, breaking from his father's court and endeavouring to establish himself as the 'Patriot King' heralded in Bolingbroke's writings. The shape-shifting

---

[190] Ibid. (12 March 1716).

[191] 'Declaration of King James', December 1743, Royal Archives (Windsor), Stuart papers, 254/92; Cruickshanks, *Political Untouchables*, pp. 43, 49.

[192] Drafted material from the *True Briton* is found in the Caryll papers, BL, Add. MSS, 28,252, and 28,231, fols 143–4, 149; *True Briton*, vol. III, 10 July 1751.

[193] Bolingbroke to Marchmont, 11 October 1746, BL, Add. MSS, 37,994, fol. 61; Alexander Pope to Viscount Polwarth, 9 January 1740, in Rose, *Marchmont Papers*, p. 206; Joseph Spence, *Anecdotes, Observations and Characters of Books and Men, collected from the Conversation of Mr. Pope and other Eminent Persons of his Time*, ed. Samuel Weller Singer (London, 1964), pp. 199, 211.

[194] *Memoirs of Sarah, Dowager Duchess of Marlborough* (1741); Nathaniel Hooke, *The glorious memory of queen Anne reviv'd, exemplify'd in the conduct of her chief favourite the Duchess Dowager of Marlborough* (1742), p. 14.

career of the ninth duke of Norfolk ended in Frederick's household, lending his London residence to the heir to the throne – who had turned down similar offers from the duke of Bedford and the duchess of Marlborough – after the estrangement from George II was formalised in 1737.[195] It was Frederick's entourage at Cliveden that extended patronage to the Catholic composer Thomas Arne, whose patriotic masque *Alfred* incorporated the score to *Rule Britannia*, to sound the iconic note for an idea of national virtue stimulated *against* government and court.[196] Moreover, in harnessing the Country rhetoric of liberty to a revived royalist iconography, with his public devotion to Charles I, Frederick held up the aura of an older Stuart lineage against his father.[197] The approach allowed some of his supporters to express their commitment with a hint of obliquity: the Tory poetry dedicated to 'the Prince of Wales' and collected by the Throckmortons was somewhat undermined when one of its authors, David Morgan, ventured into Charles Edward's rebel army.[198] Indeed, the throng of former or suspected Jacobites surrounding the prince of Wales drew Walpole's pointed remark that England now possessed two 'Pretenders to the King's crown ... one at Rome, the other at Norfolk House'.[199] For the wider political community, just like their English Catholic compatriots, the location of true allegiance was not always clearcut.

Conclusion

For Edward Blount, the demise of the Hanoverian oath scheme made for a sombre statement of the incompatibility of Catholic faith and English nationhood. He resolved instead to 'call myself a Citizen of the World ... Tho' it's a Glorious Elegy to be a Lover of one's Country, yet I don't think it so great as to be a lover of mankind.[200] Yet not all English Catholics felt the same way. For most of the recusants who abandoned Stonor and Strickland, the problem was not that the design appeared too compromising to the needs of the kingdom, but that it was not English *enough*. Rendering

---

[195] George Lyttelton to the duchess of Marlborough, 18 September 1737, BL, Add. MSS, 61,467, fol. 14; the earl of Stair to the duchess of Marlborough, 15 February 1738, BL, Add. MSS, 61,467, fol. 59; Journal of the earl of Egmont, 21 September 1737, BL, Add. MSS, 47,068, fol. 29.

[196] P. Holman and R.T. Gilman, 'Arne, Thomas Augustine', in S. Sadie, ed., *The New Grove Dictionary of Music and Musicians* (2nd edn, 29 vols, 2001), II, pp. 36–46.

[197] Gerrard, *Patriot Opposition*, pp. 212–18.

[198] David Morgan, *The country bard: or, the modern courtiers. A poem. Inscribed to his Royal Highness the Prince of Wales* (1738); 'Political poems', Warwickshire CRO, Throckmorton MSS, Box 61, Folder 2/2; Howard Erskine-Hill, 'Was there a Rhetoric of Jacobitism?', in Cruickshanks, *Aspects of Jacobitism*, pp. 49–69, at pp. 67–9.

[199] Marchmont to Stair, 28 March 1739, in Rose, *Marchmont Papers*, II, p. 113.

[200] Duffy, 'Englishmen in Vaine', p. 367.

the community pawns to the caprices of popes, emperors and diplomatists raised the dynastic conflict of Hanover and Stuart above the issue of English identity, and did not represent a positive step towards the reclaiming of a national birthright. Yet the European influences that drew Whig statesmen and Hanoverian courtiers into the Catholic oath project showed that it was not just the recusant flock whose sense of patriotic identity was overshadowed by greater international considerations. In 1716 at least, there was no clear divide between the interests of the Protestant kingdom and the concerns of the Catholic 'other'.

Most Catholics in England wanted to assert a sense of national identity without committing themselves to the extinction of the Stuart cause: the precarious nature of this objective engrossed their private commentaries, but also ensured that engagements with the political community did not end with the collapse of the oath scheme. Regardless of their feelings over the dynastic question, Catholics sought to prove that their religion was compatible with the tenets of the English constitution: in doing so they had to sideline the confessional component to their rhetoric, and push the campaign to preserve their liberties into an alternative body of political thought. By aligning their cause with the concerns of the literary and parliamentary opposition, recusants uncovered from the traditions of the 'British constitution' the rhetorical devices to press their case against penal laws and persecution. In adopting Patriot politics, they also found the haven of a political argument that allowed them to keep dynastic sympathies recondite. The Catholic link with the 'Country party' had started as a straightforward politics of self-defence against hostile governments. But the language of opposition transformed this impulse to craft a vision of political decline and renewal, corruption and virtue, liberty and oppression, which conferred a case for the public domain. The intellectual conflicts encountered by Catholicism in a Protestant country would not be quite erased by this shift, but they would at least be softened.

5

Unity, heresy and disillusionment: Christendom, Rome and the Catholic Jacobites

To be an early modern Catholic was to give voice to an international vision, to accept that certain commands towards affinity, solidarity and authority swept through the boundaries of the sovereign state or kingdom. To be an English recusant was to face especially urgent reminders of this condition: to find stigma in their own realm and protection beyond its borders as a consequence of the allegiances, obligations and institutions of the universal Roman Catholic communion. At the highest diplomatic level, the stances struck in France, Spain, Rome and the Empire would carry serious ramifications for the life of the English Catholic community. Hitherto, this discussion has concentrated on the relationship between English recusants and the demands of their native political and national community. Yet the horizons drawn after 1688 were decked by the challenges of a European arena, when the old recusant leadership had been scattered into diaspora, and the early Noncompounders of the exiled Jacobite court intoned the lesson that 'all Catholick good consists in unity', to induct their continental hosts into the experience of the fallen king. Accordingly, current scholarship has underplayed the extent to which eighteenth-century recusants experienced the tensions, anxieties and intellectual tremors of a European terrain that had as much of a tendency to fragment, as to unite. This chapter will contend that existing interpretations of the relationship between Jacobitism and English Catholicism after 1688 neglect the fact that the most decisive shifts in attitude came as responses to events in Europe.

In the decades following 1688, Jacobite commentary was absorbed by an attempt to reshape the European political environment and mobilise Catholic 'Christendom' into the mission to restore the house of Stuart. Catholic exiles claimed to represent the voices of recusants in England and linked their plight to the dispossession of the dynasty, sounding the keynotes of religious justice and political martyrdom in a bid to engage the conscience of the continent. However, these overtures encountered two significant obstacles. Firstly, in supporting the Gracious Declaration of 1693, Catholic Jacobite leaders had to moderate the confessional message by embedding their religious concerns into a larger blueprint of patriotism, public virtue and constitutional kingship. Secondly, the discord cutting across Catholic

Europe had undermined the chance of forging a grand alliance for James II, with Austria, Spain, France and the papacy proving at best insubstantial sympathisers, at worst outright opponents of the Stuart crown. Jacobites were forced to defend their position at a time when international conflict had left notions of Catholic unity contested, and when supporters of the Protestant succession had themselves appropriated the idea of 'Christendom' as a means of rallying continental opinion. Moreover, political divisions within the Catholic world ensured that the boundaries between heresy and true faith were being contested, and repeatedly redrawn. The outlook of Catholic exiles was conditioned especially by the unstable, fluctuating link between their original hosts in France and the popes Innocent XI, Alexander VIII, Innocent XII and Clement XI: a relationship that ebbed and flowed between repeated clashes of jurisdiction and combined attempts to rebuild the universal church order, by a purge of errant doctrine. The changes in French and papal attitudes were brought home in a succession of crises that hit the clergy of the Stuart royal household and the exiled colleges, with implications for the domestic recusant mission.

The chapter will study the shifting, volatile relationship between Catholic Jacobites and the international community of co-religionists, examined through the writings and correspondence of the opinion-forming circles resident in England, France and Rome. It will begin by exploring the deepening disillusionment of recusant émigrés with the court of Rome and the state of international Christendom, occasioned by the apparent acquiescence of its princes in the fall of James II. Jacobite polemics were increasingly levelled at the wider zone of Europe, and in arguing that the church had fallen prey to republicanism, irreligion and a corrupting principle of 'ragion di stato', they started to force English Catholics effectively to make a choice between prioritising their king or the loyalties due to the Pope. In putting their signatures to the *Gracious Declaration*, the leaders of the exiled court distanced the cause from the needs of the international church, putting their trust in the capacity of a Catholic monarch to judge religious settlements independently according to his conscience. As they moved towards a more strident assertion of royal authority, they took refuge in a restatement of French Gallican arguments, enlarging the role of the exiled monarchy over the religious obligations of the recusant flock. But if this argument possessed a rich intellectual lineage within the recusant community, it could give rise to serious contention when expressed by émigrés in confessional Europe. After 1693, when the king of France was seeking reconciliation with the papacy, and establishing himself as a champion of orthodoxy and order, Gallican proclamations were starting to look dangerously archaic.

The final part of the chapter will show how the vulnerability of the court was affirmed after 1701 in a series of disputes with host authorities centred on the nature of the papal prerogative and the spiritual obligations on a Catholic king. This conflict began with aspersions cast from the Holy See on the sanctity of Jacobite allegiance. It culminated when the allegation of

159

heresy and 'Jansenism' was flung repeatedly at the secular clergy who had come to dominate the entourage of James the Pretender, casting a longer shadow of suspicion over the exiled colleges and seminaries in France. I will suggest that while the defendants were largely innocent of any theological errors, they had been made vulnerable when French authorities enlarged the meaning of the term 'Jansenism' in an attempt to police the practice of Catholic faith in the Bourbon realm, and curtail the spread of anti-papal attitudes. Behind the clamour of the accusations, the detractors of the exiled court had identified a number of propositions on matters of jurisdiction, spirituality and even temporal affairs that aligned the émigrés in Paris and Douai with the controversial reform movements developing in the French capital. Ultimately, the chief source of provocation was not theological but political. If the origins of an English Jacobite 'Jansenism' lay in the diplomatic disputes with Rome in the 1690s, it was latterly the very measures, methods and rhetorical stratagems by which they lodged their public appeal to Protestant England that left them liable to interrogation. I will conclude by showing how the echo of previous conflicts destabilised Jacobite-Papal relations after the move of the court to Rome in 1718, suggesting that an afterlife of 'Jansenist' Catholicism persisted within the émigré communities into another generation.

The campaign for Christendom

English Catholics on both sides of the sea were swift to identify the fall of the house of Stuart within a setting of international conflict, pinpointing the best chance of success for James II in the permutations of great power politics. Most Jacobites initially positioned the papacy among the natural allies of James II. *The Tree of Life*, a 1689 poem by Thomas Ward, depicted kings and pontiffs resting in harmony as branches of the universal chain of being, in a conscious echo of Catholic Civil War verses. Any differences between royalist and papalist forms of Catholicism could be elided when both were brought to peril by rebels who struck at the hierarchy 'root and branch' – and both were compelled to stand together.[1] The reach of the 'Non-compounders' over the exiled court was achieved by an attempt to locate Jacobitism within an international crusade, characterised by the priest Charles Whyteford as the chance 'to restore a Catholique prince, chaised out of his Kingdoms for his virtue and religion alone'.[2]

Such voices adduced an unbroken connection between the revival of 'Christendom' on the continent, and the chance of securing an uncompromising religious settlement once the Stuarts had returned home. From the

---

[1] Thomas Ward, *The Tree of Life* (1689).
[2] Whyteford to Innes, 13 November 1694, SCA, Blairs, I, 186/15.

debris of the reign of James II, they plucked a message that could resound on the continent, when the stage of political life was littered with reminders of the principle of Catholic unity: once a motivating force for ecclesiastics, still the recipient of avowed lip-service. The most trenchant exponent of this position was the earl of Perth, whose experience of the Church was increasingly charged by a dream of restoring papal primacy over the Christian universe. On his travels through France, Italy and the Low Countries, he declared himself enraptured by relics, baroque art, and local tales of Christian martyrdom, and his entry into Rome in 1695 crowned a universalist Catholic consciousness in the process of construction.[3] 'The musick', he informed his sister, 'surpasses imagination' while 'to see all nations praise our Lord is a great joy to me, and a confirmation of the Catholique faith from China (where there are upwards already of 400,000 Christians), to Ireland … east and west round the globe'.[4] Exposure to the continent enabled Perth to see the falsity of Anglo-Scottish Protestantism – 'the diabolicall secrets of their devices and cheating solipsisms' – and the vision was made clearer when he trod the ground of Europe as the consequence of an act of martyrdom: 'I suffer for God, and with my lawful and deserving prince.'[5] A burgeoning spirituality sharpened his implacable political diagnosis.

After 1689, such sentiments directed the dispatch of Jacobite émigrés into foreign, Catholic armies to evince solidarity with the needs of an embattled faith. 1,800 soldiers marched east with Francis Taaffe, the future earl of Carlingford, to bolster Austrian and Polish forces against the Turkish advance: their commander was elected to the imperial Order of the Golden Fleece in 1694.[6] However, the Jacobite mission hinged principally on the efforts of a succession of envoys promoted by James II to ensure, in the words of John Caryll, 'that the Roman court can be made sensible of the parts and piety of a Tramontano, even in a state of persecution'.[7] The Jacobite embassy in the Holy See displayed the royal arms of the three kingdoms prominently in the English chapels and colleges.[8] Together, the representations of Sir John Lytcott, the clergymen William Leslie and Philip Ellis and, finally, Perth himself, gave a militant new voice to the interests of the house of Stuart in Rome. As Caryll insisted to the Roman Cardinalate, their remit was not simply to represent the regal cause, but to act as the official voice

---

[3] The earl of Perth to the countess of Erroll, 14 May 1694, in William Jerdan, ed., *Letters from James, Earl of Perth … to his sister the Countess of Erroll* (London, 1895), pp. 23–7.

[4] Perth to Lady Erroll, 11 June 1695, in Jerdan, ed., *Letters*, p. 79.

[5] Perth to Lady Erroll, 13 January 1689, in Jerdan, ed., *Letters*, p. 12.

[6] *Memoirs of the Family of Taaffe* (Vienna, 1856), pp. 21–31.

[7] John Caryll to Philip Ellis, 2 August 1693, HMC, *Stuart*, I, p. 7. A 'tramontano' referred to a Catholic residing north of the Alps.

[8] Sir John Lytcott to the earl of Melfort, 17 May 1692, Bodleian Library, Carte MSS, 208, fols 5–6; Ellis to Melfort, 15 June 1693, Carte MSS, 208, fols 47–8.

to draw attention 'the extreme necessities of those Catholic subjects of his Majesty's three kingdoms, who starve for their religion and their loyalty', supplying details of penal laws, parliamentary debates and instances of mob violence.[9] The condition of the recusant community had been redefined as a political rather than a pastoral matter, and Perth's letters conjured up the plight of the faithful flock with biblical drama:

> ... to see his Majesty forced to abandon them through want, who never abandoned him: a prince so holy, so generous, so much a man of true honour ... forced to abandon generous brave men and soldiers ... who had stood by him bravely to the very last. Good God! In what tongue can you express what he feels![10]

In delineating the truth to Rome, he sensed the chance to achieve what no British Catholic had manage to accomplish after a century of Reformation, and extract a promise of force to relieve the 'suffering children' of the church. The grand dream, outlined by the first Jacobite memorial to Rome in 1689, was the use of papal agency to draw the French, Spanish, Polish and Venetian governments into a militant alliance for the restoration of James II.[11] The struggle to return the Stuarts had been designated a climactic phase in the European wars of religion.

Yet in seeking to convert religious solidarity into lasting diplomatic alignments, the Jacobite embassy faced no straightforward mission, when in the stark calculus of Pope Innocent XI, 'the Prince of Orange is master, he is arbiter of Europe', and the ascendancy was aided and abetted by the majority of powers in a Catholic world that had somewhat unappreciated James II's efforts to return the true faith to his three kingdoms.[12] Jacobite commentators sensed a greater opportunity in Europe after the death of Innocent XI, before the Revolution was a year old. Even the Whig, Gilbert Burnet, who had every reason to appreciate the pro-Austrian sensibility in the Holy See, had sketched a pen-portrait of 'a jealous and fearful man', obsessed with the political decline of the papacy, concluding that 'the submitting to pope Innocent's infallibility was a very implicit act of faith, when all appearances were so strongly against it'.[13] If his actions did not quite merit Lord Ailesbury's label 'Monsieur Dykvelt's Protestant Pope', the pontiff had played, in the verdict of Lord Thomas Howard, a formidable part in 'all

---

[9] Perth to Caryll, 29 August 1695, in MacPherson, ed., *Original Papers*, I, p. 537; William Leslie to Cardinal Albani, 20 June 1690, Vatican Secret Archives, Fondo Albani, 163, fols 71–4; John Caryll to Albani, n.d. 1697, Fondo Albani, 163, fols 213–14.

[10] The earl of Perth to Pope Innocent XII, 20 July 1695, Bodleian Library, Carte MSS, 209, fols 323–4.

[11] Jacobite memorial to Pope Alexander VIII, Vatican Secret Archives, Fondo Albani, 163, fols 25–30.

[12] Perth to Caryll, 7 June 1695, in MacPherson, ed., *Original Papers*, I, pp. 532–3.

[13] Burnet, *Reign of James the Second*, pp. 92–3.

the revolutions now in England'.[14] With a new incumbent, Alexander VIII, sitting at the chair of St Peter, the dynastic conflict could, now according to one recusant commentator, be more clearly disseminated as a struggle for 'the Eternall happinesse or Misery of Millions of Souls, both in Great Brittaine, and all the Northern Parts of Europe'. It was now a 'due discharge' of the new pope's 'Pastoral Sollicitude' to 'animate by word and example Catholick Princes, and make them sensible of the Obligation they have, as sons of the Church, to assist this their Renowned Fellow-Member in his Conflict for the Faith'.[15]

The Jacobite case to Rome was brought home in the tract, 'Reflections on the League of Augsburg', drawn up by John Caryll in 1691, to denounce the conflict between France and Austria as 'a war raging in the bosome of the Church'. This work surveyed the rising spectre of Islam in the east and identified the expulsion of James II with a greater, apocalyptic moment: a time when Catholics must choose whether to 'extend the Kingdom of Jesus Christ', or accept the implosion of Christendom, 'so neare ruine and destruction'. If such words hinted at a breach with Louis XIV, who had cultivated the Sultan as an ally, the 'Reflections' nonetheless argued that the true 'Machiavel' sapping Christian strength was not the Bourbon monarch but William III. Caryll discerned behind the honeyed words of Orange diplomacy a front for the rise of militant Protestantism, and targeted the apparent indifference of his allies in Madrid and Vienna. In their moral blindness before greed and gunpowder, 'every blow they aym at France falls (without touching her) heavily upon the Catholick Church, wounding her thereby … in England, Scotland, Ireland and even Italy herself'. He mingled pathos with asperity, to contrast the profanity of his cast of fools and villains with the noble tragedy of James II, whose refusal to take either the French or the Austrian side was animated by his concern for the guarding of 'Jerusalem'. Realpolitik brought its consequences, and if James had lost just 'a temporary and transitory crown', those who acquiesced in his downfall 'run ye hazard of losing their own soules and the kingdom of heaven'.[16] Now, the old moving force of Roman power must be summoned up to bring the Stuarts their chance of deliverance.

Contested notions of the crusade marched in step with a martyrological representation of the house of Stuart that prepared the ground for the campaign to canonise James II: a chance to 'lay up a stock for eternity', in the words of Lord Perth, so that 'while our enemies have that thorn in their foot, they are not like to walk easily in their course'.[17] In Perth's judgement, James had given 'the most noble instance of being a true disciple of Jesus Christ than any age has produc'd of a Crown'd Head'; to John Caryll, the

---

14 *Monthly Account*, December 1688.
15 'Coppie of a Letter', Bodleian Library, Rawlinson MSS, D 91, pp. 24–5.
16 'Reflections on the League of Augsburg', BL, Add. MSS, 28,252, fols 26–37.
17 Perth to Caryll, 7 November 1695, Bodleian Library, Carte MSS, 209, fol. 361.

king would have been permitted to keep his crown had he allowed his son to be brought up a Protestant, and his refusal to do so could therefore be compared to the surrender of Isaac by Abraham, for 'the world must allow this to be the greatest sacrifice that a King could make to his God'.[18] Alive to the importance of striking symbolic blows, many of the campaigns in the Holy See were conducted in a specifically devotional form, exemplified by the Jacobite promotion of the Stuarts' ancestor St Margaret as a figurehead to demonstrate the importance of the British Isles to the Catholic Church. An icon for royal sainthood as the sister of the Saxon prince Edgar Atheling, and the wife of Malcolm III of Scotland, Margaret's *Vita* was penned by the Jesuit William Aloysius Leslie, in dedication to the young Prince of Wales, and in 1693, Cardinal Howard laboured successfully to shift her anniversary to 10 June, birthday of the infant prince.[19] Priests resident in the Holy See were especially alert to the politics of sainthood. James Gordon, the agent of the secular clergy in Rome, commented that Jacobite hopes rested on the fact that 'no college of Rome has furnished so many good missionaries and holy martyrs' as that of the English.[20] Through the pipeline of ideas and appeals running into Europe, the Jacobite cause had been identified as the new opportunity to place the suffering of British martyrs onto the calendar and the consciences of continental brethren.

Christendom 'at ruine'

In the first five years of exile, Jacobite diplomats had therefore internationalised English Catholic political argument, endeavouring, in the words of Lord Perth, to 'turn ye scales of Europe' by unmasking the rise of William III as a source of menace to all members of the church. The attempt to reclaim the idea of Christendom marked a break from the recusant rhetorical traditions of the previous half century, threatening to overturn the Gallican ideology that had once inspired authors like Caryll to separate the 'meerly spirituall' authority of Rome from the welfare of temporal princes.[21] This was a development that had flourished disruptively in response to the Revolution, with little intellectual grounding in the politics of the house of Stuart. Like the

---

[18] Perth, private commentary, n.d., Bodleian Library, Carte MSS, 209, fol. 370; 'Reflections on the League', BL, Add. MSS, 28,252, fol. 37.

[19] Cardinal Howard to Melfort, 14 April 1693, Bodleian Library, Carte MSS, 209, fol. 62; William Aloysius Leslie, *Vita di Sancta Margherita* (1693 edn); Mark Dilworth, 'Jesuits and Jacobites: The Cultus of St Margaret', *Innes Review*, 47 (1996), pp. 169–80. William Aloysius Leslie was cousin to the secular clergyman William Leslie, quoted elsewhere in this chapter.

[20] James Gordon to John Betham, 18 July 1703, AAW, St Gregory's Seminary MSS, fol. 223.

[21] Caryll, 'Not Guilty', BL, Add. MSS, 28,252, fol. 146.

other core components of the Noncompounders' manifesto, its strength as a point of principle depended heavily on the ability to deliver practical strategic rewards.

For all the ingenuity of the appeals, these gains were not forthcoming. Alexander VIII stuck resolutely to the political line of his predecessor, and refused to provide more than basic material support for the refugees.[22] Even the election of Innocent XII – more favourably inclined to France – in 1693 did not manage to awaken a European conscience that had, as John Caryll perceived it, been 'borne down by the violence of the stream'.[23] Indeed, unbeknown to the Stuart envoys, the curia considered seriously the suggestion of a secret embassy to William III, following the precedent of dialogue in 1560 between Elizabeth I and Pius IV, as the best way to safeguard the welfare of its flock throughout Britain.[24] A mood of hostility towards the Catholic world order became evident in Jacobite correspondence from the summer of 1692, when the envoy John Lytcott left Rome, to report on his findings to the exiled court. He lamented to Melfort: 'What now, my Lord, can be further expected from Rome? Not so much, I feare, as would make up the Hulke of one Vessel.'[25] Lytcott had found a place of veiled, conflicting interests, in which Jacobites struggled against the bluster of diplomatic enemies: he reserved particular vitriol for 'the Emperour's Ambassador, & a little pert Jesuit, who is here as a kind of Envoye from the Kg of Poland'. He concluded that the Pope 'had been so teised & even threatened by ye house of Austria that he is in a manner forc'd to Trim', adding sarcastically of the cardinals that 'were they to be as good as their words, most of them woud be perfect Pelicans, offering still to let out their blood'.[26] Other voices in the Holy See were somewhat less astounded. To the clergyman William Leslie, the 'Imperialistick' interest reached so far into Italy that papal judgement was now long entrenched. 'Be sure they will still machinat against you', he claimed: 'It is most easie to do without touching the discipline or the dogma of the Church.'[27] Moreover, his mood arose quite logically when the international interests of the papacy dwarfed the struggles of national territories, 'and there is no impietie to thinke and say boldly that we care not what becomes of kings, princes and potentates'.[28] For the Pope, as much as any

---

[22] *His Holyness the Pope of Rome's declaration against the French king, Louis the 14th* (1689).

[23] Caryll to Ellis, 21 March 1695, HMC, *Stuart*, I, p. 99.

[24] 'Padre Como' to Cardinal Albani, n.d. 1700, Vatican Secret Archives, Fondo Albani, 163, fols 195–6.

[25] Lytcott to Melfort, 20 July 1692, Bodleian Library, Carte MSS, 208, fol. 17.

[26] Lytcott to Melfort, 20 July 1692, Bodleian Library, Carte MSS, 208, fol. 22; and 5 August 1692, Carte MSS, 208, fol. 25

[27] William Leslie to Whyteford, 23 August 1693, SCA, Blairs, 1/128/33.

[28] Leslie to Whyteford, 9 November 1689, SCA, Blairs, I, 123/17.

Gallican bishop, spiritual fidelity with a Catholic prince did not seemingly translate into temporal commitment.

Between 1692 and 1695, the Jacobite court made sporadic attempts to cast the diplomatic net wider than the French court, putting John Caryll in charge of a private embassy to the Catholic Elector Palatine – an enemy of Louis XIV – and assuring the pontiff, in Perth's words, that no king of England would 'allow France to be so very powerful as to be master of Europe'.[29] Yet Stuart agents were faced with frequent reminders of the fragility of their position.[30] In 1692, Leslie reported that the cardinalate was starting to shun vespers in the British colleges in the Holy See 'because they knew it was for the King of England'.[31] Rather than reversing the direction of policy, Innocent XII exerted his leverage over Louis XIV by trying to temper French interest in the war of the British succession, playing to the weariness of a kingdom stricken by famine, bad harvests and high taxes. By 1695, the Jacobite leadership was faced with faltering Bourbon resolve, and caught the hint of the slide towards peace proceedings, with European nations apparently forgetting, according to John Caryll 'that what is unjust and irreligious in itself ought not to be done to save the whole world'.[32] Papal pleas for a settlement had grown in cogency after French forces crashed to defeat at the siege of Namur in 1695, when the Confederates started to force the Sun King back from the southern Netherlands. In 1696, the failure of the French navy to launch a planned expedition in the Channel was compounded by the exposure of the Assassination Plot against William III – a discovery that severely dented the reputation of the exiled court abroad, despite its vigorous protests of innocence, and left Louis XIV humiliated.[33] The face of Europe had turned away from St Germain, and in May 1697, the leaders of the great powers gave formal sanction to the Protestant succession, putting their signatures to the Treaty of Ryswick: in Perth's acid judgement, 'a treaty where Catholick princes exclude a Catholick king because he is a Catholick'.[34]

In Catholic Jacobite political thought, the anguished tone of literature berating England for the ills of 1688 was rapidly being replicated in broadsides inveighing against the powers of Christendom, for a corruption that displayed apparently similar contempt for monarchy and religion. As Bishop Philip Ellis claimed to have discovered in Rome, popes and potentates looked guiltily upon James II, but carried 'as little sense of his wrongs and suffer-

[29] Sheridan, 'Historical Narrative', HMC, *Stuart*, VI, p. 72; Perth to Pope Innocent XII, 29 June 1695, Bodleian Library, Carte MSS, 209, fol. 313.

[30] Caryll to Perth, 4 July 1695, in MacPherson, ed., *Original Papers*, I, p. 534.

[31] Leslie to Innes, 8 July 1692, SCA, Blairs, 1/150/13

[32] Caryll to Perth, 14 June 1695, in MacPherson, ed., *Original Papers* I, p. 533

[33] Sheridan, 'Historical Narrative', HMC, *Stuart*, VI, p. 73; Caryll to Perth, 12 July 1696, in MacPherson, ed., *Original Papers*, pp. 551–2.

[34] Perth to Caryll, 26 July 1695, Bodleian Library, Carte MSS, 209, fol. 327.

ings as if he was King of China'.[35] Drawing parallels with the fall of the first
Rome, Jacobite courtiers cast aspersions upon the Holy See that came curi-
ously close to touches of English Protestant polemic. A place of apparently
waning piety – even creeping atheism – Rome was charged with elevating
those sections of the Jesuit order hostile to royal principles, with papal preference for the Venetians as international arbitrators held as apparent proof
of a city 'full of the spirit of the republick'.[36] For Lord Perth, the events only
served to deepen a fervent spirituality: 'he reasoned well that said religion
must be true that subsists amidst such partiality and scandals'.[37] However,
for other courtiers, the image of Rome never quite recovered, and by 1696,
the Jacobite embassy had been decisively scaled down, with the Holy See
subject only to periodic appeals to money.[38] 'Great bitterness fills my heart',
Leslie wrote to the cardinalate, 'a dreadful evil has fallen upon the Church
of God.'[39] From St Germain, Lytcott issued the bleak rejoinder: 'Christen-
dome is at ruine'.[40]

Over the decade that followed the Glorious Revolution, the chances
of assembling an international coalition for the restoration of the Stuarts
appeared to have withered and died amid the spiritual and political
winds blowing through Catholic Europe. From his Paris monastery, Benet
Weldon saw the fall of James II, together with the rise of the Ottomans,
as the symptom of a loss of spiritual moorings across the continent, when
'ye idol of ambition commands the hearts of men' away from the 'Sacred
Rule' that 'our Holy Benedictine Predecessors taught there when they drew
them from their Deified Stocks and Stones'.[41] He concluded that the inac-
tivity of Innocent XII 'shall remain a blast in ye Annals of ye Church of
Christ in all Eternity', and an exhibition of the fallibility of spiritual powers
in 'humane matters'.[42] Weldon's fellow exiles similarly voiced the ending
of the dogmatic certainties that had inspired the original programme in
exile. Henry Browne appealed against the danger of dependence on any
foreign prince, when religious conscience no longer kept its place in 'reason
of state', and even a Catholic ally only 'played ye Game' as a means to
'ruin your Majesty's Kingdoms'.[43] Courtiers outside the policy-making circle
expressed similar scepticism over the dream of Catholic Christendom: Lady

---

35 Ellis to Caryll, 5 October 1694, Bodleian Library, Carte MSS, 209, fol. 131.
36 Ellis to James II, 23 March 1694, Bodleian Library, Carte MSS, 209, fols 107–8; Ellis
to James II, 9 November 1694, Carte MSS, 209, fol. 134.
37 Perth to Caryll, 14 December 1695, Bodleian Library, Carte MSS, 209, fols 202–3.
38 Leslie to Innes, 6 July 1695, SCA, Blairs, I, 124/92; Nairne to Leslie, 20 February
1696, SCA, Blairs II, 17/16.
39 Leslie to Albani, 7 September 1698, Vatican Secret Archives, Fondo Albani, 163,
fols. 165.
40 Lytcott to Leslie, 12 August 1695, SCA, Blairs, I, 134/46.
41 Weldon, 'Collection', BL, Add. MSS, 10,118, p. 365.
42 Weldon, 'Collection', BL, Add. MSS, 10,118, p. 384.
43 Henry Browne to James II, 29 September 1691, AAW, Browne MSS, 103.

Sophia Bulkeley protested to Browne about her son, serving in the Polish army 'in a war where his King nor country is noe ways concern'd in and will do little to advance his restuaration'.[44] By the middle of the decade, St Germain was already in rivalry with the Holy See in pursuit of bequests from English Catholics. David Nairne wrote morosely of Cardinal Howard's will, left entirely to the Church: 'it is not in any way mine to be a judge of these things, but *intra nos* I think it had been as well bestowed upon the King and would have been a great example to others'.[45]

If their vehemence became more overt with the prospect of an end to the war, the dashed hopes and wounded pride of the Jacobite courtiers were implicit in the principles of the Gracious Declaration, as a manifesto that obliged any restored Stuart to reject the commands of the universalist conscience, and govern, in effect, as a Protestant. In turning the Jacobite claimant into a *politique* figure, locating the needs of the state away from the demands of religion and sanctioning correspondence with Protestant Englishmen, courtiers had delivered their rebuke to continental powers. In persuading Bishop Bossuet to endorse the pragmatic needs of James II above the rigidities of faith, Jacobite leaders pitched their appeal to the strain of despondency within the French nation, glimpsed in Bossuet's abandonment of the dream of a last great campaign against the Turks, and the verdict of the future Cardinal Fleury that 'only a few of the poets clamour for crusades'.[46] The Catholic Compounders behind the manifesto grounded their case in older Gallican principles of detachment from Rome, convincing James II of its legitimacy by reminder of the dictum that recusants served as members of the 'Church not the Court of Rome': as they could expect no support from the pontiff, so they were not enjoined to bring his word into temporal affairs.[47] John Caryll's 1697 'Memoire Sommaire' incorporated the Jacobite case into a larger conception of 'Christendom' compatible with the rights of Protestant princes and all who bore 'le nom de Chretienne'. The argument for restoration was rephrased to appeal to the solidarity of 'crowned heads' and 'the peace of Europe', which could never be made safe when William had 'unhinged the law of nature and nations'.[48] Protestant Jacobite pamphleteers such as Charlwood Lawton were even permitted to espouse an anti-papal line, highlighting the threat to the Gallican Church to show how William's allies struck at the liberties of sovereign kingdoms.[49]

By the passing of the Treaty of Ryswick, the failure of the confessional 'Christendom' campaign had left a vacuum in the imagination of the exiled

---

[44] Lady Sophia Bulkeley to Browne, 17 October 1694, AAW, Browne MSS, 233.

[45] Nairne to Leslie, 29 July 1694, SCA, Blairs, I, 181/9.

[46] Hazard, *The European Mind (1680–1715)* (London, 1952), pp. 205–8.

[47] Dodd, *Church History*, III, pp. 421–2.

[48] 'Memoire Sommaire', 1697, Oxfordshire CRO, Belson MSS, F/1/4/MS/51.

[49] [Lawton], *A Reply to the answer Doctor Welwood has made to King James's declaration* (1694).

court, obliging its leaders to speak of their faith in a different language. Returning to a traditional Anglo-Gallican stance, Philip Ellis asserted that the Jacobite claimant was the true 'spirituall representative' of the nation and the worthiest recipient of recusant prayers: through his prospect of success, 'our chastisements, tho' not our faults, grow towards an end'.[50] Jacobite letters to the Holy See promoted the Stuart princes as the figures best equipped to nurture 'right doctrine and good morals in the kingdoms', without needing to submit to external direction.[51] However, in Catholic Europe, this deconstruction of the spiritual and political goods of 'Christendom' needed to be phrased somewhat tactfully. The Declaration itself was exposed to a withering assault in a series of Austrian manifestos that were put before the papacy in 1693.[52] By failing to promise his Catholic subjects parity of position with the Anglican establishment, James could not really be a redeemer for the faith, they said, and he now offered no more to the Holy See than William of Orange. An Austrian 'Answer' to the Declaration drew out the inconsistencies of the Stuart position: the failure to match claims of self-sacrificial piety with an unremittingly 'Catholic' programme, served as the proof that 'it is very hard to maintaine an ill cause'.[53] These claims highlighted the contradiction at the heart of a cause with both national and European aspirations. The anti-papal realignment may have suited the needs of an English audience, but it brought more complex repercussions for those Catholics living in exile. The Austrian line of attack offered an ominous precedent for opponents of the Jacobite court over the coming two decades.

Rome and the conflict of Catholic allegiance 1701–1716

In the wake of diplomatic disenchantment, the political thought of the statesmen in exile was being brought back into the line with the sensibility of recusants in England, whose writings continued to put up barriers against the temporal interests of the Holy See. Reflecting in 1697 on the challenges put before his co-religionists, the Oxfordshire scholar John Belson contended that 'because every Temporall action of a Christian has or may bee thought to have a connexion with Religion', his communion must resist 'a conceit that wee think our selves obliged to obey every order wch at Rome shall be

---

[50] Ellis to James Edward, 23 October 1701, AAW, St Gregory's Seminary MSS, 225.

[51] James II to Cardinal Barberini, 1697, Vatican Secret Archives, Fondo Albani, 164, fols 11–19.

[52] Ellis to James II, 13 July 1694, Bodleian Library, Carte MSS, 209, fol. 115; Royal Archives (Windsor), Sheridan, 'Political Reflexions', p. 104; Clarke, ed., *Life of James the Second*, II, pp. 510–11.

[53] 'The Answer in Dutch to the King's Manifesto', Bodleian Library, Carte MSS, 209, fols 381–4.

call'd or declared Spirituall', lest they wished to be thought of as subjects to a Forreign power even in Temporals'. The matter had implications of 'extreme import' for the dynastic question. If the impression was allowed to linger, James II 'will disgust his Protestant friends, & heighten the enmity of ye rest'.[54] Avowals of this nature became more vocal from the Pretender's Council of Regency after the death of James II. A tract of 1712 invoked Marsiglio of Padua to prove that 'the best' men of the Catholic religion 'believe and maintaine as well as Protestants, that Rome has no power over Princes in temporalls, and that whenever Popes extend their power beyond the limits prescribed by the Canon, or that they act as Secular princes, they are, and ought to be, looked upon and dealt with as such'.[55] A memorial by Lord Middleton cited the storming of Rome by Charles V, as well as French resistance to 'the decrees of Trent relating to discipline', in order to verify this precept.[56] Even Lord Perth insisted that Stuart restoration could only be guaranteed by demonstrating the temporal independence of the monarchy: 'for I venture to say the name of the Pope is more hateful to them, and much more capable of arousing a persecution'.[57] In Europe, Jacobites underplayed the fact that their chosen model offered little resemblance to the Gallicanism of Louis XIV, with the Stuart prince now disowning not merely temporal obedience to Rome, but much of the mandate to act as 'nursing father' to the faith of his people.

If courtiers had not totally relinquished the vision of a major European realignment, any hope that the pontiff could act to 'unite all the Catholick princes' in defence of 'our king and our poor Catholicks' was being persistently attenuated by international realities, especially after the 1709 agreement between Clement XI and Joseph I of Austria served to silence any pro-Stuart leanings 'under this Pontificate'.[58] Rome itself could do little to arrest the trends of great power politics after the treaty of Utrecht marked peace between Britain and France in 1713 and left the exiled court bounced around the diplomatic chessboard between Urbino, Bar-le-Duc and Avignon to serve the needs of Versailles.[59] Neither could the pontiff stop the formation of the Quadruple Alliance in 1717 – that 'four-footed monster' as it was dubbed by Stuart diplomats, which locked the improbable alliance

---

[54] John Belson, 'Concerning the effects of obedience of RC priests to orders from Rome', 1697, Oxfordshire CRO, Belson MSS, F/1/4/MS/19–20.

[55] 'Account of a politick conversation between a Catholick and a Whig upon the Hanoverian succession', 1712, Bodleian Library, Carte MSS, 210, fols 411–14.

[56] The earl of Middleton, 'On the Hanoverian succession', 1709, HMC, *Stuart*, VII, p. 597.

[57] James Edward and the earl of Perth to Cardinal Imperiali, 12 June 1714, HMC *Stuart*, I, pp. 329–32.

[58] Dicconson to Mayes, 23 August 1714, AAW, Epistolae Variorum, V/62; Nairne to Gualterio, 15 February 1714, BL, Add. MSS, 31,259, fols 14–15.

[59] Berwick to James Edward, 9 December 1714, 5 February 1715, HMC, *Stuart*, I, pp. 337–8, 346–7.

between France and Austria into a pact of friendship with the Hanoverian crown in London.[60] The sense of estrangement from 'weak and wicked measures' in Catholic Europe rendered it as feasible by 1715 that a Jacobite diplomat would be sent to courts outside the sphere of his own religion: George Jerningham concentrated on impressing 'the justice and right of the cause' on Swedish and Russian ministers during his operations in the Baltic after 1716.[61] However, recusants in England continued to articulate their bitterness at the European loss of faith considered responsible for the plight of their congregation. Bishop Bonaventure Giffard saw international frailty encapsulated by the reluctance of ambassadors to open their London chapels to public worship. He obsereved that, 'our poor Ca: are all strangely abandoned by Ca: princes, worse than in ye time of Cromwell'.[62] Overall blame was still laid at the door of the Holy See. To the court preceptor John Ingleton, 'the King has the glory to suffer for his religion, and methinks he should be more respected, especially by Rome, than if he was on the throne'.[63] Instructing secular clergymen in the Holy See to 'ring you such a peal as would make them ashamed', Giffard could only pronounce: 'God grant they may never want the charity they refuse to us.'[64]

Papal neglect was not the only source of Jacobite concern. After the death of James II, relations with the papacy deteriorated as the result of a new and unwelcome development: the growing conflict over dynastic allegiance within the English Catholic community, which starkly exposed the risks created for Stuart affairs by a posture of confrontation with Rome. When the peace of Ryswick gave Rome the chance to involve itself more in the mission to the three kingdoms, the Jacobite court was faced with recurrent complaints from papal offices about its intervention on recusant religious life. In 1697, the Holy See had protested that 'ye temporall interest' in England, Scotland and Ireland 'is starting to usurpe upon ye spirituall or ecclesiasticall power', with priests ministering less to common pastoral needs than the worldly requirements of the Stuart cause.[65] In 1703, a papal edict acted upon these concerns, and moved to forbid English missioners from making themselves 'odious to the government' and becoming involved with anything save affairs of the spiritual realm.[66] James Gordon, agent for the

---

[60] George Jerningham to the earl of Mar, 20 December 1718, HMC, *Stuart*, VII, pp. 659–60.

[61] Jerningham to Mar, 20 September 1718, HMC, *Stuart*, VII, p. 317; Jerningham to Vice-Chancellor Schapiroff, 17 August 1718, HMC, *Stuart*, VII, p. 318; John J. Murray, *George I, the Baltic and the Whig Split of 1717* (1969), pp. 112–14, 146–56.

[62] Giffard to Mayes, 21 November 1717, AAW, Epistolae Variorum, VI/65.

[63] Ingleton to Mayes, 14 April 1714, AAW, Epistolae Variorum, V/76.

[64] Giffard to Mayes, 15 September 1718, AAW, Epistolae Variorum, VI/ 96.

[65] 'Paper on the Irish bishops', 1697, Bodleian Library, Carte MSS, 208, fol. 231.

[66] George Witham to Betham, 13 March 1703, AAW, St Gregory's Seminary MSS, 203. The suggestion was first raised in a *Supplica* put before the Pope by the Cardinalate in 1700, Vatican Secret Archives, Fondo Albani, 163, fols 193–4.

secular clergy of England and Scotland, confessed to deep misgivings about the decree: 'I own that I do not like the wording ... it gives some suspicion that many great folks here are not too tender of the King's title.'[67] The same concern impelled clergymen close to James Edward to seek a stronger institutional status for the exiled court in Rome, and a formal recognition of its interest as spiritual guardian of the three kingdoms. They submitted an official nomination for Fillippo Antonio Gualterio, one of the few avowedly Jacobite voices in the Holy See, as Cardinal-Protector of the three kingdoms in 1704, and struck out angrily when voices in the curia objected to their right to make the choice. 'To speak frankly, the Cardinal is a true servant of the King of England', Betham insisted in a letter to Rome. To 'suffer the King of England to be dependent on France' for his voice in the Holy See would mock 'the incontestable authority of a sovereign and legitimate prince' torn from his throne 'for his inviolable attachment to the Catholic religion'.[68] Gualterio's elevation was accepted – with little enthusiasm – but Jacobite credit had been damaged in Rome, at a time when St Germain was notably void of political strength.[69]

Enmity with Catholic powers came at a cost. In Britain and Europe, Catholic opponents of the Jacobite cause reacted to signs of a breach by making recourse to the Holy See, as an instrument to drive the Stuart cause apart from the English Catholic laity. After the failure of the 1715 rebellion, as has been seen, the oath campaign contrived by John Stonor and Thomas Strickland utilised the language of unity and orthodoxy with particular skill, confident that the reconstruction of an alliance between Hanover, Austria and the Papacy would present English recusants with an alternative idea of where true conscience ought to reside.[70] By diplomatic necessity as much as heartfelt conviction, the affair of the Catholic oath therefore brought a final flowering of the ideal of militant Christendom in Jacobite circles, in a last-ditch attempt to sway the sympathies of Rome. The clergy of Douai sent their own memorials to Gualterio in the Holy See, exhorting the papal court against a design that came with great peril for peril for 'the lives and liberties of all Catholics' through 'the injustice done to a legitimate prince matched by no-one in his zeal for the true religion, whose hopes increase every day'.[71] The campaign to canonise James II was renewed overtly to restore the religious conscience into world politics, when Nicholas Dempster, secretary to Mary of Modena, urged the court to

[67] Gordon to Betham, 10 July 1703, AAW, St Gregory's Seminary MSS, 215.
[68] 'Memorial concerning the reasons why the King of England persisted in the nomination of Cardinal Gualterio as Protector of England and of the difficulties and objections raised against the nomination', n.d. 1704, BL, Add. MSS, 20,311, fols 211–13; Cardinal Paulucci to Cardinal Gualterio, 12 January 1705, BL, Add. MSS, 20,311, fols 217–18.
[69] Gordon to Betham, 15 February 1705, AAW, St Gregory's Seminary MSS, 161.
[70] See Chapter 4 above.
[71] Declaration of the Vicars Apostolic, 1716, BL, Add. MSS, 20,311, fols 281–3.

follow his mistress's conviction that 'the interests of the crown depend so much upon the memory of the Holy King'.[72] The idea of Jacobite sanctity was enlarged by polemical narratives dispatched in memory of the executed rebels into the English College, Rome, with Robert Witham printing a prayer for the earl of Derwentwater as a 'holy martyr of the church', who 'therefor died a saint'.[73] The Benedictine president Thomas Southcott drew the larger recusant community into his diagnosis, insisting that the confessional interest of the Whig party prevented any chance of safety for Catholics in Hanoverian England: the likely effect of the oath plan was instead 'a schism, and probably a persecution'. Southcott evoked images of the siege of Jerusalem to shape an apocalyptic narrative for 'the daughter of Zion in her agony' – valiantly withstanding 'the malice and the rage of her enemies', as the number of her martyrs 'blossoms and multiplies'.[74]

Ostensibly, these overtures enjoyed some success. By 1721, the signs of division within English Catholicism had turned the Holy See against Strickland's design, suspending the chance of papal intervention in recusant politics.[75] Yet this *volte face* did not lead to any perceptible thaw in the attitudes of the Jacobite secular clergy. The superiors in Douai and Paris drew little comfort from the caprices of the Holy See, voicing suspicions that the prime motive for the switch lay more in concerns for the authority of Rome than any true interest in the Stuart regal right. The Pope's real objection, they surmised, arose after Strickland's lay associates had proposed importing into the oath a renunciation of the 'deposing power'.[76] Therefore, although support for the Stuarts had been salvaged, the scent of anti-Jacobite feeling in Rome was nonetheless believed to lie behind a train of events, 'so unexpected and so mortifying' to John Ingleton, bringing the threat of 'unspeakable damage to the mission of England'.[77] A place long perceived by George Witham to be crawling with spies, where 'ye unhappy maxims of ... ragion di stato' hold 'more weight with many then ye Interests of true religion' was confirmed as an insufficient barrier against the threat to consciences

[72] Nicholas Dempster to Nairne, April 1713, Douai Abbey, Dempster Letter-book; List of miracles at the tomb of James II, n.d., BL, Add. MSS, 20,311, fol. 13; 'On the life of the Holy King James II', n.d., BL, Add. MSS, 20,311, fol. 17.
[73] Robert Witham to Lawrence Mayes, 20 July 1716, AAW, Epistolae Variorum, VI/19; *Diary of Edward Dicconson*, p. 35; 'Account of Colonel Roxburgh's death', n.d. November 1716, EPSJ, Notes and Fragments, 102.
[74] Southcott to Gualterio, 31 May 1723, 14 June 1723, BL, Add. MSS, 20,309, fols 31–2, 34–5.
[75] Plowden to Eberson, 17 January 1720, Kennett to Eberson, 17 February 1720, both in EPSJ, Notes and Fragments, 107.
[76] Ingleton to Mayes, 21 October 1716, AAW, Epistolae Variorum, VI/34; Kennett to Eberson, n.d. November 1716, EPSJ, 102.
[77] Ingleton to Mayes, 22 September 1716, AAW, Epistolae Variorum, VI/27; Ingleton to Gualterio, 15 December 1716, BL, Add. MSS, 20,310, fol. 173.

from within the British Isles.[78] In turn, Edward Dicconson began to use anti-papal language against Strickland, proclaiming that it was the Catholic Hanoverians who were guilty of meddling with 'the court of Rome', acting as 'enemies to kinges', by raising the power of the Pope over the three kingdoms: the very crime of which Jacobite recusants had been accused in decades past. All oath proposals since 1688, he said, had emanated from 'strangers to our mission', backed by 'Itallian politicians', and the new design simply represented the reappearance of these same 'republickan' interests.[79] Ingleton's judgement stepped into equally provocative territory. In characterising the oath project as 'the work of foreign divines, who are strangers to the constitution and the laws of England', he declared dissent against forces in Rome so ready in 'sacrificing the King's unquestionable right, and yet so tenacious of an authority that at the best can only be put in the class of school opinions'.[80]

The shock that the papal interest might be used to coerce recusants against the Jacobite interest sealed the sea-change in the worldview of the Paris and Douai clergymen. In the following decade, the Douai alumnus Robert Manning returned to the theme for the benefit of Protestant pamphlet readers. He assured them that the Holy See had no mandate to make an intervention in the matter of dynastic allegiance, and any such action would represent the interests of the 'temporal court, not the Church' of Rome, which English Catholics had the right to resist. Indeed, bringing the pope into the dynastic contest would set a positively dangerous precedent: a 'blunder' identical to the Holy League's invocation of papal powers against Henri of Navarre in the French Wars of Religion, which had been rightly rejected by all good Catholics. He concluded that 'if any subject of a Catholick Sovereign Prince on this side of the Alps would venture to maintain the notion, he would pass his time but very uncomfortably'.[81] Such words fell within the logic of the Anglo-Gallican tradition, but their reassertion marked the climax of twenty years of growing distrust between the Holy See and the Jacobite clergy. The grip of the Catholic world in temporal affairs had been shaken in a section of recusant opinion, by the splits and shifts occasioned since 1688. For those who had sought to revive the militant Counter-Reformation in 1689, the wheel had turned full circle.

---

[78] George Witham to Whyteford, 26 December 1702, SCA, Blairs, II, 79/12.
[79] Dicconson to Mayes, 16 August 1715, AAW, Epistolae Variorum, V/100; Dicconson to Ingleton, 23 April 1717, AAW, St Gregory's Seminary MSS, 389.
[80] Ingleton to Mayes, 21 October 1716, AAW, Epistolae Variorum, VI/34.
[81] Robert Manning, *The case stated between the Church of Rome and the Church of England in a second conversation betwixt a Roman Catholick lord, and a gentleman* (2 vols, 1721), I, pp. 92, 94, 236, 244–6.

English 'Jansenism' and the Jacobite cause

Disputes breaking out between English Catholics and the court of Rome were not configured solely by diplomatic conflict. After 1701 especially, clashes of allegiance and jurisdiction possessed a new and troubling component: a rising tide of doctrinal contention that brought a section of the émigrés into conflict not merely with the Holy See, but with their hosts in France. Up to the death of James II, Rome had offered little intervention in the religious and political discussions that contributed to the formation of the Jacobite manifesto. Accepting the overtures of Bishop Bossuet, the curia made no contribution to the debates over matters of conscience that preceded the 1693 Gracious Declaration. Yet by the second decade in exile, the situation was changing. Once it had been Stuart circles berating the papacy for its apparent loss of the principle of Catholic unity; now the positions of the dispute were reversed, and Jacobite invective against the court of Rome was countered by the claim that James Edward Stuart was being led into treacherous spiritual ground, in his search for compromises to win back the three kingdoms. In 1712, the anti-Jacobite Brussels Nuncio began to voice suspicions of an anti-papal mood developing among the exiles.[82] In 1716, a letter to Cardinal Gualterio denounced the Stuarts for bringing their Protestant entourage into the Papal States, and concluded that 'I find the court lacking in zeal and vigilance for the glory of Jesus Christ and for the good of the Church.'[83] Later, the clergyman Lawrence Mayes warned of a view from the Holy See that 'they run down with a strange liberty ye Pope's power, and constitution as if they were only to be laught at, and seem to have forgotten at least yt he is head of ye Church, and as such can make laws and be obeyed'.[84] The tension between Stuart interests, the native culture of English Catholicism, and the demands of the international church had been brought to a head.

The challenge to the exiled court appeared most violently in allegations that the Jacobite milieu harboured the heresy of Jansenism, projecting into the heart of St Germain the single most rancorous issue to strike at the unity of Catholic Europe in the early eighteenth century. In 1705, Dr John Betham was forced to resign his post after French imputations that he had been corrupting the seventeen-year-old Pretender with heterodox teachings.[85] In 1710, the English College, Douai faced an inquisition over suspi-

---

[82] Vincenzo Santini to Gualterio, n.d. 1712, BL, Add. MSS, 20,499, fol. 95; Santini to Paulucci, 23 November 1713, Vatican Secret Archives, Segretaria di Stato: Nunziatura di Fiandra, 105, fols 807–8; Henry Paston to Mayes, December 17 1714, AAW, Epistolae Variorum, V/80.

[83] Anon., letter to Cardinal Gualterio, 1716, BL, Add. MSS, 20,311, fol. 369.

[84] Mayes to Ingleton, 4 June 1726, AAW, St Gregory's Seminary MSS, 563.

[85] Mary of Modena to Cardinal de Noailles, February 1704, HMC, *Stuart*, I, pp. 190–1; Betham, 'Ruff Draught of the Reasons Given and the Methods Taken for Removing

cious doctrine.[86] The mood of animosity was intensified after the passing of the bull, Unigenitus, of 1713, when new restrictions on Catholic reading forced the resignation of Dr Thomas Witham as president of St Gregory's, Paris.[87] The same decree brought peril upon the Scots College, Paris, when the opinions of Lewis Innes's brother, Thomas, prompted calls for an investigation into the conduct of the clergy in Scotland, and the bishop of Tournai complained that through the same influence 'many unfit scandalous persons were sent on the mission' in England.[88] In the Low Countries, the issue exacerbated strains between the different exiled communities, with the English Franciscans accused by their Irish counterparts of disregard for 'the rights of orthodoxy'.[89] In 1718, English colleges were ordered to keep their pupils away from doctoral studies at St Gregory's, which was judged contaminated by false doctrine.[90] Concerns over the exiled colleges had originally been raised by Cardinal Albani, the future Clement XI, before his enthronement, with a suggestion that the Holy See should monitor pastoral and priestly training far more decisively if any 'scintilla' of religion was to survive in the three kingdoms.[91] However, John Ingleton professed himself 'surprised, disturbed, confounded and afflicted' by the ferocity of the assaults, which he predicted would bring 'irredeemable damage to English Catholicks'. The clergy at York pleaded for protection from the Jacobite court in an affair grave enough to be regarded the 'business of state'.[92]

The Jansenist movement in *ancien régime* society has been subject to a febrile and highly contested historiography, tracing the transmutation of a theological heresy into a set of propositions concerned with the function of the temporal and spiritual powers in public affairs. With its devotional

---

from St Germain John Betham, Preceptor to King James ye 3rd', January 1705, AAW, St Gregory's Seminary MSS, fols 231–245; Scott, 'Education of James III', pp. 275–6.

[86] James Edward to Cardinal Caprara, 9 March 1710, HMC *Stuart*, I, p. 236; Caryll to Caprara, 11 March 1710, AAW, Old Brotherhood MSS, III, fols 104–6; John Ingleton and Lewis Innes, 'Attestio from St Germains', 1710, AAW, Old Brotherhood MSS, III, fols 110–111.

[87] James Davies to Plowden, 13 December 1714, EPSJ, Notes and Fragments, 93; Thomas Eyre to Plowden, May 1715, EPSJ, Notes and Fragments, 99.

[88] Andrew Michael Ramsay to Thomas Innes, 14 September 1720, SCA, Blairs, II, 229/8; James F. Macmillan, 'Thomas Innes and the Bull Unigenitus', *Innes Review*, 33 (1982), 23–31.

[89] Santini to Paulucci, 6 August 1716, Vatican Secret Archives, Segretaria di Stato: Nunziatura di Fiandra, 108, fols 383–4.

[90] Cardinal Paulucci to Robert Witham, n.d. 1719, *Diary of Edward Dicconson*, p. 62; Ingleton to Mayes, 11 May 1722, AAW, Epistolae Variorum, VII/109; Santini to Witham, 19 August 1719, in *Register Book of St Gregory's* (CRS, 19, Paris, 1917), p. 124.

[91] Cardinal Albani to Pope Innocent XII, n.d., Vatican Secret Archives, Fondo Albani, 163, fols 247–8.

[92] Bryan Tunstall to Ingleton, 4 January 1710, AAW, St Gregory's Seminary MSS, 307; Ingleton to Mayes, 21 August 1719, AAW, Epistolae Variorum, VI/120; James MacMillan, 'Jansenism and the Scots College Books', *Innes Review*, 44 (1993), pp. 73–5.

centres at Utrecht and the Parisian convent of Port Royal, Jansenism was built upon the spiritual writings of Cornelius Jansen, Antoine Arnauld and Pierre Nicole: a theology of 'grace' with undertones reminiscent of Calvinism, and an Augustinian view of the gulf between God and man. But the heresy itself was a notoriously protean phenomenon, a spectre created just as much by the decision of Louis XIV to align himself with Pope Clement XI, pose as a champion of orthodox faith, and launch a major inquisition to purge errant teachings from church and state.[93] Under pressure of interrogation, the creed fragmented, according to Konrad Hecker, into 'a certain mentality and spirituality rather than an explicit and dogmatic theology', far harder to police, but deemed equally inimical by the French crown.[94] Popular among aristocratic circles in Paris and anti-Jesuit sections of the Benedictine and Oratorian clergy, this refined Jansenism harked back to the concern for moral reform and the Christological strain of individual piety present at the birth of the Counter-Reformation, with its preference for inward spirituality, private reading and devotional submission before God. The crown's reaction, beginning with the prosecution of forty Sorbonne doctors in 1701, proceeding through the desecration of Port Royal in 1709, and, culminating in attempts to strike the works of Pasquier Quesnel from Catholic libraries with the bull Unigenitus, introduced strains of clandestinity, persecution and martyrdom into the movement. Jansenist partisans availed themselves of near-mystical intensity, when the miracles reported in Paris cemeteries gave stimulus to claims that 'the Earth is becoming empty of saints, while heaven is filling up'.[95]

The affiliation between St Gregory's, Paris, and the Sorbonne provided the alleged incubus of English Jansenism. To inquisitors such as Vincenzo Santini, the Brussels nuncio, the heresy was endemic within an English communion 'steeped in Quesnellism'; to the defenders, the claim was a phantom raised by those seeking to advance their own power.[96] French 'Jansenism' was certainly used as a brickbat, highly effective in sullying an ecclesiastical career, and it was partly in this context that the phenomenon entered England, as Eamon Duffy has shown, out of a power struggle between the Jesuits and the seculars for control of the domestic mission.[97] However,

[93] Jacques Reboulet, *Histoire de Clément XI* (Avignon, 1752); Owen Chadwick, *The Popes and European Revolution* (Oxford, 1981), pp. 273–86.

[94] Hecker quoted in Clancy, *English Jesuits*, p. 219.

[95] John McManners, 'Jansenism and Politics in the Eighteenth-Century', in Derek Baker, ed., *Church, Society and Politics* (Studies in Church History, 12, 1975), pp. 253–73; Dale Van Kley, 'Piety and Politics', pp. 119–20.

[96] Santini to Paulucci, 23 November 1713; Vatican Secret Archives, Segretaria di Stato: Nunziatura di Fiandra, 105, fols 807–8; *Diary of Edward Dicconson, 1704–7, 1714* (CRS, 1972), pp. 102–104; Robert Witham to Mayes, 12 January 1719, AAW, Epistolae Variorum, VI/106.

[97] Eamon Duffy, 'A Rubb-up for Old Soares: Jesuits, Jansenists and the English Secular Clergy 1705–17', *Journal of Ecclesiastical History*, 28 (1972), pp. 291–317.

there remained an undercurrent to recusant religious life to raise suspicion that the absence of effective papal scrutiny had brought about a divergence from orthodox teaching. Charles Dodd, the clergyman and pamphleteer, acknowledged of his fellow 'seculars', that 'the System of their Theology, as to what touch'd upon Grace, was contrary to the Jesuits Schools'.[98] The Jacobite priests in Rome, George Witham and William Leslie, confessed to fears of 'being clapt up in prison by the Inquisition' for precisely this reason.[99] The widened category of 'error' outlined by Louis XIV and Pope Clement XI could create grounds for convergence between Jansenist calls for the revival of holy life, and the rigorist form of worship developed by recusants to erase aggressive and confrontational elements from their faith. John Betham identified the issue as the smoke-screen for Roman assaults on the pastoral model exemplified by the handbooks of Gother, whose Augustinian 'morals and maxims', he admitted, could be judged 'too severe on the corruption of this Age'.[100] Robert Witham, more loyal than many of his coevals to the will of Rome, nonetheless saw the ambitions of French dioceses behind the controversy: an attack on the rights and exemptions of the exiled colleges.[101] Both however, were being somewhat disingenuous. The same college printing presses disseminating the works of Gother had also ushered outlawed literature into the British Isles, to leave the teachings of Quesnel 'mighty common and much in use amongst the Catholicks', as the Norfolk priest Henry Paston conceded, before and after the passing of the bull.[102]

It was not coincidental that the suspicion of St Germain as a nursery of heresy grew at a time when relations with Douai and St Gregory's were especially close, when the English secular clergy dominated confession and instruction at the exiled court, and the influence of the Society of Jesus, was, according to one of its superiors, lamentably thin.[103] The English Benedictines in Paris also possessed connections to Port Royal, affirmed when Weldon's manuscript celebrated the miracle of the Holy Thorn growing within the convent garden and recalled the support of the nuns for Charles II in his own time of exile.[104] The Jacobite monk Thomas Southcott had aroused particular distrust in Rome as an alleged translator of Quesnel,

[98] RC [Charles Dodd], *The History of the English College at Doway from its first foundation in 1568, to the present time* (1713), p. 32.

[99] George Witham to Betham, 29 August 1701, AAW, St Gregory's Seminary MSS, 163.

[100] Betham to James Gordon, 16 March 1704, AAW, Epistolae Variorum, I/21; Betham, 'Mr Gother on Indulgences', n.d., AAW, Epistolae Variorum, 1/34.

[101] Witham to Mayes, 24 April 1718, AAW, Epistolae Variorum, VI/83.

[102] Henry Paston to Mayes, 12 June 1714, AAW, Epistolae Variorum, V/56.

[103] Geoffrey Holt, ed., *The Letter-book of Lewis Sabran 1713–1715* (CRS, 1971), pp. 61, 66, 249. 291.

[104] Weldon, 'Collection', BL, Add. MSS, 10,118, fol. 42.

albeit before Unigenitus came into force.[105] Among the exiled lay contingent, the Hamilton siblings – a Scots-Irish family who had married into the French aristocracy – served as patrons of Port Royal and the lords Berwick, Middleton and Perth went in worship to the same congregation, at the time they sat on the Council of Regency.[106] Here, beneath the hints and the aspersions was the whisper of a challenge to Rome. According to the bishop of Toul, St Germain was 'a holy court, and that party [the Jansenists] has always tried to cover itself with appearances of piety to seek the support of good people'.[107] When the primary concern over the heresy lay in its potential 'corruption of youth', the eye of the French state fell especially upon the activities of John Betham as royal preceptor: provoked by the Jansenist strains imported into his educational *Treatise* and his preference for a curriculum that echoed the teachings at Port Royal.[108] The bishop of Toul made his case for Betham's dismissal with the verdict that 'it is easy to see how dangerous it is to have a person of this character and these opinions with a young Prince every day, and it is very difficult to erase first impressions formed in youth'.[109] Circles close to the exiled throne appeared to be announcing their affinity with a movement that was becoming rapidly more subversive.

By voicing his belief that Arnauld was worthy of a cardinal's cap, and introducing James Edward to the books of Nicole and Pascal, Betham had certainly provided provocation for the ecclesiastical authorities. But he himself described the ensuing storm in patriotic terms, as the latest stage in a battle to keep control over Catholic religion, its books and its teaching, 'in the hands of our English fathers' and so prevent it becoming 'governed by forraigners'.[110] It was perhaps more accurate to identify the origins of English Jansenism in a clash between Rome and the tendency among recusants and Jacobites that had been shaped by the older Gallican opinion, when political alienation from the Holy See brought them back to the original French critique of papal decrees on discipline and church governance. The outlook of the secular clergy had been crafted from what Henry Paston called 'our Sorbonnick erudition', loyal to the university from which had they received their doctorates, and which was now under increasing assault, when the 1705 bull Vinem Domine attacked its 'respectful silence' on the status of

---

105 Ingleton to Mayes, 29 January 1719, AAW, Epistolae Variorum, VI/107.

106 *Ruth Clark, Anthony Hamilton: His Life, his Works and his Family* (London, 1921), pp. 109–19; Clark, *Strangers and Sojourners at Port Royal; Being an Account of the Connections between British Isles and the Jansenists of France and Holland* (Cambridge, 1932), pp. 164, 241.

107 Bishop of Toul to Madame de Maintenon, November 1703, HMC, *Stuart*, I, p. 188.

108 Betham, *Brief Treatise*, p. 16; H.C. Barnard, *The Little Schools of Port Royal* (1913), pp. 45–6, 112–24.

109 Bishop of Toul to Madame de Maintenon, November 1703, HMC, *Stuart*, I, p. 188.

110 Betham to Gordon, 18 April 1705, AAW, Epistolae Variorum, I/34.

Jansenist propositions.[111] The tension between Rome and France resonated through the exchanges between clergymen on the continent. John Ingleton voiced characteristic Sorbonne attitudes when he declared his wariness of priests from the Holy See in October 1722, 'for I have often observed in young men who come from thence a bitterness and intemperat zeal which does not edify'.[112] Conversely, his correspondent Lawrence Mayes reported papal displeasure at such enthusiastic immersion into 'ye air of Paris ... as infectious as ever'.[113] It was no coincidence that English institutions in southern parts of Europe, including the college of the seculars at Lisbon were spared the furore surrounding Unigenitus.

After the attack on the Sorbonne, the patriotic undertone in Jansenist thought rose to a louder pitch, overwhelming the original theological focus of contention. Shifting its focus from 'grace' to 'liberty', the movement underwent a radical inner transformation. The name 'Jansenist' became the watchword for a campaign of self-assertion within the Paris *parlement*: a move to defend 'Gallican liberties' against the caprices of the Pope and the tyranny of Louis XIV, who in deferring to Rome was accused of shattering the sovereign unity of people, church and monarchy.[114] The opening gambit from the *parlement* came in an attack on Unigenitus, inflamed by the excommunication of errant French clergymen in 1718 and, the incorporation of the bull as state law in 1730. But Parisian jurists could unite with reform-minded clergy in declaring excess papal power a threat to the customs of the kingdom. The partisans found new targets, harnessing the grievances of the lesser clergy against episcopal wealth, striking at aloof luxury and absolutism in Versailles, and finding their greatest success with the agitation that brought the expulsion of the Jesuits from France in 1763.[115] Fragmented Jansenist forms flowered in different shapes and hues across Catholic Europe, obtaining royal patronage in Spain, parts of Italy and the German territories: a movement that would scarcely have been recognised by its founders, but which shared the aim of reducing papal power and cutting back the histrionics of baroque piety.[116]

Because of their long immersion in the traditions of political theology within the French Catholic Church, British recusants were undoubtedly

---

[111] Henry Paston to Mayes, 12 October 1714, AAW, Epistolae Variorum, V/56. Duffy, 'The English Secular Clergy and the Counter-Reformation', *JEH*, 34 (1983); John McManners, *Church and Society in Eighteenth-Century France, Vol. 1: The Clerical Establishment and its Social Ramifications* (Oxford, 1998), pp. 45–68; Emmanuel Le Roy Ladurie, *The Ancien Régime: A History of France 1610–1774* (London, 1996 translation), p. 256.

[112] Witham to Mayes, 25 November 1720, AAW, Epistolae Variorum, VII/29; Ingleton to Mayes, 26 October 1722, AAW, Epistolae Variorum, VII/134.

[113] Mayes to Ingleton, 4 June 1726, AAW, St Gregory's Seminary MSS, 563.

[114] McManners, *Church and Society*, I, pp. 210, 213, 519, 601.

[115] Dale K. Van Kley, *The Jansenists and the Expulsion of the Jesuits from France, 1757–1765* (New Haven, 1975).

[116] Chadwick, *Popes and European Revolution*, pp. 392–5.

receptive to aspects of the Jansenist worldview. After the Restoration, English clergymen such as George Leyburne and Serenus Cressy and the Irish Franciscan Peter Walsh had cultivated Jansenist sympathisers in the Sorbonne, in an effort to work out a viable oath to Charles II that would break the dominance of Rome, 'the city of fortune', over the domestic mission, and make themselves more acceptable to Protestant opinion.[117] Walsh had dedicated his Louvain philosophy thesis to Cornelius Jansen, and he drew from Jansenist teachings a language to reconcile submission to temporal authority with the religious conscience, crediting the state with the provision of order on earth, and confining the role of the church to the dispensing of grace to the individual soul.[118] Correspondingly, it was the jurisdictional, rather than theological aspects of Jansenism that most incriminated the Jacobite circle. In voicing their concerns against 'odly principled men' present on the English mission and among 'the king's chaplains' at St Germain, Jesuit missioners alluded not just to the ubiquity of Quesnel's works in their provinces, but to the justifications given to legitimise it. 'The Old Gentleman's [Pope's] authority is not of much weight with 'em', William Kennett warned as early as 1709, adding that 'Infallible is a banished term in these parts.'[119] The stance of Thomas Innes was duly crystallised by scholarly resistance against the right of Rome to introduce the 'intolerable yoke' of the bull Unigenitus – this 'new kind of Inquisition' – which would only bring about 'the decay of solid piety'.[120] Yet Rome could only be resisted effectively when dissidents invoked the protection of an alternative religious authority. Kennett and Richard Plowden reported that the seculars had appealed first to conciliarist tenets concerning the governance of the Church – they would not 'allow of an Obligation of submitting unless decided by a General Council'. However, as they 'chime their discourses with Jansenists abroad', the dissidents were starting to look to another institution for support. Increasingly, 'they claim the King's name'.[121]

As the Jesuit correspondents hinted, it was no coincidence that the allegations of heresy struck at the same set of men who were encouraging the Pretender to seek distance from the Holy See after the disappointments of the 1690s. Echoing the rhetoric of the *Parlement*, Lewis Innes contended that the papacy had erred in seeking to impose Unigenitus on the British colleges without consulting James Edward Stuart, since it was 'a known maxim, received and practised in all Catholick countries that no Decree of this kind can be imposed by any spiritual power without the consent and

---

117 Peter Walsh, *Letter to the Catholics of England, Ireland and Scotland, &c.* (1674); 'Declaration by the doctors of theology at Paris', 1680, Oxfordshire CRO, Belson MSS, F/1/4/MS/32–33.

118 O'Connor, *Irish Jansenists*, pp. 71, 320–35.

119 Kennett to Plowden, n.d., August 1709, EPSJ, Notes and Fragments, 78.

120 Thomas Innes to William Stuart, 4 November 1721, SCA, Blairs, II, 33/121.

121 Kennett to Plowden, July 1709, April 1714, EPSJ, Notes and Fragments, 78, 94.

approbation of the soverain'.[122] Moreover, it had become visibly apparent in the prosecution of John Betham that Jacobite 'Jansenism' extended far beyond the issue of the right to read Quesnel, with the preceptor subject to a set of discrete allegations that related as much to secular policy as questions of spirituality. Betham admitted that his instructions to James Edward included a brusque rejection of the papal infallibility, grounded in the simple formula that 'if the Pope should say two and three makes not five, I will not believe it'.[123] He had insisted that his royal pupil address Protestant fears that Catholics craved to raise the pontiff as 'temporal lord of the world', for 'if they thought our King assumed him infallible, it might prove a paid obstacle to his restoration'. As the canard of foreign allegiance must fall, so too Betham sought to demolish a Catholic dynasty's association with arbitrary rule and 'notions of government incompatible with ye constitution of England', citing specifically the methods used to enforce uniformity in France. Hence, he discoursed against the government in Versailles and the practice of *lettres de cachet*, expressing a preference for the rule of Charles II over that of Louis XIV.[124]

Sentiments of this nature were hardly polemical or unusual in the context of English gentry households, even under Jesuit chaplaincy. The 'Religio Laici' composed by Stephen Tempest attacked papal claims towards 'Temporal powers of which they have no title', as a mark of the 'ridiculous things' practised 'in some churches abroad'.[125] Even in Europe, the theories behind English Jansenism did not amount to an *avant-garde* phenomenon. In previous decades, the attitudes expressed by Betham had gained protection from French clergymen who had travelled in a similar ideological direction, resisting the temporal powers of the Holy See, and resiling from baroque strains in Catholic worship. But by repositioning himself alongside Rome after 1693, Louis XIV had left anti-papal voices within his own kingdom somewhat exposed. Against the background of a continental struggle against heresy, clergymen who wished to remodel the Stuart monarchy in a Gallican form could now be accused of adopting a position 'derogatory to the mandate of the late King Louis XIV'.[126] Thomas Strickland aimed to court both the See of Rome and the Regency at Versailles by highlighting instances of Gallican disobedience within the Jacobite community, cultivating his diplomatic connections by arguing that the elevation of the Stuarts to spiritual status characterised the errors of a 'Jansenisticall part of the clergy'.[127] Robert Witham warned from Douai that their enemies wished

---

[122] Lewis Innes to Bishop Gordon, 14 August 1733, SCA, Blairs, II, 33/118.
[123] Betham, 'Ruff Draught', AAW, St Gregory's Seminary MSS, 238.
[124] Betham, 'Ruff Draught', AAW, St Gregory's Seminary MSS, 239.
[125] Tempest, 'Religio Laici', Tempest MSS (private collection).
[126] Francis Kearney to Santini, 28 July 1716, Vatican Secret Archives, Segretaria di Stato: Nunziatura di Fiandra, 108, fols 385–6.
[127] Robert Witham to Mayes, 18 September 1716, AAW, Epistolae Variorum, VI/45.

to impose Hanoverian claims on the recusant community with a bull 'as formal as Unigentius', with Jesuit reports adding that Strickland pledged to 'keep better order and submission to His Holiness' on the mission than any remedy riddled with the interests of Douai and St Gregory's.[128]

However, throughout the storm of allegations between 1705 and 1718, the Jacobite court failed to wilt under pressure of doctrinal assault. John Caryll and Lewis Innes worked to shield Betham after his dismissal, and in choosing Ingleton, a man cut from the same Gallican cloth, to succeed him as royal preceptor, they signalled that there would be no willing submission to the inquisitors.[129] In 1710, under Caryll's direction, the court issued a passionate defence of the English College, Douai, and by 1713, the Jansenist element in the royal entourage had achieved its own 'expulsion of the Jesuits', with the Society forbidden to join James at Bar-le-Duc, as a body seemingly offensive to English opinion.[130] A rare voice of papal loyalty, Queen Mary Beatrice lamented the hostility to Rome that she found around her, but her protests were unable to stop a vigorous court campaign to restore the reputation of St Gregory's, Paris, instructing English colleges to continue sending their students there, against the wishes of the Holy See.[131] English Jansenism had been created out of a concoction of political and devotional attitudes, experienced on both sides of the Channel. But its most striking contribution to the law of unintended consequences was to open up an avenue into opposition for Catholics disillusioned with the politics of Rome, who nonetheless considered themselves neither heretics to the church nor adversaries in the state.

The afterlives of British 'Jansenism'

Allegations of Gallican and Jansenist heresy hit the Jacobite court hardest while it resided in France, as a ramification of the confessional pressures created in the Bourbon territory. The relocation of the court in Rome in 1718 henceforth calmed the spirit of opposition, and it was perhaps for this

---

[128] Robert Witham to Mayes, 17 October 1716, AAW, Epistolae Variorum, VI/54; Thomas Parker to Richard Plowden, 13 December 1716, EPSJ, Notes and Fragments, 101.

[129] Royal Archives (Windsor), Sheridan, 'Political Reflexions', p. 106; Tunstall to Ingleton, 15 October 1709, AAW, St Gregory's Seminary MSS, 307.

[130] Caryll to Cardinal Caprara, 10 May 1710, AAW, Old Brotherhood MSS, III, 104; Caryll to Cardinal Caprara, 10 May 1710, AAW, Old Brotherhood MSS, III, 104; James Edward, 'Reasons for not assisting at Te Deum at Perth, January 1716', HMC, Stuart, V, p. 12.

[131] Mary of Modena to earl of Mar, 4 October 1717, HMC, Stuart, II, p. 385; Clark, Strangers and Sojourners, p. 241; Ingleton to Witham, n.d., AAW, St Gregory's Seminary MSS, 455; Nairne to Ingleton, 23 February 1722, AAW, St Gregory's Seminary MSS, 477.

reason that William Dicconson, the main defender of the seculars in Stuart circles, had tried to avert the move, proposing negotiation with the German Catholic princes to find an alternative base.[132] With the Jesuits resuming their place at court – the English College, Rome supplying chaplains and confessors – the emphasis of Jacobite officers fell on reviving the sapped strength of religious solidarity. In 1720, the Pope endorsed a decree that obliged the English colleges and convents to commemorate certain national saints venerated in the Jacobite calendar: St Margaret, St Thomas Becket and St Anselm.[133] With the marriage of the Pretender to the Polish princess Maria Clementina, the antagonism of the previous decade appeared to have been drowned out by a renewed search for concord within the Catholic world. After Austrian authorities intercepted the bride *en route* to Rome, the Jesuit rector at the English College, Valladolid felt confident enough to appeal to the Pope against 'ye scandal of ye world', the 'great and manifest ambition of ye ministers of Vienna', bent on 'extinguishing ye male line & Catholick family of ye Stuarts ... which will fill with horror even ye most barbarous nations'.[134] Three years later, with the marriage safely confirmed, the president of the English College could report 'ye unspeakable joy of all Rome' at the birth of Prince Charles Edward, with a new prayer printed, and the pontiff himself saying mass at the English College. The president instructed his brethren in France to 'give notice of this news as you think may be most proper in England & elsewhere'.[135]

Yet the harmony of the first three years did not endure uninterrupted. Although most signs of English 'Jansenism' had loosened their hold on the Stuarts, the frictions that had created the allegations remained largely unsolved. The priest Alexander Paterson predicted trouble over James's desire to maintain a partly Protestant entourage, discerning a spirit of intolerance in Rome that suggested 'the Italians had more faith than charity'.[136] James Edward was felt to be uncomfortable within the religious culture of the Holy See, the Cardinals, in turn, expressed disquiet over the 'Protestant' concessions outlined in the Jacobite settlement proposal, and the Jesuits at the English College lamented the ease with which hotheads on either side could allow altercations between prince and pontiff to escalate into a clash of the religious conscience. Thomas Eberson warned of 'jealousy' between the Jacobites and the cardinals over the governance of the royal chapel, adding that James himself 'appears before His Holynesse only upon

---

[132] William Dicconson, November 1716, HMC, *Stuart*, III, p. 567.
[133] Congregation of Rites for James III, 3 February 1720, Ushaw College, Durham, LC, Roman Documents.
[134] Michael Connell to Thomas Eberson, 8 March 1719, EPSJ, LPC, 73.
[135] Eberson to Plowden, 4 January 1721, EPSJ, LPC, 75.
[136] James Edward to Gualterio, 11 March 1718, BL, Add. MSS, 20,312, fols 47–8; Alexander Paterson to William Stuart, 20 June 1718, SCA, Blairs II, 10/16.

necessary occasions' and 'many talk sourly of ye Old Gent'.[137] Increasingly, the disputes of jurisdiction appeared to have been simply driven inwards, into the affairs of the royal household. In 1724, as a later chapter will show, papal pressure forced the resignation of Andrew Michael Ramsay as tutor to Charles Edward. A year later, a serious crisis ensued with the near-breakdown of the royal marriage after Maria Clementina's refusal to countenance a Protestant governor for her son, and the feeling in her entourage that the Catholic tutor, the younger Thomas Sheridan was offering somewhat less of a rigid defence of the faith than his Noncompounding father.[138] The suspicion that the young prince was being nurtured to hold derisory attitudes towards baroque ceremony brought the Inquisition onto the scene, with rumours of Charles Edward's impending kidnap by Catholic fanatics.[139] By December 1725, the royal household was threatened with the loss of half of its pension, and James had left the Holy See, taking the secular clergyman Lawrence Mayes as his chaplain to Bologna. ''Tis thought he intends to return no more to Rome', lamented the rector of the English College.[140]

In 1726, James *did* resume his place, but the bout of hostility reminded many of his following of their old unhappiness with the temporal interests of the court that now impinged more closely on their lives. The belief – correctly surmised – that Cardinal Giulio Alberoni, one of the most vociferous supporters of Maria Clementina, had been pushing a pro-Hanoverian line at the court of Madrid, served especially to revive doubts as to the integrity of the European ecclesiastical order in world politics.[141] The Pretender authorised William Dicconson to send an account of the affair to Catholics in England, alleging that 'the Pope was acting intirely in the interests of our ennemies', and bemoaning that 'it was to be found his Holiness would carry his resentments to a great extent against the king'.[142] Financial circumstances meant that James Edward could not follow the advice of Lewis

[137] Eberson to Plowden, n.d. 1721, EPSJ, LPC, 76; 'Agent Walton', November 1724, National Archives, State Papers, Italian States, 14, fol. 257.

[138] James Edward to Francis Atterbury, 5 December 1725, Royal Archives (Windsor), Stuart papers, 87/154; Thomas Sheridan to the duke of Wharton, 4 August 1725, Stuart papers, 85/8; Frank McLynn, *Charles Edward Stuart: A Tragedy in Many Acts* (London, 1988), pp. 15–32.

[139] Cardinal Palluci to Gualterio, 24 July 1725, BL, Add. MSS, 21,896, fol. 11; Report of agent 'Walton', December 1725, National Archives, State Papers, Italian States, 15, fol. 497; Lewis Innes to John Hay, 10 December 1725, Royal Archives (Windsor), Stuart papers, 88/15.

[140] Plowden to Eberson, n.d. 1725, EPSJ, LPC, 163; Agent 'Walton', February 1726, National Archives, State Papers, Italian States, 15, fol. 504.

[141] John Hay to the duke of Wharton, 5 January 1726, Royal Archives (Windsor), Stuart papers, 89/32; the duke of Wharton to Hay, 26 January 1726, Stuart papers, 90/21; McLynn, *Charles Edward Stuart*, p. 17.

[142] 'His Majesty's Reasons for a separation from his Queen', November 1725, Lancashire CRO, Scarisbrick MSS, 78/1.

Innes, who urged him to leave Rome permanently, lest his own reputation and the religious freedoms of his following be disabled.[143] However, the Pretender declared it a point of principle to resist papal edicts where they concerned the nurturing of his children: 'it shall now be my greatest and chief desire to give them an education so that my people may be happy in them afterwards', and the courtiers gave vocal applause to some precocious utterances on the part of the young Charles Edward in support of the Paris Parlements.[144] Since the nurturing of his son should be 'under the direction of ye same counsel as his political affairs', it was essential to James that 'any Catholic named for the charge should be of such a Character for Moderation in Religion as less likely to offend'.[145] The conviction was declared repeatedly, even as the Jacobite court became more fully absorbed into the life of the city.

Outside Rome, the colleges and seminaries of the secular clergy still laboured in the shadow of an inquisition. Two decades after the storm hit Douai, secular priests such as Edward Dicconson renewed their appeals to the exiled court as 'the Tribunal which alone can take a legal cognizance', to protect the English faith against papal attack.[146] Questions of heresy continued to tear into the small émigré community left in St Germain. In an ironic epitaph to his father's wounded sense of Catholic universalism, Lord Edward Drummond, son of the earl of Perth, attended Jansenist assemblies and embraced the cause of the parlement, actions for which he was banned from entering Paris. Charles Radcliffe, brother to the 'martyred' Lord Derwentwater, was also expelled from the gates of the city. From the height of the French episcopate, Francis Fitzjames, grandson to James II, imperilled his position as bishop of Soissons with a series of sermons dedicated to the virtue of patriotism, attacking the corruption and decadence on show at Versailles.[147] In the following decade, the allegations ran into Scotland, with the Paris Nuncio fixing his sights upon the Vicars Apostolic, Alexander Smith and James Gordon, and the clergymen ministering to Bishop Nicolson's Highland seminary at Scalan, where Unigenitus was believed to be held in contempt.[148] For all their defiance, the dissidents were

---

[143] Lewis Innes to James Edward, 30 June 1727, Royal Archives (Windsor), Stuart papers, 107/151.

[144] James Edward to Francis Atterbury, 19 November 1727, Royal Archives (Windsor), Stuart papers, 87/97; Stuart papers, 151/124.

[145] Francis Atterbury to James Edward, 2 January 1726, Royal Archives (Windsor), Stuart papers, 89/20; James Edward to Gualterio, 17 September 1727, BL, Add. MSS, 20,311, fols 21–2.

[146] Edward Dicconson to William Dicconson, 13 February 1735/6, Lancashire CRO, Dicconson letter-book, pp. 501–12.

[147] Clark, Strangers and Sojourners, pp. 236, 243, 248–50, 254; Donald Maclean, The Counter-Reformation in Scotland (Edinburgh, 1932), p. 244.

[148] Alphons Bellesheim, History of the Catholic Church in Scotland, trans. D.O. Hunter Blair (4 vols, Edinburgh, 1887–1890), IV, pp. 169, 204, 395, 408.

running against the currents of the time. Forced to leave the Scots College in 1732, to spare the house a full visitation, Thomas Innes surveyed the state of the Catholic world and gave voice to a gloomy vision. The 'fires of division' were billowing through Christendom, he said, and the appearance of 'false prophets' such as Unigenitus was only enhancing wickedness a time when 'the world is too full of division already, not only in Church but in State'.[149] Innes could contemplate only one solution. He prayed for a Jacobite return, not to advance the writ of the Holy See, but to bring shelter and protection for English and Scottish recusants, a chance to 'avoid all the noise' of continental disturbances. When unified Christendom had dissolved into crisis, Innes concluded, 'you know we never had any other physician' but James III.[150]

Conclusion

In tracing the connection between the transformation and prosecution of European 'Jansenism', and the allegations threatening the Jacobite émigrés, the historian is taken into the innate contradictions of early modern recusant identity: the tensions that tore between the universalist outlook of the Catholic Church and the traditions of a community conscious of their unusual minority status in their native kingdom. Most scholars touching upon the affairs of the early modern recusant community have concentrated on the way in which European allegiances threatened to compromise Catholics in England, Scotland and Ireland, leaving a province of doubt in Protestant minds as to whether they could ever represent true, loyal patriots. Yet the discomfort of divided allegiance could turn in both directions. The routes taken by British political and religious exiles after 1688 in France, Rome and the Low Countries forced them to confront a state of disunity in the realm of Catholic Christendom, in which their own distinctively national religious assumptions would be subject to interrogation. The agents, statesmen and literary champions of the Jacobite cause had marched onto the scene carrying hopes to 'turn ye scales' of Europe, and incorporate the justice of the Stuart cause into the mission of a last great crusade. To this end, they failed, and the process of reaction, disillusionment and recrimination was starkly illustrated in the Catholic Jacobite trajectory, from self-proclaimed arbiters of the European conscience to dissidents, critics and suspected guardians of heresy, facing the pressures of religious inquisition.

Before 1688, contention over matters of allegiance had been fought

---

[149] Thomas Innes to Bishop Gordon, 17 October 1732; Innes to William Stuart, 12 October 1733; Innes to Stuart, 19 April 1734; Lewis Innes to Bishop Wallace, 1 November 1732, all Innes letters, SCA, Blairs, II. William Clapperton, 'Memoirs of Scotch missionary priests', 1871, SCA, CC 1/11.

[150] Thomas Innes to Bishop Gordon, 5 January 1726, SCA, Blairs, II.

largely in the realm of theory, because, as John Caryll had commented, the Pope stood 'at a great distance from us'.[151] Now, the presence of the exiled court on the continent, and the high stakes of the Jacobite cause, brought the contested relationship between church, nation and monarchy very directly into their public and private lives. For the population of the Catholic Jacobite diaspora, Rome remained a source of spiritual authority. But, as a voice in politics, the Holy See could only ever be another temporal court, and political circumstances required them to harbour, nurture and restate that distinction in their public addresses. The Pretender himself took up the tools of Gallican rhetoric to disseminate a political manifesto into England, but he spoke at a time when its more contentious expressions were liable to be judged as falling outside orthodox faith. Increasingly, Catholic experiences in the diaspora gave rise to a more natural affinity with the discourse of continental religious dissenters, even if such a stance risked the provocation of the societies that hosted them. Out of this combination arose an explosive mix of conflicts, centring on theological rectitude, the liberty of the free conscience, and the rights of national Catholic kingdoms. The result was that by the middle of the eighteenth century, the institutions of the diaspora continued to protect 'rebellious' forms of the faith, even as they intoned ideals of Catholic unity. Certainly, the conflicts of loyalty towards faith and nation became no less urgent for the exiles transplanted into Catholic Europe, and no less troubling.

---

[151] Caryll, 'Not Guilty', BL, Add. MSS, 28,252, fol. 147.

4. Dr John Ingleton (d. 1739), portrait from Douai Abbey, Woolhampton. Printed by kind permission of Abbot Geoffrey Scott.

5. Stephen Tempest of Broughton (1689–1771), portrait from Broughton Hall, Yorkshire. Printed by kind permission of Henry Tempest.

6

The English Catholic clergy and the creation of a Jacobite Church

The taint of a 'priest-ridden' reputation bedevilled the Jacobite movement. Whispers of shadowy clerics directing secret counsels filtered into the descriptions of St Germain, circulated by Williamite agents within England to fan the flames of the popular imagination.[1] Accounts of Stuart conspiracies claimed to expose the craft of James II's 'fatal scorpions', who 'swarm'd over from Doway and St Omers, greedily gaping after preferments'.[2] Jacobitism gave a new lease of life to old archetypes of Catholic clergymen as exotic figures, inspired by the missionary and martyrological zeal of the Counter-Reformation to hold up a crucifix to Protestant England. This chapter will aim to explore the reality behind these judgements, investigating the connection between the English Catholic clergy and the dynastic contest to produce a political reading of recusant ecclesiastical history in the early eighteenth century. I will argue that, although the Stuart cause did *not* breed religious extremism among the priesthood, it injected new political zeal into their ranks, enough to change the priorities of the domestic mission. Ambitious émigrés used the cloth, the cowl and the mitre to advance dynastic service in the corridors of the *ancien régime*, and formulate a new *modus operandi* that could unite devotion to order, faith and king in the defence of 'our afflicted church, which has suffered so long under an unjust usurpation' as John Ingleton described the struggle.[3]

The study of an active clerical Jacobitism calls into question the existing scholarly depiction of Georgian Catholicism, with its stress on the drift into an insular, denominational status that banished any longing to revive the 'ghost church' of pre-Reformation England. In the words of one leading church historian, detachment from post-Tridentine Europe left the clergy's 'political dreams removed' so that they 'could quietly get on with their

---

1 Macky, *View of the Court*, pp. 14–15; Matthew Prior to the earl of Jersey, 14 February 1698, HMC, *Bath*, III, p. 190.
2 Richard Ames, *The character of a bigotted prince, and what England may expect from the return of such a one* (1691), pp. 1–3.
3 Ingleton to Gualterio, 21 August 1717, BL, Add. MSS, 20,310, fols 180–1.

more traditional skills: priestcraft, education and the religion of the heart'.[4] But the primacy given to sources from the domestic mission has brought neglect of the ideological context to clerical lives, overlooking in particular the direction that came from the diaspora across the seas. While the clerical community at home may have functioned in new urban mission stations and gentry households, I will argue that these centres were viewed as outworks of a larger continental operation, with émigré priests pushing the case to reinvigorate a lost English Church from their strongholds in Paris, Rome and the exiled Stuart court. An alternative reading of recusant ecclesiastical history, incorporating the correspondence of the exiled religious houses, would set the social and pastoral element to priestly lives against the background of a contest for leadership between the rival religious orders, which echoed from the manor houses of England, through the cloisters of the diaspora, to the heights of the Holy See.

This chapter will first survey the involvement of the clergy within the international Jacobite movement: the simultaneous attempt to tighten the grip of the Stuart cause on the lives of Catholics at home and promote the interests of recusants before an international audience. Secondly, I will look at the political component to the running of the exiled colleges and convents, where English clerics exploited the public and material benefits of support from the Stuarts, and strong-armed their pupils towards Jacobite service. However, the chapter will centre on the most controversial project undertaken by the priesthood in exile: an attempt to strip power from Rome and bind recusant religious life financially and jurisdictionally to the Jacobite cause. The secular clergy of France and the Low Countries, closely shadowed by the Benedictine leadership in Paris, began the construction of their own subterranean church in the three kingdoms, seeking to put James Edward Stuart in control of the senior clerical appointments, aiming to establish a cadre of fully ordained bishops, and jousting for positions in the hierarchy. In the wake of controversies over Jansenism and the Hanoverian oath, these projects were stimulated by disenchantment with the court of Rome, and underpinned by trenchant expressions of Anglo-Gallican thought. Moreover, the polemicists aimed to find a public platform for the Catholic faith by cultivating support among Anglican Protestants, and mapping out their ideas in partisan readings of England's Medieval past that echoed the discourse of disaffected High Churchmen. However, as the final part of the chapter will show, their efforts came at a cost: exacerbating strains between the secular and regular clergy, courting controversy with defenders of the Holy See, and heightening the political stakes in an already-fragile moment for recusant England.

---

[4] Lunn, *Benedictines*, p. 142.

The emergence of clerical Jacobitism

The Jacobitism of the clergy represented the culmination of a growing and intimate involvement between the house of Stuart and the English Catholic Church. The accession of James II brought into the open clerical ambitions that had flitted through the court with figures such as Serenus Cressy and Philip Howard. New ambitions for English Catholicism had been developed in a nexus of London cloisters, including the secular clergy chapel at Lyme Street, the Jesuit seminary at Savoy House, and the Benedictine congregations in Whitehall and St James's Palace. Clerical superiors became royal preachers, their sermons communicating the project of religious awakening, and pronouncing the duty of allegiance at a time of political change.[5] In 1689, therefore, with the uprooting of the mission, the mob attacks on schools and chapels, and the imprisonment of the leading ecclesiastics, the Catholic clergy felt the force of the downfall of James II, and a generation of priests wrote that they entered into the spiritual drama of the fallen monarchy. Jesuit letters throbbed with lamentation: 'But behold! An unexpected star blighted these hopes, and destroyed the abundant harvest white to the sickle ... Our Fathers were scattered in flight and sought safety in rough and impassable spots during the depths of winter ... venturing only to travel by night.'[6] For those re-established in exile, the memory of 1688 haunted spiritual commentaries, linking the fortunes of the faith to the shield of legitimate monarchy. Henry Joseph Johnston, Prior of the Benedictine Monastery of St Edmunds, prayed: 'God preserve his Majesty in all doings he undergoes, Restore him to his rightful kingdoms, and with him the Catholick Religion.'[7] From far beyond another sea, on the Quebec mission, the monk Bonaventure Eyston recalled a prophecy whispered to him in Paris, on the accession of James II:

> a man of middle age unknown to me ... took me aside and whispered in my ear 'Do ye know what has been foretold of ye King of England?' 'No', quoth I. 'It has been' said he, 'fortold yt he shall bare ye sway but four years, and for all his destiny to restore ye true Religion to his Dominions, he's not so far to prevail. But he shall get a son, yt shall restore it ...'[8]

The exiled clergy believed that they had found a spark of providence, a

---

5   Ellis, ed., *Ellis Correspondence*, I, pp. 68, 123, II, p. 63; Douai Abbey, Woolhampton MSS, Weldon, 'Memorials', IV, pp. 311–12; Dodd, *Church History*, III, pp. 418–19.

6   Foley, *Society of Jesus*, V, pp. 151–3, 157.

7   Henry Joseph Johnston to Mary of Modena, 1710, Bodleian Library, Carte MSS, 210, fol. 375.

8   'A Note from new France to James III', in Weldon, 'Collection', BL, Add. MSS, 10,118, fol. 34.

last hope that might return true religion to England, in the person of the Jacobite claimant.

For all the jeremiads, the English clergy contrived, in reality, to mount a swift recovery from the effects of the Revolution. In contrast to the outcome of the Popish Plot, the various orders actually experienced less disruption than their lay brethren, and, by 1704, numbers in England had risen to 400, including 250 of the 'secular' clergy, seventy Jesuits, forty Benedictines, thirty Franciscans, and twelve Dominicans, ministering over John Betham's projected figure of 'four score thousand' recusants.[9] This was itself a conservative estimate, since Jesuit records and recent studies of the Benedictines have yielded double the conjectured total.[10] Indeed, the eighteenth-century came to embody the high age of the mission, with priests attaining a foothold for the faith in new urban and provincial centres, not least in London itself, extracting converts out of the lower and 'middling sort', who raised the tally of recusants in the English nation by a purported thirty per cent.[11] However, the priesthood could not operate in isolation from the pressures of the public realm. With a regular supply of informers willing to alert the government to the practice of Catholic rites, a Wiltshire Benedictine voiced his bitterness that: 'My ease, my property and my life are at the disposal of every villain ... tomorrow his humour may vary, and I shall then be obliged to hide in some dark corner, and fly from this land of boasted liberty.'[12] As Vicar Apostolic in London, the ageing Bonaventure Giffard was forced to change his residence fourteen times in 1714 alone.[13] Submitting their thoughts to Cardinal Howard in 1694, the spokesmen for the Scottish clergy had identified the political context behind this plight: 'To whom does a missioner service? To the usurper? Or to his Majesty?'[14] The combination of a galvanised mission with a sense of political fragility made the clergy highly susceptible to the promotion of the Jacobite message.

Clerical networks provided abundant opportunities for Jacobite service. In the decade after the Revolution, the Benedictines Augustine Tempest and Henry Joseph Johnston, marshalled the movement of arms and horses through the northern counties; the former taking the codename 'Pastor

---

[9] Betham to Gordon, 14 September 1704, AAW, Epistolae Variorum, I/149.

[10] Geoffrey Scott has estimated that between 1690 and 1720 an average of 80 Benedictine monks trod the mission, as Revolutionary disruption was reversed, *Gothic Rage*, pp. 41, 82–3. In 1701 the Society could muster 350 members of its English congregation; between 1708 and 1711 it claimed to have ministered to 2,082 baptisms and 2,476 general confessions. Approximately 154 served in England in 1708 as opposed to 92 in 1683. Foley, *Society of Jesus*, V, pp. 195, 215.

[11] Duffy, '"Poor Protestant flies"', pp. 289–91.

[12] J.A. Williams, 'Benedictine Missions in Wiltshire in the 17th and 18th Centuries', *Downside Review*, 78 (1960), pp. 263–73, at p. 263.

[13] Bonaventure Giffard, 7 October 1714, AAW, Epistolae Variorum, VI/67.

[14] Appeal of missioners in Scotland to Cardinal Norfolk, 1699, AAW, Main Series, vol. 36, 154–5.

Storm'.[15] In their guardianship of the manorial chapels, priests nourished the political faith of the recusant elites, using relics, devotional aids and the function of the liturgy to domesticate Jacobite piety. The order of service recorded by Thomas Anderton at Towneley Hall showed the affections of the lay family reconstituted by masses, celebrated five times a month 'Pro Rege Jacobus III', alongside prayers for Jacobite soldiers while the younger sons served in the rebellion of 1715.[16] However, the influence of the priesthood was made most explicit within the diaspora communities across the Channel, among clerics who enjoyed a liberty denied to co-religionists across the British Isles. After 1688, the exiled superiors played an increasingly important directorial role in the running of the mission, and the shift in the power-base was aptly confirmed in 1710, when the Benedictines declared that their general chapter would be held outside England until the Stuarts were restored.[17] Many talented members of the orders spent most if not all of their careers on the continent. As Assistant Prelate to Innocent XII, Bishop Philip Ellis resisted pressure to return to the mission: he had, he said, discovered 'more frequent opportunities to serve my religion and my country ... by reflecting many person's understandings, taking off prejudices, and sweetening sharp humours ... procuring friends and shelter to our cause'.[18] If the forty clerics at St Germain posited by Anthony Hamilton represented an exaggeration, it has been seen how many of the sixteen tutors, confessors and almoners, who served between 1689 and 1713, played a critical role in conditioning the Jacobite political worldview.[19]

Under the direction of court chaplains, Jacobite clergymen advanced across the continent. James II sponsored the establishment of a Benedictine office in the Holy See, approved the choice of Jesuit fathers as rectors of the English College, and dispatched George Witham to Rome as agent of the English secular clergy, armed with pictures of the Prince of Wales, to 'labour in ye concernes of ye Royall family ... for ye common good of our nations and our religion', in 1696.[20] Twenty years later, the Scottish Protestant, Captain John Ogilvie urged James Edward to 'send churchmen of the

---

15 Porteous, 'New Light', pp. 1–60. Nairne Diary, 10 September 1693, National Library of Scotland; Geoffrey Scott, 'A Benedictine Conspirator: Henry Joseph Johnston', *Recusant History*, 20 (1990–1).

16 *Towneley Hall Papers* (CRS, II, 1906), pp. 306–7.

17 Augustine Howard to Francis Rookwood, 19 June 1712, Downside Abbey, Birt papers, A/139; Scott, *Gothic Rage*, p. 50.

18 Philip Ellis to James Edward, 11 April 1695, HMC, *Stuart*, I, p. 69; Ellis to Bonaventure Giffard, 12 January 1702, in W.M. Brady, *Annals of the Catholic Hierarchy in England and Scotland A.D. 1585–1876* (London, 1877), pp. 283–4.

19 List of residents at St Germain, BL, Egerton MSS, 2517; Edward Corp, 'The Jacobite Chapel Royal at Saint-Germain-en-Laye', *Recusant History*, 1993 (1999–97), pp. 528–44, at p. 527.

20 Mary of Modena to Cardinal Altieri, 25 August 1694, HMC, *Stuart*, I, p. 91; George Witham to Lewis Innes, 8 December 1699, SCA, Blairs, II, 63/15; Witham to Innes,

same orders the confessors are of, where they go, and let them cry out of the miseries they suffer … only from an inveterate malice to their religion'.[21] Carrying a moral weight that would be absent from men of secular estate, priest-diplomats could be relied upon to express devotion to the dynastic cause as a point of spiritual fervour. In Rome, William Leslie declared the promotion of Stuart interests 'the pol starre by which I rule myself and my actions', and, in France, the Capuchin monk Archangel Graeme ran himself into penury, sickness and obloquy from fellow priests 'for my attachment to the king'.[22]

It suited the Jacobite leadership that their priests should become powerful figures, to grant social entrée in foreign countries, and allow them to persist in political activity, sheltered from the pressures of their own hierarchies. Captain Ogilvie pressed the court to secure a diocese for Father Graeme, since:

> The Regent never meddles with ecclesiastics, so he will have the power to go where he pleases. I cannot express how useful this will be for the King's service, for he will have all the inferior priests under his subjection, and, consequently, can find out many things …[23]

Accordingly, court officers laboured to obtain abbacies, canonries and bishoprics for their followers of the cloth, and the more enterprising seized the potential of the Jacobite cause to establish the building blocks for high-profile international careers. Philip Ellis argued that an English bishop should always reside in the Holy See, capitalising on the support of Secretary Caryll to gain promotion to the diocese of Segni in 1705.[24] Thomas Southcott, at ease with the mechanics of European power and patronage, took credit for averting the threatened two-thirds levy on recusant lands after the Atterbury Plot in 1723, exploiting friendly aristocratic and literary circles in Paris to gain access to French ministers, whom he convinced to intercede with their allies in the English government, against 'the extirpation of the Roman Catholics … for no other reason but religion itself'.[25] Fortified by his success, Southcott proclaimed confidence in his ability to

---

2 June 1697, AAW, Main Series, 36, 142/577; Cardinal Howard to the earl of Melfort, 17 November 1693, Bodleian Library, Carte MSS, fol. 84.

[21] 'Instructions sent by Capt. John Ogilvie', August 1716, HMC, *Stuart*, IV, p. 63.

[22] Leslie to Innes, SCA, Blairs, I, 152/4; Archangel Graeme to the earl of Mar, HMC, *Stuart*, VII, p. 122.

[23] John Ogilvie to Mar, 29 December 1718, HMC, *Stuart*, VII, p. 680.

[24] Ellis to James Edward, 11 April 1695, HMC, *Stuart*, I, p. 69; Mary of Modena to Pope Clement XII, 6 November 1705, HMC, *Stuart*, I, p. 204.

[25] Southcott to James Edward, 4 January 1723, Royal Archives (Windsor), Stuart papers, 64/127; Southcott to James Edward, 24 May 1723, Stuart papers, 67/35. Southcott to Gualterio, 'Letter on the affairs of Catholics in England', n.d. 1723, BL, Add. MSS, 20, 309, fol. 95; Hatton, *George I*, p. 257.

'save the estates of all the Roman Catholicks in both of the kingdoms'.[26] In gratitude, court officers pressurised Rome to increase funding for the English Benedictines, and assisted Southcott in his pursuit of the abbacy of Ville-neuve, in 1728. 'You monks are cunning folk from what I can find' was the Protestant secretary of state John Hay's arch remark.[27]

For all their cosmopolitan grandeur, Jacobite clerics retained the consciousness of the recusant 'country', typically originating as the younger sons of gentry families. With an influence that ranged eastwards across the Alps and westwards over the Channel, they could provide the bridge between the contrasting theatres of Catholic life. 'I know the greatest part of the Catholick families in London, and those in Oxfordshire, and by their marriages about what age their children will be' boasted Robert Witham from Douai in 1728, as he prepared to enter into England to scour the recu-sant counties in search of pages for 'a certain noble Prince, who has a great love for the English nation'.[28] With these connections, they spun a web that drew the lives of recusants ever closer to the exiled milieu. From Rome, Lawrence Mayes and Philip Howard forged contacts with laymen venturing upon the Grand Tour, and left their own families' English mansions stocked with Stuart portraits and medals.[29] From Paris, Thomas Southcott commu-nicated a vigorous assertion of English Catholic interests at the exiled court, gleaned through communication with families such as the Consta-bles, Howards and Carylls. In 1715, he promoted the possibility of marriage between the Pretender and the widowed recusant noblewoman, Lady Cath-erine Petre.[30] If they pledged to impose Jacobitism upon the lives of their client families, the court's priest-agents also resolved to bring the concerns of recusants reciprocally into an international environment, creating an axis to bind contrasting worlds. Their actions illustrated the way in which cler-gymen might become less the chief victims than the major beneficiaries of the diaspora of 1688.

26 Southcott to James Edward, 9 December 1722, Stuart papers, 63/41.
27 Thomas Southcott to Colonel John Hay, 31 October 1724, Royal Archives (Windsor), Stuart papers, 77/129; Hay to Southcott, 31 October 1724, Stuart papers, 77/132; Hay to Southcott, 28 November 1724, Stuart papers, 78/31.
28 Robert Witham to Mayes, 19 February 1728, AAW, Epistolae Variorum, IX/66.
29 Lord Rivers to Mayes, 18 July 1721, AAW, Epistolae Variorum, VII/65; Philip Howard to Mayes, 20 February 1723; Sir Edward Gascoigne to Mayes, 13 May 1726, AAW, Epis-tolae Variorum, IX/19.
30 Southcott to James Edward, 27 July 1728, 118/112; John Paul Stafford to James Edward, 17 October 1728, Royal Archives (Windsor), Stuart papers, 121/57; South-cott to John Caryll, 30 April 1740, BL, Add. MSS, 28,237, fol. 24; Sir Marmaduke to Constable to John Bede Potts, 27 February 1739, Hull University, Brynmor Jones Library, Constable MSS, DDEV/56/30, fols 147–8.

Jacobite culture in the colleges and convents

The politics of the Jacobite clergy brought the most tangible impact upon the exiled religious houses entrusted with propagating the moral and religious mettle of recusant England. In Rome and Douai, the feast day of St Thomas of Canterbury was seen as an opportunity for royal and patriotic solidarity, with representatives of all the British orders holding prayers together for the Stuarts.[31] The dynastic spirit was supported by persistent Jacobite patronage, and the appearance of new office-holding opportunities. Each of the twelve Jesuits at St Germain had occupied posts at St Omer, while the president of the college, Richard Plowden, was nephew to two senior Jacobite officers, Francis Plowden and John Caryll.[32] From Douai, Edward Dicconson travelled to the exiled court every June to make 'the compliments of the college' upon the Pretender's birthday.[33] Families used the institutions to train their children for the etiquette of court life: John Caryll dispatched his great-nephew to the Scots College in 1699, while Francis Strickland was applauded by Dicconson, as 'a fine innocent child' when he left Douai in 1705, ready for his role as page to the Queen.[34] Obtaining physical and ideological proximity with the Stuart court, clerical institutions sought to strengthen their status as transplanted dots of English land on a foreign soil.

Jacobite politics colluded with the vital but precarious sense of nationhood that animated worship and education at the colleges, and made them resist complete immersion into a foreign Catholic culture. By 1688, many of the exiled institutions were under pressure from their host authorities to submit to greater local control, a conflict made especially evident when the cloisters of Valladolid, Madrid and Seville had fallen under native Jesuit governance, and the originally anti-Jacobite stance of the Spanish throne yielded scant sympathy for English émigrés.[35] The college at Seville was rapidly becoming English in name alone, after its governors stopped admitting students from the British Isles in 1693, and passed the foundation

---

[31] James Gordon to John Betham, 13 March 1703, AAW, St Gregory's Seminary MSS, 203; Eberson to Plowden, 15 February 1721, EPSJ, LPC, fol. 76.

[32] Foley, *Society of Jesus*, V, p. 157; Holt, ed., *Sabran letter-book*, pp. 118, 249.

[33] *Diary of Edward Dicconson*, p. 78; Royal Archives (Windsor), Sheridan, 'Political Reflexions', p. 93.

[34] Gillow and Trappes-Lomax, eds, *Diary of the 'Blue Nuns'*, pp. 244, 413–14; Foley, *Society of Jesus*, IV, pp. 541–9; Philip Harris, ed., *Douai College Documents 1639–1794* (CRS, 113, London, 1972), pp. 95–6; John Caryll to John Caryll of West Harting, 4 March 1700, BL, Add. MSS, 28,226, fols 107–8.

[35] Michael Connell to the General of the Jesuits, 15 May 1720, EPSJ, LPC, 73; Edwin Henson, ed., *The English College at Madrid 1641–1767* (CRS, 29, London, 1929), pp. ix–xii.

into the hands of the Irish Dominicans seventeen years later. The priest Henry Gerard appealed to Cardinal Howard to order a return to the ancient national rules of the foundation, 'or else ye colledge is quite ruined'.[36] In the annals of these houses, references to 'the king' would more commonly refer to the crown in Madrid, even after the rapprochement between Spain and the house of Stuart in 1717.[37] By contrast, the Jacobite experience had become entrenched as a form of national self-assertion in the colleges of France and the Low Countries, closer to the original base of the exiled court, with institutions in Brussels, Antwerp and Ghent emboldened to defy pro-Austrian religious authorities and maintain contact with James Edward Stuart. Edward Dicconson was gratified that dynastic loyalties had prevented the English 'factories' in northern and western Europe going the way of 'the Houses of Valladolid and at Seville, into the Spaniards' hands and management', and superiors drew upon Stuart patronage in their bid to protect congregational rights and exemptions.[38] In 1699, John Caryll marshalled an appeal to Versailles against plans by the bishop of Guise to enforce amalgamation between the Benedictine convent of Dunkirk, and the Irish nuns at Ypres.[39] Between 1721 and 1736, Lady Mary Rose Howard of the Brussels Dominicans used her familiarity with James Edward to 'take yr Powerfull Protection for our security', urging him to lobby Rome on her behalf against the city diocese.[40]

An emotive relationship had therefore developed between the Stuart crown and the English Catholic cloisters – unmatched since the Reformation – to accentuate the exiles' sense of separation from the host societies in which they resided. For the Benedictines, the height of intimacy with the exiled court was attained in 1701, by the burial of James II in St Edmund's, Paris: an act that immortalised the monastery as a place of pilgrims, mysteries and miracles, with the Benedictines paid a yearly sum of 3,000 livres to maintain the chapel, and draw up a detailed record of supernatural occurrences.[41] Under the watch of the monks, the body of the king was treated with a series of actions designed to stimulate reliquary devotion.

[36] 'Paul Savage' [Henry Gerard] to Cardinal Norfolk, 20 June 1693, AAW, Main Series, 36/75; Martin Murphy, ed., *St. Gregory's College, Seville, 1592–1767* (CRS, Southampton, 1992), p. 25.

[37] Henson, ed., *English College at Madrid*, pp. 321, 335.

[38] Witham to Mayes, 25 November 1720, AAW, Epistolae Variorum, VII/29; Dicconson to Stonor, 11 May 1736, Lancashire CRO, Dicconson letter-book, p. 516.

[39] Maura Knightley to John Caryll, 2 January 1700, BL, Add. MSS, 28,226, fols 117–18, 119.

[40] Mary Rose Howard to James Edward, 1 February 1725, Royal Archives (Windsor), Stuart papers, 79/124.

[41] Douai Abbey, Woolhampton MSS, Weldon, 'Memorials', V, pp. 519–21; Weldon, 'Collection', BL, Add. MSS, 10,118, p. 38; Douai Abbey, Woolhampton MSS, Dempster letter-book, 13 February 1718, p. 113; James Edward to Thomas Southcott and Lewis Innes, 1 September 1734, BL, Add. MSS, 38,851, Hodgkin Papers, vol., VI, fol. 127.

James's heart was sent to reside in the convent at Chaillot; his bowels were delivered to St Omer, and parts of his flesh were taken for embalmment to Anne Tyldesley of the Paris Augustinians in 1704.[42] In the next decade, the Douai superiors echoed this process by taking charge of the memory of Lord Derwentwater, printing a prayer in tribute to his life and dispatching a formal account of his death into Rome.[43] The Benedictine nuns of Pontoise assumed possession of his heart, his portrait hung on the walls at Louvain, and in Paris, Lady Tyldesley promised 'devout reflexions on his memory' with the singing of Te Deums every 24th February.[44] If Jacobite martyrs had not passed through the rigorous canonisation tests set in Rome, many exiled superiors retained the judgement of the Jacobean convert Toby Mathew that 'the church walks on with a foot of lead' in such matters, and decided to place the affair in their own hands.[45] The heavenly status of James II and Lord Derwentwater could be legitimised for English recusants by the direction taken in Douai and St Edmund's.

The Jacobite spirit of the colleges was gamely emulated within the ranks of the English nuns.[46] The exiled convents were swiftly established as lynchpins of the diaspora, providing shelter, securing passports, and offering vocations, with the queen herself standing sponsor to girls who wished to take the veil.[47] Commitment to the monarchy informed a style of devotion by turns homespun or starkly baroque. In 1688, Abbess Maria Wigmore of the Antwerp Carmelites had sent a relic of St Teresa of Avila, to be worn in the last days of labour: the miraculous properties would confer safe deliverance for a queen 'whose illustrious virtues are sufficient to reduce to the waie of truth and sanctity the whole nation'.[48] 1725, Gilbert Haydock, chaplain to the Augustinians at Louvain, attested to feverish excitement at the birth of Prince Henry: 'Can the young Prince talk? Are his teeth come through? Has his Majesty trusty friends about him?' These concerns, 'trivial to some' meant much to a house 'entirely devoted to his Majesty's interest, prosperity

---

[42] Douai Abbey, Woolhampton MSS, Weldon, 'Memorials', V, pp. 517–19; Downside Abbey, Annals of the Augustine Convent of our Lady of Syon in Paris, 2 vols, II, p. 164.

[43] Douai Abbey, Woolhampton MSS, Weldon, 'Memorials', V, pp. 515–25; Witham to Mayes, 20 July 1716, AAW, Epistolae Variorum, VI/19.

[44] Downside Abbey, Annals of the English Augustinians at Paris, II, p. 152.

[45] J.T. Rhodes, 'English Books of Martyrs and Saints of the Late 16th and Early 17th Centuries', Recusant History, 22 (1994), pp. 7–25, at p. 23.

[46] The study of English nuns is yielding a rich secondary literature. See especially Claire Walker, Gender and Politics in Early Modern Europe: English Convents in France and the Low Countries (Basingstoke, 2003) and Niall MacKenzie, 'Gender, Jacobitism and Dynastic Sanctity', unpublished PhD thesis, Cambridge, 2003.

[47] Matthew Prior to James Vernon, 18 December 1694, HMC, Bath, pp. 40–1. Mary Skelton to James III, 26 June 1724, Royal Archives (Windsor), Stuart papers, 75/29; Margaret Oxburgh to James III, 2 January 1725, Stuart papers, 79/7.

[48] Maria Wigmore to Mary of Modena, 23 May 1688, BL, Add. MSS, 28,225, fol. 276.

and both temporal and eternal good'.[49] The convents nurtured a tradition of political involvement harking back to the Interregnum, when the sisters of Ghent had provided a mailbox for royalist correspondence, and commitments were resumed after 1688, with Jacobite letters entrusted to Mary Caryll, the abbess at Dunkirk.[50] After 1721, the role was adopted by Mary Rose Howard in Brussels, who obtained papal permission for 'receiving and transmitting letters', against the trepidation of her Dominican superiors and the attention of political authorities in the Austrian Netherlands.[51] Jacobite piety responded to a partiality towards the heroic virtues, glimpsed when English nuns left testimonies of their conventual worlds. From the Poor Clares at Rouen, Mary Joseph Swinburne wrote to her family in 1704 that she had experienced a 'spring of grace' through spiritual ascent: 'I never had a yeare of such joy, consolation, peace, health ... it seems to me all my life before was slavery, stupidity, a dream, a time lost at best.'[52] After 1688, nuns started to speak the language of Jacobite martyrdom. 'We glory to suffer with your Majesty and are banished from our country for our religion', proclaimed Lady Howard, 'we are animated to suffer all persecutions'.[53]

Clerics cut a channel between the world of James III, and the offspring of families, by no means all active Jacobites, but denied the liberty of an education in England. 'We teach all our young gentlemen here their duty to their King next to God', Robert Witham impressed upon the exiled court, assuring parents such as Bernard Howard in Winchester that their sons were 'being bred up in such principles as I know you approve'.[54] The religious superiors chiselled a Jacobite ideology into the scholarly and aesthetic life of their institutions. At Douai, President Witham resolved to dedicate a 1725 translation of the New Testament to 'King James the Third', to render his work 'the Royall Catholick edition' just as 'the Protestant version is called the Royal Bible being dedicated to James the First'.[55] In the weekly prayers of the Benedictine monasteries, in the embroiderings of the royal arms put

[49] Gilbert Haydock to Mayes, 10 April 1725, AAW, Epistolae Variorum, VIII/9.

[50] Dodd, *Church History*, III, p. 496; Lewis Innes to John Caryll of West Harting, 5 June 1708, BL, Add. MSS, 28,227, fol. 73; National Library of Scotland, Nairne Diary, 27 October 1702.

[51] Mary Rose Howard to James Edward, 11 July 1725, Royal Archives (Windsor), Stuart papers, 84/5; 'Dominicana' (CRS, 25, 1927), pp. 208–9.

[52] Mary Joseph Swinburne to Lady Isabella Swinburne, 1 July 1701, Northumberland CRO, Swinburne MSS, 322, Box 5.

[53] Mary Rose Howard to James Edward, 2 June 1724, Royal Archives (Windsor), Stuart papers, 74/113.

[54] Witham to Mayes, 7 January 1721, AAW, Epistolae Variorum, VI/39; Witham to Bernard Howard, 28 April 1734, Arundel Castle, Howard of Norfolk MSS, Howard Letters, 42B.

[55] Witham to Mayes, 22 April 1727 and 5 July 1727, AAW, Epistolae Variorum, IX/67, 94.

together by the nuns at Louvain, and the exchange of relics, crosses and healing 'touchpieces' bearing the Stuart image, the English houses created a ceremonial culture of Jacobite worship.[56] The chalice veil at Ghent was fashioned out of Jacobite military banners, and bore the legend 'J.R.', while the poetry of the Paris Augustinians hailed the Stuart cycle of martyrdom and deliverance, from 'Holy King James' to the 'Mighty Infant', waiting at the threshold of destiny.[57] When James Edward visited Douai in 1710, he met a tumultuous show of support among the students.[58] Thirty years later, the composer John Francis Wade was resident in the college when he composed the carol, *Adeste Fideles* (latterly famous as *O Come, all ye Faithful*), in dedication to Charles Edward Stuart.[59]

The spiritual spring of college life was an 'autodidactic' style of teaching; the communication of an ideal of martyrdom expressed in Benet Weldon's conception of his monastery as 'a citadel or a fortress where we maintain our ground against the devil'.[60] Lessons and prayers kindled imaginative affinity with Englishmen who had perished for the faith, encouraging students to internalise what Weldon called the 'fruitful harvest' sown by 'the seed ... which never fails to bring forth a hundred fold, which is the blood of martyrs'. For all the weight of theological instruction, 'we may fully learn more from men than books'.[61] The English College, Douai exalted the memory of its 130 martyred alumni in the night of fireworks and feasting that commemorated its 150th anniversary in July 1718.[62] The idea flowered in religious theatre – exemplified by Jesuit plays such as the *Captiva Religio* (1614) – which was brought back into the Douai curriculum through the pressure of parents in 1717.[63] Against the background of the dynastic contest, a curriculum hitherto driven towards *internalising* heroism in heart and conscience now obtained a worldly, thoroughly physical goal in the form of Stuart restoration. It was no coincidence that Douai was becoming associated with a constituency in the militant north: the president's cousin George Collingwood was executed in Preston, and the college provided

[56] Gilbert Haydock to Mayes, 30 May 1721, AAW, Epistolae Variorum, VIII/58; Witham to Mayes, 7 January 1721, AAW, Epistolae Variorum, VII/39; Mary Rose Howard to James III, 9 December 1723, Royal Archives (Windsor), Stuart papers, 71/19; 'Prayers for ye Prosperity of ye Royal Family', 1725, Downside Abbey, Birt papers, A/299.

[57] *Annals of the English Benedictines of Ghent* (Stafford, 1894), p. 42; Anne Hardman, *Two English Carmelites* (London, 1939), pp. 111–12; Downside Abbey, Journal of the English Augustinians at Paris, p. 91.

[58] Ingleton to Mayes, 17 January 1716, AAW, Epistolae Variorum, VI/1.

[59] Bennet Zon, 'The Origin of *Adeste Fideles*', *Early Music*, 24 (2) (1996), pp. 279–88.

[60] Douai Abbey, Woolhampton MSS, Weldon, 'Memorials', V, p. 550.

[61] Weldon, *Chronological Notes*, p. 119.

[62] Witham to Mayes, 20 July 1718, AAW, Epistolae Variorum, VI/93.

[63] Witham to Mayes, 20 February 1716, AAW, Epistolae Variorum, VI/ 3; Thomas Brockholes to Mayes, 10 December 1717, AAW, Epistolae Variorum, VI/ 71; Shell, *Catholicism*, pp. 169–72, 188, 199.

sanctuary for refugees, including the vice-president's brother, Roger Dicco-nson.[64] Concurrently, under the presidency of Lewis Innes, more alumni of the Scots College, Paris fought in the Jacobite wars than entered the ministry, an astonishing statistic in view of the clerical function of the school.[65] When asking why so few recusant families made their peace with George I, the answer can be found in their formative years of contact with the exiled world. It was in the colleges that Jacobite priests attained their grip over the recusant community, drumming the virtue of the cause into the minds of their charges in an oral exhortation made all the more vital when censorship curtailed the opportunities for disseminating Stuart doctrine in England.

The campaign for a Jacobite Church

The prime ambition of the Jacobite priesthood was the extension of control over the English Catholic provinces by the powerbase of the exiled court. Inclined to promote a conception of the laity as passive, victimised figures, in need of moral guidance, their concerns intensified in the wake of the 1716 oath controversy, amid fears of a crisis of recusant loyalty in England. To Lewis Innes, the lesson was that the Jacobite court must take a more vigilant role in the affairs of the flock: 'The measures they take and their motives shall be so watched that I hope it shall not be in their power to do anything that may prejudice your Majesty's interest.'[66] As the clergy knew well, Jacobitism was essentially a voluntary position, drawn from a sense of political right rather than religious compulsion. Affairs on the continent made this allegiance appear still more precarious. After 1716, a key part of the agenda of the Catholic Hanoverians was the attempt to isolate the colleges of France and the Low Countries from the English mission, branding them the incubus not merely of treason but of Jansenism. At St Grego-ry's, Paris John Ingleton was threatened by Strickland 'not to talk against K. George and that if he did and brought up his young men in rebellion, he would take care to have him removed from this seminary' by papal decree.[67] By bringing the exiled institutions to heel, Strickland assured Whig minis-ters that it would be possible for the Holy See to 'Govern these missions without any relation to ye Chev_'s interest'.[68] The superiors of Douai and Paris therefore saw themselves under attack alongside their Stuart masters.

[64] Witham to Mayes, 4 March 1716, AAW, Epistolae Variorum, VI/4; Elizabeth Meynell to Mayes, 26 April 1716, AAW, Epistolae Variorum, VI/11.
[65] Halloran, The Scots College, Paris, p. 75.
[66] Lewis Innes to James III, 2 August 1728, Royal Archives (Windsor), Stuart papers, 118/137.
[67] Witham to Mayes, 21 September 1718, AAW, Epistolae Variorum, VI/98.
[68] 'Papers relating to a scheme', BL, Stowe MSS, 121, fols 1–8.

Lewis Innes regretted that, in a time of 'many miseries and afflictions' for the recusant community, Rome had 'taken advantage of your Majesty's present condition to enlarge their own power'.[69] As 'the spring head from whence all these matters flowe', they urged the court to take a more decisive stand in Europe, and protect the imperilled bases of English Catholicism.[70] To this end, they aimed to bring about the creation of a formal Jacobite Church, in a bid to bind the recusant heartlands permanently and institutionally to the monarchy in exile.

For almost twenty years before the oath controversy, notables in the Stuart entourage had begun to raise the idea of a new ecclesiastical structure in the three kingdoms, governed from the exiled court, with senior positions appointed on a mandate to advance the Jacobite interest. The claim was first presented by renewing traditional Stuart claims over the Irish dioceses, when, according to John Caryll, 'in this tyme of usurpation there is more need of Bishops to keep the Priests and layity to their duty' and James II claimed to be receiving 'testimonies from all parties recommending candidates for the vacant Sees'.[71] However, within ten years of the Revolution, voices linked to the exiled court started to expand the dynastic interest into England and Scotland, proposing a formal status for the Vicars Apostolic as nominated agents of St Germain.[72] Writing to the cardinals in 1698, the earl of Perth declared the matter an urgent pastoral concern: the failure of ecclesiastical discipline on the English mission threatened the decay of religious life, among families reduced to poverty and starvation by penal constraints.[73] George Witham duly re-entered Rome in 1701 'resolved to insist on ye K's nomination'.[74] This enterprise sprang naturally from the concerns of the secular clergy, not least the superiors of Douai and St Gregory's, where three of the four original Vicars had been schooled. According to one supporter, William Leslie, 'the making of a Bishop should be a matter of pietie in a Christian prince ... fulfilling the precepts and just teachings of Christ', and the ability of the Stuarts to do so was a touch-

[69] Lewis Innes to James Edward, 17 March 1727, Royal Archives (Windsor), Stuart papers, 105/7.

[70] Edward Dicconson to William Dicconson, 13 February 1735/6, Lancashire CRO, Dicconson letter-book, RCWB/5, pp. 501–12.

[71] 'List of Irish Bishops & when they were named to their severall Bishopricks by his Maty's letters to the Pope', 1694, Bodleian Library, Carte MSS, 208, fol. 246; Caryll, 'Answers to ye Exceptions', n.d. 1697, Carte MSS, 208, fols 249–50; James II to Cardinal Barberini, 1697, Vatican Secret Archives, Fondo Albani, 164, fols 11–19.

[72] Cardinal Howard to the earl of Melfort, 25 August 1693, Bodleian Library, Carte MSS, 209, fol. 66; Betham to James Gordon, 1 December 1704, AAW, Epistolae Variorum I/26.

[73] Perth to Albani, 31 August 1698, Vatican Secret Archives, Fondo Albani, 163, fol. 162.

[74] George Witham to Betham, 15 February 1701, AAW, St Gregory's Seminary MSS, 147.

stone of their enduring legitimate right.[75] In England, lay supporters such as John Belson suggested that reform would help to separate Catholics from 'extraordinary dependence on the Court of Rome', with an administration subject to the 'lawfull magistrates of the temporall realm'.[76] The Benedictine Alban Dawnay recommended the centralised control of clerical appointments developed under the Grand Dukes of Tuscany as the model for the small recusant community.[77] But the argument displayed greater partisanship than its proponents implied. Behind their claims was a lineage of controversy between rival religious orders, stretching back through half a century of contention over the command and control of the domestic mission.

The desire to rebuild an institutional Catholic Church in England represented a cherished goal among leaders of the secular clergy, articulated for seventy years after Bishop Richard Smith sensed an opening to promote the recusant interest through the marriage of Charles I to Henrietta Maria.[78] In a formal 'Declaration of Allegiance' to Charles II in 1661, the seculars had shaped their plea for liberty of conscience through the rhetoric of episcopal discipline, seeking fully ordained bishops to 'inculcate ye due observation of ye Divine Precepts to ye faithfull under their Charge', and so prevent their flock from being 'misled by passion or interest, to mistake opinions for matters of faith'.[79] Both the recusant community and their royal masters would benefit from a visible, accountable church in the three kingdoms, when, they argued, 'Bishops proceed by Canons, where every body may see what they have, or have not power to command.'[80] But this was a contested standpoint, in the context of a mission where approximately forty per cent of working priests were drawn from the regular orders, asserting their own rights and exemptions, and able to engage lay patrons adamant that a beleaguered communion could only prosper in the hands of its patrician families.[81] Henry Howard, the future duke of Norfolk, fulminated against the 'hot-headed fancy' of the seculars' president, George Leyburne, in 1667. 'At a time when 'our Enemyes accuse us for so much dependence in secular affairs from Rome', he was appalled by the prospect of 'alterations or Innovations or new rules of authoritys to bee procured'.[82] In clerical discourse, this argument disclosed the conflict of interpretations between those who traced

---

[75] Leslie to Melfort, 21 October 1692, SCA, Blairs, I, 152/9.

[76] John Belson, 'On a Catholick rule of faith', n.d., Oxfordshire CRO, Belson MSS, F/1/4/MS/57.

[77] Dawnay letter-book, BL, Add. MSS, 28,254, fol. 48.

[78] Questier, Catholicism and Community, pp. 433–72.

[79] Dean and Chapter of the English secular clergy, Declaration of Allegiance to his Majesty (1661).

[80] John Sergeant, 'Concerning the effect of obedience of Roman Catholick priests to orders from Rome', 1687, Oxfordshire CRO, Belson MSS, F/1/4/MS/20.

[81] W.M. Brady, The Episcopal Succession (3 vols, Rome, 1877), III, 309.

[82] Henry Howard to William Leslie, 30 August 1667, Arundel Castle, Howard of Norfolk MSS, Autograph letters, 399.

continuity between the English nation and its pre-Reformation heritage, and others, notably from Jesuit ranks, who saw the mission as virgin territory, glimpsed in the same light as China, Japan and the Americas, to be captured by conversion, confession and heroic individual effort.

However, in the eyes of the seculars, the moral case for the church was transformed by the events after 1685, when, in John Betham's words, the British Isles possessed 'a Catholick king that onely in all Europe now suffers this day for the true faith'.[83] The grounds for action were not straightforward. Although the Vicars Apostolic *were* consecrated as bishops, their position in a Protestant country denied them full episcopal status: they took their titles from ancient Sees of the East – Madura, Aurelianople, and Callipolis – and the Stuart crown enjoyed only a nebulous power of 'recommendation'.[84] Yet the case was grist to the mill for the reformist minds who had immersed themselves in the Gallican theology of the French Church. Writing to Pope Innocent XII in 1699, Betham decried those voices in Rome that denied James II his regal right – 'no concordat ever proving to justify such a pretension' – and concluded his letter with a veiled threat. Should papal intransigence come to public knowledge, it would:

> I fear, cast a blemish on that pontificate which has, in other things, far excelled all we have heard of for many years past. Nothing could be more sensible to us, in the midst of so many afflictions than an accident of this nature, for none can be more concerned for the honour of the Holy See.[85]

To deal with Rome in such a strident manner was dangerous, and, as has been seen, Betham was to pay the price with the allegations of Jansenism that led to his dismissal as royal preceptor. Yet, by this time in St Germain, the seculars had beaten off Jesuit claims in the battle to control the education of the royal household, with the result that the Pretender was being nurtured on Gallican convictions, with books drawn from the curriculum at Douai. For the following thirty years, the issue of the Vicars Apostolic and the royal nominations would equip the secular leadership to inform the Jacobite claimant that it was 'in his interest to support the Clergy [rather] than the Regulars' in the construction of a new ecclesiastical order, when any other outcome would be 'particularly dangerous and hurtful to the Publick Welfare'.[86]

---

[83] John Betham, copy of a petition to the Pope, 1699, AAW, Main Series, 36, 197.
[84] Brady, *Annals*, pp. 140, 151, 201.
[85] John Betham, copy of a petition to the Pope, 1699, AAW, Main Series, 36, 197; see also Betham to James Gordon, 1 December 1704, AAW, Epistolae Variorum, 1/26.
[86] George Witham to John Betham, 20 March 1703, AAW, St Gregory's Seminary MSS, fol. 205; Robert Witham to Lawrence Mayes, 19 February 1728, AAW, Epistolae Variorum, IX/66; Royal Archives (Windsor), Sheridan, 'Political Reflexions', pp. 91–4;

The campaign to resurrect 'dignified Ecclesiasticks' on the English mission was embellished in the letters of Edward Dicconson, and supported in the pamphlets of his protégé Charles Dodd, whose *History of the English College at Doway* (1713) was written in the wake of the Jansenist storm, three years before his *Catholick System of Allegiance* adopted a radical, if somewhat tran-sient, case for a state oath. The episcopal case was presented with full public ramifications. Both authors spoke from a patriotic perspective, celebrating secular institutions as 'the college and hospital of the English nation', the heirs to an Oxbridge tradition of humanist learning that had rebuffed Ital-ianate forms of the Counter-Reformation.[87] To Catholic laymen, the estab-lishment of bishops would be presented as a legitimising influence, bringing them a step closer to 'the tolleration' on the model of Charles II's Decla-ration of Breda, never yet delivered within their own realm. Dodd and Dicconson judged the rise of the Jesuits the catalyst for 'a kind of Anarchy amongst the Papists', which had defeated the hopes of 'the best Catholicks', for engagement with the crown.[88] Drawing his conclusions from a study of High Church treatises, Dicconson suggested that a Catholic hierarchy could work to kindle civil loyalty, proving to Protestants that any lingering traces of 'popery' had been purged from their Catholic fellow subjects.[89] Dodd went a stage further, overtly targeting an audience outside his own confession by assuming the voice of an Anglican chaplain. In a partisan review of the Jansenist dispute at Douai, he struck parallels between the Jesuits and the radical Dissenters perceived by Tories to be tearing at the Anglican communion. The eventual victory of Douai over its accusers could be portrayed as a triumph for the forces of order, against religious fanaticism and social subversion, and made into grounds for establishing a common interest between seculars and High Churchmen, with the lesson, 'let us take a warning at their Divisions'.[90]

The issue, however, gained a further dimension by dint of Dicconson's Jacobite credentials. Using his brother William as the mouthpiece, Dicco-nson aimed to impress upon James Edward Stuart 'what interest he himself has in the affair'. He contended first that Vicars Apostolic on royal appoint-ment would strengthen Catholic support for the Stuarts, obliging recusants to tender their allegiance to the exiled throne. However, the benefits would mainly be reaped in the aftermath of any restoration, when accountable

Edward Dicconson to William Dicconson, n.d. 1736, Lancashire CRO, Dicconson letter-book, p. 513.

[87] Edward Dicconson, 'Maurice Clennog, his life', 1735, Lancashire CRO, Dicconson letter-book, p. 11; RC [Dodd], *History of Doway*, pp. 12–13.

[88] RC [Dodd], *History of Doway*, pp. 16–20; Edward Dicconson to William Dicconson, n.d., Lancashire CRO, Dicconson letterbook, p. 513.

[89] Edward Dicconson to William Dicconson, 29 July 1736, Lancashire CRO, Dicconson letter-book, p. 519.

[90] RC [Dodd], *History of Doway*, p. 32.

ecclesiastics would help the Stuarts show the nation that Catholicism could be made compatible with patriotism and moderation. A diocesan structure for English Catholicism would be 'much less apprehended and by consequence less odious' than anything offered by their regular opponents, and, in demonstrating detachment from Rome, would raise the reputation of all Catholics in the realm.[91] By contrast, Jesuit ideas – 'greatly offensive to men in power' – were rooted in the conflicts of the Reformation, and could never be welcome in the Protestant kingdom. Moreover, the Society's manifesto could be no less dangerous for a restored Catholic monarch. The Jesuit philosophy was, Dicconson contended, anti-monarchic at root ('no bishop, no king') and was stained with the residue of ultramontane principles, propagating the canard that 'deposing kings' was an 'article of faith' within the Catholic Church. Hence, 'Father Parsons his Doctrine' had brought inspiration to the Whig extremists 'who so hotly pursued the Bill of Exclusion in King Charles ye 2d's time': an incorrigible threat to thrones and altars of whatever faith.[92] The return of bishops was therefore made the concomitant of secure Catholic monarchy, the way in which the Stuarts could liberate themselves from claims of a hidden confessional agenda and bring their religion peacefully into the open.

If the blueprint for a new English church originated with clashing interests in the recusant community, it gained dramatic expansion when the exiled Stuarts brought a political component to affairs on the mission. The Benedictines, previously more inclined to the Jesuit position, had gained one of the first four Vicars Apostolic with the election of Philip Ellis, and the monks of Paris subsequently threw their weight behind the drive for episcopal status. Benet Weldon voiced alarm that Rome's failure to grant James III his full powers implied tacit disregard for Stuart legitimacy, 'as if the Royall family had no Power like other Princes in such things'.[93] Wedding itself to Gallican doctrines, the exiled court also began to flex its muscles over ecclesiastical appointments. A letter of 1714, sent to Rome by James III and Lord Perth, asserted that 'it is in my interest that every Bishop, who by his dignity is a peer of my kingdom, should know that he owes his nomination to me'.[94] Fortified by the sense of dynastic support, the ambitions of the clergy became more pronounced. John Ingleton was emboldened to propose systemic changes to the mission, including the creation of

[91] Edward Dicconson to William Dicconson, 13 February 1735/6, Lancashire CRO, Dicconson letter-book, p. 486.

[92] Private commentary, Lancashire CRO, Dicconson letter-book, pp. 463–9.

[93] Whyteford to Leslie, n.d. 1690, SCA, Blairs, I, 133/4; Douai Abbey, Woolhampton MSS, Weldon, 'Memorials', V, pp. 527–8.

[94] James Edward to Cardinal Imperiali, 12 June 1714, HMC, Stuart, I, pp. 329–32; James Edward to Gualterio, 15 November 1711, HMC, Stuart, I, p. 241. See also National Library of Scotland, Nairne Diary, 23 August 1706.

a fully 'national Cardinall', subject to royal appointment.[95] By 1727, Lewis Innes saw the papal appointment of a new cardinal with responsibility for Scotland as 'an encroachment upon your Majesty's indisputable right', and a matter deserving of contention.[96] The presence of the Jacobite cause had given the clerics their mandate to promote ecclesiastical change within the church. Any ensuing controversy could be justified by public and patriotic needs.

The Jacobite Church and the writing of Catholic history

Gallican claims had long rested on a sense of historical authenticity, roused as much by national legend as the finer points of jurisdiction. In France, the image of the past was used to endorse national traditions within the Catholic Church against Tridentine claims to governance. During Henri II's disputes with the papacy in the 1550s, clerics had appealed to the dynastic church of 'Gallo-Francia', a theme renewed in the following generation when the antiquarian Claude Fauchet invoked the example of Merovingian governance, in his *Traicte des Libertez de l'eglise Gallicane*, to reassure those concerned by the Protestant possibility of Henri IV.[97] Later in the seventeenth-century, Maurist Benedictine scholars looked to the Medieval kingdom to legitimise their questions over the temporal authority of Rome.[98] The Jacobite clerics linked to Paris and Douai marched in step with this intellectual turn, and began to prise out the matter of Britain, from calendars and chronicles, annals and hagiographies, to support claims of royal authority within the Catholic Church. Here they sought not merely to generate a dialogue within their own community, but to cultivate a section of English Protestant opinion.

The inspiration behind Catholic Jacobite history emerged from antiquarian enthusiasts in the Benedictine Congregation. Philip Ellis had illuminated his sermons with dedications to 'the apostles of religion in this kingdom, the planters, the propagators and the preservers of it ... a Sigebert, an Alfred and an Ethelred'. He hailed King Edgar as 'to our nation what Romulus was to Rome, Cyrus to ye Persians, Charles ye Great to ye French ... and even Theodosius to ye Christians', a prince whose alliance with St

---

[95] Ingleton to Mayes, 2 July 1717, AAW, Epistolae Variorum, VI/52.

[96] Lewis Innes to James Edward, 17 March 1727, Royal Archives (Windsor), Stuart papers, 105/7.

[97] J.H.M. Salmon, 'Catholic Resistance Theory, Ultramontanism and the Royalist Response, 1580–1620', in Burns and Goldie, eds, *History of Political Thought*, pp. 219–53, at pp. 231–5.

[98] McManners, *Church and Society*, I, pp. 594–6, 605.

Dunstan 'brought ye nation to ye utmost part of flourishing'.[99] This idea was incorporated into the planned official history of the Benedictine Congregation by the young novice Benet Weldon, who promoted the Jacobite cause as the chance to return to a halcyon age of pious Catholic monarchy. Looking back to the cradle of the nation, Weldon summoned up the authorities of William of Malmesbury and Orderic Vitalis and ascribed to a partnership of crown and cloister the creation of the unique 'English Church ... comprehended within the limits of that nation and confined to the nature thereof'.[100] Reconstructing the historical experience of English Catholicism, he argued that the monks had 'collected such rules as were proper for the circumstances they were in, not only from the Roman Church, but also the Gallican or any other', and this sensitivity to national character denoted the creation in England of 'a certain peculiar Congregation very different from the Order of St Benedict in other Provinces'.[101] One of the greatest reasons to lament the Reformation was that it had placed the Benedictines out of royal hands, under Spanish ecclesiastics. Now, 'unwilling to make any application to Rome, where we are much misrepresented', the monks 'cast ourselves at His Majesty's feet ... to do what was his pleasure', and he decried as an 'absurd proposition' the papal desire to retain control, 'so groundless and dishonourable to England'.[102]

Written privately for his fellow monks, Weldon's manuscript echoed an older genre of monastic writing, conceived to assert ancient rights and exemptions, by demonstrating the 'wonderfull familiarity' between 'the Diadem of England and ye Rule of St Bennet'.[103] However, echoes of his concerns moved into commercial print. The antiquarian John Stevens – a former pupil of the Benedictines in Douai – and the secular clergyman Robert Manning both extrapolated ancient regal rights over the ecclesiastical foundations in the kingdom.[104] The most substantial work of Anglo-Gallican scholarship emerged with the four-volume *Church History of England* (1738–1743) written 'especially with regard to Catholicks' by Charles Dodd, then serving as chaplain at Harvington Hall, and obtaining patronage from his Throckmorton patrons, alongside lay supporters of the secular clergy such as Edward, duke of Norfolk and Cuthbert Constable.[105] In a first sign that the

---

[99] Quoted in Douai Abbey, Woolhampton MSS, Weldon, 'Memorials', p. 10, and Weldon, 'Collection', BL, Add. MSS, 10,118, fol. 83.

[100] Douai Abbey, Woolhampton MSS, Weldon, 'Memorials', IV, p. 10.

[101] Weldon, *Chronological Notes*, pp. 18–19.

[102] Ibid., pp. 62, 139; Douai Abbey, Woolhampton MSS, Weldon, 'Memorials', IV, pp. 5–8.

[103] Weldon, 'Collection', BL, Add. MSS, 10,118, fol. 83; Scott, *Gothic Rage*, pp. 58–63.

[104] Stevens, *History of Ancient Abbeys* (4 vols, 1722), I, p. III; Robert Manning, *England's conversion and reformation compared* (Antwerp, 1725).

[105] Charles Butler, *Historical Memoirs of the English, Irish, and Scottish Catholics since the Reformation* (3rd edn, 1822), pp. 451–3; *Catholicon*, 3 (1816), pp. 120–3.

the author was altering his earlier political stance, the work garnered extensive Jacobite subscription through the efforts of William Dicconson in St Germain.[106] Dodd duly found monarchical principles embedded in the foundations of the English Church.[107] He turned to the Saxon kingdoms to discover kings who chaired synods, consecrated bishops, and enacted the laws concerning fasting, feasting and clerical celibacy. Dodd praised Edgar as the model of a reforming prince: berating bishops who had 'slept over their duty' and wielding 'the sword of Constantine' to 'purge the house of God'. The kings of Wessex were hailed as Christian knights, who replenished the church, guarded monastic discipline as they preserved the civil laws, and planted 'pious foundations' across the land.[108]

Royal claims over the church could be sanctioned when Benedictine scholars identified a continuum of thirty 'holy kings' from the Saxon dominions who had either been canonised, attained martyrdom or become monks: Serenus Cressy had believed that no other realm could muster such a 'numerous Variety of Heavenly Patterns' in the performance of her monarchs.[109] The superiors at St Edmund's drew especially on this saintly bloodline, and held up the memory of Edward the Confessor – that 'glorious King and Bountifull Benefactor of the Benedictine Monks' – as a model for the conduct of the house of Stuart.[110] In 1710, Henry Joseph Johnston published a new edition of a *Life* of the Confessor, written a century earlier by the monk, Jerome Porter and now 'Revis'd and Corrected', to fit the genre of 'mirror for princes' literature, with a preface dedicated to the Pretender.[111] To the Jacobite court, the example conferred instruction on the responsibilities of a Catholic ruler: John Caryll reminded his charges that 'in the reigne of Edward the Confessor before the Conquest it is declared that the King ... shall governe and rule the people of the land, and above all the Holy Church'.[112] Edward's actions set the template for subsequent English monarchs – 'priests in ye temporalls' – from Richard II and Henry VI to the

---

[106] William Dicconson to Matthew Beare, 21 January 1742, Lancashire CRO, Scarisbrick MSS, 44/14.

[107] Charles Dodd, *The Church History of England* (3 vols, 1737–42), I, p. xxvi, III, p. 440.

[108] Dodd, *Church History*, I, pp. 33–5, 56–8.

[109] Hugh Serenus Cressy, *The Church History of Brittany from the beginning of Christianity to the Norman Conquest* (1667), Preface, 'priests in ye temporalls'; Douai Abbey, Woolhampton MSS, Weldon, 'Memorials', IV, pp. 9–10.

[110] Douai Abbey, Woolhampton MSS, Weldon, 'Memorials', IV, p. 9; John Gybbon, *Edovardus Redivivus, The Piety and Vertues of Holy Edward the Confessor, Revivd in the Sacred Majesty of King James II* (1688).

[111] Jerome Porter, *Life of St Edward, King and Confessor* (1710 edn), Preface. Henry Joseph to Johnston to Queen Mary of Modena, 1710, Bodleian Library, Carte MSS, 210, fol. 375.

[112] John Caryll, instructions to royal printers, 1710, Bodleian Library, Carte MSS 180, fol. 517.

example of James II, whose 'courage and intrepidity' were daringly defended by Dodd even where his political naivety was conceded.[113] The religion of the Stuarts was judged no bar to the throne of their ancestors, for the constitution of England was threaded with 'Christian laws' forged by the Anglo-Saxon revival of the Catholic faith. The settlement in 1689 insulted the fact that it was a line of Catholic monarchs who had laid the foundations of the civil and ecclesiastical order, and propelled the nation towards its future greatness.

In casting an Anglo-Gallican glow on the gothic bequest, recusant historians presented the narrative to articulate a larger sense of Catholic patriotism. In Porter's rendering of the dream of Bishop Brithwold of Winchester, St Peter bestows the promise of deliverance from pagan Danish assault, since 'the Kingdom of England belongeth unto God himself, who will provide a King according to the Divine Ordinance of his own will and pleasure'.[114] Crossing swords with the scholarship of John Milton and William Fuller, who argued that excessive royal devotion sapped the virility of the body politic, Dodd insisted that if 'building churches, erecting pious foundations, and relinquishing all this life for the sake of the other, must be censured, traduced, and ridiculed, Christianity itself has but a very feeble prop to support it against infidelity and atheism'.[115] Jacobite historians transmitted ideas beyond the court circle. They offered much to hold the affections of recusant readers such as Charles Eyston of East Hendred – a published historian of Glastonbury Abbey – the Haggerston family in Northumberland, who buried their dead on Holy Island, and Stephen Tempest of Broughton, sceptical of exclusively classical or confessional learning, who urged his son that 'the History of your own nation is what you ought to make yourself master of', in order to 'lay up a stock of knowledge, against the Time'.[116] The support for Catholicism not so much as the true faith but as the truly *English* religion provided consolation for Gallican minds angered at neglect by co-religionists in Europe. Bonaventure Giffard pledged to 'awaken ye devotion of my people' by prayers to hallowed Saxon heroes, declaring that 'it shall not be my fault if our saints are not honoured in the future ... No place stands more in need of such powerful advocates'.[117]

These arguments hinted at more than simple patriotic sentiment. The Gallican perspective was applied to offer a striking departure from some

---

[113] Dodd, *Church History*, IV, p. 441; Douai Abbey, Woolhampton MSS, Weldon, 'Memorials', IV, pp. 10–11.

[114] Porter, *Life*, p. 8.

[115] Dodd, *Church History*, I, p. 54; Graham Parry, *The Trophies of Time: English Antiquarians of the Seventeenth Century* (London, 1993), p. 271; R.J. Smith, *The Gothic Bequest: Medieval Institutions in British Thought, 1688–1833* (Cambridge, 1987).

[116] Stephen Tempest, 'Religio Laici', Tempest MSS (private collection); Thomas Hearne to Charles Eyston, 17 May 1717, Bodleian Library, Rawlinson letters, 5, fol. 12.

[117] Giffard to Mayes, 21 November 1717, AAW, Epistolae Variorum, VI/65.

of the older Catholic historical narratives born in the cut and thrust of Reformation polemic. Dodd did not discern a church springing up in isolation from the Holy See, but neither did he genuflect to the 'ultramontane' idea adumbrated in Persons's *Treatise of Three Conversions* (1603) or Richard Verstegan's *Restitution of Decayed Intelligence* (1605).[118] Instead, his defence rested on an argument for English Catholic exceptionalism, appropriating the Protestant foundation myth that attributed the origins of the church to the efforts of Joseph of Arimathea, consolidated by King Lucius, and suggesting that the first contact with the Holy See came with St Peter preaching in Britain after the expulsion of Jews from Rome.[119] Christian foundations, according to this theory, did not fall with the retreat of the Roman Empire, and as the nation was protected by its heroic princes, so providence would guard the primitive roots from which flowered 'the constant tradition of the British Church', free of 'foreign influence or jurisdiction'.[120] The idea carried appeal across the hierarchy of the secular clergy – Bonaventure Giffard evinced particular interest in St Joseph, lamenting that 'we keep no commemoration of him'.[121] However, it posed weighty questions of political theology. By positing an unbroken stream of religion from the Celtic kingdoms to the Saxon heptarchy, scholars would diminish the significance of St Augustine's venture into Kent – once totemic to the Catholic imagination.[122] To Dodd, the See of Canterbury *did* restore links with the continent, but by de-emphasising disputes over doctrine and jurisdiction, he could paint Augustine's mission in an Erasmian hue. British princes were assured that, though many of their customs were 'opposed' to the rites of the Church, Rome was 'willing to sink every minor consideration, and demand their submission only in matters that are essential'. In adopting the Roman computation of Easter and the ritual of baptism, the priesthood would manifest 'their attachment to Catholic unity' and the papacy could 'leave them at full liberty to retain their other customs, and enjoy whatever other immunities they may claim'.[123]

Gallican authors believed that this conception of the English past possessed an importance beyond the confines of their own community. Declaring 'my design being not to enter into any capital quarrel about religion', Dodd searched for the common ground to invite Anglicans into the narrative, and littered his study with references to the scholarly works of Peter Heylin, Jeremy Collier and Bevill Higgons. He looked to court especially the sympathies of the antiquarian school that had developed after

118 Donna B. Hamilton, 'Catholic Use of Anglo-Saxon Precedents, 1565–1625', *Recusant History*, 26 (2002–3), pp. 537–55.

119 Dodd, *Church History*, I, pp. 2–7, 311–17; Parry, *Trophies of Time*, pp. 169–71.

120 Dodd, *Church History*, I, pp. 10, 13, 18, 21.

121 Giffard to Mayes, 21 November 1717, AAW, Epistolae Variorum, VI/65.

122 Daniel Woolf, *The Idea of History in Early Stuart England* (1990), pp. 36–44.

123 Ibid., p. 25.

1660, among High Church divines who sought to separate the Anglican tradition from the ties of radical continental Protestantism, by outlining its uniquely national provenance.[124] Strains of Gallican thought could walk hand-in-hand with the old Laudian anatomy of 'a Church reformed, not made new', alongside a body of High Church writings pervaded with forlorn reflections upon the loss of the monasteries, 'the greatest blow to antiquities that ever England had', in William Dugdale's words.[125] After 1688, the prospect of scholarly commerce was enhanced when converts such as Henry Joseph Johnston – who had undertaken research for Dugdale – and Benet Weldon carried a Tory language into the Catholic fold.[126] The Tory author William Cole was entertained by the Benedictines in Paris, while Thomas Hearne, the Non-juring fellow of St Edmund Hall, Oxford, became the 'Honoured and Much Esteemed' confidante of Charles Eyston, with whom he exchanged Medieval manuscripts and martyrologies, and discoursed on their content.[127]

Common sociability brought the possibility of a deeper ideological convergence between Anglo-Gallicans and High Churchmen. In rewriting the relationship between the See of Rome and the Medieval Church in England, Dodd suggested that the conflict of traditions imposed a false dichotomy, which 'unprejudiced' Catholics and Anglicans were duty-bound to rectify. When the English church had been subject repeatedly to 'true Catholic reformation' under monarchs such as Edgar, he argued that it was already at a substantial remove from Rome, and scarcely in need of Henry VIII's tyrannical and tendentious measures to purge it of papal power.[128] He pressed the case that it was not Roman ambitions, but corruption in the state that historically did most to threaten the liberties of the English Church. The precedent for Tudor conflicts could hence be traced back to 1066, when the Conquest broke the temporal and spiritual balance of the kingdom, and 'church and state began to struggle for power, and make reprisals on one another', while public virtue diminished and cynical courtiers colluded with bishop-placemen to despoil the realm.[129] This vein of anti-Normanism also offered provocative hints over the ecclesiastical condition after 1688, targeting growing Anglican anxieties over the welfare of their church in the hands of its Calvinist or Lutheran kings, latitudinarian bishops and

---

[124] David C. Douglas, *English Scholars* (London, 1939), pp. 1–10, 60, 91–4.

[125] William Dugdale, *The Antiquities of Warwickshire* (1656), Preface.

[126] Scott, 'A Benedictine Conspirator', pp. 59–61.

[127] Thomas Hearne, *Collections*, ed. H.E. Salter (12 vols, London, 1914), VIII, pp. 267–8; Charles Eyston to Thomas Hearne, 15 September 1721, Bodleian Library, Rawlinson MSS, D732.185; Scott, *Gothic Rage*, pp. 159–62.

[128] Dodd, *Church History*, I, pp. 62, 311–17.

[129] Dodd, *Church History*, pp. 80–1.

centralising governments.[130] To the Tory author Bevill Higgons, the brutal conquest of one invading William in 1066 had prefigured the strike of the Prince of Orange, with equally lamentable consequences for the clerical order.[131] To Jeremy Collier, in an account closely followed by Dodd, the oppression and humiliation of St Anselm at the hands of William II brought a thinly veiled parallel with the treatment of the church in the 1690s.[132] In embarking on the search for historical precedents, Jacobite clergymen therefore set the case for reviving an English Catholic Church among the scholarly themes, motifs and controversies disrupting the Anglican public domain. If they did not succeed in their boldest objective – a stream of conversions from the Nonjuring fold – Dodd and his contemporaries still demonstrated the potency of a Gallican argument that based its platform on the familiar narratives of the English regal and ecclesiastical past.

The creation of the Jacobite Church

If it was never formally endorsed on either side of the Channel, the Jacobite Church was becoming a reality in recusant lives soon after the 1715 rebellion. Indeed, the rhetorical conflict fashioned with Rome proved something of a phony war. The Jacobite campaign was able to capitalise on a seeming withdrawal of papal interest in the ecclesiastical state of England; a pusillanimity at appointing Vicars Apostolic that saw no successor elected to succeed Philip Ellis in his Western district between 1705 and 1713, and a four-year hiatus after the death of James Smith in the north in 1711, rendering half the English vicariates vacant for two years.[133] Concurrently, most of the recommendations supplied by James met with little opposition in the Holy See, though the chief advocate of Gallican ideas, John Ingleton, was twice rebuffed, in 1715 and 1717.[134] Whenever a vicariate fell empty, the exiled court was bombarded with letters pressing the case for preferred candidates, and claiming to represent a groundswell of opinion in England.[135]

130 G.V. Bennett, *The Tory Crisis in Church and State 1688–1730: The Career of Francis Atterbury* (London, 1975).

131 Weldon, 'Collection', BL, Add. MSS, 10,118, fol. 410; Douai Abbey, Woolhampton MSS, Weldon, 'Memorials', V, p. 496. The view is shared in Higgons, *Short View*, p. 50.

132 See also Collier, *Ecclesiastical History*, I, p. 101.

133 J.A. Williams, 'Bishops Ellis, Giffard and the Western Vicariate 1688–1715', *Journal of Ecclesiastical History*, 15 (1964), pp. 218–28.

134 David Nairne, 'Mon memoire au Pape', 6 July 1717, Bodleian Library, Carte MSS, 208, fol. 290; Thomas Eyre to Plowden, May 1715, EPSJ, Notes and Fragments, 99; Ingleton to Mayes, 26 October 1722, AAW, Epistolae Variorum, VII/134.

135 Ingleton to Mayes, 6 July 1716, AAW, Epistolae Variorum, VI/18; Ingleton to Gualterio, BL, Add. MSS, 20,310, fol. 173; Southcott to James Edward, 26 December 1722, Royal Archives (Windsor), Stuart papers, 64/65; Robert Witham to James Edward, 21 June 1724, Stuart papers, 83/103.

In 1725, the choice fell upon a Dominican, John Dominic Williams, his campaign spearheaded by the incongruous pairing of the Protestant Bishop Atterbury and the exiled lay leader Charles Radcliffe, whose letters accentuated the sensibilities of 'the North of England, where the King may well want a man of his zeal to keep His Majesty's Roman Catholique subjects firm in their allegiance and their loyalty'.[136] In 1741, James addressed Laurence York, the newly appointed coadjutor of the Western district, acknowledging 'the share I had in your promotion', and adding: 'I doubt not the less in your answering my expectation'.[137] York proffered an understanding of his mandate: 'Nothing can encrease my zeal for your service, in which I would willingly lay down my life, and make my way through any danger ... as long as I should be thought worthy to receive your commands.'[138] This was an ecclesiastical structure that made Stuart allegiance extremely difficult to dislodge.

The pressures of the Jacobite Church crossed into the English country, where priests refused to accept that the power of the Stuart prince was confined to mere 'recommendation'. Thomas Southcott ransacked Weldon's historical theories in his campaign to secure a Benedictine Vicar Apostolic. He insisted to James Edward, 'I would have you remember Father Huddleston's brethren who saved King Charles's body first, and his soul, I hope afterwards.'[139] The fruits of centuries of royalist labour could still be witnessed, he claimed, on the Benedictine mission, where ''tis certain that the best principled families in England are of our education'.[140] Struggles for dominion could be played out among recusant squires, with a breach occurring between two Jacobite houses in 1713, when Roger Dicconson promoted the interests of the seculars in the Lancashire mission against the stance of the Jesuits' patron Sir Nicholas Shireburne.[141] The exiled court was increasingly called upon to arbitrate between the competing bodies, entreated from Suffolk by Sir Francis Mannock, to protect the rights of chaplains and patrons threatened by the Vicars Apostolic, and so enhance 'the good of

---

136 Charles Radcliffe to John Hay, 23 July 1725, Royal Archives (Windsor), Stuart papers, 84/95.
137 James Edward to Matthew Prichard, 27 April 1722, Royal Archives (Windsor), Stuart papers, 59/61; James Edward to Lawrence York, 11 October 1741, Stuart papers, 236/197; Ingleton to Mayes, 17 April 1714, AAW, Epistolae Variorum, V/50.
138 Lawrence York to James Edward, 20 August 1741, Royal Archives (Windsor), Stuart papers, 235/115.
139 Thomas Southcott to James Edward, 4 September 1723, Royal Archives (Windsor), Stuart papers, 68/138.
140 Southcott to James Edward, 17 January 1722, Royal Archives (Windsor), Stuart papers, 55/116; Southcott to James Edward, 22 June 1722, Stuart papers, 60/32; Southcott to James Edward, 9 December 1722, Stuart papers, 63/41.
141 Edward Dicconson to Mayes, 22 October 1713, AAW, Epistolae Variorum, V/32; Edward Plowden to Sir Nicholas Shireburne, 30 March 1717, Lancashire CRO, Shireburne MSS, 97/21.

the mission'.[142] But the competition to control the hierarchy created new animosities between the different orders, at a time when Catholic interests could ill afford internal conflict. In 1714, Jesuit reports warned of altercations in London coffeehouses over the appointments in Vicars Apostolic, hardly the environment in which to flaunt a Catholic clerical identity.[143] From the ranks of the Society, John Constable subjected Dodd's *Church History* to scholarly attack, arguing that the author's reliance on High Church narratives left a work vitiated by 'very bad doctrine', if not overt Jansenism, with a series of 'Insolencies against the See Apostolick'.[144] Sir Francis Mannock lamented that 'as for religion, there is hardly any, they all putting first there different interests. It is melancholy to see and worse to know ye ignorance ye poore are bred up in, in account of these feuds.'[145]

The Jacobite clergy did not create all of these divisions, but they aggravated them, by making displays of loyalty to the Stuarts the watchword to prove one's integrity as a good English Catholic, and vying aggressively with each other to vindicate their credentials. Political activity brought a collision between worlds: the ideological purity of the cloister confronting the lives of compromise and discretion with which recusants were long-habituated. It was increasingly the view of Bonaventure Giffard that those on the continent failed to grasp the messy complexity of life on the mission. 'I have always envied the glory of martyrs' he once conceded: 'Great God! How little these great men understand our circumstances. I wish one of them were in my place for a month or two.'[146] There was an indisputable conflict between the spiritual and political vocation, and on the Benedictine mission, under Southcott's auspices, numbers grew in only one district, the ardently Jacobite northern counties. Further south, where the eye of the government could see further, his pursuit of power came at a cost, sacrificing a small number of individuals, not just from his order, but from the faith itself. William Denis Huddleston resettled in the Anglican ministry and attacked the ambition of priest-politicans in his *Recantation Sermon* of 1729.[147] Faced with such assaults, Southcott confided his nightmare that his enemies 'will do something to bring an outcry upon my back from all our

---

[142] Francis Mannock to William Mannock, 25 August 1725, Royal Archives (Windsor), Stuart papers, 85/92; William Mannock to John Hay, Stuart papers, 12 November 1725, 87/71.

[143] Kennett to Plowden, April 1714, EPSJ, Notes and Fragments, 94.

[144] Clerophilius Alethes [John Constable], *A Specimen of Amendments candidly proposed to the compiler of a work, which he calls The Church History of England* (1751), p. 27.

[145] Sir Francis Mannock to William Mannock, 25 August 1725, Royal Archives (Windsor), Stuart papers, 85/92.

[146] Brady, *Annals*, pp. 152–3; Duffy, 'A Rubb-up for Old Soares', p. 306.

[147] Scott, *Gothic Rage*, pp. 55–6; Duffy, 'Over the Wall', pp. 31–2; William Denis Huddleston, *Recantation Sermon* (London, 1729).

own people, who ... if there be any change at all, will lay it at my door'.[148] He protested that 'my business is peace-making', but continued to tilt at the windmills of 'Strickland, the Bishop [Stonor] and Mr Fenwick' until they totally clouded his horizon.[149] In 1728, James himself confessed to advice from the Holy See not 'to load my conscience with ecclesiastical matters', informed that 'I am no ways in the situation of meddling with the court of Rome'.[150]

Yet the Jacobite Church retained an appeal that was demonstrated by Southcott's re-election on four occasions as Benedictine president, and the monks' choice of Cuthbert Farnworth, Jacobite chaplain to the Swinburnes of Capheaton as his successor.[151] The creation of ecclesiastical bonds remained one of the most effective ways of forging connections between the diaspora and the shires, evidenced when Farnworth's candidacy was backed as vigorously in letters to the continent from his patron Sir John Swinburne.[152] Indeed, even the resolutely Hanoverian Bishop Stonor was compelled to communicate with exiled courtiers, via Edward Dicconson, between 1733 and 1735, in the interest of the seculars' mission.[153] On his retirement in August 1741, Southcott waxed nostalgically of 'my old trade', professing satisfaction that he had kept the Benedictines 'loyal' and Catholic England 'in great peace and tranquillity'.[154] James thanked him, 'I see your heart towards me is always the same', and signalled the appointment of Southcott's ally, Laurence York, as coadjutor of the Western district: a final acknowledgement by the court of one of its most indefatigable servants.[155] Political awareness, as much as pastoral devotion, remained a coveted virtue on the domestic mission into another decade: deemed the vital prerequisite for those who wished to see the rebirth of an organised Catholic Church. This conviction kept alive the pressures on priests, monks and patrons,

---

[148] Southcott to James Edward, 2 September 1723, Royal Archives (Windsor), Stuart papers, 68/138.
[149] Southcott to James Edward, 3 August 1722, Royal Archives (Windsor), Stuart papers, 61/73; Southcott to James Edward, 23 September 1735, Stuart papers, 182/166.
[150] James Edward to Southcott, 12 September 1723, Royal Archives (Windsor), Stuart papers, 69/14; James Edward to Lewis Innes, 28 June 1728, Stuart papers, 117/126.
[151] James Edward to Cuthbert Farnworth, 11 October 1741, Royal Archives (Windsor), Stuart papers, 236/198; 'Will of Ralph Cuthbert Farnworth', 19 April 1745, Northumberland CRO, Swinburne MSS, 322, Box 5.
[152] Sir John Swinburne to anon., 17 September 1741, Northumberland CRO, Swinburne MSS, Box 5.
[153] John Stonor to William Dicconson, 9 November 1736, Lancashire CRO, Dicconson letter-book, p. 88.
[154] Southcott to James Edward, 21 August 1741, Royal Archives (Windsor), Stuart papers, 235/117.
[155] Brady, Annals, p. 292; James Edward to Southcott, 11 October 1741, Royal Archives (Windsor), Stuart papers, 236/116.

renewed the influence of the refugee world, and bound the prayers and the finances of recusant chapels to the service of the exiled dynasty.

Conclusion

In the half-century after the Revolution, the recusant mission was transformed into the front line of an ecclesiastical operation that sought to reclaim the spiritual and doctrinal realms of English Catholicism for the Stuart monarchy, casting the Jacobite cause as the authentic expression, not merely of religious faith, but of patriotic virtue. Uncovering the Jacobite Church exposes a public character to the English Catholic clergy, versed in international diplomacy, patronage and political ambition, which casts doubt on the received picture of a communion falling into denominational status. The silent undergrowth of clerical activity in England was opened up to the pressures of a controversial and charismatic environment in the diaspora, where Jacobite priest-statesmen perceived their community on the verge of ruin, and sought to generate a political strategy to save it. In justifying their ideas, they offered a guide to the exiled Stuarts on how to reconcile Catholic allegiance with the recovery of the British Isles. By mapping out the claims of the Stuarts over their church through the irenic language of the Gallican tradition, Catholic priests were able to adopt a less aggressive and defensive tone towards their compatriots, and aimed to challenge the idea of anti-popery as an inveterate component of English national identity. Yet in sending the priests of the exiled society across the seas, their mission retained a bellicose purpose: an attempt to infuse the blood of Jacobite martyrs into the veins of recusant England. The effect was to make the lives and liberties of their brethren even more fragile.

The Jacobite Church did not attain a lasting place in the eighteenth-century domestic mission, and its hold diminished in the next generation, under Vicars Apostolic such as Richard Challoner, less caught up with the drama of dynastic politics, who proved more scrupulously deferential to Rome. Edward Dicconson complained that this Douai protégé 'I fear, has too much of the Dove', and hoped that by judging 'what is transacted in this business', he may 'see the necessity of joining to his present qualifications so much of the serpent as is recommended from the best Hand'.[156] However, the pursuit of a Jacobite ecclesiastical order satisfied two generations of priests who had drunk deep of Gallican ideas, and looked away from the Holy See towards the spiritual anchorage of national kingdoms. Political circumstances gave their case a lease of life. As long as there was a need to

---

[156] E.H. Burton, *The Life and Times of Bishop Challoner* (2 vols, London, 1909), I, pp. 232, 237; II, pp. 210–11; Sheridan Gilley, 'Challoner as a Controversialist', in Duffy, ed., *Challoner and his Church*, pp. 90–111; Edward Dicconson to Stonor, 30 March 1736, Lancashire CRO, Dicconson letter-book, p. 492.

import a physically distant prince into the imagination of English subjects, as long as the image of religious martyrdom was engraved into that prince's identity, and as long as his cause was sponsored by the ranks of the faithful in exile, the Jacobite movement would cast its shadow over the life of the recusant missionary church.

7

The English Catholic reformers
and the Jacobite diaspora

In 1737, an obscure novel of ideas emerged from the London printing press. Acclaimed in *The Gentleman's Magazine* as 'a beautiful fiction', and 'sublime allegory', *The Adventures of Signor Gaudentio di Lucca* presented a new vision of man's state of nature, centred on the encounters of an explorer with a people 'such as nations might be supposed to be, who had retained in their Purity … the original ideas of the arts, manners, religion and government of the first men in the infancy of the world'.[1] The inhabitants of Mezzorania had survived their own voyage through exile, cast out of their native land by religious persecution. Resettled 'in the midst of the Deserts of Africa', they had constructed a society that was 'the most humane and civilized I ever saw', anchored in agrarian economics, a public meritocracy shaped by intellectual achievement, and the protection of benign, paternalist monarchy. Above all, they propounded toleration in affairs of the soul, being 'not so inhuman as to put people to death, because they were of a different opinion from their own'. These 'gentle and innocent children of nature', had been set free to follow 'the dictates of pure reason' and 'natural justice', and their kingdom had ascended to a state of unity, bound not by coercion, but the love that made each man and woman view each other as part of the same family. Their experience offered a salutary rebuke to 'the horrid injustices, frauds and oppressions among Christians', and the prejudices that lead to Gaudentio's arrest by the Inquisition, for 'unguarded remarks' made on his return to Europe.[2]

By 1737, thanks to Defoe and Montesquieu among others, the utopian undertone to travel literature had been established as a scholarly motif of the century, and most critics assumed that the printing of *Gaudentio* recaptured an early rendering of the theme, from the pen of Bishop Berkeley.[3] But Berkeley was *not* the hand behind this work, and the revelation of its true

[1] [Simon Berington], *The Adventures of Signor Gaudentio di Lucca* (1737); 'A Register of Books for April', *Gentleman's Magazine* (April 1737).
[2] Berington, *Gaudentio*, pp. 4, 27, 32, 76.
[3] Lee Monroe Ellison, '*Gaudentio Di Lucca*: A Forgotten Utopia', *Periodical of the Modern Language Association*, 5 (1935), pp. 494–509, at p. 496.

authorship may have met with less certain appreciation. Simon Berington was a former professor of poetry at the English College, Douai, resettled on the Catholic mission in London, and variations on his book had circulated in manuscript through recusant libraries before penetrating the commercial print domain.[4] For thirty years, his own 'family' had been his fellow émigrés in the Jacobite diaspora. His own benign, paternal monarch was James Edward Stuart, hailed in a previous verse as the 'destin'd champion of providence', who would bring the light of faith and virtue back to his benighted lost kingdoms.[5] Yet, far from offering just another example of Jacobite polemic, Berington's ideas appeared to tilt in a different direction. His discontent fell chiefly upon the papal inquisition, and the Roman cardinals shamed into silence as Gaudentio spells out his meditation on naturalistic innocence.[6] He aimed to locate the principle of religious toleration as an essential tenet of the public spirit lost in European society. In seeking to rediscover Simon Berington's hidden radical voice, this chapter will argue that his imagination was stirred by the religious anxieties that had gripped a wider cohort of his English co-religionists after 1688, when a series of confrontations had exposed the tension that tore between the Catholic orthodoxy of the continent and the devotional culture of recusant communities across the Channel. Berington's thoughts, I will show, were not conceived in isolation: he was merely one of the most prolific of a generation of English Catholic reformers.

In the pamphlet literature of eighteenth-century England, one of the central charges levelled against recusants was that they stood irredeemably opposed to tenets of tolerance, 'politeness' and enlightenment, a group who would 'without doubt have erected such a bloody Tribunal as they have among the Spaniards', should they acquire the opportunity.[7] English Catholicism, in this verdict, offered a pathway into obscurantism: the mark of a faith that was inimical to new learning, brutal towards rival religious opinions and despotic in its politics.[8] For later historians, the Jacobite movement was believed to take this tendency to its height, but even if recusants could throw off the chains that bound them to a failed dynastic cause, the chance of a Catholic 'enlightenment' would still, in received opinion, be stifled by the forlorn nostalgia of a gentry caste whose grip on the faith hastened the trend towards cultural retreat. Yet, in the face of this caricature, the half-century after the Glorious Revolution brought the emergence of a loose network of recusant authors calling for political and religious reform in England and Europe, making a case for acceptance in their native

---

[4] *Diary of Edward Dicconson*, pp. 21–3, 37–8; Kirk, *Biographies*, pp. 20–21.
[5] Simon Berington, *To his Most Excellent Majesty James III* (1708).
[6] Berington, *Gaudentio*, pp. 251, 288–91.
[7] Quoted in Haydon, *Anti-Catholicism*, p. 8.
[8] Andrew C. Thompson, 'Popery, Politics and Private Judgement in Early Hanoverian Britain', *Historical Journal*, 45 (2002), pp. 333–58.

country that was accompanied by rejection of the most oppressive traits found throughout the Catholic continent. Their ideas aimed to reposition the Catholic faith as the friend of 'tolerance', 'reason' and 'natural philosophy' and their vocabulary was redolent of the discourse associated with early 'Enlightenment'. The paradox was that most of them owed their patronage to the magnates of recusant society, while their ranks included many champions of the house of Stuart, who had conceived their ideas in the networks and enclaves of the Jacobite diaspora.

The literature of the English Catholic reformers was embedded in novels, histories, spiritual reflections, treatises on government and appeals for liberty of conscience. The principal contributors were Simon Berington, Nathaniel Hooke, Charles Dodd and George Flint. In Europe, their ideas were promoted by the Benedictine, Thomas Southcott; in England, the same motifs inspired the clergymen Robert Manning and – most famously – the poet Alexander Pope. Their friendships introduced a like-minded Scottish émigré, Andrew Michael Ramsay, into recusant discourse. While some of Pope's Catholic correspondents have received a cursory scholarly attention, they have not hitherto been captured as part of any coherent persuasion in recusant life, nor connected with a cosmopolitan flowering of thought in the Jacobite diaspora: Ramsay has usually been characterised as a figure on the fringes of the 'radical Enlightenment'.[9] However, reformist writings arose out of half a century of contention among the Catholic exiles in Europe, when the interrogation over errant doctrine at Douai and Paris forced a contingent of writers to reappraise their thoughts on the function of civil and religious estates. Their experiences brought them into contact with the dissidents, radicals and indicted heretics of the French Church; in some cases driving them closer to the mystical and Masonic undercurrents of Parisian religious life. Their activities altered the ideological complexion of at least one part of the Jacobite diaspora. In 1723, correspondents of the British envoy to Turin, John Molesworth, were astounded to find among the exiles a type of man who 'though a Jacobite', still 'hated slavery as much as the greatest Whig in England'.[10]

This chapter will begin by uncovering the links of English exiles to a defeated and fragmenting reformist tendency in French politics, before exploring the political and religious models they chose to promote. I will then show how their thoughts came to exercise a disproportionate influence over the rhetoric of the Jacobite movement, as the exiled Stuart princes strained for ways to prove their fitness for a Protestant kingdom. In England, reformist writings helped to incarnate a language of patriotism that could

9 Erskine-Hill, *Social Milieu*, pp. 74–102; Scott, *Gothic Rage*, pp. 114, 154, 184–94; Jonathan I. Israel, *Radical Enlightenment: Philosophy and the Making of Modernity, 1650–1750* (Oxford, 2001), pp. 574, 585.
10 *Abbate* Niccolini to John Molesworth, 3 February 1725, HMC, *Reports on Various Collections*, VIII (1913), pp. 381–2.

justify a push for Catholic involvement in domestic politics. Set within this context, Simon Berington's utopian fantasy can be pinpointed as part of a larger intellectual movement, a recusant variation of the 'Christian *philosophe*' identified in rediscoveries of the Catholic German and Italian states.[11] Though the works of Locke could be found in libraries at Douai and Paris, the scholarship of the reformers owed less to the international lineage of the Enlightenment than a re-engagement with the Erasmian, humanist strain present in recusant tradition.[12] Most of the ideas aroused in the diaspora found echoes in English Catholic discourse because they worked with the intellectual raw materials that had shaped a communion detached from the militant Counter-Reformation and set against Protestant pressures in their own kingdom. In building on these foundations, the reformers pushed their community into a wider rhetorical and intellectual world. Their activities call for a re-evaluation of recusant politics, culture and ideology in the time of the Enlightenment.

English Catholics and French dissidents

As earlier chapters have illustrated, many of the troubles encountered by English Catholics in Europe arose after Louis XIV's bid for rapprochement with the papacy, and the attempt to purge the French domain of ideas deemed destructive of Catholic unity. Most of the English Catholic pronouncements interrogated on suspicion of Jansenism represented beliefs that had been legitimate in France in the 1680s, and commonplace in recusant thought over a longer period. Resistance had its limits, and all of the British institutions signed up, however regretfully, to the bull Unigenitus. But the professor of poetry Simon Berington, left the English College, Douai 'abruptly' and 'without leave' in a sign of protest shortly before the Vice-President committed his signature, venturing to serve as confessor to the Augustinian nuns at Louvain before entering the mission in London.[13] Other émigrés chose to seek solace through scholarship, drawing from their experiences an alternative vision of how the Catholic world ought properly to function, and seeking to reveal to English audiences the state of solidarity that bound recusant writers to the threatened dissidents in Paris.

Catholic literature in England highlighted familiarity with the disaffected traditions within the French Church. The Jacobite journalist, George Flint lamented that Unigenitus had wrenched by 'Malice and Ignorance', a set of 'Propositions that are truly Orthodox' into the realm of heresy: the

---

[11] Blanning, 'Enlightenment in Catholic Germany', pp. 118–26; Davidson, 'Toleration in Enlightenment Italy', pp. 230–49.

[12] Robert Witham to Mayes, 19 February 1728, AAW, Epistolae Variorum, IX/66.

[13] *Diary of Edward Dicconson*, pp. 37–8; John Ingleton, private commentary, 1719, AAW, St Gregory's Seminary MSS, 433.

resultant 'jarrs' and 'dissensions' now constituted a serious threat to Christendom.[14] If Simon Berington's critique appeared allusively in The *Adventures of Gaudentio di Lucca*, his concerns took overt form in a series of tracts written against the inquisition, which he claimed was not 'any part of faith or religion', when no Pope should be allowed to 'bind the nation in chains'. Berington maintained that the extension of temporal powers out of Rome was judged illegitimate by the 'Doctors of Sorbon', and the best 'Catholick Kings and Princes withstood it to the best of their power'.[15] In two pamphlets conceived for English Protestant readers, another Douai alumnus, the historian Robert Manning, maintained that 'Pretensions to infallibility ... neither are now, nor ever were, *Terms of Communion*', when Bede's *Ecclesiastical History* offered 'innumerable instances' of 'Churches maintaining their privileges against the See of Rome'.[16] Manning extrapolated from the Jansenist disputes a view of the distribution of authority within the Catholic world. He argued that the body of the church lay not solely in 'the City, nor the Diocese of Rome', and that even the most dispersed congregations had a right to assist the resolution of doctrinal disputes. Recalling the longer lineage of reformist writings from the Sorbonne, he concluded that 'tho one Church be supreme, yet the best part of Roman Catholicks place not their Infallibility there, but in a General, or Oecumenical Council', with delegates appointed by kings of the faith. The right to act as 'Supreme Judge and Tribunal' could not be established in an arbitrary alliance of Rome and Versailles. Members of the Catholic communion might legitimately oppose any decree that diverged from 'the true spirit of Christianity'.[17]

In appropriating Gallican and conciliarist arguments, the English reformers aimed also to showcase the constitutionalist and patriotic attitudes that they believed equipped recusants to act as faithful subjects within their own realm. The English political nation could find abundant proof that, even in the heart of *ancien régime* Europe, their Catholic compatriots were urgently refuting 'all those infamous characteristicks fastened upon them'. Manning added that withstanding the Holy See over the right to read Jansenist books represented no more a 'derogation' of true spiritual authority 'than a subject is supposed to derogate from the just prerogatives of the Crown when he goes to Law with his Sovereign; or a son to disown the authority of a Father ... when he refuses to obey a command that appears unreasonable to him'. The crucial distinction was that while Rome could wield spiritual authority, the Pope was no 'universal bishop': he enjoyed

---

14 George Flint, *The Shift Shifted*, 23 June 1716; 25 August 1716.
15 Simon Berington, *A modest enquiry into how far Catholicks are guilty of the horrid tenets laid to their charge: how far their principles are misrepresented* (1749), pp. 140–43.
16 Robert Manning, *England's conversion and reformation compared* (1725), pp. 123–7, 141–2.
17 Robert Manning, *The case stated between the Church of Rome and the Church of England* (2 vols, 1721), pp. 92–100, 235–42, 265.

no right to usurp the ecclesiastical freedoms of a nation, just as he had no 'deposing power' to use against temporal princes.[18] The Jansenist disputes carried implications across the Channel. Manning quoted with approval the opinion of the High Church divine Thomas Hearne that 'Popery' could be a legitimate description for the '*Errors* of the Church of Rome', and those mistaken enough to subscribe to them, but not an appellation to account for *all* Roman Catholics.[19] Ten years later, Charles Dodd used his *Church History* to argue that struggles against self-aggrandisement from the Holy See represented an apt way for Protestants to distinguish between 'papists' and 'true, loyal Catholicks'.[20] The closer an individual stood to the genuine articles of the Catholic faith, the better they would perform their duties as a subject of the crown.

While reformers such as Berington could agree with Jansenist partisans on the issue of papal power, their thoughts were starting to sweep beyond the precise concerns that agitated Port Royal and the *Parlement*. Unigenitus would be decried instead in more universal terms as a symptom of the 'inhumanity of persecution for consciences sake' that was all too prevalent across the fractured terrain of Christian Europe. The final editions of George Flint's *The Shifted Shifted* surveyed the Jansenist struggle against the background of west-ward advances from the Ottoman Empire, to identify a providential judgement on the 'oppressing, wronging and butchering' that scarred 'the great Bulwark of Christendom'. While 'Infidels pray', the men that 'call themselves true believers are *cursing* each other … and talk demurely about cutting the throats of our Fellow Christians'. He proclaimed: 'Heavenly God! What is Protestant or Papist, that we so quarrel about Names, whilst not one Soul of us regards the Reality of Religion.'[21] The English 'Jansenist' tendency that had begun as a hard-headed bid to prise power from Rome was transmuting into a deeper critique of the authorities that suppressed and coerced the free conscience. Reflecting on the affair, recusant writers started to foray across a wider corpus of French writings, searching for other resources to sustain a case for protest and reform.

Fénelon, Ramsay and the English Catholic reformers

In moving beyond the narrowly Jansenist canon, Catholic reformers drew their political authority from a varied tapestry of authorities. Manning and Dodd took inspiration from Louis-Ellies Dupin, the religious author indicted by Bossuet with the contradictory position of being 'at once a Jansenist and a demi-Pelagian', whose support for Port Royal moved in step with a call

---

[18] Manning, *England's Conversion and Reformation*, pp. 127–46.
[19] Ibid., p. 205.
[20] Dodd, *Church History*, I, pp. i–iii, 99.
[21] Flint, *Robin's Last Shift*, 18 February 1716, 3 March 1716.

for the tempering of papal powers, denying that 'the Diocese of Rome and the Catholick Church pass for synonymous terms', and beginning a search for dialogue with Protestant churches.[22] The affiliation more likely to resonate with an English readership emerged however, not from Paris, but Cambrai, where Archbishop Francois Fénelon's *Lettre à Louis XIV* (1694) had pronounced a stinging assault on Bourbon policy, castigating the expulsion of the Huguenots, the luxury of Versailles, the limitless succession of wars and the ruin of the economy that had turned France into 'nothing more than a great hospital, devastated and without provisions'.[23] The development of these ideas in his epic *Telemachus*, a thinly veiled satire on Machiavellian abuses of temporal and spiritual power, made Fénelon sufficiently potent a name outside France to attract a visit from the duke on the Marlborough on the campaign trail in 1708. The archbishop's pious rage against religious persecution provided an enticing precedent for recusant scholars hit by the storms at Douai and Paris. From the 'angelic wisdom' of 'Monsieur de Cambray', as Thomas Southcott put in, a contingent of English Catholics could establish the platform of political and religious opinions that would keep reformist ideas alive, beyond the first phase of doctrinal interrogation.[24]

Though recusant links to the Fénelonian tradition developed mainly as a posthumous act of homage, the associations had started to spring up during the lifetime of the archbishop, facilitated by the English Benedictine nuns in Cambrai.[25] From Douai, Edward Dicconson took tutees into the diocese, attracted by Fénelon's reputation as a pedagogue, with the eighth and future ninth dukes of Norfolk obtaining private conversations in 1705.[26] Among the Paris exiles, Lady Elizabeth Hamilton, a patron of Port Royal, received spiritual instruction from the archbishop, and the same networks paved the way for Fénelon's widely reported meeting with the Pretender, attained for the purposes of political education in 1709.[27] Ostensibly, these connections presented something of a conundrum: Fénelon had expressed hostility to the Augustinian worldview that underpinned Jansenist belief. His reputation was defined instead by the quietist mystical way articulated originally by Madame Jeanne Marie Guyon, and spelt out in Fénelon's own *Explication des Maximes des Saints* (1697). Moving away from the Jansenist sense of sin and grace, Guyon's vision of 'Pure Love' attained in private prayer would enable

---

[22] Manning, *The Case Stated*, I, pp. 92–4; Bossuet, *Oeuvres* (Versailles, 1817), XXX, p. 475; Dodd, *Apology*, pp. iii–v; Constable, *Specimen*, p. 27.

[23] J.H. Davis, *Fénelon* (Boston, 1979); Frank E. Manuel and Fritzie P. Manuel, *Utopian Thought in the Western World* (Oxford, 1979), pp. 381–6; Le Roy Ladurie, *The Ancien Régime*, p. 210.

[24] Southcott to Gualterio, 20 September 1722, BL, Add. MSS, 20,309, fol. 11.

[25] Booth to Middleton, 19 May 1709, Bodleian Library, Carte MSS, 210, fol. 116.

[26] *Diary of Edward Dicconson*, May 1705, p. 92.

[27] Ramsay, *Life*, p. 101; Clark, *Anthony Hamilton*, pp. 109–19.

the worshipper to rouse 'an inward Sentiment and Feeling of the Divinity', to take primacy over the outward structures of the Church, and even the mediating function of the sacraments.[28] However, the grounds for convergence between the different persuasions were created by the fragmentation of the original Jansenist persuasion, and the erosion of its theological core. As the movement filtered into a looser spiritual mood, later Jansenism drew closer to the quietist tenets of restrained, perfectionist stillness in worship: a form of mysticism that aimed to soften the baroque mortifications of the earlier Spanish tradition and induce in its disciples a sober, active spirit of faith, loyal to the writings of St Francis de Sales. In France, the Jansenist monk Gabriel Gerberon evinced sympathy for aspects of 'Pure Love' as a feature of the Christian way of life. English Benedictines explored the links between Fénelon's teachings and the creed of the Medieval mystics, Julian of Norwich and Walter Hilton, revived by spiritual authors such as Augustine Baker, Serenus Cressy and Gertrude More, and promoted as the authentic ethos of Catholicism within the British Isles.[29]

The principal source of affinity between Fénelon and the English Catholic reformers concerned shared experiences of the Bourbon heresy hunt. Quietism had been declared heterodox in 1688, and the machinery of Rome and Versailles fell upon Fénelon: confined to Cambrai and monitored by state officials to prevent the dissemination of his ideas.[30] By the middle of the eighteenth century Dominique de Colonia, the Jesuit professor at Lyons, reflected that Jansenists and quietists posed a common threat to church orthodoxy that was far more important than their apparent conflicts in belief.[31] The most prolific English Fénelonian, the Benedictine Thomas Southcott, had once stood under the shadow of Jansenist suspicion, but he now asserted that quietist teachings were winning dozens of Anglican souls to the Catholic faith, and impressed upon his friends at the Sorbonne that the ideals voiced by the archbishop could serve to rebuild the threatened church.[32]

[28] Michael de la Bédoyère, *The Archbishop and the Lady: The Story of Fénelon and Madame Guyon* (London, 1956).

[29] Ramsay, *Life*, pp. 34, 146, 154; Charles Butler, *The Life of Fénelon, Archbishop of Cambrey* (London, 1810), pp. 82–3; Hugh Serenus Cressy, *The Church History of Brittany from the beginning of Christianity to the Norman Conquest* (1667); T.A. Birrell, 'English Catholic Mystics in Non-Catholic Circles', *Downside Review*, 94 (1976), pp. 94–117.

[30] Fénelon, *L'Explication des Maximes des Saints sur la vie intérieure* (1697); A.T. Gable, 'The Prince and the Mirror: Louis XIV, Fénelon, Royal Narcissism and the Legacy of Machiavelli', *Seventeenth-Century French Studies* 15 (1997), pp. 243–68.

[31] In its original French title: *Les aventures de Telemaque, fils d'Ulysse* (1699); Dominique de Colonia, *Dictionnaire des livres jansenistes, ou qui favorisent le jansenisme* (4 vols, Antwerp, 1752).

[32] Southcott to James Edward, 19 January 1722, Royal Archives (Windsor), Stuart papers, 57/64; Southcott to Gualterio, 20 September 1722, BL, Add. MSS, 20, 309, fol. 11; N. Sykes, *William Wake* (2 vols, Cambridge, 1957), I, pp. 261–75.

Southcott was especially struck by the fact that the most resounding defence of Fénelon's ideas was emerging from a fellow Briton in Paris, the Chevalier Andrew Michael Ramsay, who had been drawn into Guyon's circle from the Episcopalian mystic communities of north-east Scotland, and received into the Catholic Church in conversation with the archbishop. Before his first contact with Jacobite society, the publication of a *Life of Fénelon* and an *Essay on Civil Government* had won Ramsay the protection of a circle of reform-minded Paris aristocrats; later he returned to the utopian motifs that had inspired *Telemachus* with his own novel of ideas, *The Travels of Cyrus* (1727), and a *Plan of Education for a Young Prince* (1732).[33] Southcott professed himself captivated: 'Tho I have all the opinion in the world of the late archbishop of Cambray, I look upon Ramsay himself as yet a greater man than he.'[34]

Devotion to the legacy of Fénelon reinvigorated the old networks of émigrés who had suffered at the hands of the anti-Jansenist inquisition. Southcott pursued the acquaintance of Andrew Ramsay, and introduced him to the exiled clergymen in Paris and St Germain, arranging evenings of conversation with John Ingleton and the Innes brothers at the Scots College.[35] In 1723, Thomas Innes drafted the Chevalier into a formal defence of the Scottish mission against Jansenist charges before the Cardinal-Archbishop of Paris: Ramsay concurred that 'though we disagree in some speculative principles', the world should be 'tolerant as to persons of singular merit, virtue and piety'.[36] Later that year, he was co-opted into a campaign to save English Catholics from recriminations after the exposure of the Jacobite 'Atterbury Plot', obtaining access for Southcott to Bishop Fleury and Regent Orleans, and enabling Jacobites to force the matter onto the diplomatic agenda when the ministers consorted with their English allies.[37] Southcott brought his new inspiration before a circle of friends in England, initiating correspondence between Ramsay and Alexander Pope, and emboldening Nathaniel Hooke to translate the Chevalier's works for the London print market.[38] From Douai, Robert Witham spoke of the 'high commendation'

---

33 Andrew Michael Ramsay, *Essay on Civil Government* (1722); Ramsay, *Life of François de Salignac de la Motte Fénelon* (1723); Ramsay, *The Travels of Cyrus* (2 vols, 1727); Ramsay, *A Plan of Education for a Young Prince* (1732); Gabriel Glickman, 'Andrew Michael Ramsay, the Jacobite Court and the English Catholic Enlightenment', *Eighteenth-Century Thought*, 3 (2007), pp. 293–329.
34 Thomas Southcott to James Edward, 19 January 1722, Royal Archives (Windsor), Stuart papers, 57/64.
35 *The Diary of the 'Blue Nuns' or Order of the Immaculate Conception of Our Lady, at Paris, 1658–1710*, ed. J. Gillow and R. Trappes-Lomax (CRS, London, 1910), pp. 84–5.
36 Ramsay to Thomas Innes, 14 September 1720, SCA, Blairs, II, 229/8; see also Blairs, II, 245/11; 266/13.
37 Southcott to James Edward, 9 December 1722, Royal Archives (Windsor), Stuart papers, 63/41; Southcott to James Edward, 24 January 1723, Stuart papers, 64/171.
38 G.D. Henderson, *Chevalier Ramsay* (London and New York, 1952), pp. 126, 135–46.

felt for the Chevalier by the recusant lay leaders introduced to his work.[39] Quietist principles, like aspects of Gallican and Jansenist belief, had been appropriated to provide a voice for the recusant imagination. Ten years after the imposition of the bull Unigenitus, the suppressed reformist impulse had gained a vital lease of life, and its identifying themes would start to resurrect themselves in English Catholic scholarship.

Quietist thought and the case for toleration

For the Jacobite exiles, the defining trait of quietist belief was a revitalised argument for the freedom of religious conscience: a protest against what Ramsay called the 'abominable infractions against human liberty' that was conceived to carry implications for Catholic and Protestant countries alike. Fénelon's disciples asserted the primacy of the religious interior and the 'sovereign mind', over the weapons of coercion and inquisition. The 'inner light' of true religion would respond to no coercive power, he believed, and Christianity would be corrupted by the adoption of any such method. For Ramsay, the persecuting state took the beauty and truth out of religion: encouraging kings to 'intermeddle' in things outside their domain, while its churchmen stripped the universe to a state of 'invincible fatality', reducing faith to mere authority and obedience, and shutting out the hope of redemption from the minds of men.[40] Though churches could supply 'salvatory aids' to worship, it was contemplation alone that unlocked the door to the true spirit of faith: expressed through an Erasmian belief that in the moment of prayer, worshippers would be able to distinguish for themselves between 'the Religion of Means and that of the End, the Forms and the Essence, the Substance and the Ceremonies'.[41] This case for liberty of conscience was made therefore not from the customary Montaignian scepticism about the truth of the universe, but its opposite: a pious hope that the human mind could leap towards the divine mysteries, when unfettered by persecution and inquisition.

Quietist beliefs served to amplify the older form of recusant polemic that had recommended the contemplative traditions of the Catholic faith as a better route to peace and toleration than Protestant discourse founded in a spirit of competition and self-aggrandisement. In 1710, the Benedictine James Maurus Corker had accused the High Churchman Henry Sacheverell of betraying 'the peaceful and charitable Spirit of an upright Christian' after his famous sermon of invective against 'false brethren' within the Dissenting congregations. For Corker, the resort to 'Varnishes and Flour-

---

[39] Robert Witham to Mayes, 3 June 1728, AAW, Epistolae Variorum, IX/72.
[40] Ramsay, *Essay on Civil Government*, pp. 102–105; Ramsay, *Cyrus*, II, pp. 21–7; Ramsay, *Plan of Education*, p. 10.
[41] Ramsay, *Plan of Education*, p. 10.

ishes of Rhetorick and Sophistry', in the attempt to 'bugbear Men out of their Reason and Christian Liberty' was the hallmark of those who 'mistrust the integrity of their Cause', when true religion rested pre-eminently upon the inward experience.[42] However Ramsay's *Travels of Cyrus* offered a startling enlargement of the older argument. The author believed that the revelations glimpsed through 'mental prayer' attacked the basic grounds for persecution, by revealing the underlying unity of the world's faiths, the common tenets of religion scattered through the different nations and cultures. Contemplation, he argued was not merely the centre of Christian religion, but the keystone to all mature spiritual beliefs, alerting worshippers to the same common truth, when 'the Mysteries of Religion' lay concealed 'under Symbols, Hieroglyphics and Allegories'. Glimmerings of the Trinity could hence, be adduced in the mystical thought of Judaism and Zoroastrianism, the last echo of a Golden Age when all faiths were as one, before 'an Immortal Fire of Discord, Hatred and Confusion' left 'Dispers'd, deluded Souls', groping towards a sense of the truth. In a setting clouded by ignorance, Catholicism might represent the surest pathway to God, but outward forms embodied only the shell, not the substance of pure faith. No one church could offer the only source of blessing from a God who had allowed 'different Societies' and 'different systems' to come into being, who 'overlooks all these imperfections and demands only the heart'.[43]

The origin of such ideas lay outside the Catholic Church, and disclosed Ramsay's debt to the Cambridge Platonist Ralph Cudworth's *True Intellectual System of the Universe*, which had captured the Fall as a diaspora of knowledge as much as a descent into sin.[44] However, *Cyrus* also caught the echo of the Figurist doctrines expounded by Jesuit missionaries returning from the Far East, who had drawn attention to the spiritual threads that bound Confucianism to the Judaeo-Christian corpus.[45] Aspects of this vision informed the development of recusant reformist literature, with authors accentuating the grander scheme of human life to justify a call for toleration and moderation in exchanges between different faiths. Simon Berington's reflection on *The Great Duties of Life* (1738) traced commonalities in Jewish and Chaldean teachings, set alongside the scholarship of 'the divine Plato', to extract a narrative of man's salvation so concurrent among 'the most ancient writers, sacred and profane, that it might almost be called the *Vox Populi* of the whole Earth'.[46] Enhancing the theme in his *Dissertations on*

---

[42] James Maurus Corker, *Queries to Dr Sacheverell from North Britain* (1710), pp. 3–6.

[43] Ramsay, *Cyrus*, I, pp. 100–101, 106, 194–8, II, p. 14; Ramsay, *Plan of Education*, pp. 15–17. This vision was given more detailed expression in Ramsay's last, posthumously published work, *The Philosophical Principles of Natural and Revealed Religion unfolded in a Geometrical Order* (2 vols, 1748–49).

[44] Ralph Cudworth, *The True Intellectual System of the Universe* (1678).

[45] Jonathan Spence, *The Memory Palace of Matteo Ricci* (London, 1985).

[46] Simon Berington, *The Great Duties of Life. In three parts* (1738), pp. iii–xix.

the Mosaical creation (1750), he accepted that the 'Deluge' and the 'building of Babel' left divine truth flung haphazardly across the far corners of the earth. However, 'the confusion was of tongues, or languages, not of Confessions', with even inchoate pagan mythologies asserting common belief in 'the unity of the Godhead of any people in the World'.[47] Alexander Pope's *Universal Prayer* found God's 'Temple' in the 'earth, sea, skies' of the world, and saw 'Nature's Incense' rising in the chorus of devotion by 'saint, by savage, and by sage', venerating the common 'Father of all', in whatever church they chose:

> Let not this weak, unknowing hand
> Presume Thy bolts to throw,
> And teach damnation round the land
> On each I judge Thy foe.[48]

The sense of spiritual wealth and variety reaffirmed his desire to be 'a Catholick in the strictest sense of the word ... not a Roman Catholick, or a French Catholick, or a Spanish Catholick, but a true Catholick'.[49] The effectiveness of persecution was confounded by the complexity and fecundity of God's creation: those dreaming of unity must instead wait for man's salvation, when all divisions would finally dissolve.

Ramsay and his supporters had crafted a case for toleration to speak not just for English Catholics, but all dispossessed peoples across Europe, encompassing the French Protestant Pietist and Scottish Episcopalian circles that had shared their devotion to Guyon's legacy.[50] Contemplative teachings wrought an influence especially suited to the plight of a minority congregation under political pressure, creating a language of spiritual forbearance that widened the space for communication with the Protestant majority. In the previous century, the Benedictine Augustine Baker had formed friendships with Nicholas Ferrar's Anglican mystic community at Little Gidding; now the Jacobite poet Jane Barker translated Fénelon's Lenten meditations as *The Christian Pilgrimage* (1718), endeavouring to make the archbishop 'speak English and the dialect of the Church of England'.[51] Barker's work tempered the bellicosity of her Jacobite politics to endorse a quietist vision of stoicism in the face of worldly defeat, sublimating hopes of Catholic revival into a cosmic struggle for spiritual redemption, and ending with a

---

[47] Simon Berington, *Dissertations on the Mosaical creation, deluge, building of Babel, and confusion of tongues, &c* (1750), pp. 31, 122–4.

[48] Alexander Pope, *Universal Prayer* (London, 1738).

[49] Pope to Francis Atterbury, 20 November 1717, in Pope, *Correspondence*, I, p. 453.

[50] Henderson, *Ramsay*, pp. 17–23; Butler, *Life*, pp. 82–3.

[51] Jane Barker, *The Christian Pilgrimage or a Companion for the Holy Season of Lent* (London, 1718), p. 2; King, *Jane Barker, Exile*, p. 157; T.A. Birrell, 'English Catholic Mystics in Non-Catholic Circles', *Downside Review*, 94 (1976), pp. 58–78; 99–117.

prayer for the conversion of the Jews. If the details of the Figurist vision remained somewhat exclusive to Ramsay, Pope and Berington, a larger section of the English Catholic community called upon the quietist idea of the sacred conscience to raise an iron wall between the areas of religious faith in which kings and popes might or might not intervene. Recusant subscribers such as Stephen Tempest of Broughton who acquired The Travels of Cyrus in Paris, could bolster their own Erasmian spirituality through the creed of 'Pure Love'.[52] Nathaniel Hooke – described by William Warburton as 'an odd sort of Catholic, in his own mystic way' – sought explicitly to defend his religious faith by translations of Ramsay, and in 1727, Southcott reported that the earl of Stafford and the duke of Norfolk had 'conceived such a high notion' of the Chevalier that they were envisaging him as an envoy for recusant interests before the Whig government.[53] A Catholic alignment – however retrospective – with the opponents of Louis XIV would meet Pope's advice that 'the best piece of service one could do to our religion' would entail a purge of 'all those artifices and pious frauds which it stand so little in need of, and which have laid it under so great a scandal among our enemies'.[54]

By establishing recusants on a foundation apart from 'popery', quietist precepts could also prepare the ground for a bold appeal for Catholic civil emancipation. Translations from the works of Paris dissidents dramatised the maladies of the French dominion, resuscitating Fénelon's plea to Louis XIV to 'call off your dragoons' from terrified Protestants, but the same arguments could be turned back against an English audience to make a case for seeing recusants in equivalent terms to the harassed Huguenot congregations.[55] If persecution, according to Robert Manning, sprung principally from 'human politicks', cloaked in religious guise, it could appear just as chillingly in the calculations of Protestant 'reason of state'.[56] For Simon Berington, Bourbon oppression struck parallels with the confessional tendencies of the Whig-Hanoverian kingdom, where 'the dreams of enthusiastic Puritans' had unleashed 'furious and fanatical invectives against Papists, in the magazines and common newspapers ... which, one would think, were calculated expressly to excite the populace to cut their throats at once'. By contrast, Berington argued that the Fénelonian conception of

---

52 Tempest library, Broughton Hall.

53 Joseph Spence, Anecdotes, Observations and Characters of Books and Men, collected from the Conversation of Mr. Pope and other Eminent Persons of his Time, ed. Samuel Weller Singer (London, 1964), pp. 199, 211; Southcott to James Graeme, 27 June 1727, Royal Archives (Windsor), Stuart Papers, 107/135. The quietist defence of the Catholic faith was evident in Hooke's privately written Six letters to a lady of quality ... upon the subject of religious peace and the true foundation of it (London, 1816).

54 Pope to John Caryll, 19 July 1711, in Pope, Correspondence, I, pp. 126–7.

55 Ramsay, Life, pp. 13–19.

56 Manning, England's Conversion, pp. 286–7, 310–11.

toleration walked hand-in-hand with England's claim to represent a 'Polite Nation': the defining mark of the ideal would be the dissolution of rancour between religions. No realm, he suggested, could claim the status of 'politeness', until it had laid aside such 'black and bloody aspersions' as 'the odious name of papist', labels that forever beckoned England back to the 'fire and faggots' of the reign of Mary I, and the 'gibbets and butchering knives' that had corrupted the Elizabethan state.[57] Moreover, it was not just the moral moorings of the realm that would be loosened by religious coercion, but its temporal stature, as attested by the state of exhaustion that Louis XIV had bequeathed to the realm of France. Persecuting nations, for Ramsay, turned inexorably into declining nations, because they brought their subjects to the 'dreadful precipice' over which Christian charity, public virtue and civic bonds would ultimately descend.[58]

'Pure Love' and 'pure reason'

Ramsay, Berington and their contemporaries aimed to respond to the changing trends of European learning, and align themselves with contemporary moves to reform the intellectual ethos of the Catholic Church. An appeal to the wisdom of foreign cultures and customs had been prefigured in the works of the Oratorian, Louis Thomassin, and sustained in the historical inquiries of the Maurist Benedictine Jean Mabillon, who framed the conclusion that 'all truth is of God, and by consequence one must love it. All truth can carry us to God.'[59] Such influences had ushered cosmopolitan components into the monastic and university curricula of Catholic Bavaria, Swabia and Franconia.[60] Ramsay's 'universal system' was especially shaped by his membership of the Masonic order: he issued a passionate defence of the fraternity as a model of Christian morality, and used his oration to the Paris Grand Lodge in 1737 to call for the brotherhood across Europe to combine in the creation of an encyclopedia, 'a universal library of all that is beautiful, great, and luminous'.[61] Freemasonry provided the original environment to open up Ramsay's ideas into the recusant world, when

---

[57] Berington, Modest Enquiry, pp. 6–7, 146, 151, 159–62.
[58] Ramsay, Cyrus, II, pp. 21, 153–7.
[59] Chadwick, From Bossuet to Newman (2nd edn, Cambridge, 1987), pp. 57–62; McManners, Church and Society, I, pp. 594–6, 605.
[60] Blanning, 'Catholic Germany', p. 119.
[61] Ramsay, An Apology for the Free and Accepted Masons (1738), in Rev. George Oliver, The Golden Remains of the Early Masonic Writers, illustrating the institutions of the order (5 vols, London, 1847–50), III, pp. 78–133; Virginia Thorpe, 'Mysterious Jacobite Iconography', in Corp, ed., Stuart Court in Rome, pp. 95–110; Peter Partner, The Murdered Magicians: The Templars and their Myth (Oxford, 1982), pp. 103–6; J.M. Roberts, The Mythology of the Secret Societies (London, 1972), pp. 34–8.

many Catholic exiles had found in the lodges an ethos of corporate seclusion not dissimilar to the clubs and fellowships that nourished Jacobite convictions at home. Charles Radcliffe of Derwentwater and the former St Germain courtiers Charles Booth, James Porter, and Thomas Neville joined Ramsay as members of St Thomas's Lodge, founded in Paris in 1726, while émigrés from the Sheldon, Howard and Constable families established affiliate branches in Avignon and Rome. The support of Jacobite émigrés proved critical for the Chevalier in 1734, when he was raised to the Grand Chancellorship of the Freemasons of France.[62] For displaced recusants, advocacy of the Masonic ideal came to entail a denial of the will of Rome; an intimation of discord between the traditions of English Catholicism and the strictest ideas of orthodoxy on the continent confirmed after the Holy See issued its edict against the lodges in 1737.[63]

Masonic and quietist influences inspired Ramsay to break down the barriers between intellectual endeavour and mystical contemplation. He compared prayer to an 'experimentall science', as a quest to 'know', 'feel' and 'desire' the truth, contending that faith and new learning must stand together, as pathways to discover the truth of the universe, when 'contempt for religion can only arise from ignorance'.[64] Ramsay's supporters shared the hope that contemplation might purge the religious interior of delusion and fanaticism, and so elicit the sparks of virtue and learning. Thomas Southcott lamented that 'a great deal of pedantry mingles in the schools of piety and divinity', and wished to imbue in his young nephew instead the education fit for a 'master of philosophy', resolving that 'this young man must see a great deal of the world' beyond the monastic teaching room.[65] Charles Dodd believed that 'there should be nothing in faith contrary to reason', condemning 'undue attachment to Rome' and 'the wrangling temper of schoolmen', as the force behind persecution in the Medieval church and state.[66] Simon Berington suggested that defenders of religion must rise to the challenges posed by Newton, 'the greatest man that has ever appeared in the World since the Revival of Learning and Sciences, and the particular Glory of this Nation'. He duly centred his *Dissertations* on 'the just and rational way of arguing', in a bid to 'shew our Unbelievers that Revelation does not clash with any certain Discoveries of Nature', and argued that scientific strides in the study of geology, which traced the outlines of the

---

62 Thorpe, 'Mysterious Jacobite Iconography', p. 99; A. Kervella, *La Passion écossaise* (Paris, 2002), pp. 165–88; William J. Hughan, *The Jacobite Lodge at Rome, 1735–7* (Torquay, 1910), pp. 9, 10, 37.

63 Margaret C. Jacob, *The Radical Enlightenment: Pantheists, Freemasons and Republicans* (London, 1981), pp. 256–60.

64 Ramsay, *Cyrus*, II, p. 184.

65 Thomas Southcott to James Edward, 25 July 1731, Royal Archives (Windsor), Stuart papers, 147/64.

66 Dodd, *Church History*, I, p. 145; RC [Dodd], *History of Doway*, p. 25.

biblical Flood, ran as one with the rediscovery of Hebrew and Chinese texts to prove the overwhelming logic of a scattered theistic truth.[67]

The Catholic reformers voiced an ideal, rather than a fully formed scientific theory, but if few of them engaged with the intricacies of 'natural philosophy', they nonetheless aimed, in Ramsay's words, to 'surprise and open a sense of great ideas in the truly learned' to be 'followed with very important consequences against Deists, Socinians and Freethinkers'.[68] Berington left his testament in a body of works setting out to confute contemporary opponents of traditional faith – John Toland and Conyers Middleton – by proving that the Christian God, more than the amorphous divinity of the Deists, had the claim to be the 'Supreme Reason' and 'Perfect Creator'. He insisted that the clergy must appeal to that 'substance in man endow'd with the noble faculties of thinking, judging, chusing, forseeing, willing', setting the flock 'free to examine the interior grounds of belief' in the 'just and natural use of Liberty and Reason'.[69] By contrast, the perverse logic of 'this new [Deistic] system of no religion' was exemplified when it strove to deny heavenly truths even as the full scientific wonder of the Christian universe was being gloriously unveiled.[70] Ramsay had, contentiously, described himself as a 'Christian freethinker', and Berington could concur in fixing himself on a territory 'diametrically opposite to both scepticism and credulity'.[71] The stance required an ecumenicist outlook that, he admitted, others in his church had been somewhat reluctant to adopt. However, Berington sought to rise above 'Scholastick' contention: he wished to avoid 'all disputes between Christians and Christians of any denomination', aiming to unite all 'who glory in the dignity of being members of the Christian Church'.[72] For Ramsay, it was a source of frustration that so few Catholic leaders were prepared to rally to this challenge, and, for all the glittering sociability of Paris, he anguished that 'I live in a country where true, noble Christian freethinking, is not allowed, nor even tolerated'.[73]

Against suspicions of heterodoxy, the dispersed society of British recusants represented one religious world that *did* embrace the reformist minds of the continent. Not all of the English monks had responded warmly to Thomas Southcott's promotion of Pope's *Essay On Man*, but he informed the poet that subscription to reformist texts fell in line with the historic Benedictine spirit, when the Order had been the guardian of Medieval learning against

---

[67] Berington, *Dissertations*, Preface.

[68] Ramsay to Thomas Carte, 22 November 1736, Bodleian Library, Carte MSS, 226, fol. 419.

[69] Berington, *Dissertations*, pp. 24, 209–12; Chadwick, *Bossuet to Newman*, pp. 55–7.

[70] Berington, *Great Duties*, p. xxviii.

[71] Ramsay to Carte, 22 November 1736, Bodleian Library, Carte MSS, 226, fol. 419; Berington, *Great Duties*, p. xxxv.

[72] Berington, *Great Duties*, pp. xxxii–xxxiii.

[73] Ramsay to Carte, 22 November 1736, Bodleian Library, Carte MSS, 226, fol. 419.

a descent into superstition.[74] Berington too assured Protestant audiences that recusants received in their colleges 'a liberal and polite education', alert to the highest achievements of a 'Monkish Age' that had preserved 'the remains of the greatest part of learning we have, when the inundation of many barbarous nations had almost extinguish'd it'.[75] Ramsay himself applauded the monastic life in *The Travels of Cyrus*, with a description of a religious house that conflated mystical prayer with 'the study of wisdom' and his links to the Benedictines were immortalised in 1743, when he was given burial in St Edmund's, Paris.[76] Two years later, the congregation's Society of St Edmund's was founded as a forum for scientific and philosophical discussion, to ripen the legacy of exchanges between Southcott and the Chevalier: capitalising on the new spirit of philosophical inquiry promoted by Pope Benedict XIV, its members discoursed on subjects as wide-ranging as Jewish learning, Newtonian theory and the writings of Diderot and Voltaire. In an opening address, Thomas Welch exhorted his brethren 'to take reason for their guide in all things that belong to Nature', to render their theses not in Latin but in English, 'which has been long neglected amongst us to our dishonour' and so reclaim 'the noble and sublime Sciences of Antiquity'. The society's president, Augustine Walker, hoped to push back the 'Gothick deluge' by resurrecting the 'banished arts' that would 'lead us into a new world of light'.[77]

In England, the vision of Catholicism purified through a revival of learning was endorsed by the cohort of recusant leaders who had stocked their libraries with reformist texts from the Paris print market. In Warwickshire, Sir Robert Throckmorton developed his devotion to the writings of Mabillon in a private collection of European books; Stephen Tempest fashioned a similar scholarly self-image, depicted in his portrait holding a copy of Pope's *Essay on Man*.[78] In Oxfordshire, John Belson took from his tutor John Sergeant the *avant-garde* doctrines of the Blacklowist movement, sparked among a generation of scholars at the English College, Lisbon who had sought to meld Catholic theology with the search for 'pure reason', rejecting the 'well-worn path of Aristotelian philosophy', as their college annals put it, to pursue 'whatever is hidden in nature, whatever is abstruse in theology', and so equip the church to meet the challenge of Cartesian thought.[79] At the limits of the tradition, Sergeant and his mentors Thomas

74 Scott, *Gothic Rage*, p. 74.
75 Berington, *Modest Enquiry*, Preface.
76 Ramsay, *Cyrus*, I, pp. 60–61, 84; Henderson, *Ramsay*, 197.
77 Memoirs of the Society of St Edmunds, 1748, Douai Abbey, 4 vols, I, pp. 13–26, 37–49; Scott, *Gothic Rage*, pp. 155–62; Hanns Gross, *Rome in the Age of Enlightenment* (Cambridge, 1990), pp. 239–43.
78 Elizabeth Throckmorton to Sir Robert Throckmorton, 1 April 1720, Warwickshire CRO, Throckmorton MSS, 47/2; Commonplace book, Throckmorton MSS, LCB/72.
79 John Sergeant to John Belson, n.d. 1705, Oxfordshire CRO, Belson MSS, F/1/4/C1/7;

White and Kenelm Digby had risked papal anathema in attempting to push back the authority of Rome from Catholic intellectual life, while White's bid for *détente* with the Cromwellian regime eroded much sympathy in recusant opinion.[80] But admirers such as Belson preserved aspects of the creed. One of his scholarly transcriptions, Sergeant's poem 'To Science, Virtue's hand-maid' saw the study of natural philosophy scattering knowledge of divine truths across the universe 'as blossom from the Rose full blown', conveying an idea of God, just as the first glimpse of 'the early Sun/ New sprung from the cool morning Horizon' heralded the heat of the day. Scientific advances interwoven with Christian virtue could 'rescue nature ... From that originall offence' caused by Adam's 'besotted soul', and lower the 'rare, rich chain of gold ... Wch ties the earth, His foot-stoole to Jove's chair'.[81]

Other, less recondite elements in recusant society were similarly recep-tive to cosmopolitan influences generated on the continent. Indeed a mood of scholarly and scientific inquiry had colluded with the very marginality of the recusant faith, with squires freed from the expenses of public duty and electioneering, and seeking to style themselves exemplars of amateur intel-lectual recreation. When John Aubrey visited Charles Howard of Deepdene in 1672, he described a house 'made not for grandeur', yet 'neat, elegant and suitable to the modesty and solitude of a Christian philosopher'.[82] The history of the Towneley family – receivers of Jansenist books disseminated on the secular clergy mission in York – attested to 150 years of interest in science, translation and collecting, on both sides of the Channel.[83] Richard Towneley's work in the family laboratory left him accredited by the Royal Society as a figure who paved the way for Boyle's Law. His nephew John extended the scholarly tradition in Jacobite exile, joining the salon of Mme Doublet de Breuilpont in Paris, and penning a translation of Butler's *Hudi-bras* in response to a challenge by Voltaire – his labours won the approba-tion of Horace Walpole. John Towneley's nephew Charles flourished late within the diaspora, amassing a collection of antique sculptures, which were donated to the British Museum after his death in 1805.[84] From Lancashire

Sharratt, ed., *Lisbon College Register*, pp. 173–6; Dorothea Krook, *John Sergeant and his Circle: A Study of Three Seventeenth-Century English Aristotelians*, ed. Beverley C. South-gate (1993).

[80] Robert Pugh, *Blacklo's Cabal* (1680).

[81] John Sergeant, 'To Science Virtues Handmaid', Oxfordshire CRO, Belson MSS F/1/4/MSS/77.

[82] John Aubrey, *The Natural History and Antiquities of the county of Surrey* (5 vols, 1719), IV, p. 164.

[83] Richard Short to Richard Towneley, 14 August 1708, Ushaw College MSS, Durham, 1/98; C. Webster, 'Richard Towneley, the Towneley Group and Seventeenth-Century Science', *Transactions of the Historical Society of Lancashire and Cheshire*, 118 (1966–67), pp. 51–76.

[84] Spence, *Anecdotes*, p. 89; J.G. Alger, 'The Towneleys in Paris, 1709–80: The Trans-lator of *Hudibras*', *Palatine Note-Book*, 3 (1883), pp. 84–6.

to Paris, the family had participated in a European theatre of intellectual life that refused to be constrained by the fluctuating definition of orthodox religion. In the hands of such custodians, the dissenting works banished from continental libraries could be sheltered from the pressures of the inquisition, and resuscitated in recusant households. Though they took a variety of different intellectual routes, the squires showed how the vision of Catholic faith driven towards 'pure reason' was not confined to secret ruminations in colleges and monasteries.

The quietists, the Jacobite court and the revival of kingship

In exploring 'the true Anatomy of Man', Fénelon's disciples dwelt upon the earthly, as much as the spiritual estate. The break with earlier forms of Counter-Reformation mysticism came because quietist doctrines were conceived to flourish not in self-lacerating retreat but as responses to the temporal world: 'animated by the tender sentiments of a newborn love we exercise ourselves with a noble and masculine vigour in the labours of active virtue'.[85] Andrew Ramsay argued that peaceful self-examination would calm the rages within a body politic as inside an individual's soul, when civil distemper came from an inability to see beyond the imperfect forms and shadows of a fallen state. In the moment of prayer 'the Soul will bring forth, as Plato says, not the Shadows of Virtue, but the Virtues themselves', fostering the 'Desire of imitating the Sovereign Truth, Justice and Goodness'.[86] Cultivation of the inward spirit would allow the worshipper to extrapolate a sense of the values that must govern human life: 'From these same principles are derived all the Moral and Social duties, both of publick and private life: from the same source flow all the Maxims of Politicks and Government.'[87] It was most explicitly the political idea drawn out of quietist teachings that fostered correspondence between Paris dissidents and the exiled Stuarts, and laid the ground for the most ambitious bid for influence attempted by the Catholic reformers: the promotion of Ramsay to the exiled court.

If, as Nathaniel Hooke put it, 'the Chevalier was unable to leave out the mystical doctrine', this was because Ramsay claimed to intuit grounds for civil as well as religious renewal from prayerful contemplation.[88] As they wished to revive the church through tolerance and reason, so the Catholic reformers raised a manifesto to regenerate the temporal *polis*, their works declaring that love of country gave man the impulse to love humanity and

---

85 Ramsay, *Life*, p. 74; Ramsay, *Cyrus*, I, p. 175.
86 Ramsay, *Cyrus*, I, pp. 6–7; Ramsay, *Plan of Education*, pp. 15–16.
87 Ramsay, *Essay on Civil Government*, pp. iv–vii; Ramsay, *Plan of Education*, p. 16; Henderson, *Ramsay*, p. 126.
88 Ramsay, *Essay on Civil Government*, Preface, p. iv.

heaven. Ramsay was gripped by the search for a kingdom that could merit the highest fraternal loyalties, inducing 'strict Probity', 'severe honour', and 'Delicacy in love' in its subjects, to bring the body politic closer to divine Natural Law.[89] Yet, for all his loathing of tyranny and inquisition, the Chevalier's idealism was tempered by a Christian sense of sin: haunted by the fallibility of human institutions when 'all men are not reasonable, therefore reason is only a chimera'. He trembled at the ease with which unfettered liberty could descend into 'wild licentiousness', through 'the terrible ends of popular government', and against the optimism of some early Enlightenment authors, reflected that the corruptible *form* of the polity mattered less than the moral and spiritual conditions that underpinned it.[90] He suggested that 'Men will never find their happiness in outward Establishments nor in the most curious Schemes invented by Human Wit, but in the principles of Virtue', to be kindled through methods of education rather than political restructuring.[91] The roots of the contemporary political malaise, but also the seeds of potential renewal, lay with the dynastic leaders of European states, and the instruction they received. He concluded that 'the Safety and Happiness of a Kingdom does not depend so much upon the Wisdom of Laws as upon that of Kings'.[92]

Ramsay drew upon a traditional regal imagery, conceiving of the prince as a father to his people, on the principle that private 'family love' planted the seeds that grew into 'love of one's country'.[93] Yet the Chevalier endeavoured to reconcile this patriarchal sense of the roots of royal power with civic humanist claims of a patriotic obligation on the man who held the throne. He sought to provide a counterblast to the image of the confessional and absolutist 'universal monarch' inhabited by Louis XIV, prescribing a model of princely rule directed to 'the great Law of the Publick Weal' and the 'Liberties of the Body Politick'.[94] The wellspring of this idea could be found in an older lineage of 'mirror for princes' literature, with the influence of Erasmus's *Institutio principis Christiani* especially inspiring a genre of French reformist texts.[95] The *Institution d'un Prince* (1739) by the Jansenist Abbe' Duguet, stressed the shared responsibilities of the monarch and his 'citizens' to diffuse virtue across the realm in imitation of Augustine's City

---

[89] Ramsay, *Cyrus*, I, pp. 140–44.

[90] Ramsay, *Cyrus*, I, pp. 218–19; Ramsay, *Plan of Education*, p. 18; Ramsay, *Essay on Civil Government*, pp. 20, 62–4, 107.

[91] Ramsay, *Essay on Civil Government*, p. 195.

[92] Ramsay, *Cyrus*, II, p. 51.

[93] Ramsay, *Essay on Civil Government*, pp. 20, 62–4, 107.

[94] Ramsay, *Life of Fénelon*, pp. 375–6.

[95] Anthony Grafton, 'Humanism and Political Theory', in Burns and Goldie, eds, *Cambridge History of Political Thought*, pp. 9–29.

of God.[96] However, the Fénelonian critique was also stimulated by Figurist reflections on the high morality and sophisticated thought present in non-Christian cultures, and communicated through a series of imaginary Utopian landscapes, raised to invite contemplation and judgement on contemporary European affairs. In Fénelon's *Telemachus*, the invigorating prosperity of the kingdom of Salentum is offset by a journey into the Underworld, where defective monarchs face punishment, with mocking Furies holding up mirrors to show royal vices reflected into eternity.[97] On his odyssey through the East, Ramsay's hero Cyrus sees 'nothing but sad examples of the Weakness and Misfortunes of Princes': a host of monarchs usurped, expelled and striving to recover their thrones.[98] Such was the fate of those who fell in thrall to the Machiavellian 'three Empires' of 'Opinion', 'Ambition' and 'Sensuality'.[99]

Through *The Travels of Cyrus* and the *Plan of Education for a Young Prince*, Ramsay aimed to help kings to navigate the pathway through temptation, delusion and deception, engaging with men who must take on a mantle fraught with loneliness, to 'resemble the Immortals, who have no Passion'.[100] He claimed that the 'fatal Circle' of 'Conquest, Luxury, Anarchy' could only be beaten by a prince with the courage to resist the urge towards tyranny, imparting instead 'Humanity, the publick Good, and the true Love of our Country'.[101] Cyrus, whose mythic power rose not as a conqueror, but as the liberator of the Jews from captivity, became the exemplary model. Purged of ignoble desires by reason and contemplation, the sovereign following his path would be inspired to gain 'an Empire over [the] Passions, more glorious than the false Lustre of Royalty'.[102] Ramsay's reforming king would rebuild the Ciceronian bonds of friendship and civility in his dominions: the 'true interests' of princes and people being 'necessarily united, whatever pains are taken to separate them'.[103] It was 'not reasonable', the Chevalier argued, that 'the Royal Authority should be the only power of the state'; neither laws nor taxes should 'depend entirely upon his absolute will', without the scrutiny of a parliament.[104] Emancipating subjects to worship as they chose, the prince must likewise set them free from the tyranny of mercantile restrictions, opening up the trade of the realm to proclaim an

---

96 Marisa Linton, 'Citizenship and Religious Toleration in France', in *Toleration in Enlightenment Europe*, ed. Porter and Grell, pp. 157–74.
97 Gable, 'Prince and the Mirror', pp. 241–6; Manuel and Manuel, *Utopian Thought*, pp. 367–91; J.C. Davis, 'Utopianism', in Burns and Goldie, eds, *Cambridge History of Political Thought*, pp. 329–44, at pp. 341–2.
98 Ramsay, *Cyrus*, II, pp. 134–7.
99 Ibid., I, p. 7.
100 Ibid., I, pp. 145–6; Ramsay, *Plan of Education*, pp. 2–5; Ramsay, *Life*, pp. 22–4.
101 Ramsay, *Cyrus*, I, p. 7; II, pp. 134–7.
102 Ibid., I, p. 86; Ramsay, *Plan of Education*, pp. 7, 14–15.
103 Ramsay, *Cyrus*, I, pp. 140–4, 175.
104 Ramsay, *Essay on Civil Government*, pp. 176–8.

example of peace and patriotism across the world.[105] Ramsay's ideal had therefore moved far beyond Fénelon's original prescription. Denouncing 'the parasitical principles of an unbounded Passive Obedience', attacking the fallacy that 'Princes, being the Vicegerents of God, may act like them', and declaring that sovereign legitimacy only fell to those who governed by 'free and unbribed consent', the Chevalier was inviting his reader to reject canons sacred to the *ancien régime*.[106] If few enthroned dynasts would take up the manifesto, logic made him look to the inchoate potential of a prince who was yet to see his own dominion.

Meditations on royal virtue, linked to the narrative vision of a prince defeating injustice to restore God's blessing to his promised land, opened up the channels of contact between Fénelonian circles and the Jacobite court. Ramsay's *Essay on Civil Government* fulminated against the 1688 Revolution, as an event that left Britain in thrall to 'Cabals, Hatreds, Division and Deceit'.[107] In November 1721, the *Life of Fénelon* had been dedicated to James Edward Stuart: written, according to its author, 'to maintaine your rights and endeavour to undeceive my countrymen of their errours'.[108] The Chevalier suggested that the trial of Stuart banishment should be seen as a chance to enlarge moral and mental worlds, the magus Zoroaster reporting to Cyrus that, through the opportunities for study and travel, 'my Exile prov'd a new source of happiness to me. It depends upon ourselves to reap Advantage from Misfortunes.'[109] Ramsay reminded the Pretender that, having 'seen the world in all its shapes', he could prove 'a model to future Princes of moderation in their grandeur', using the experience of displacement to guard his dynasty against any danger of regal self-delusion: 'Is there any knowledge more useful to make you one day reign a true father of your people, and to forewarn you against an ambition of absolute government?[110] Echoes of the quietist idea of kingship entered into a wider corpus of recusant reformist writing. Pope's enigmatic yearning to discover 'not a King of Whigs, of King of Tories but a King of England' was developed in George Flint's overtly Jacobite 'Proposal for Christian Re-union', exhorting the Pretender to fulfil the ecumenicist dream put before James I by Hugo Grotius.[111] Simon Bering-

---

[105] Ramsay, *Cyrus*, I, pp. 283–6; II, pp. 77–83.

[106] Ramsay, *Plan of Education*, pp. 19–20; *Essay on Civil Government*, pp. 77, 92–4; Ramsay, *Cyrus*, I, p. 140.

[107] Ramsay, *Essay on Civil Government*, pp. 168–9.

[108] Ramsay, 'To the King of Great Britain', n.d., Bodleian Library, Rawlinson MSS, D1198.247.

[109] Ramsay, *Cyrus*, I, pp. 86, 306–307; II, pp. 150–3.

[110] Ramsay, 'To the King of Great Britain', Bodleian Library, Rawlinson MSS, D1198.247.

[111] Pope to Atterbury, 20 November 1717, in Pope, *Correspondence*, I, p. 453. W.B. Patterson, *James VI and I and the Reunion of Christendom* (Cambridge, 1997). Extracts of the 'Proposal' are in Flint to John Caryll, 1 August 1744, BL, Add. MSS, 28,230, fol. 873.

ton's *Gaudentio* repeated Ramsay's conjunction of the prince as a father *and* a patriot: a self-denying leader to his people in the mould of Moses, the original 'divine legislator'.[112] However, the task outlined for James Edward was becoming increasingly daunting. No longer imagined simply as Britain's 'king over the water', the Pretender was being invited to link his name to a challenge to vital elements of the European realm.

In bringing Ramsay's name before the exiled court, the exiled reformers therefore sought to fashion an image for the Stuarts that would finally over-throw the myth of 'popery and arbitrary government'. Ramsay's stock rose in Jacobite circles due to the lingering memory of James Edward's 1709 encounter with Fénelon; the renewed emphasis on the regal duty to sustain liberty and virtue also made for a continuation of the teachings taken from the prince's first preceptor, John Betham. By 1721, quietist principles were being voiced at court as the language in which a Catholic king might convince Protestant subjects of his fitness to rule. A pamphlet written purportedly by a young Whig nobleman recalled James invoking 'my friend the late Arch-bishop of Cambray' to declare his good will towards Protestant subjects, and his desire 'to become a good King to all my people without distinction'. The conversation closely imitated Fénelon's published instructions to the royal duke of Burgundy: 'From infancy he had made it his business to acquire the knowledge of the laws, customs and families of his country, so as he might not be reputed a stranger, when the Almighty pleased to call him thither.'[113] In a panegyric to the *Life of Fénelon*, Lord Lansdowne predicted that 'in all events of life, your Majesty may have recourse to this book, as an oracle either for consolation or advice'; its lessons would make him 'an example to all succeeding Kings'.[114] The Jacobite secretary of state, John Hay, was moved to offer similar acclamation for Ramsay, as the guardian of the Fénelon legacy and one whose 'sound judgments and zealous heart I look upon to be the chief support of the cause at this time'.[115] The quietist revival had moved daring east-wards across the Alps. In November 1723, these overtures found their reward when, on Southcott's recommendation,

---

112 Berington, *Gaudentio*, pp. 27, 98.

113 Anon., *A Letter from an English Traveller at Rome to his Father, of the 6th of May, 1721. O. S.* (London, 1721), pp. 7–8. The authenticity of the letter remains open to doubt, but it has been attributed to William Godolphin, 2nd Marquis of Blandford. See Daniel Szechi, 'The Image of the Court: Idealism, Politics and the Evolution of the Stuart Court 1689–1730', in Corp, ed., *The Stuart Court in Rome*, pp. 49–64; Lionel Rothkrug, *Opposition to Louis XIV: The Political and Social Origins of the French Enlighten-ment* (Princeton, 1965), pp. 284–5.

114 Henderson, *Ramsay*, pp. 85–6.

115 John Hay to Francis Atterbury, 5 September 1724, Royal Archives (Windsor), Stuart papers, 72/112.

Ramsay received a summons to Rome, to serve as tutor to the young Charles Edward Stuart.[116]

By framing their manifesto to suit the ambitions of the exiled court, the reformers in Jacobite Paris appeared to have found a chance of rehabilitation. However, this was a moment seemingly too precarious to endure. Within a year, Ramsay was returning from Rome, his tenure ended and his mission seemingly defeated, to the surprise and disquiet of his patrons in France. Conventionally, the conclusion of the Chevalier's posting has been attributed to the destructive factionalism that wracked the exiled court – the credit of Jacobites in Paris had been blasted by evidence of their patron the earl of Mar's disloyalty to the cause.[117] Yet if he appeared to some observers an incongruity in the court milieu – 'an owl among lesser birds' according to one Whig agent – there had been no sign of Ramsay meeting serious enmity from within the Stuart household.[118] Nine months into the tutor's tenure, James Edward signalled his approbation: 'I thank God he has given my son all that can be wished for a child of his age.'[119] The sources of animosity appeared to fall instead from outside the royal palace. A year before Ramsay's appearance, Cardinal Alberoni, a senior member of the curia, had dubbed *Telemachus* a 'very dangerous for princes to read', with James crisply instructed to reject the Chevalier's dedication of his life of Fénelon.[120] Soon, there were whispers in Rome that pressure had fallen on James Edward to relinquish the new tutor. The Italian radical *Abbate* Niccolini insisted that Ramsay 'is hated by the great bigots' in the Holy See, 'who say that such a man is not fit to bring up a Roman Catholic prince'.[121] Snapshots of the Chevalier's own conversation pinpointed the same antagonists. He described Pope Benedict XIII as a man who 'delights in the trifles of religion and has no notion at all of the true spirit behind it'.[122] Taking this evidence into account, Ramsay's dismissal can best be identified among the series of confrontations ignited between the Jacobite entourage and

---

[116] Thomas Southcott to James Edward, 13 December 1723, Royal Archives (Windsor), Stuart Papers, 71/38.

[117] John Hay to Francis Atterbury, 12 November 1724, Royal Archives (Windsor), Stuart papers, 77/154; Edward Gregg, 'The Jacobite Career of John Earl of Mar', in *Ideology and Conspiracy: Aspects of Jacobitism, 1689–1759*, ed. Eveline Cruickshanks (Edinburgh, 1982), pp. 179–200; Pauline McLynn, *Factionalism among the Exiles in France: The Case of Bishop Atterbury and Chevalier Ramsay* (Royal Stuart Society, Huntingdon, 1989).

[118] Report of agent 'Walton', December 1724, National Archives, State Papers, Italian States, 15, fol. 216.

[119] James Edward to Lewis Innes, 13 August 1724, Royal Archives (Windsor), Stuart papers, 72/23.

[120] Spence, *Anecdotes*, p. 49; Thomas Southcott to James Edward, 24 January 1723, Royal Archives (Windsor), Stuart papers, 64/171.

[121] Niccolini to Molesworth, 3 February 1725, HMC, *Reports on Various Collections*, VIII (1913), pp. 381–2.

[122] Spence, *Anecdotes*, p. 52.

the papacy of Benedict XIII, when, as has been seen, the suggestion that a heterodox religious life was bring sponsored in the Palazzo Muti revived old suspicions against the exiled community, and climaxed in 1725 with a temporary separation between the Pretender and his queen.

Such altercations exposed the gulf between Jacobite Paris and the hardening idea of religious orthodoxy at the heart of the Catholic world. However diligently they pursued the humanist Holy Grail of a chance to counsel kings, the reformers in the Catholic diaspora would remain confined to a maverick status, with their thoughts more likely to reify in a context of protest and dissent. Yet if Ramsay's return from Rome marked a dispiriting end to raised hopes, the reformers' affiliation with the international Jacobite movement was not completely attenuated. Ramsay himself remained a salaried agent of the court, and retained his support among the English Catholics in France, who lobbied unsuccessfully for him to return to Rome, as under-governor to the young Prince Henry in 1728.[123] In 1735, his private affairs took him back to the heart of the exiled movement, with marriage to Marie, daughter of Sir David Nairne.[124] In the following decade, Charles Edward himself displayed traces of affinity with the man who had nurtured him in infancy. The Young Pretender's interest in promoting himself as a reforming prince was evinced in his reputed sympathies for the Masonic order, and his support for a late flourishing of radicalism in Jacobite manifestos that offered Britain extended press freedom, triennial parliaments and a foreign policy designed to shake the autocracies of Europe.[125] From the Paris cloisters in 1745, Augustine Walker hailed Charles's voyage into Scotland as the return of a 'patriot' prince 'who neglects his own to heal his people's wounds' and who would rock the thrones of 'haughty tyrants' with a restoration of 'liberty'.[126] Propaganda images dressed the prince in the Enlightenment raiment of noble Roman virtue; one portrait captured his study stocked with volumes of Locke.[127] If much of their activity was clandestine, the reformers had nonetheless brought a sense of what Ramsay called 'the taste of true liberty' into the discourse of the exiled world, ensuring that the Chevalier's placement in Rome was more than just the last hurrah for a defeated manifesto.[128] If they had run up against the constraints inherent in the lives of political and religious refugees, they hoped to find a wider public space for their opinions on the other side of the English Channel.

---

123 Ramsay to James Edward, 28 June 1727, Royal Archives (Windsor), Stuart papers, 107/128; Ramsay to James Edgar, 8 March 1732, Stuart papers, 152/18; Robert Witham to Lawrence Mayes, 3 June 1728, AAW, Epistolae Variorum, IX/72.

124 Henderson, *Ramsay*, pp. 151, 156, 178–85.

125 *An authentic account of the conduct of the young Chevalier* (1749); Szechi, *The Jacobites*, pp. 150–1; Monod, *Jacobitism*, pp. 300–303.

126 'Memoirs of the Society of St Edmunds', II, pp. 303–307.

127 Monod, *Jacobitism*, p. 84.

128 Ramsay, *Plan of Education*, p. 19.

The Catholic reformers in English politics

When the ambitions of exiled reformers appeared thwarted by the intellectual mainstream in Catholic Europe, the English terrain of penal laws, 'popery' scares and the Protestant succession provided scarcely greater grounds for optimism. Yet the radical circles linked to Jacobite Paris spoke with conspicuous confidence about the chance of gaining a favourable reception in their own country. Simon Berington believed that when the relationship between the crown, parliament and the law functioned to full effect, the kingdom possessed 'the best constitution in the world'.[129] Nathaniel Hooke announced that the reasons to live in England could be expressed in the simple chant 'liberty, liberty, liberty!' while Ramsay surmised that Fénelon would have acquired a greater chance to voice his radical conscience had he lived across the Channel.[130] The writings of the reformers therefore aimed not just to raise Jacobite hopes, but to offer a redescription of the origins of English civil society, framed to encourage Catholic participation in a Protestant domain. Bringing the humanist and utopian register into contact with French contemplative traditions, they recast the principles behind mystic piety to meet the language of patriotism and 'politeness' present within the English public realm.

From his *Essay on Civil Government* to *The Travels of Cyrus*, Ramsay made clear that he was imparting instructions to the 'citizenry' as much as the rulers of a royal dominion. He claimed that 'in the Body Politic, as in the Natural, all the Members contribute something to the common Life', rendering it the civic duty of subjects to 'enter into conference with their prince'. Kingdoms 'perish more through want of having good Subjects, than because there are bad Sovereigns'.[131] But if Whigs drew the genealogy of English liberties from a succession of providential Protestant triumphs, Ramsay argued that the desire to defend freedom and foster virtue actually arose from the divinely inspired 'Sovereign Reason' lingering within the human soul: an idea of the 'eternal and immutable laws of universal good' that was expressed firstly in private friendship and sociability, but rose to nurture civil societies from Catholic France to Confucian China.[132] Interpreted in this light, the laws and customs of a realm should be adhered to for the sake of public peace, but they could never represent more than the shadow of a greater natural law.[133] When the sources of corruption and degeneration clung innately to human institutions, subjects should not cease their attempts to promote

---

[129] Simon Berington, *A dialogue between the gallows and a freethinker* (1744), p. 5.
[130] Spence, *Anecdotes*, pp. 21, 199; Henderson, *Ramsay*, p. 84.
[131] Ramsay, *Cyrus*, I, pp. 140–44, 175; Ramsay, *Essay on Civil Government*, pp. 23, 92–4; Ramsay, *Plan of Education*, pp. 18–21.
[132] Ramsay, *Essay on Civil Government*, p. 26.
[133] Ibid., pp. 68–9.

renewal. This diagnosis created grounds for the revival of Catholic political life in England. An independently formed language of 'virtue', 'politeness' and the 'public good', could converge on the territory inhabited by Protestant patriots, while nonetheless rejecting the idea that the Whig settlement of 1689 represented the fount of liberty in the realm.[134]

Quietist writers turned their political thought to suit the experiences of Catholic laymen who already maintained a set of relations with Protestant friends, kinsmen and county authorities. From the writings of Grotius, Ramsay counselled that it was viable to uphold civic life even under the rule of a usurper, when outward civility, rather than anguished isolation, was the mark of 'evenness of soul', and the surest way of overthrowing illegitimate powers was to confront them with the true patriotic ethos.[135] Concurring, Simon Berington argued that English recusants had already proved themselves exemplars of the patriotic spirit by the frequency with which they had 'spent their lives and fortunes for Protestant Princes', over the previous century, and 'never made the religion of their King the Standard of their Allegiance'.[136] His exhortation to stand against 'Fury of Parties, Abuse of Power' was written in imitation of the language of the 'Country' movement, and Catholic reformers used French-inspired rhetoric to deepen their links to a parliamentary opposition that was increasingly diagnosing the Whig state not as the guardian, but the potential enemy of ancient national liberties.[137] Nathaniel Hooke carried old reformist strains into his *Roman History*, dedicated to the Patriot Whig earl of Marchmont and inspired by the Chevalier's own reflections on the classical world.[138] Describing the emasculation of the Roman republican spirit by a ruling oligarchy, he departed from the common iconography of English classical authors, refusing to pay homage to the aristocratic leadership of the senate. Instead, he forayed further back, tracing the root of corruption to the defeat of Tiberius Gracchus – 'the most accomplished Patriot that Rome ever produced' – who had sought to restore the virtue of the founders through a programme of political and social reform.[139]

Hooke dramatised the doomed campaign in the senate to revive Rome's old agrarian law – which had prevented any citizen from possessing more than 500 acres of the public lands – and so 'save the state' from rapacious 'grandees'. The mission reached a shuddering end with the killing of Gracchus by his political enemies on the day of elections, with 300 of the Gracchi slaughtered and their friends cast into exile. In Hooke's judgement:

134 Ramsay, *Cyrus*, I, pp. 218–19; Ramsay, *Essay on Civil Government*, pp. 168–9.
135 Ramsay, *Essay on Civil Government*, p. 57.
136 Berington, *Modest Enquiry*, pp. 17–18.
137 Ibid., pp. 151–2.
138 *Essay on Civil Government*, p. 54.
139 Nathaniel Hooke, *Roman History* (4 vols, 1738–71), II, p. 539; Philip Ayres, *Classical Culture and the Idea of Rome in Eighteenth-Century England* (Cambridge, 1997).

'the popular cause never recovered of the wound it received, by the murder of those illustrious Patriots, there remained little more than the form of the ancient constitution'. Despite appearances, the author was no social revolutionary, as he was quick to assure his aristocratic patrons: it was not so much the economic as the political consequence of Roman land-holding that offered instruction. Gracchus's aim was 'not to make poor men rich, but to strengthen the Republic by an increase of useful members'. The landed estates in Rome were embodiments of the public interest, which was equally in danger of bleeding dry in Georgian England, when the citizens were deprived of their stake in the realm by the government patronage and bribery that was undermining the independence of borough corporations. In Rome, as in England, 'Virtue and the Republic' were but 'cant words when men 'put their own liberty and the Commonwealth to sale', and a polity 'losing its inhabitants of free condition' would face 'being overrun with slaves and barbarians, that had neither affection for the Republic, nor interest in her preservation'. The new oligarchy, 'if not destroyed, would infallibly produce another monster, more hideous, if possible, *Monarchic Despotism*' and this, after much 'effusion of blood' was to be the city's tragic destination, when 'the final catastrophe was the Utter Ruin of Roman Liberty'.[140] The degenerative conditions of arbitrary rule, social injustice and weakness abroad were diagnosed as the symptoms of a long-term national decline, as Hooke's later editions brought the language of Country politics into contact with the first glimmer of Wilkesite radicalism.[141]

Much as Jacobites might abhor the alliance, the consolidation of Anglo-French relations in the two decades after the Treaty of Utrecht increased English interest in affairs across the Channel, and positioned Catholics versed in Parisian intellectual culture for dialogue with Protestant compatriots. Archbishop Wake of Canterbury, who professed his attachment to the precedents of the Gallican Church, could enter correspondence with the Benedictine missioner Gilbert Knowles over the readership of *Cyrus* – dubbed by the latter 'the finest system of the morality I ever saw'.[142] Translations, classical histories and political treatises inspired by the French reformers caught the timbre of English Patriot rhetoric, and were reshaped to subject the Whig oligarchy to the same satirical, morally rigorist critique levelled at Bourbon tyranny. As early as 1705, the publication of *Telemachus* was attacked from a pro-government perspective in Bernard Mandeville's *The Grumbling Hive*, for raising a false 'Eutopia' with which to assail the

---

[140] Hooke, *Roman History*, II, pp. 523–60.
[141] Linda Colley, 'Eighteenth-Century English Radicalism before Wilkes', *Transactions of the Royal Historical Society*, 5th ser., 31 (1981), pp. 1–20.
[142] Gilbert Knowles to William Wake, n.d., Wake letters, Christ Church, Oxford, 22/339.

political and economic legacy of the Glorious Revolution.[143] Undeterred, the Huguenot author Abel Boyer combined with the Whig radical Isaac Littlebury in a translation of Fénelon's work in 1721.[144] *Telemachus* was translated into English twelve times over the course of the century, and was to cross the seas again to transplant a vision of civic virtue in the minds of American authors.[145] It gave a new set of references to political reformers, and widened the Patriot consciousness to posit a larger international context to the struggle for liberty. In 1740, Pope suggested to Lord Marchmont that a collapse into 'slavery abroad' prefigured the trajectory of 'the church and state we may find at home', when Britain could not long remain 'the only corner [of Europe] left still free'.[146] From the same perspective, the opposition Whig leader George Lyttelton qualified his support for the Anglo-French alliance with consistent sympathy for the Jansenist leadership in Paris.[147] Solidarity among the ranks of European patriots could transcend the religious divide.

Such exchanges gave Nathaniel Hooke his space as a Catholic author to transmit commentary on English affairs, and it was chiefly through his agency that Andrew Michael Ramsay began to gather a reputation outside France. The Chevalier was awarded an honorary degree from Oxford University in 1730, initiating correspondence with David Hume, the duke of Argyll and the Tory scholars William King and Thomas Carte.[148] In Paris, Bolingbroke sought Ramsay's acquaintance through membership of the crypto-Jansenist Entresol Club, and he channelled Fénelonian imagery into his own 'Idea of a Patriot King': the inspiration for the circle around Frederick, Prince of Wales.[149] By the end of the following decade, the quietist manifesto had been refigured outside the confines of Catholic Europe. In 1748, the Tory MP Charles Gray exhorted Frederick to rally his country around a 'patriot scheme' that recalled *Telemachus*, *Gaudentio* and Hooke's *Roman History*, aiming to 'elevate the public welfare' through reform of the poor laws and

---

143 Bernard Mandeville, *The Grumbling Hive: or, Knaves turn'd Honest* (London, 1705); Istvan Hont, 'The Early Enlightenment Debate on Commerce and Luxury', in Mark Goldie and Robert Wokler, eds, *The Cambridge History of Eighteenth-Century Political Thought* (Cambridge, 2006), pp. 379–418.

144 Abel Boyer and Isaac Littlebury, eds, *The Adventures of Telemachus, the Son of Ulysses: In 24 Books* (1721).

145 Leslie A. Chilton and O.M. Brack, their Introduction to Fénelon, *The Adventures of Telemachus, the Son of Ulysses*, trans. Tobias Smollett (Georgia, 1997 edn), pp. iii and x–xx; Manuel and Manuel, *Utopian Thought*, p. 391.

146 Pope to Marchmont, 22 June 1740, Rose, ed., *Marchmont Papers*, p. 216.

147 Robert Phillimore, ed., *Memoirs and Correspondence of George, Lord Lyttelton* (2 vols, London, 1845), I, pp. 39–40.

148 Henderson, *Ramsay*, pp. 135–46; Ramsay to Thomas Carte, 22 November 1736, Bodleian Library, Carte MSS, 226, fol. 419.

149 N. Childs, *A Political Academy in Paris 1724–1731: The Entresol and its Members* (Oxford, 2000), pp. 87–91, 114–15; Gerrard, *Patriot Opposition*, pp. 12–16.

the electoral system, accompanied by an end to inequitable trade protection barriers. These remedies would finally purge the ills of a 'revolution system' distorted by William of Orange to 'favour the interests of Holland' while 'beggaring all the ancient gentry of the kingdom'.[150] If they never succeeded in ushering in a wave of political and social reforms, such commentaries nonetheless supplied increasingly common motifs in Augustan thought. The legacy they left was somewhat paradoxical. The outcome of the Catholic dalliance with English politics was to domesticate a quasi-Jacobite critique into the realm, even as the regal claims and assertions of the house of Stuart began to fall into the background.

Conclusion

Reviewed in isolation, the reformers of the Jacobite diaspora offered deeply personal interpretations of a Catholic exile's place in the world between the religious wars and the time of Enlightenment. Lamenting the demise of Andrew Michael Ramsay in 1743, David Hume reflected that he preached 'a philosophy peculiar to himself'.[151] Yet a reconstruction of the networks of friendship and patronage sheds light on the shared ambitions and anxieties of a group of authors who set out to reform tastes and direct public actions amid the scattered society of their co-religionists. The Christian Utopianism that inspired Ramsay, Hooke, Berington and their contemporaries may not have matured into a uniform doctrine, but their writings assembled certain consistent propositions that reacted against coercive power politics in church and state, and pointed towards peace between different confessions through a revival of learning and civic life. Moreover their ideas gathered a constituency from the disenchanted Anglo-Gallican minds of Paris and Douai, carried an appeal to recusants straining for a voice in English politics, and enlivened a host of exiles who drank in the intellectual ferment of the century as freemasons, collectors and translators. Common political and religious pressures allowed their thoughts to travel across denominations and amongst troubled consciences on both sides of the English Channel.

As Roman Catholics proclaiming the virtue of syncretistic toleration, mystics who relished the challenge of scientific reason, disciples of Fénelon who defended alleged Jansenists, and champions of Jacobite kingship who cherished constitutional liberties, the blueprint of the recusant reformers drew upon a series of seemingly irreconcilable stances. That each individual received a measure of acclaim within his lifetime – and equally, that their fame did not outlast their own century – suggests that some of these conjunc-

---

[150] Charles Gray to Egmont, 5 June 1749, BL, Add. MSS, 47,012, fols 34–5; Earl of Egmont to Charles Gray, n.d. July 1749, BL, Add. MSS, 47,012, fols. 118–20.
[151] Henderson, *Ramsay*, p. 232.

tions might not have appeared so implausible to a certain contemporary mindset. Further, their careers strike against the old perception that Jacobitism inescapably meant dogma and reaction, that the exiled court formed no more than a milieu of shadows and mental provincialism, a barrier to the regeneration of the English Catholic intellect. The Fénelonian undertone in the diaspora may never have risen to be the single, dominant note in Jacobite thought, but the world of the exiled Stuarts was still capacious enough to find a place for its authors. In English recusant society, the writings of European reformers animated an older discourse that had separated the flock from the mainstream of the Catholic *ancien régime*, professing detachment from the court of Rome, and counselling separation between the spiritual and the temporal power in human affairs. Though their worldview was cosmopolitan, the new writers offered a language to affirm loyalty towards the English realm, to imagine a beneficent Jacobite future, but also push for a prior participation in civic life. That ideas stirred in the dissident colleges and seminaries of Paris burgeoned within the broader setting of the Country movement calls into question the notion of all things Romish as the ostracised 'Other' against which Englishmen defined their own identity.

Conclusion

Three decades after the last shot was fired in the siege of Preston, the Jacobite challenge was once again pressed upon the consciousness of the nation. During the course of the 1745 rebellion, there were significant signs that elements within the English Catholic community had not abandoned the dream of reversing the Revolution, and reclaiming their perceived birthright within the kingdom on the back of Stuart re-conquest. In the East Anglian recusant enclaves of Norwich, Wymondham and Bungay, Catholic priests were reported to be exhorting their flock to rebellion.[1] In Yorkshire, the duke of Norfolk's steward, Andrew Blyde, rode out to rally under the standard of Prince Charles Edward.[2] Further north, military exertions by members of the Strickland, Charlton, Collingwood and Clavering families showed that old traditions of Stuart royalist action would take more than one generation to wither away.[3] These scattered bursts of insurrection represented a slight threat compared to the rising of 1715, or the organised system of weapon-holding and conspiracy that linked together recusant manors during the reign of William III. However, they served to hint that, just because the Catholic community had been demilitarised by the recriminations after 1715, it was not necessarily drained of fervour.

While Jacobite conspiracy slowly diminished, Jacobite *convictions* would still linger into later decades in the English recusant consciousness. In Lancashire, Anne Hawarden and Mary Standish exchanged political poetry during the '45, and ran to salute the rebel troops on their southward march.[4] After the collapse of the rebellion, the Catholic north found a new, martyred hero in Colonel Francis Towneley – if a lack of royal blood meant that he could not generate a cult in quite the manner of Lord Derwentwater, his head was still preserved as a stimulus to reliquary devotion in the family seat.[5] In Wiltshire, Francis Cottington of Fonthill cherished the title conferred

---

[1] Nicholas Rogers, 'Popular Jacobitism in a Provincial Context: Eighteenth-Century Bristol and Norwich', in Cruickshanks and Black, eds, *The Jacobite Challenge*, pp. 123–41, at p. 133.

[2] National Archives, SP 36/85, fols 442–3.

[3] Gooch, *Desperate Faction?*, pp. 160–70.

[4] Anne Hawarden to Mary Standish, November 1745, Lancashire CRO, Scarisbrick MSS, 44/15.

[5] Alexander B. Grosart, ed., *English Jacobite Ballads, Songs and Satires etc. from the MSS. At Towneley Hall, Lancashire* (Manchester, 1877), pp. 121–5.

upon him by James Edward in 1748, while Henry Jerningham exported his family's Jacobite traditions from Norfolk into Maryland, where he settled, married, and named his eldest son Charles Edward in 1749.[6] It was only as a very gradual process that Jacobite loyalties elided into a less immediate part of the recusant conscience, a pietistic ethos of fidelity and forbearance. From Lisbon, the composer John Francis Wade prefaced his setting of liturgical plainchant, *The Evening Office of the Church* (1773) with an engraving of Charles Edward Stuart, encircled by the Irish harp, the English rose, the thistle and fleur-de-lis and framed by a cross formed from the Stuart laurels.[7] His collection of liturgical texts, *The Roman Gradual*, incorporated a prayer for the 'People of Zion' whose Lord 'shall come to save the Gentiles'.[8] Across the Channel, at Danby Hall, the Scrope family's smuggled weapons were carefully sealed away; at Stonyhurst, the Shireburnes' royal portraits were moved into a more concealed part of the mansion; in Scotland, the ancient gateway into Traquair Castle was closed by the Maxwell Stuarts, kept out of use until some distant moment of national re-awakening.[9]

Jacobite gestures and affectations represented not so much facile sentimentality among recusants as a way of keeping private integrity in politics, against the pressures of the time. The preservation of a national recusant tradition depended on the transmission of a certain habit of mind, as much as a theological doctrine. The intransigent vocabulary of English Catholicism – 'the noble power of suffering bravely', as Pope put it – would be re-kindled generation-by-generation, and in seeking to appropriate those virtues, Jacobites brought dynastic and religious loyalties into a tight embrace.[10] In the private domain, recusants imagined the possibility of an alternative England whenever they tended to their 'little commonwealths', moved among the displaced communities abroad, or entered into scholarly reflections upon their nation's history. They had brought themselves, however unwittingly, into a context of opposition, and successive governments responded in kind. Of all rebel titles stripped away by the state, the earldom of Derwentwater was the only one not to be returned to descendants in later years.[11]

However, the trajectory of Jacobite *ideas* after the collapse of the cause was far more complex. The Stuart cause did not leave any uniform legacy over the English Catholic community, and leading recusants moved in different directions, once the prospect of success began to diminish. In the diaspora, the Carylls and Towneleys became less resistant to assimilation

---

6 W.J. Hoare, *History of Modern Wiltshire* (1821), p. 21; Mann, 'Nuns of the Jerningham Letters', p. 365; Guilday, *Refugees*, p. 388.

7 John Francis Wade, *The Evening Office of the Church* (1773).

8 John Francis Wade, *The Roman Gradual* (1767 edn).

9 Castle, ed., *Jerningham Letters*, II, p. 185; Mark Bence Jones, *The Catholic Families* (London, 1992), pp. 31–2.

10 Pope, *Correspondence*, I, p. 512

11 Arnold, *Northern Lights*, p. 258.

and were slowly absorbed into the cultural and military life of the French kingdom.[12] Others took the opposite path, and damned, in the words of Charles Edward Stuart, 'the Roman Catholick Religion … the artful system of Roman Infallibility [that] has been the ruin of my family'.[13] Apostasy remained a source of recusant anxiety, though its effects were compensated by the rise of new Catholic houses, such as the Silvertops in Northumberland, enriched by commercial wealth.[14] Between the extremes, a core of gentry families consolidated their hold over the culture of English Catholicism, and the prosperity of many estates, flaunted by the Palladian designs brought in by the Arundells of Wardour, suggested that theirs' was not a dying order.[15] Recusant lay leaders adopted a variety of political postures in engagement with the Hanoverian kingdom. Catholic stances could range from the loyalist Toryism of the Welds, as friends of George III, to the Whig grandeur of the house of Norfolk, to the radical spirit that rose among the Swinburnes of Capheaton, who 'scandalised' the ageing Jacobites of their county with histrionic displays of support for the revolution in France.[16] Barbara Charlton of Hesleyside recalled Sir John Swinburne, Lord Grey and Dr John Fenwick 'riding about with one spur on and calling themselves Citizen Swinburne, Citizen Fenwick and Citizen Grey', while Lady Swinburne 'lisped out "all for equality!" as her carriage and four greys drove up to the Capheaton door'.[17]

The lack of a common 'party' trajectory among English Catholic families is not altogether surprising. Beyond its central dynastic goal, Jacobitism had imposed no single manifesto; it presented instead a variety of intellectual challenges to heighten the political consciousness of the community, and resist the drift into cultural isolation or denominationalism. The cause obliged all but the most unyielding 'Noncompounders' to think about how they could achieve a settlement with their compatriots, distinguish Catholicism from 'popery' and return the Stuarts on the basis of consent. In amplifying recusant thought beyond the religious boundaries, Jacobitism therefore left a legacy deeper than simple dynastic choice or party alignment. Whatever position they took after 1745, the majority of Catholic writers thought of themselves as participants in the context of a *nation*, and they aimed to speak outside the fold of the faith. Studying the debates aroused by the Stuart cause allows us to move towards a new judgement on the evolution

---

[12] Alger, 'The Towneleys in Paris', pp. 84–6; Sir Charles Petrie, *The Jacobite Movement: The Last Phase 1716–1807* (London, 1950), p. 171.

[13] Aveling, *Handle and the Axe*, p. 254.

[14] Leo Gooch, '"Incarnate Rogues and Vile Jacobites": Silvertop vs Cotesworth, 1718–1726', *Recusant History*, 18 (1987), pp. 277–81.

[15] Bence Jones, *The Catholic Families*, pp. 39–44.

[16] Wilton, 'Early Eighteenth Century Catholics', pp. 277–87.

[17] Barbara Charlton, *The Recollections of a Northumberland Lady 1815–66*, ed. L.E.O. Charlton (London, 1949), p. 194.

of English Catholic identity, with conclusions that ramify across a larger period.

In releasing the Catholic flock from the clutches of scholarly orthodoxy, it becomes possible to make a judgement on the political and religious environments in which they moved, and the worlds to which they wished to belong. Despite their fears of persecution, Catholic commentators after 1688 pursued a vigorous engagement with the demands of English – and British – national identity. From the promotion of Fénelonian ideas within the 'Country' opposition movement to the convergence with High Church historians, they aimed to defend themselves by importing Catholic discourses into the vocabulary of the public sphere. Indeed, the paradox surrounding Catholic Jacobite ideology was that a cause that did so much to extend the gallery of anti-popish myths was itself shot through with patriotic and irenic ideas, offering loyal overtures to the nation, but wedded to the service of a different dynasty. The rhetoric of Jacobite commentators such as Betham, Ingleton and Dicconson brought into dynastic politics that persuasion in recusant life that sought to reform relations between the civic and religious estates; following the spirit, in Pope's words, of 'good Erasmus in an honest mean'.[18] The existence of a Catholic court, a cause and a claimant emboldened recusants to turn their ideas into ambitions, voicing their design to engage the Protestant nation, renew the Erasmian project, and so refigure the English body politic. The Catholic conception of Englishness remained above all an identity of *aspiration*, a frustrated yearning to change the central assumptions on which state politics turned. But this was not an unfamiliar motif in eighteenth-century patriotism. For many Hanoverian Protestant pamphleteers, the idea of a kingdom whose glory was as yet unfulfilled, a new Israel whose promise remained fragile, was equally potent.[19] The energy of the recusant 'patriot' culture, together with the encounters they *were* able to establish in the national domain, challenges the 'forged', 'constructed' and exclusively Protestant understanding of eighteenth-century Britain. Ideas of nationhood after the Glorious Revolution were far more fluid and contested than British statesmen, monarchs and governors desired.

By demystifying the lives of the recusant gentry, the historian opens up avenues that lead beyond the English nation. The ambitions roused in recusant life came from the wider diaspora; the disputes within the exiled colleges served a reminder that the architecture of their world was framed just as intensely by contention in Catholic Europe. Moreover, when the European Catholic landscape was itself fragmented over political, religious

---

18 Pope, *Imitation of Horace, Satire, II* (1733), l. 66.
19 Tony Claydon and Ian McBride, 'The Trials of the Chosen Peoples: Recent Interpretations of Protestantism and National Identity in Britain and Ireland', in Claydon and McBride, eds, *Protestantism and National Identity: Britain and Ireland c.1650–c.1850* (Cambridge, 1998), pp. 3, 14.

and diplomatic conflict, the questions of divided affinity and allegiance, of private conscience and public behaviour that had cut across the recusant world only rose to a louder pitch. Before 1688, as one late-Georgian Catholic recalled, the principal canons of recusant thought had been formed 'under the shelter of Gallican liberties and Gallican maxims': the French Church providing a model for forms of rigorist spirituality and claims of detachment from the 'court of Rome'.[20] However, after Louis XIV began to retreat from Gallican rhetoric, pursuing reconciliation with the papacy and purging his domain of heterodox ideas, recusant authors were stripped of a vital shield of support. The patriotic language used by Catholics in England was therefore fashioned from a moral, political and religious critique originating in France and the Low Countries: a movement of dissent against Versailles that sought to reclaim the traditions of the church from the state strategies of coercion and conformity. The afterlife of such exchanges ran into the later eighteenth-century. With the English Catholic mindset nourished by certain constructions on French opposition ideas, the genesis of a shift from Jacobite to *Jacobin* among Northumbrian families is made less perplexing.

In 1791, the Scottish Catholic Whig Alexander Geddes opined that 'a kind of secret reformation', had swept through the British recusant communities over two hundred years, jettisoning all the worst dogmas and pretensions of the faith in Europe, and disowning those dangerous convictions that an English Protestant branded 'papist'.[21] He articulated a stock theme of the liberal Cisalpine movement that had coalesced in the households of the Howards, Petres and Throckmortons to promote the cause of Catholic Relief. The recusants' suitability as subjects of the crown could be proved by the way in which they had rejected successive papal inquisitions from the reign of James I onwards – with the final point of departure coming over the bull Unigenitus.[22] Geddes and his supporters could stir some very immediate memories. When two of the most prolific Cisalpines were the priests Charles and Joseph Berington – respectively cousin and nephew of the secret Utopian novelist, and the Throckmortons took as their tutor the Benedictine reformer of learning Augustine Walker, the campaigners quarried their political theology from a discourse formed within the Jacobite world.[23] In England, John Lingard returned to Anglo-Saxon precedents to unearth the foundations of a distinctively national Catholic Church, while Joseph Berington marvelled of Dodd's *Church History* that 'I have seldom known a writer, and that writer a Churchman, so free from prejudice, and

---

[20] Alexander Geddes, *A Modest Apology for the Roman Catholics* (London, 1800), pp. 217–18.

[21] Ibid., p. 8.

[22] Chinnici, *English Catholic Enlightenment*, pp. 4–5, 92–6; Goldie, 'Bishop Hay, Bishop Geddes and the Scottish Catholic Enlightenment', pp. 82–6.

[23] Kirk, *Biographies*, pp. 20–21; John Thorpe to Lord Arundell, 12 March 1774, transcript at Douai Abbey. I am grateful to Geoffrey Scott for this latter reference.

the degrading impressions of party zeal.'[24] Charles Butler published a life of Fénelon, which vaunted the archbishop as a figure comparable to Grotius, whose works paved the way for the 'reunion of Christians'. He acknowledged a particular debt to Andrew Michael Ramsay, a proponent of 'the purest principles of religion and virtue'.[25] Across the Channel, the last flowering of the reformers' manifesto was provided in the career of Luke Joseph Hooke, nephew of Nathaniel, who won the friendship of Diderot, promoted ideas of harmony between the churches, but lost his Sorbonne chair over suspected Deist leanings in 1764.[26] Some of the most tenacious defences came from his former students at the English Benedictine monastery of St Edmund's.[27]

The historian is therefore confronted with the paradox of a body of Catholic Jacobite writings that reached beyond the dynasty itself, emboldened recusants to resist ultramontane challenges, and inspired 'ecumenical' ideas that burned brightly enough to be recovered in the hands of later Whig campaigners. The political literature generated after the Revolution forces us therefore to redraw the genealogy of English Catholic thought away from traditional themes of hagiography and martyrology. The German Catholic *Fruhaufklärung* has been located as a significant feature of European intellectual life, but, among the English communion, the 'enlightened' trend is considered negligble before the rise of the Cisalpine movement in the later part of the eighteenth century. Yet these campaigners did not write out of a vacuum, and this book has aimed to expose the vitality of an earlier tradition, a lost mentality and a set of manuscripts that fall outside the conventional English Catholic bibliographies. The lineage of Catholic writings after 1688 looked back to an older manifesto that placed limits on Rome, pressed for detachment between church and state interests and enlarged the idea of religious toleration. However, the international pressures of the 'Jacobite' period had opened up the horizons of the recusant community. If they found little contemporary comfort in France, Rome or their own country, the unpromising setting of exile and defeat had still sown the seeds of a frail but resilient English Catholic Enlightenment.

[24] John Lingard, *The Antiquities of the Anglo-Saxon Church* (1776); Joseph Berington, *Memoirs of Panzani* (1775), preface, p. ix.

[25] Charles Butler, *The Life of Fénelon, Archbishop of Cambray* (London, 1816), pp. 209, 233–5.

[26] Thomas O'Connor, *An Irish Theologian in Enlightenment France: Luke Joseph Hooke, 1714–96* (1995).

[27] Dom John Bede Brewer produced an English translation of Hooke's *Religionis naturalis et revelatae principia* in 1774. Scott, *Gothic Rage*, p. 165.

Appendix I

English Catholics and their families in residence at the court of St Germain c. 1694–1701

Sources: Marquis of Ruvigny and Raineval, *The Jacobite Peerage* (Edinburgh, 1904); C.E. Lart, *The Parochial Registers of St Germain-en-Laye: Jacobite Extracts of Birth, Marriage and Death* (2 vols, London, 1920–22); 'List of Englishmen with King James', *CSPD, William and Mary, 1690*, p. 375; 'The Establishment of Salaries, Pensions & c. Commencing in the month of January 1709', BL, Egerton MSS, 2517.

Henry Arundell of Wardour, Wiltshire
Thomas Belassis of Lincolnshire
Dr John Betham of Rowington, Warwickshire
Richard Biddulph of Biddulph Grange, Staffordshire
Charles and Mary Booth of Brampton, Herefordshire
Robert and Catherine Brent of Lark Stoke, Gloucestershire
Henry and Mary Browne of Cowdray, West Sussex
Sir Henry and Lady Sophia Bulkeley of Anglesey
*Sir Richard and Lady Bulstrode of Horton, Buckinghamshire
Joseph Bryerly of Belgrave, Leicestershire
Sir Charles Carteret of Toomer, Somerset
John Caryll of West Harting, Sussex
Thomas Codrington of Sutton Mandeville, Wiltshire
Dr Michael Constable SJ
William and Juliana Dicconson of Wrightington, Lancashire
Sir John Gifford of Burstall, Leicestershire
Fergus Grahme of Netherby, Lancashire
William and Elizabeth Herbert, Marquis and Marchioness of Powis.
George Holman of Warkworth, Northamptonshire
Colonel Bernard Howard of Glossop, Derbyshire
Dr John Ingleton of Lancashire
Charles Leyburne of Nateby, Yorkshire
Sir John Lytcott of Oxfordshire
*Charles, Earl of Middleton (lands in Scotland and Goodwood, Sussex)
Thomas Neville of Holt, Leicestershire
Roger Palmer, Earl of Castlemaine of Dorney Court, Buckinghamshire
Edmund Perkins of Ufton, Berkshire
Francis and Mary Plowden of Plowden Hall, Shropshire
James Porter of Aston-sub-Edge, Gloucestershire
Andrew Poulton SJ of Desborough, Northamptonshire
Francis Sanders SJ of Worcester

Ralph and Dominic Sheldon of Winchester
*Bevil Skelton of Raveley, Huntingdonshire
Francis Stafford
John Stafford (landowner in Staffordshire, Shropshire and Gloucester-
    shire).
Sir Thomas and Lady Winifred Strickland of Sizergh, Westmorland
Robert and Bridget Strickland of Catterick, Yorkshire
Admiral Sir Roger Strickland
Lord Waldegrave of Chewton, Somerset
Sir William Waldegrave of Borley, Essex
John Warner SJ

* Converted to the Catholic faith in exile.

Appendix II

*Commissions to English Catholics given out by the exiled court,
1689–1693*

Source: Bodleian Library, Carte MSS, 181, fols 9, 559–561.

Colonel John Parker's regiment of horse, 1689
Colonel John Parker
Captains Thomas Giffard, John Metham, John Mannock, Edward
 Widdrington
Lieutenants Robert Charnock, Charles Skelton
Cornet Edward Hales

Parker's regiment, 1693
Colonel John Parker
Captains Hugh Smithson, Thomas Errington, Ralph Standish, Thomas
 Salkeld, Thomas Charnock, George Porter, John Swinburne

Richard Towneley's Regiment, 1693
Colonel Richard Towneley, Colonel William Standish
Captains Francis Towneley, Robert Standish, William Dicconson

Stephen Tempest's Regiment
Colonel Stephen Tempest, Colonel Simon Scrope
Major Ralph Widdrington
Captains Edward Charlton, Nicholas Tempest, John Clavering, William
 Haggerston, Richard Tempest, Charles Fairfax, George Meynell, Philip
 Langdale

Dragoons (1)
Colonel Thomas Tyldesley, Colonel John Eglinton
Captains George Leyburne, Henry Butler, Thomas Carus, Edward Tyld-
 esley, Ralph Tyldesley, William Fleetwood, Edward Winkley

Dragoons (2)
Colonel James Hungate, Colonel Robert Dalton

Appendix III

Vicars Apostolic in England 1685–1750

1685–1688: John Leyburne, Bishop of Adrumentum, Vicar Apostolic of all England and Wales

London District
1688–1702: John Leyburne
1703–1734: Bonaventure Giffard, Bishop of Madura
1735–1758: Benjamin Petre, Bishop of Prusa

Midland District
1688–1703: Bonaventure Giffard
1703–1716: George Witham, Bishop of Marcopolis
1716–1756: John Stonor, Bishop of Thespia

Western District
1688–1705: Philip Michael Ellis, Bishop of Aureliopolis
1713–1750 – Matthew Prichard, Bishop of Myra

Northern District
1688–1711: James Smith, Bishop of Callipolis
1716–1725: George Witham
1726–1740: Dominic Williams, Bishop of Tiberiopolis
1740–1752: Edward Dicconson, Bishop of Malla

Appendix IV

The Howards of Norfolk
(salient family members)

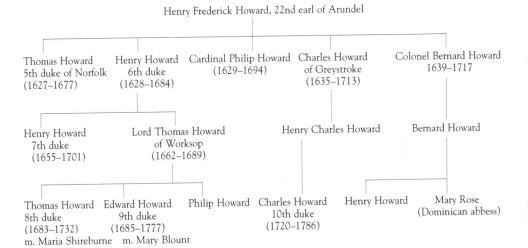

Henry Frederick Howard, 22nd earl of Arundel

Thomas Howard
5th duke of Norfolk
(1627–1677)

Henry Howard
6th duke
(1628–1684)

Cardinal Philip Howard
(1629–1694)

Charles Howard
of Greystroke
(1635–1713)

Colonel Bernard Howard
1639–1717

Henry Howard
7th duke
(1655–1701)

Lord Thomas Howard
of Worksop
(1662–1689)

Henry Charles Howard

Bernard Howard

Thomas Howard
8th duke
(1683–1732)
m. Maria Shireburne

Edward Howard
9th duke
(1685–1777)
m. Mary Blount

Philip Howard

Charles Howard
10th duke
(1720–1786)

Henry Howard

Mary Rose
(Dominican abbess)

The Carylls of West Harting
(salient family members)

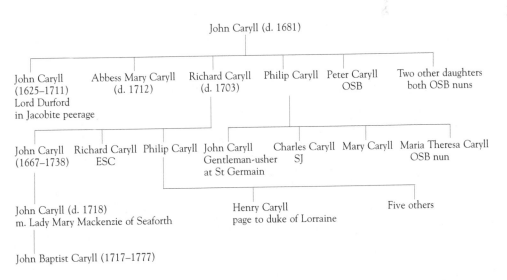

John Caryll (d. 1681)

John Caryll
(1625–1711)
Lord Durford
in Jacobite peerage

Abbess Mary Caryll
(d. 1712)

Richard Caryll
(d. 1703)

Philip Caryll

Peter Caryll
OSB

Two other daughters
both OSB nuns

John Caryll
(1667–1738)

Richard Caryll
ESC

Philip Caryll

John Caryll
Gentleman-usher
at St Germain

Charles Caryll
SJ

Mary Caryll

Maria Theresa Caryll
OSB nun

John Caryll (d. 1718)
m. Lady Mary Mackenzie of Seaforth

Henry Caryll
page to duke of Lorraine

Five others

John Baptist Caryll (1717–1777)

263

Bibliography

Manuscript sources

Archives of the Archbishop of Westminster, Kensington
Main Series, A 36, 37, 38; B 36, 37.
Epistolae Variorum, I, IV, V, VI, VII, VIII, IX.
Old Brotherhood papers, III.
Browne MSS.
St Gregory's Seminary MSS.

Arundel Castle
Howard of Norfolk MSS.

Bodleian Library, Oxford
Carte MSS 180, 181, 203, 205, 208, 209, 210, 211, 212, 226, 228, 254.
Rawlinson letters, 5, 6.
Rawlinson MSS A, D.
Clarendon MSS.

British Library, Additional Manuscripts
10,118, Henry Joseph Johnston and Benet Weldon, 'A Collection of Sundry things yt may contribute to ye History of Great Brittain's late Glorious Monarch', 1705–08.
20,309, 20,310, 20,311, 20,499, 21,896 – Gualterio papers.
21,621 – Jane Barker, 'A Collection of Poems Referring to the Times', 1700.
28,224; 28,226; 28,227; 28,228; 28,229; 28,230; 28,231; 28,237, 28,238, 28,239, 28,240; 28,250, 28,252; 28,253 – Caryll papers.
28,254 – Letter-book of Alban Dawnay, 1710.
29,981 – 'A Collection of Loyal Poems Made in the years 1714, 1715 and 1716'.
33,954 – Historical Tracts.
34,510; 34,512 – States General correspondence.
34,523 – MacKintosh Collection, Vol. 37.
36,296 – John Stevens, 'An Account of my Travels since the Revolution'.
38,847 – Hodgkin papers, Vol. II.
38,851 – Hodgkin papers, Vol. III.
38,864 – Household accounts of William Herbert, 3rd earl of Powis, 1686–1700.
39,661 – Letter-book of the earl of Melfort.
39,662 – Letter-book of Henry Browne.
41,842 – Middleton papers.
61,620 – Blenheim papers.
65, 138; 65,139 – Clifford papers.

British Library, Egerton Manuscripts
1671 – Jacobite papers.
2517 – 'The Establishment of Salaries, Pensions & c. Commencing in the month of January 1709'.
3683 – Bulstrode papers.

British Library Stowe Manuscripts
53 – 'Papers relating to a scheme for inducing the English Catholicks in general to become, by degrees, truly and heartily well-affected to His Majesty's Government', 1719.

Cambridgeshire County Record Office, Cambridge
Huddleston MSS.

Douai Abbey, Woolhampton
Ralph Benet Weldon, 'Memorials' (5 vols).
Letter-book of Nicholas Dempster, 1717–18.

Downside Abbey, Stratton-on-the-Fosse
Mannock MSS.
Birt MSS.
Journal of the English Augustinians at Paris.
Annals of the English Augustinians at Paris (2 vols).

English Province of the Society of Jesus, Farm Street, London
Notes and Fragments.
Liège Procurators' Correspondence.

Gloucestershire CRO, Gloucester
D5563/11 – Paston Inventory.

Hull University, Brynmor Jones Library
DDEV – Constable MSS.

Lambeth Palace Archives
Main series, 929–941.

Lancashire County Record Office, Preston
DDBl – Blundell MSS.
DDM – Molyneux MSS.
DDSc – Scarisbrick MSS.
DDSt – Shireburne of Stonyhurst MSS.
DDPt – Walmesley MSS.
RCWB – Letter-book of Edward Dicconson.

National Archives, Kew
State Papers 36, 78.
State Papers, Italian States, 14, 15.

National Library of Scotland – from microfilm
Diary of Sir David Nairne.

Northumberland County Record Office, Newcastle
5828, M15/A49a – Radcliffe MSS.
67 (ZSW) – Swinburne MSS.
322, Box 5, Box 20 – Swinburne and Radcliffe papers.

Oxfordshire County Record Office, Oxford
F/1/4 – Belson MSS (photocopied transcripts from Berkshire County Record Office).

Private collection, Leeds
Tempest MSS.

Royal Archives, Windsor – from microfilm
Stuart papers, including Thomas Sheridan, 'The King of Britain's Case', Miscellany, V, and 'Political Reflections', Miscellany, VII.

Scottish Catholic Archives, Edinburgh
Blairs Letters, I, II.

Suffolk County Record Office, Ipswich
HA 246 – Mannock MSS.

Ushaw College, Durham
Book Archive, 89 – Letter book of Edward Jones.
Main Series.
Roman Documents.

Vatican Secret Archives, Rome
Fondo Albani, 163–165.
Segretaria di Stato: Nunziatura di Fiandra, 105–109.

Warwickshire County Record Office, Warwick
CR 1998 – Throckmorton MSS.

Printed primary sources

Acton, Lord, ed., *Letters of James II to the Abbot of La Trappe* (London, 1876).
An Account of the VICTORY obtain'd at Preston over the REBELS by the King's forces under the command of General WILLS (1716).
Ailesbury, Thomas Bruce, earl of, *Memoirs, written by himself*, ed. W.J. Buckley (2 vols, Roxburgh Club, 1890).
Allanson, Athanasius, *Biographies of the English Benedictines* (Ampleforth, 1999 edn).
Ames, Richard, *The character of a bigotted prince, and what England may expect from the return of such a one* (1691).

Anderton, Chistopher, *A Catechism for the Use of his Royal Highness, the Prince of Wales* (Paris, 1692).

Annals of the English Benedictines of Ghent (Stafford, 1894).

Ashley Sykes, Arthur, *The reasonableness of mending and executing the laws against papists* (1746).

Aubrey, John, *The Natural History and Antiquities of the county of Surrey* (5 vols, London, 1719), IV.

Barker, Jane, *The Christian Pilgrimage or a Companion for the Holy Season of Lent: Being Meditations upon the Passion, Death, Resurrection, and Ascension of Jesus Christ* (London, 1718).

Barker, Jane, *The Galesia Trilogy and Selected Manuscript Poems*, ed. C. Shiner Wilson (Oxford, 1997).

Barker, Jane, *The Lining of the Patchwork Screen* (1726).

Barker, Jane, *A Patchwork Screen for the Ladies, or Love and Virtue Recommended* (1723).

Bedingfield Papers (CRS, 7, London, 1909).

[Berington, Simon], *The Adventures of Signor Gaudentio di Lucca* (1738).

Berington, Simon, *A dialogue between the gallows and a freethinker* (1744).

Berington, Simon, *Dissertations on the Mosaical creation, deluge, building of Babel, and confusion of tongues, &c* (London, 1750).

Berington, Simon, *The great duties of life. In three parts* (London, 1738).

Berington, Simon, *A modest enquiry how far Catholicks are guilty of the horrid tenets laid to their charge* (London, 1749).

Berington, Simon, *A popish pagan the fiction of a protestant heathen* (1743).

Berington, Simon, *To His Most Excellent Majesty James III* (Douai, 1704).

Berwick, James Fitzjames, duke of, *Memoirs* (2 vols, London, 1779).

Betham, John, *Brief Treatise of Education, with a Particular Respect to the Children of Great Personages; for the use of His Royal Highness the Prince* (Paris, 1693).

Blackmore, Sir Richard, *A True and Impartial History of the Conspiracy against the Person and Government of King William III of Glorious Memory in the Year 1696* (London, 1723).

Blundell, Margaret, ed., *Cavalier: The Letters of William Blundell to his Friends 1620–1688* (London, 1933).

Bolingbroke, Henry St John, Viscount, *Letter to Sir William Wyndham* (1717).

Bossuet, Jacques-Benigne, *Oeuvres* (20 vols, Paris, 1841), XVII.

Boyer, Abel, *The Political State of Great Britain* (40 vols, London, 1711–40).

Brady, W.M., *Annals of the Catholic Hierarchy in England and Scotland A.D. 1585–1876* (London, 1877).

Bretonneau, François, *Life of James II*, trans. R. Wilson (1704).

Bulstrode, Sir Richard, *Miscellaneous Essays*, ed. Whitlocke Bulstrode (1724).

Burnet, Gilbert, *History of My Own Time* (5 vols, Oxford, 1816 edn).

Burton, E.H., and Nolan, E., eds, *The Douai College Diaries: The Seventh Diary 1715–78* (CRS, 28, London, 1928).

Butler, Charles, *The Life of Fénelon, Archbishop of Cambray* (London, 1816).

Calendar of State Papers Domestic, James II, 1686–7, 1687–9; William and Mary, 1689, 1690, 1690–91, 1694–5, 1698.

Canes, John Vincent, *Fiat Lux, or, A general conduct to a right understanding ... about religion here in England* (1661).

Caryll, John, 'Brisseis to Achilles', in J. Dryden, ed., *Ovid's Epistles, Translated by Several Hands* (London, 1681), pp. 245–54.

Caryll, John, *The English Princess, or the Death of Richard III, a Tragedy* (London, 1667).

Caryll, John, 'Fabius Maximus', in *Plutarch's lives translated from the Greek by several hands; to which is prefixt the life of Plutarch* (5 vols, London, 1683), I, pp. 600–651.

Caryll, John, *The Hypocrite*, in G. de F. Lord, ed., *Poems on Affairs of State: Augustan Satirical Verse 1660–1714* (London, 1965), pp. 219–21.

Caryll, John, *Naboth's Vineyard, or the Innocent Traytor*, in Lord, *Poems on Affairs of State*, pp. 206–18.

Caryll, John, *The Psalms of David, Translated from the Vulgate* (St Germain, 1701).

Caryll, John, 'Virgil's First Eclogue', in J. Dryden, ed., *Miscellany Poems* (2 vols, London, 1684), II, pp. 303–23.

Castle, E., *The Jerningham Letters, 1780–1843* (2 vols, London, 1896).

Castlemaine, Roger Palmer, Earl of, *A Full Answer and Confutation of a Scandalous Pamphlet* (1673).

Catholic hymn on the birth of the Prince of Wales (1688).

Catholic Record Society, 25 'Dominicana' (1927).

Catholic Record Society, *Miscellanea*, II (1906).

Catholic Record Society, *Miscellanea*, IV (1907).

Catholic Record Society, *Miscellanea*, XI (1917).

Catholic Record Society, *Miscellanea*, XVII (1935).

Cellier, Elizabeth, *An Answer to Queries, concerning the Colledg of Midwives* (1688).

Challoner, R., *Britannia Sancta: or, The Lives of the most celebrated British, English Scottish and Irish saints who flourished in these islands, from the early times of Christianity, down to the change of religion in the sixteenth century* (London, 1745).

Challoner, Richard, *The Garden of the Soul* (London, 1740).

Chandler, Richard, *The History and Proceedings of the House of Commons from the Restoration to the Present Time* (7 vols, 1742), VI, VIII.

Charlton, Barbara, *The Recollections of a Northumberland Lady 1815–66* (ed. L.E.O. Charlton, London, 1949).

Clarke, J.S., ed., *The Life of James the Second, King of England & c. Collected out of Memoirs Writ in His Own Hand* (2 vols, London, 1816).

Clerophilius Alethes [John Constable], *A Specimen of Amendments candidly proposed to the compiler of a work, which he calls The Church History of England* (1751).

Clifford, Lady Anne, *Collectanea Cliffordiana* (Paris, 1817).

Cobbett, William, ed., *The Parliamentary History of England*, II, III, 1722–1733.

Copley, Anthony, *A Fig for Fortune* (1596).

Corker, James Maurus, *Queries to Dr Sacheverell from North Britain* (London, 1710).

Corker, James Maurus, *Roman Catholick Principles in Reference to God and King* (1680).

Cressy, Hugh Serenus, *The Church History of Brittany from the beginning of Christianity to the Norman Conquest* (1667).

Cressy, Hugh Serenus, *Exomologesis* (1647).

Cressy, Hugh Serenus, *Fanaticism Fanatically Imputed to the Catholic Church* (1672).

de Colonia, Dominique, *Dictionnaire des livres jansenistes, ou qui favorisent le jansenisme* (4 vols, Antwerp, 1752).

Declaration of the Archbishop of Canterbury, and the Bishops in and near London, Testifieing their Abhorrence of the Present Rebellion (1716).

Defoe, Daniel, *A Tour through the Whole Island of Great Britain*, ed. G.D.H. Cole and D.C. Browning (2 vols, London, 1902).

The Design of France against England and Holland (1686).

Diary of Edward Dicconson, in P. Harris, ed., *Douai College Documents 1639–1794* (CRS, 113, 1972).

Diary of Mary, Countess Cowper 1714–60 (1864).

Dodd, Charles, *Apology for the Church History of England* (1742).

Dodd, Charles, *The Church History of England ... chiefly with regard to Catholicks* (4 vols, London, 1737–1742).

Dryden, John, *Britannia Rediviva* (1688).

Dryden, John, *The Hind and the Panther* (London, 1687).

Dugdale, William, *The Antiquities of Warwickshire* (1656).

Ellis, G.A., ed., *The Ellis Correspondence* (London, 1829).

Ellis, Philip Michael, *A Select Collection of Sermons Preach'd before their Majesties* (London, 1741).

Estcourt, E.E., and Payne, J.O., eds, *The English Catholic Nonjurors of 1715* (Farnborough, 1969 edn).

Evelyn, John, *The Pernicious Consequences of the New Heresie of the Jesuites against the King and the State* (1673).

A Faithful Register of the Late Rebellion (London, 1717).

Fénelon, François de Salignac de la Mothe, *The Adventures of Telemachus, the Son of Ulysses*, trans. Tobias Smollett (1776), ed. Leslie A. Chilton and O.M. Brack (Athens, Georgia, 1997).

Fénelon, François de Salignac de la Mothe, *L'Explication des Maximes des Saints sur la vie intérieure* (Paris, 1697).

Ferguson, Robert, *Whether the Preserving the Protestant Religion was the motive unto or the end that was designed in the late Revolution* (1695).

Fiennes, Celia, *Through England on a side-saddle in the Reign of William III and Mary II* (1888).

Fitzherbert, Thomas, *A Treatise of Policy and Religion* (2 vols, 1695 edn).

Fleetwood, William, *The Life and Miracles of St Wenefrede* (1713).

Flint, George, *Robin's Last Shift: or Weekly Remarks and Political Reflections upon the most Material News Foreign and Domestick* (London, 1717).

Flint, George, *The Shift Shifted* (London, 1716).

Foley, Henry, *Records of the English Province of the Society of Jesus* (8 vols, London, 1877).

A free conference touching the present state of England both at home and abroad in order to the designs of France (1678).

A Full and True Account of the Horrid and Bloody Conspiracies of the Papists ... In the North of England (London, 1689).

Gaquéré, François, *Vers l'Unité Chretienne: James Drummond et Bossuet, Leurs Correspondance 1685–1704* (Paris, 1956).

Geddes, Alexander, *A Modest Apology for the Roman Catholics* (London, 1800), pp. 217–18.

Gillow, Joseph, *The Haydock Papers: A Glimpse into English Catholic Life* (London, 1888).

Gillow, Joseph, and Hewiston, Alexander, *The Tyldesley Diary. Personal Records of Thomas Tyldesley ... During the Years 1712–14* (Preston, 1873).

Gillow, Joseph, and Trappes-Lomax, Richard, *The Diary of the 'Blue Nuns' or Order of the Immaculate Conception of Our Lady, at Paris 1658–1810* (CRS, 8, London, 1910).

Gother, John, *Instructions and Devotions for hearing Mass, for Confession* (London, 1744).

Gother, John, *A Papist Represented and Misrepresented* (London, 1682).

Gother, John, *Spiritual Works* (2 vols, London, 1718).

Grosart, Alexander B., ed., *English Jacobite Ballads, Songs and Satires etc. from the MSS. At Towneley Hall, Lancashire* (Manchester, 1877).

Gybbon, John, *Edovardus Redivivus, The Piety and Vertues of Holy Edward the Confessor, Revivd in the Sacred Majesty of King James II* (1688).

Hamilton, Anthony, *Memoirs of the Life of the Count of Grammont* (London, 1714).

Hamilton, Anthony, *Oeuvres* (4 vols, Paris, 1762).

Hearne, Thomas, *Collections*, ed. H.E. Salter (12 vols, London, 1914).

Henson, Edwin, ed., *The English College at Madrid 1641–1767* (CRS, 29, London, 1929).

Henson, Edwin, ed., *Registers of the English College at Valladolid 1589–1862* (CRS, 30, London, 1930).

'Herbertiana', *Montgomeryshire Collections*, 2 (1873), 19 (1886).

Hervey, John, Lord, *Memoirs of the reign of George the Second*, ed. J.W. Croker (2 vols, 1848).

His Holyness the Pope of Rome's declaration against the French king, Louis the 14th ... written by a person that is lately arrived from Germany (1689).

His Majesty's Gracious Declaration to His Loving Subjects (London, 1693).

Historical Manuscripts Commission, *Calendar of Manuscripts of the Marquis of Bath* (3 vols, 1901–1908).

HMC, *Calendar of the Stuart Papers at Windsor Castle* (7 vols, 1902–1923).

HMC *Manuscripts of A.G. Finch* (4 vols, 1913–1965).

HMC *Manuscripts of Lord Kenyon* (1894).

HMC *Reports on Various Collections*, VIII (1913).

Holt, Geoffrey, ed., *The Letter-book of Lewis Sabran SJ* (CRS, 112, 1971).

Holt, Geoffrey, ed., *St Omer and Bruges Colleges, 1593–1773* (CRS, 119, 1979).

House of Commons Journal, XIII (1700–1701).

Hooke, Nathaniel, *The glorious memory of queen Anne reviv'd, exemplify'd in the conduct of her chief favourite the Duchess Dowager of Marlborough* (1742).

Hooke, Nathaniel, *Roman History* (4 vols, 1738–1771).

Howell, T.B., *State Trials* (34 vols, 1809–28), XII, XIII, XV, XVI, XIX.

Huddleston, John, *The Phoenix, the Sepulchre and the Candle* (1691).

Huddleston, William Denis, *Irresistible Evidence against Popery* (London, 1731).

Huddleston, William Denis, *Recantation Sermon* (London, 1729).

Hughan, W.J., ed., *The Jacobite Lodge at Rome 1735–7* (Torquay, 1910).

[Hunter, Thomas], *A Modest Defence of the Clergy and Religious* (1714).

Imago Regis, or the Sacred Image of His Majesty, in all his Solitudes and Sufferings, written during his retirements in France (1692).

Innes, Thomas, *A Critical Essay on the Ancient Inhabitants of the Northern Part of Britain, or Scotland* (London, 1729).

James III, *Proclamation to all His Loving Subjects of what Rank and Degree soever ... 10 October, 1710* (1710).

James III, *To His Subjects of England ... 25 October, 1715* (Perth, 1715).

Jarvis, Rupert C., ed., *The Jacobite Risings of 1715 and 1745: Documents in the Cumberland County Record Office* (Cumberland, 1954).

Jerdan, W., ed., *Letters from James, Earl of Perth ... to his sister the Countess of Erroll* (London, 1895).

The Jesuit's memorial for the intended reformation of England under their first popish prince (1690).

Johnston, Henry Joseph, *A Vindication of the Bishop of Condom's Exposition of the Doctrine of the Catholic Church* (London, 1686).

Johnston, Nathaniel, *The Assurance of Abbey and Other Church Lands in their Possessors* (London, 1687).

King William's toleration being an explanation of that liberty of religion, which may be expected from His Majesty's declaration (1689).

Lang, C.Y., *The Swinburne Letters* (2 vols, Lancaster, 1960).

Lart, C.E., *The Parochial Registers of St Germain-en-Laye: Jacobite extracts of Birth, Marriage and Death* (2 vols, London, 1920–1922).

Lawton, Charlwood, *A French Conquest neither practicable nor desirable* (London, 1693).

[Lawton, Charlwood], *A Reply to the answer Doctor Welwood has made to King James's declaration* (1694).

Leslie, William, *Vita di Sancta Margherita* (1693).

A Letter from an English Traveller at Rome to his Father, of the 6th of May, 1721. O. S. (London, 1721).

Lingard, John, *The Antiquities of the Anglo-Saxon Church* (1776).

Lord, G. de F., ed., *Poems on Affairs of State: Augustan Satirical Verse 1660–1714* (London, 1965).

Lukis, W.C., ed., *The Family Memoirs of the Rev. William Stukeley, M.D. and other Correspondence* (Surtees Society, 73, 1882).

Luttrell, Narcissus, *A Brief Historical Relation of State Affairs from September 1678 to April 1714* (6 vols, Oxford, 1857).

Macky, John, *A view of the court of St Germain, advanced to the malcontent Protestants in England* (London, 1692).

MacPherson, James, ed., *Original Papers: Containing the Secret history of Great Britain from the Restoration to the Accession of the House of Hanover* (2 vols, London, 1776).

Madan, Falconer, ed., *Stuart papers relating chiefly to Queen Mary of Modena and the Exiled Court of King James II* (2 vols, Roxburgh Club, 1889).

Maimbourg, Louis, *History of the League*, trans. John Dryden (1684).

Mandeville, Bernard, *The Grumbling Hive: or, Knaves turn'd Honest* (London, 1705).

Manning, Robert, *The case stated between the Church of Rome and the Church of England* (2 vols, 1721).

Manning, Robert, *England's conversion and reformation compared. Or, the young gentleman directed in the choice of his religion* (1725).

Mannock, John Anselm, *The Christian Sacrifice* (London, 1726).

Mannock, John Anselm, *The Poor Man's Catechism* (London, 1752).

Marvell, Andrew, *Account of the Growth of Popery and Arbitrary Government in England* (1677).

Memoirs of the family of Taafe (Vienna, 1856).

Modern history, or, A monthly account of all considerable occurrences (1688).

'M.T.', *A Letter from a Gentleman at Rome to his Friend in London, Giving an Account of some very Surprising cures of the King's Evil by the Touch, lately Effected in the Neighbourhood of that City* (London, 1721).

Murphy, Martin, ed., *St Gregory's College, Seville, 1592–1767* (CRS, Southampton, 1992).

Murray, R.H., ed., *The Journal of John Stevens* (Oxford, 1912).

Nary, Cornelius, *Case of the Roman Catholics in Ireland* (Dublin, 1746).

Neville, Anne, *Annals of the Five Convents of English Benedictine Nuns in Flanders, 1598–1687* (CRS, 6, London, 1909).

Nichols, John, *Literary Anecdotes of the Eighteenth Century* (6 vols, London, 1817).

Nicole, Pierre, *De l'education d'un prince, divisée en trois parties, dont la dernieere contient divers traittez utiles a tout le monde* (Paris, 1671).

An Ode upon the Death of the late King James … Dedicated to his son the Prince (London, 1701).

P.R. [Charles Dodd], *The Freeman, or Loyall Papist* (1718).

P.R. [Charles Dodd], *A Roman Catholick System of Allegiance in Favour of the Present Establishment* (1716).

Papers of Devotion of James II (Roxburghe Club, 1925).

Pastoral Letter from the four Catholic Bishops to the Lay Catholics of England (1688).

Patten, Robert, *The History of the Late Rebellion* (1717).

Payne, J.O., ed., *Records of the English Catholics of 1715* (London, 1889).

Penrise, G., *Genuine and Impartial Letters of the Life and Character of Charles Radcliffe esq.* (1748).

Pope, Alexander, *Epitaph on John, Lord Caryll*, in J. Butt, ed., *Poems of Alexander Pope* (6 vols, London, 1967), VI, p. 18.

Pope, Alexander, *Imitation of Horace, Satire, II* (1733).

Pope, Alexander, *The Rape of the Lock* (1708).

Pope, Alexander, *Universal Prayer* (London, 1715).

Popish Treaties not to be rely'd upon: In a letter from a Gentleman at York to his friend in the Prince of Orange's camp, Addressed to all members of the next parliament (1689).

Porter, Jerome, *The Life of St Edward, King and Confessor* (London, 1710 edn).

The Present French king demonstrated an enemy to the Catholick as well as Protestant religion (1691).

Rae, P., *The History of the Rebellion Rais'd against His Majesty King George I: By the Friends of the Pretender* (London, 1746).

Ramsay, Andrew Michael, *An Apology for the Free and Accepted Masons* (1738), in Rev. George Oliver, *The Golden Remains of the Early Masonic Writers, illustrating the institutes of the order* (5 vols, London, 1847–1850), III, pp. 78–133.

Ramsay, Andrew Michael, *Essay on Civil Government: wherein is set forth, the Necessity, Origine, Rights, Boundaries, and Different Forms of Sovereignty. With Observations on the Ancient Government of Rome and England. According to the Principles of the late Archbishop of Cambray. Translated from the French* (London, 1722).

Ramsay, Andrew Michael, *Life of François de Salignac de la Motte Fénelon Archbishop and Duke of Cambray* (London, 1723).

Ramsay, Andrew Michael, *The Philosophical Principles of Natural and Revealed Religion unfolded in a Geometrical Order* (2 vols, Glasgow, 1748–1749).

Ramsay, Andrew Michael, *Plan of Education for a Young Prince* (London, 1732).

Ramsay, Andrew Michael, *Some few Poems composed by the Chevalier Ramsay, Author of the Celebrated Travels of Cyrus* (Edinburgh, 1728).

Ramsay, Andrew Michael, *The Travels of Cyrus* (2 vols, London, 1727).

RC [Charles Dodd], *History of the English College at Doway, from its First Foundation in 1568, to the Present Time* (London, 1713).

Reasons for Abrogating the Test (1688).

Reboulet, Jacques, *Histoire de Clément XI* (Avignon, 1752).

Register Book, College of St Gregory's, Paris (CRS, 19, London, 1917).

The Register of the Estates of Roman Catholics in Northumberland (Surtees Society, 81, 1918).

Reresby, John, *Memoirs of Sir John Reresby*, ed. Andrew Browning (Glasgow, 1936).

Roebuck, Peter, ed., *Constable of Everingham Estate Correspondence 1726–43* (Yorkshire Archaeological Society, 136, 1976).

Rose, Sir George Henry, *A Selection from the Papers of the Earl of Marchmont* (3 vols, London, 1831).

Saint-Pierre, Charles Castel de, *Mémoires pour render la paix perpetuelle en Europe* (Cologne, 1712).

Saint-Simon, Duc de, *Memoirs*, ed. F. Arkwright (6 vols, London, 1918).

Sanders, Francis, *A Short Relation of the Life and Death of James the Second, King of England & c.* (St Germain, 1703).

Scarisbrick, Edward, *Catholic Loyalty upon the subject of Government and Obedience* (London, 1686).

Scarisbrick, Edward, *The Life of Lady Warner* (1691).

Scott, Walter, ed., *A Collection of Scarce and Valuable Tracts* (Somers Collection, London, 1814).

Sharratt, Michael, ed., *Lisbon College Register 1628–1813* (CRS, Southampton 1991).

Sherburn, George, ed., *The Correspondence of Alexander Pope* (5 vols, Oxford, 1956).

A Short Account of Intrigues Transacted both at home and abroad to restore the late King James (1694).

Singer, Samuel Weller, ed., *Correspondence of Henry Hyde, earl of Clarendon and of his brother, Laurence Hyde, earl of Rochester* (2 vols, London, 1828).

Some reflections on the oaths & declaration appointed in an act past in the first year of the reign of King William and Queen Mary in reference to the Roman Catholicks of England / by Sir D.W. Baronet, of the church of Rome (1695).

Southcott, Thomas, *Translations of the Prayer of Jeremy paraphras'd*, in *Miscellaneous Poems and Translations, by several hands* (1712), pp. 109–116.

Spence, Joseph, *Anecdotes, Observations and Characters of Books and Men, collected from the Conversation of Mr. Pope and other Eminent Persons of his Time*, ed. Samuel Weller Singer (London, 1964).

Stevens, John, *History of Ancient Abbeys* (4 vols, 1722).

Towneley Hall Papers (CRS, 2, 1906).

A True Account of the Horrid Conspiracies against the Life of His Sacred Majesty William III, King of England, Scotland, France and Ireland (London, 1696).

The True Briton, vol. III, 10 July 1751.

A True Copy of the Paper Delivered to the Sheriffs of London by Colonel Henry Oxburgh, Who Was Drawn, Hang'd and Quarter'd at Tyburn for High Treason against His Majesty King George, Monday the 14th Day of March, 1716 (1716).

A True Copy of the Paper Delivered to the Sheriffs of London by Richard Gascoigne (1716).

The True Interest of the Princes of Europe in the Present State of Affairs (1689).

Tyrer, Frank, and Bagley, J.J., eds, *The Great Diurnall of Nicholas Blundell of Little Crosby, Lancashire* (3 vols, 1958–1962).

A view of the true interest of the several states of Europe since the accession of their present Majesties to the imperial crown of Great Britain (1689).

Wade, John Francis, *The Evening Office of the Church* (1773).

Wade, John Francis, *The Roman Gradual* (1767 edn).

Ward, Thomas, *England's Reformation: From the Time of King Henry VIII, To the End of Oates's Plot, a Poem* (1716).

Ward, Thomas, *The Tree of Life* (1688).

Warner, John, *History of the Presbyterian Plot* (2 vols, printed by Catholic Record Society, London, 1953).

Weldon, Ralph Benet, *Chronological Notes Concerning the Rise, Growth and Present State of the English Congregation of the Order of St Benedict* (London, 1881 edn).

Witham, Robert, 'Advice to a President', in E.H. Burton and E. Nolan, eds, *The Douay College Diaries: The Seventh Diary 1715–1778* (CRS, 8, London 1928), pp.308–26.

Wood, Anthony, *Athenae Oxoniensis* (3 vols, 3rd edn, London, 1817).

Select secondary works

Alger, J.G., 'The Towneleys in Paris, 1709–80: The translator of *Hudibras*', *Palatine Note-Book*, 3 (1883), pp. 84–6.

Allison, A.F., 'The English Augustinian Convent of our Lady of Syon at Paris', *Recusant History*, 21 (1993), pp. 451–96.

Allsop, J.D., 'John Macky's 1717 account of the English Seminaries in Flanders', *Recusant History*, 15 (1981), pp. 537–41.

Anderson, Benedict, *Imagined Communities: Reflections on the Origins and Spread of Nationalism* (London, 1991).

Anstruther, Godfrey, *The Seminary Priests* (4 vols, 1968–1977).

Arnold, Ralph, *Northern Lights: The Story of Lord Derwentwater* (London, 1959).

Aveling, J.H.C., 'The Eighteenth Century English Benedictines', in Duffy, E., ed., *Challoner and his Church* (London, 1981), pp. 152–73.

Aveling, J.H.C., *The Handle and the Axe: The Catholic Recusants in England from Reformation to Emancipation* (London, 1976).

Aveling, J.H.C., *Northern Catholics: The Catholic Recusants of the North Riding of Yorkshire 1558–1790* (London, 1966).

Ayres, Philip, *Classical Culture and the Idea of Rome in Eighteenth-Century England* (Cambridge, 1997).

Barnard, Howard Clive, *The Little Schools of Port Royal* (1913).

Beales, A.C.F., *Education under Penalty: English Catholic Education from the Reformation to the Fall of James II* (London, 1963).

Beales, Derek, 'Christians and Philosophes: The Causes of the Austrian Enlightenment', in Derek Beales, and Geoffrey Best, eds, *History, Society and the Churches: Essays in honour of Owen Chadwick* (Cambridge, 1985).

Beaumont, W.M., ed., *The Jacobite Trials at Manchester in 1694* (Chetham Society, 18, 1853).

Bellenger, Aidan, ed., *Opening the Scrolls* (Downside, 1987).

Bellesheim, Alphons, *History of the Catholic Church in Scotland*, trans. D.O. Hunter Blair (4 vols, Edinburgh 1887–1890), IV.

Bence Jones, Mark, *The Catholic Families* (London, 1992).

Bennett, G.V., *The Tory Crisis in Church and State 1688–1730: The Career of Francis Atterbury* (London, 1975).

Birrell, T.A., 'Catholic Allegiance and the Popish Plot', *Downside Review*, 68 (1950), pp. 439–61.

Birrell, T.A., 'English Catholic Mystics in Non-Catholic Circles', *Downside Review*, 94 (1976), pp. 58–78, 99–117.

Black, Jeremy, *The British Abroad: The Grand Tour in the 18th Century* (Stroud, 1992).

Black, Jeremy, *The English Press in the Eighteenth Century* (London, 1987).

Blackwood, B.G., 'Lancashire Catholics, Protestants and Jacobites in the 1715 Rebellion', *Recusant History* (1994), pp. 41–59.

Blanning, T.C.W., 'The Enlightenment in Catholic Germany', in R. Porter and M. Teich, eds, *The Enlightenment in National Context* (Cambridge, 1981).

Bloch, Marc, *The Royal Touch: Sacred Monarchy and Scrofula in England and France*, trans. J. Anderson (London, 1973).

Blom, F., Blom, J., Korsten, F., Scott, G., *English Catholic Books 1701–1800: A Bibliography* (Aldershot, 1996).

Blundell, F.O., *Old Catholic Lancashire* (3 vols, London, 1925, 1938, 1941).

Bosher, J.F., 'The Franco-Catholic Danger, 1660–1715', *History* 79 (1994), pp. 5–30.

Bossy, John M., *The English Catholic Community* (London, 1976).

Bossy, John M., 'English Catholics after 1688', in Grell, Israel and Tyacke, eds, *Persecution to Toleration*, pp. 369–87.

Bredvold, Louis I., *The Intellectual Milieu of John Dryden* (London, 1956).

Brennan, Gillian E., 'Papists and Patriotism in Elizabethan England', *Recusant History*, 19 (1988–9), pp. 1–15.

Brietz Monta, Susannah, *Martyrdom and Literature in Early Modern England* (London, 2005).

Bruckmann, Patricia, '"Paradice it selfe": Hugh Cressy and Church Unity', in Kevin L. Cope, ed., *Ideas, Aesthetics and Inquiries in the Early Modern Era*, I (New York, 1997), pp. 83–107.

Burns, J.H. and Goldie, M.A., eds, *Cambridge History of Political Thought 1450–1700* (Cambridge, 1991).

Burton, E.H., *The Life and Times of Bishop Challoner* (2 vols, London, 1909).

Callow, John, 'The Last of the Shireburnes: The Art of Death and Life in Recusant Lancashire 1660–1754', *Recusant History*, 26 (2002–3), pp. 589–615.

Callow, John, *The Making of James II* (Stroud, 2000).

Camm, Bede, *In the Brave Days of Old* (London, 1899).

Campbell, Kenneth L, *The Intellectual Struggle of English Papists in the Seventeenth Century: The Catholic Dilemma* (New York, 1986).

Cannadine, David, 'British History: Past, Present – and Future?', *Past and Present*, 116 (1987), pp. 169–91.

Cannon, John, *Aristocratic Century: The Peerage of Eighteenth-Century England* (Cambridge, 1984).

Carswell, John, *The Descent on England* (1969).

Cavelli, Marquise Campana de, *Les Derniers Stuarts à Saint Germain-en-Laye* (Paris, 1871).

Chadwick, Owen, *From Bossuet to Newman* (2nd edn, Cambridge, 1987).

Chadwick, Owen, *The Popes and European Revolution* (Cambridge, 1981).

Champion, Justin, *The Pillars of Priestcraft Shaken: The Church of England and its Enemies 1660–1730* (Cambridge, 1992).

Chauncy, Maurice, *The Passion and Martyrdom of the English Carthusian Fathers* (London, 1935).

Cherry, A., 'The Scots College Books in Paris', *IR*, 44 (1993), pp. 69–72.

Childs, John, *The Nine Years War and the British Army 1688–97* (Manchester, 1991).

Childs, Nicholas, *A Political Academy in Paris 1724–1731: The Entresol and its Members* (Oxford, 2000).

Chinnici, Joseph, *The English Catholic Enlightenment: John Lingard and the Cisalpine Movement 1780–1850* (Shepherdstown, 1980).

Clancy, Thomas H., 'A Content Analysis of English Catholic Books 1615–1719', *Catholic Historical Review*, 86 (2000), pp. 258–72.

Clancy, Thomas H., *English Catholic Books 1640–1700* (Chicago, 1974).

Clancy, Thomas H., *A Literary History of the English Jesuits: A Century of Books 1615–1714* (London, 1996).

Clark, J.C.D., *English Society 1660–1832: Religion, Ideology and Politics during the Ancien Régime* (2nd edn, Cambridge, 2000).

Clark, J.C.D., 'On Moving the Middle Ground: The Significance of Jacobitism in English Historical Studies', in Cruickshanks and Black, eds, *The Jacobite Challenge* (Edinburgh, 1989), pp. 177–85.

Clark, Ruth, *Anthony Hamilton: His Life, his Works and his Family* (London and New York, 1921).

Clark, Ruth, *Strangers and Sojourners at Port Royal; Being an Account of the Connections between British Isles and the Jansenists of France and Holland* (Cambridge, 1932).

Claydon, Tony, *Europe and the Making of England 1660–1760* (Cambridge, 2007).

Claydon, Tony, 'Protestantism, Universal Monarchy and Christendom in William's War Propaganda, 1689–1697', in Esther Mijers and David Onnekink, eds, *Redefining William III: The Impact of the King-Stadtholder in International Context* (Aldershot, 2007), pp. 125–42.

Claydon, Tony, *William III and the Godly Revolution* (1996).

Claydon, Tony, and McBride, Ian, 'The Trials of the Chosen Peoples: Recent Interpretations of Protestantism and National Identity in Britain and Ireland', in Claydon and McBride, *Protestantism and National Identity: Britain and Ireland c.1650–c.1850* (Cambridge, 1998).

Cokayne, George Edward, *The Complete Peerage* (12 vols, London, 1910).

Colley, Linda, *Britons: Forging the Nation 1707–1837* (London, 1992).

Colley, Linda, 'Eighteenth-Century English Radicalism before Wilkes', *Transactions of the Royal Historical Society*, 5th ser., 31 (1981), pp. 1–20.

Collins, Jeffrey R., 'Thomas Hobbes and the Blackloist Conspiracy of 1649', *Historical Journal*, 45 (2002), pp. 303–31.

Corns, Thomas N., ed., *The Royal Image: Representations of Charles I* (Cambridge, 1997).

Corp, Edward T., ed., *L'autre exil: Les Jacobites en France* (Paris, 1993).

Corp, Edward T., 'Catherine of Braganza and Cultural Politics', in Clarissa Campbell Orr, ed., *Queenship in Britain 1660–1837: Royal Patronage, Court Culture and Dynastic Politics* (Manchester, 2002), pp. 53–73.

Corp, Edward T., ed., *A Court in Exile: The Stuarts in France 1689–1718* (Cambridge, 2003).

Corp, Edward T., 'The Jacobite Chapel Royal at Saint Germain', *Recusant History*, 23 (1997).

Corp, Edward T., 'James II and Toleration: The Years in Exile at St Germain-en-Laye', *Royal Stuart Society* (1997).

Corp, Edward T., ed., *The Stuart Court in Rome: The Legacy of Exile* (Aldershot, 2003).

Cottret, Bernard, and Cottret, Monique, 'Le Sainteté de Jacques II et les miracles d'un roi défunt', in Corp, ed., *L'autre exil: Les Jacobites en France* (Paris, 1993), pp. 79–106.

Cruickshanks, Eveline, ed., *By Force or by Default: The Revolution of 1688–9* (Edinburgh, 1989).

Cruickshanks, Eveline, ed., *Ideology and Conspiracy: Aspects of Jacobitism 1689–1759* (Edinburgh, 1982).

Cruickshanks, Eveline, and Black, Jeremy, eds, *The Jacobite Challenge* (Edinburgh, 1988).

Cruickshanks, Eveline, and Corp, Edward T., eds, *The Stuart Court in Exile and the Jacobites* (London, 1995).

Cruickshanks, Eveline, and Erskine-Hill, Howard, *The Atterbury Plot* (Basingstoke, 2004),

Cruickshanks, Eveline, and Erskine-Hill, Howard, 'The Waltham Black Act and Jacobitism', *Journal of British Studies*, 24 (1985), pp. 358–65.

Davidson, Nicholas, *The Counter-Reformation* (1987).

Davidson, Nicholas, 'Toleration in Enlightenment Italy', in Porter and Grell, eds, *Toleration in Enlightenment Europe*, pp. 230–49.

Davis, J.H., 'Utopianism', in Burns and Goldie, eds, *History of Political Thought*, pp. 329–44.

Davis, R.H., *Fénelon* (Boston, 1929).

de la Bédoyère, Michael, *The Archbishop and the Lady: The Story of Fénelon and Madame Guyon* (London, 1956).

Delumeau, Jean, *Catholicism between Luther and Voltaire: A New View of the Counter-Reformation* (London, 1977).

Dillon, Anne, *The Construction of Martyrdom in the English Catholic Community, 1535–1603* (Aldershot, 2002).

Dilworth, Mark, 'Jesuits and Jacobites: The Cultus of St Margaret', *Innes Review*, 47 (1996), pp. 169–80.

Ditchfield, Simon, 'Martyrs on the Move: Relics as Vindicators of Local Diversity in the Tridentine Church', in D. Wood, *Martyrs and Martyrologies*, Studies in Church History, 30 (1993), pp. 283–95.

Dolan, J.G., 'James II and the Benedictines in London', *Downside Review*, 18 (1899), pp. 94–103.

Douglas, David C., *English Scholars 1660–1730* (London, 1939).

Doyle, F.C., 'St Edmunds, Paris', I, *Downside Review*, 22 (1913), pp. 125–47; II, *Downside Review*, 33 (1924), pp. 250–75.

Duckett, Sir George, *The Penal Laws and the Test Acts* (2 vols, London, 1882, 1883).

Duffy, Eamon, ed., *Challoner and his Church* (London, 1981).

Duffy, Eamon, 'The English Secular Clergy and the Counter-Reformation', *Journal of Ecclesiastical History*, 34 (1983), pp. 214–30.

Duffy, Eamon, '"Englishmen in Vaine", Roman Catholic Allegiance to George I', in Stuart Mews, ed., *Religion and National Identity*, Studies in Church History, 18 (Oxford, 1982), pp. 345–67.

Duffy, Eamon, '"Over the Wall": Converts from Popery in Eighteenth-Century England', *Downside Review*, 94 (1976), pp. 1–25.

Duffy, Eamon, *Peter and Jack: Roman Catholics and Dissent in Eighteenth Century England* (London, 1982).

Duffy, Eamon, '"Poor Protestant flies": Conversions to Catholicism in Early Eighteenth Century England', in Derek Baker, ed., *Studies in Church History*, 15 (London, 1978), pp. 289–304.

Duffy, Eamon, '279"A rubb-up for old soares": Jesuits, Jansenists and the English Secular Clergy 1705–17', *Journal of Ecclesiastical History*, 28 (1972), pp. 291–311.

Durant, C.S., *A Link between Flemish Mystics and English Martyrs* (London, 1925).

Ellison, Lee Monroe, '*Gaudentio Di Lucca*: A Forgotten Utopia', *Periodical of the Modern Language Association*, 5 (1935), pp. 494–509.

Erskine-Hill, Howard, 'John, First Lord Caryll and the Caryll Papers', in Cruickshanks and Court, *Stuart Court*, pp. 73–91.

Erskine-Hill, Howard, 'Literature and the Jacobite Cause: Was there a Rhetoric of Jacobitism?' in Eveline Cruickshanks, ed., *Aspects of Jacobitism* (London, 1981), pp. 49–69.

Erskine-Hill, Howard, 'Poetry at the Exiled Court', in Corp, *A Court in Exile*, pp. 215–34.

Erskine-Hill, Howard, *Poetry and the Realm of Politics* (Oxford, 1996).

Erskine-Hill, Howard, *Poetry of Opposition and Revolution* (London, 1996).

Erskine-Hill, Howard, *The Social Milieu of Alexander Pope* (London, 1975).

Evetts-Secker, Joanna, 'Jerusalem and Albion: Ralph Buckland's Seaven Sparkes of the Enkindled Soul', *Recusant History*, 20 (1990–1), pp. 149–63.

Fendley, John, 'The Pastons of Horton and the Horton Court Library', *Recusant History*, 22 (1994–5), pp. 501–28.

Foley, Brian, *Some People of the Penal Times: Aspects of a Unique Social and Religious Phenomenon* (Lancaster, 1991).

Fritz, Paul S., *The English Ministers and Jacobitism between the Rebellions of 1715 and 1745* (Toronto, 1975).

Gable, A.T., 'The Prince and the Mirror: Louis XIV, Fénelon, Royal Narcissism and the Legacy of Machiavelli', *Seventeenth-Century French Studies*, 15 (1997), pp. 243–68.

Garrett, Jane, *The Triumphs of Providence* (Cambridge, 1984).

Geiter, Mary K., 'William Penn and Jacobitism: A Smoking Gun?', *Historical Research*, 73 (2000), pp. 213–17.

Genet-Rouffiac, Natalie, 'Jacobites in Paris and Saint Germain-en-Laye', in Cruickshanks and Corp, eds, *Stuart Court*, pp. 15–39.

Gerrard, Christine, *The Patriot Opposition to Walpole: Politics, Poetry and National Myth 1725–42* (Oxford, 1994).

Gilley, Sheridan, 'Challoner as Controversialist', in Duffy, ed., *Challoner and his Church*, pp. 90–111.

Gillow, Joseph, *Biographical Dictionary of the English Catholics* (5 vols, London, 1985 edn).

Goldie, Mark, 'Bishop Hay, Bishop Geddes and the Scottish Catholic Enlightenment', *Innes Review*, 45 (1994), pp. 82–6.

Goldie, Mark, 'James II and the Dissenters' Revenge', *Historical Research*, 66 (1993).

Goldie, Mark, 'Restoration Political Thought', in Glassey, *The Reigns of Charles II and James VII and II* (1997), pp. 12–35.

Goldie, Mark, 'The Revolution of 1689 and the Structure of Political Argument', *Bulletin of Research in the Humanities*, 83 (1980), pp. 473–564.

Goldie, Mark, 'The Scottish Catholic Enlightenment', *Journal of British Studies*, 30 (1991), pp. 20–62.

Goldie, Mark, 'The Theory of Religious Intolerance in Restoration England', in Grell et al., *From Persecution to Toleration: The Glorious Revolution and Toleration in England* (Oxford, 1991), pp. 331–68.

Goldie, Mark, and Jackson, Clare, 'Williamite Tyranny and the Whig Jacobites', in Esther Mijers and David Onnekink, eds, *Redefining William III: The Impact of the King-Stadtholder in International Context* (Aldershot, 2007), pp. 177–200.

Gosden, Christopher, *Social Being and Time* (Oxford, 1994).

Gooch, Leo, *The Desperate Faction? The Jacobites of North East England 1688–1745* (Hull, 1995).

Gooch, Leo, '"Incarnate Rogues and Vile Jacobites": Silvertop vs Cotesworth, 1718–1726', *Recusant History*, 18 (1987), pp. 277–81.

Gooch, Leo, 'Priests and Patrons in the Eighteenth Century', *Recusant History*, 20 (1990–1), pp. 207–22.

Gooch, Leo, '"The Religion for a Gentleman": The North Country Catholics in the Eighteenth Century', *Recusant History*, 23 (1997), pp. 543–68.

Gorski, Konrad, 'La Naissance des états et le "roi-saint": problème de l'idéologie féodale', in T. Mantcuffel and A. Gieysztor, eds, *L'Europe aux IXe–Xie siècles: aux origins des états nationaux* (Warsaw, 1968), pp. 425–32.

Grafton, Anthony, 'Humanism and Political Theory', in Burns and Goldie, eds, *History of Political Thought 1450–1700*, pp. 9–29.

Gregg, Edward, 'New Light on the Authorship of the Life of James II', *English Historical Review*, 108 (1993), pp. 947–62.

Gregg, Edward, 'The Politics of Paranoia', in Cruickshanks and Black, *Jacobite Challenge*, pp. 42–53.

Grell, Ole Peter, Israel, Jonathan I. and Tyacke, Nicholas, *From Persecution to Toleration: The Glorious Revolution and Religion in England* (Oxford, 1997).

Grell, Ole Peter, and Porter, Roy, eds, *Toleration in Enlightenment Europe* (Cambridge, 2000).

Guilday, Peter, *English Catholic Refugees on the Continent, 1558–1795* (London, 1914).

Haigh, Christopher, 'Catholicism in Early Modern England: Bossy and beyond', *Historical Journal*, 45 (2002), pp. 481–94.

Haigh, Christopher, 'The Fall of a Church or the Rise of a Sect? Post-Reformation Catholicism in England', *Historical Journal*, 21 (1978), pp. 181–6.

Halloran, Brian M., *The Scots College, Paris 1603–1792* (Edinburgh, 1997).

Hamilton, Donna B., 'Catholic Use of Anglo-Saxon Precedents, 1565–1625', *Recusant History*, 26 (2002–3), pp. 537–55.

Hardman, Anne, *Two English Carmelites, Mother Mary Xaveria Burton (1668–1714) and Mother Mary Margaret Wake (1617–1678)* (London, 1939).

Harris, Tim, 'London Crowds and the Revolution of 1688', in Cruickshanks and Miller, eds, *By Force or Default?*, pp. 44–65.

Harris, Tim, Seaward, Paul, and Goldie, Mark, eds, *The Politics of Religion in Restoration England* (London, 1990).

Harth, Philip, *Pen for a Party: Dryden's Tory Propaganda and its Contexts* (Princeton, 1993).

Hartmann, Cyril Hughes, *Clifford of the Cabal* (London, 1937).

Hatton, Ragnhild, *George I: Elector and King* (London, 1978).

Haydon, Colin, *Anti-Catholicism in 18th Century England c.1714–80: a Political and Social Study* (Manchester, 1993).

Haydon, Colin, '"I love my King and my Country, but a Roman Catholic I hate": Anti-Catholicism, Xenophobia and National Identity in Eighteenth-Century England', in Tony Claydon and Ian McBride, eds, *Protestantism and National Identity: Britain and Ireland c.1650–c.1850* (Cambridge, 1998), pp. 33–52.

Haydon, Colin, 'Samuel Peploe and Catholicism in Preston, 1714', *Recusant History*, 20 (1990–1), pp. 76–80.

Hazard, Paul, *La crise de la conscience européenne (1680–1715)* (Paris, 1935).

Hazard, Paul, *The European Mind (1680–1715)* (London, 1952).

Hazard, Paul, *European Thought in the Eighteenth Century* (London, 1954).

Hemphill, Basil, *The Early Vicars Apostolic of England 1685–1750* (London, 1954).

Henderson, G.D., *Chevalier Ramsay* (London and New York, 1952).

Hibbert-Ware, Samuel, *Lancashire Memorials of the Rebellion, 1715* (Chetham Society, 5, 1843).

Hill, Christopher, 'The Norman Yoke', reprinted in *Puritanism and Revolution* (London, 1958), pp. 57–73.

Hill, P.K., *The Oglethorpe Ladies and the Jacobite Conspiracies* (Atlanta, 1977).

Hodgetts, Michael, 'The Yates of Harvington, 1631–1696', *Recusant History*, 22 (1994), pp. 152–81.

Holmes, Geoffrey, *The Making of a Great Power: Late Stuart and Early Georgian Britain 1660–1722* (London, 1993).

Holmes, Geoffrey, and Szechi, Daniel, *The Age of Oligarchy: Pre-Industrial Britain 1722–83* (London, 1993), p. 90.

Holt, Geoffrey, 'Edward Scarisbrick (1639–1709): A Royal Preacher', *Recusant History*, 23 (1996–7), pp. 159–65.

Holt, Geoffrey, *The English Jesuits and the Age of Reason* (Tunbridge Wells, 1993).

Holt, Geoffrey, 'Some Chaplains at the Stuart Court at St Germain', *Recusant History*, 25 (2000–1), pp. 43–51.

Holt, Geoffrey, 'Two Seventeenth-Century Hebrew Scholars: Thomas Fairfax and Edward Slaughter', *Recusant History*, 22 (1994–5), pp. 482–90.

Hopkins, P.A., 'The Commission for Superstitious Lands of the 1690s', *Recusant History*, 15 (1980), pp. 265–82.

Hopkins, P.A., 'Sham Plots and Real Plots in the 1690s', in Cruickshanks, *Aspects of Jacobitism*, pp. 89–110.

Hopkins, P.A, 'Sir James Montgomery of Skelmorlie', in Cruickshanks and Corp, *Stuart Court*, pp. 39–61.

Hoppitt, Julian, *A Land of Liberty? England 1688–1727* (Oxford, 2000).

Hornyold-Strickland, Henry, *Genealogical Memoirs of the Family of Strickland of Sizergh* (Kendal, 1928).

Israel, Jonathan I., *The Anglo-Dutch Moment: Essays on the Glorious Revolution and its World Impact* (London, 1988).

Israel, Jonathan I., *Radical Enlightenment: Philosophy and the Making of Modernity, 1650–1750* (Oxford, 2001).

Israel, Jonathan I., 'William III and Toleration', in Grell, Israel and Tyacke, eds, *Persecution to Toleration*, pp. 129–70.

Jacob, Margaret C., *The Radical Enlightenment: Pantheists, Freemasons and Republicans* (London, 1981).

Jenkins, Philip, 'Jacobites and Freemasons in 18th Century Wales', *Welsh Historical Review*, 9 (1979), pp. 391–406.

Jones, George Hilton, *Charles Middleton: The Life and Times of a Restoration Politician* (London, 1967).

Jones, George Hilton, *The Main Stream of Jacobitism* (Harvard, 1954).

Jones, J.R., 'James II's Whig Collaborators', *Historical Journal*, 7 (1960), pp. 65–73.

Jones, J.R., *The Revolution of 1688 in England* (London, 1972).

Joyce, M.B., 'The Haggerstons: The Education of a Northumberland Family', *Recusant History*, 19 (1978), pp. 175–92.

Kelly, J.N.D., *Oxford Dictionary of Popes* (Oxford, 1986).

Kenyon, John, *The Popish Plot* (London, 1972).

Kenyon, John, *Revolution Principles: The Politics of Party, 1689–1720* (London, 1977).

Kervella, A., *La Passion écossaise* (Paris, 2002).

Kidd, Colin, *Subverting Scotland's Past: Scottish Whig Historians and the Creation of an Anglo-British Identity, 1689–1830* (Cambridge, 1993).

King, Katherine, *Jane Barker, Exile: A Literary Career 1675–1725* (Oxford, 2000).

Kirk, John, *Biographies of English Catholics in the 18th Century* (London, 1905 edn).

Knoppers, Laura L., 'Reviving the Martyr: Charles I as Jacobite Icon', in Corns, ed., *The Royal Image*, pp. 263–87.

Knox, Ronald A., *Enthusiasm: A Chapter in the History of Religion with Special Reference to the XVII and XVIII Centuries* (Oxford, 1950).

Lacey, Andrew, *The Cult of King Charles the Martyr* (Woodbridge, 2003).

Langford, Paul, *A Polite and Commercial People: England 1727–1783* (Oxford, 1989).

Leighton, C.D.A., *Catholicism in a Protestant Kingdom: A Study of the Irish Ancien Régime* (Basingstoke, 1994).

Lenman, Bruce, 'The Scottish Episcopal Clergy and the Ideology of Jacobitism', in Cruickshanks, *Aspects of Jacobitism*, pp. 36–48.

Le Roy Ladurie, Emmanuel, *The Ancien Régime: A History of France 1610–1774* (London, 1996 translation).

Lindley, Kenneth, 'The Part Played by Catholics', in Brian Manning, ed., *Politics, Religion and the English Civil War* (London, 1973), pp. 127–78.

Luckett, Richard, 'Bishop Challoner: The Devotionary Writer', in Duffy, ed., *Challoner and his Church*, pp. 71–89.

Lunn, David, 'The Anglo-Gallicanism of Dom Thomas Preston, 1567–1647', Studies in Church History, 9 (1972), pp. 239–46.

Lunn, David, *The English Benedictines 1540–1688: From Reformation to Revolution* (London, 1980).

Lunn, John, *The Tyldesleys of Lancashire: The Rise and Fall of a Great Patrician Family* (Altrincham, 1966).

MacDonald, G., 'The Lime Street Chapel', *Dublin Review* (1927) 180, pp. 261–5 and 181, pp. 2–6.

Maclean, Donald , *The Counter-Reformation in Scotland* (Edinburgh, 1932).

Mann, M.J., 'Nuns of the Jerningham Letters: Eliz Jerningham (1727–1807) and Frances Henrietta Jerningham (1745–1824), Augustinian Canonesses of Bruges', *Recusant History*, 22 (1994–5), pp. 350–69.

Manuel, Frank E., and Manuel, Fritzie P., *Utopian Thought in the Western World* (Oxford, 1979).

Mathew, David, *Catholicism in England 1540–1935* (London, 1936).

McCann, Timothy J., 'Henry Houghton, SJ., Chaplain to the Caryll at West Grinstead, Sussex, 1736–50', in Aidan Bellenger, ed., *Opening the Scrolls*, pp. 91–100.

McCann, Timothy J., 'On the Alleged Murder of his Chaplain by Henry Browne, 5th Viscount Montagu of Cowdray', *Sussex Archaeological Collections*, 131 (1999), pp. 126–8.

McGoldrick, T.J., 'Jacobitism and English Catholics', *Ushaw Magazine*, 46 (1936), pp. 1–20.

McInnes, Angus, 'The Revolution and the People', in G. Holmes, ed., *Britain after the Glorious Revolution*, pp. 80–95.

McKenna, J.M.W., 'Popular Canonisation as Political Propaganda', *Speculum*, 45 (1978), pp. 608–23.

McLynn, Frank, *Charles Edward Stuart: A Tragedy in Many Acts* (London, 1988).

McLynn, Frank, *The Jacobites* (London, 1985).

McLynn, Pauline, *Factionalism among the Exiles in France: The Case of Bishop Atterbury and Chevalier Ramsay* (Huntingdon, Royal Stuart Society, 1989).

McManners, John, *Church and Society in Eighteenth-Century France*, I, *The Clerical Establishment and its Social Ramifications* (Oxford, 1998).

McManners, John, 'Jansenism and Politics in the Eighteenth Century', in Derek Baker, ed., Studies in Church History, 12 (1975), pp. 253–73.

McMillan, James F., 'The Innes Brothers and the Scots College, Paris', in Cruickshanks and Corp, eds, *Stuart Court*, pp. 91–100.

McMillan, James F., 'Jansenism and the Scots College Books', *Innes Review*, 44 (1993), pp. 73–5.

McMillan, James F., 'Thomas Innes and the Bull "Unigenitus"', *Innes Review*, 33 (1982), pp. 23–31.

Michaud, Eugene, *Louis XIV et Innocent XI* (3 vols, Paris, 1883).

Middleton, Dorothy, *The Life of Charles, Second Earl of Middleton 1650–1719* (London, 1957).

Miller, John, 'Catholic Officers in the Stuart Army', *English Historical Review*, 88 (1973).

Miller, John, *James II: A Study in Kingship* (London, 1978).

Miller, John, 'James II and Toleration', in Cruickshanks, *By Force or by Default?*, pp. 8–28.

Miller, John, *Popery and Politics in England 1660–88* (Cambridge, 1973).

Monod, Paul, 'Jacobitism and Country Politics in the Reign of William III', *Historical Journal*, 30 (1987), pp. 289–310.

Monod, Paul K., *Jacobitism and the English People* (Cambridge, 1989).

Monod, Paul K., 'The Politics of Matrimony: Jacobitism and Marriage in England', in Cruickshanks and Black, eds, *The Jacobite Challenge*, pp. 26–41.

Morrill, John, 'The Sensible Revolution', in Israel, ed., *The Anglo-Dutch Moment*, pp. 73–104.

Morris, John, *The Troubles of our Catholic Forefathers* (3 vols, London, 1872–1877).

Mullett, Michel A., *Catholics in Britain and Ireland, 1558–1829* (London, 1998).

Murphy, Martin, 'A House Divided: The Fall of the Herberts of Powis 1688–1715', *Recusant History*, 26 (2002–3), pp. 88–101.

Murphy, Martin, 'A Jacobite Antiquary in Grub Street: Captain John Stevens', *Recusant History*, 24 (1998–9), pp. 437–54.

Murray, John J., *George I, the Baltic and the Whig Split of 1717: A Study in Diplomacy and Propaganda* (London, 1969).

Newman, P.R., 'Catholic Royalist Activities in the North 1642–6', *Recusant History*, 14 (1977), pp. 26–38.

Newman, P.R., 'Roman Catholics in pre-Civil War England: The Problem of Definition', *Recusant History*, 15 (1979), pp. 148–52.

Newman, P.R., 'Roman Catholic Royalists: Papist Communities under Charles I and Charles II 1642–60', *Recusant History*, 15 (1981), pp. 396–405.

Nicholson, Albert, 'Lancashire in the Rebellion of 1715', *Transactions of the Lancashire and Cheshire Antiquarian Society*, 3 (1885), pp. 66–88.

Norman, Edward, *Roman Catholicism in England from the Elizabethan Settlement to the Second Vatican Council* (Oxford, 1985).

Norman, Marion, 'John Gother and the English Way of Spirituality', *Recusant History*, 11 (1972), pp. 306–19.

Nuttall, Geoffrey F., and Chadwick, Owen, eds, *From Uniformity to Unity* (London, 1962).

O'Brien, Susan, 'Women of the English Catholic Community: Nuns and Pupils at the Bar Convent, York 1690–1790', in J. Loades, ed., *Monastic Studies* (1990), pp. 270–2.

O'Ciardha, Eamonn, 'A Fatal Attachment': *Ireland and the Jacobite Cause 1688–1788* (Cambridge, 2001).

O'Connor, Thomas, *Irish Jansenists 1600–1670* (Dublin, 2008).

O'Connor, Thomas, *An Irish Theologian in Enlightenment France: Luke Joseph Hooke, 1714–96* (Blackrock, 1995).

O'Leary, J.G., 'The Last of the Southcotes of Witham', *Essex Recusant*, 2 (1969), pp. 21–9.

Owen, John B., *The Eighteenth Century 1714–1815* (London, 1974).

Parry, Graham, *The Trophies of Time: English Antiquarians of the Seventeenth Century* (London, 1993).

Partner, Peter, *The Murdered Magicians: The Templars and their Myth* (Oxford, 1982).

Patterson, W.B., *James VI and I and the Reunion of Christendom* (Cambridge, 1997).

Petrie, Sir Charles, *The Jacobite Movement: The First Phase* (London, 1948).

Petrie, Sir Charles, *The Jacobite Movement: The Last Phase* (London, 1950).

Pincus, Steven C., 'The European Catholic Context of the Revolution of 1688–89: Gallicanism, Innocent XI and the Catholic Opposition', in Allan I. MacInnes and Arthur H. Williamson, eds, *Shaping the Stuart World 1603–1714: The Atlantic Connection* (Leiden, 2005).

Pincus, Steven C., 'From Butterboxes to Wooden Shoes: The Shift in English Popular Sentiment from anti-Dutch to anti-French in the 1670s', *Historical Journal*, 38 (1996), pp. 333–61.

Pincus, Steven C., '"To protect English liberties": The English Nationalist Revolution of 1688–1689', in Tony Claydon and Ian McBride, eds, *Protestantism and National Identity: Britain and Ireland c.1650–c.1850* (Cambridge, 1998), pp. 75–104.

Pittock, Murray G.H., 'Jacobite Ideology in Scotland and at Saint-Germain-en-Laye', in Cruickshanks and Corp, ed., *Stuart Court*, pp. 113–24.

Pittock, Murray G.H., *Jacobitism* (London, 1998).

Plumb, Sir John, *The Growth of Political Stability in England 1675–1775* (London, 1969).

Pocock, J.G.A., *The Ancient Constitution and the Feudal Law* (1957).

Porteous, T.C., 'New Light on the Lancashire Jacobite Plot, 1692–4', *Transactions of the Lancashire and Cheshire Antiquarian Society*, 50 (1934–5).

Porter, Roy, and Teich, Mikulas, eds, *The Enlightenment in National Context* (Cambridge, 1981).

Price, W., 'Three Jesuits at Plowden Hall in Shropshire in the Eighteenth Century', *Recusant History*, 3 (1965), pp.165–75.

Purcell, Peter, 'The Jacobite Risings of 1715 and the English Catholics', *English Historical Review*, 44 (1929), pp. 418–32.

Questier, Michael C., *Catholicism and Community in Early Modern England: Politics, Aristocratic Patronage and Religion c.1550–1640* (Cambridge, 2006).

Questier, Michael C., 'Catholicism, Kinship and the Public Memory of Sir Thomas More', *Journal of Ecclesiastical History*, 53 (2002), 476–509.

Rhodes, J.T., 'English Books of Martyrs and Saints of the Late 16th and Early 17th Centuries', *Recusant History*, 22 (1994), pp. 7–25.

Ridyard, Susan J., *The Royal Saints of England: A Study of West Saxon and East Anglian Cults* (Cambridge, 1988).

Roberts, J.M., *The Mythology of the Secret Societies* (New York, 1972).

Robinson, John M., *The Dukes of Norfolk* (Oxford, 1982).

Roebuck, Peter 'An English Catholic Tour in Europe 1701–3', *Recusant History*, 9 (1971), pp. 156–9.

Rosa, Susan, 'Bossuet, James II and the Crisis of Catholic Universalism', in James G. Buickerood, ed., *Eighteenth Century Thought*, 1 (New York, 2003), pp. 52–61.

Rosenheim, James M., *The Emergence of a Ruling Order* (1998).

Rothkrug, Lionel, *Opposition to Louis XIV: The Political and Social Origins of the French Enlightenment* (Princeton, 1965).

Rowlands, M., 'The Iron Age of Double Taxes', in *Staffordshire Catholic History*, III (1963), pp. 45–61.

Ruvigny and Raineval, Marquis of, *The Jacobite Peerage* (Edinburgh, 1904).

Salmon, J.H.M., 'Catholic Resistance Theory, Ultramontanism and the Royalist Response, 1580–1620', in Burns and Goldie, eds, *History of Political Thought*, pp. 219–53.

Scott, Daniel, *The Stricklands of Sizergh Castle* (Kendal, 1908).

Scott, Geoffrey, 'A Benedictine Conspirator: Henry Joseph Johnston', *Recusant History*, 20 (1990–1), pp. 58–74.

Scott, Geoffrey, 'The Collector: A Look at Benedictine Archives through the Eyes of Brother Benet Weldon, 1674–1713', *Catholic Archives*, 6 (1986), pp. 25–43.

Scott, Geoffrey, 'The Court as a Centre of Catholicism', in Corp, *A Court in Exile*, pp. 235–56.

Scott, Geoffrey, 'The Education of James III', in Corp, *A Court in Exile*, pp. 257–79.

Scott, Geoffrey, *Gothic Rage Undone: English Monks in the Age of Enlightenment* (Downside, 1992).

Scott, Geoffrey, 'Sacredness of Majesty: The English Benedictines and the Cult of James II', *Royal Stuart Society* (1984).

Shagan, Ethan H., ed., *Catholics and the 'Protestant Nation'* (Manchester, 2005).

Sharpe, J.S., 'Last Dying Speeches: Religion, Ideology and Public Execution in 17th Century England', *Past and Present*, 107 (1985), pp. 144–67.

Sharratt, Michael, '"Excellent Professors and an Exact Discipline": Aspects of Challoner's Douai', in Duffy, ed., *Challoner and his Church*, pp. 112–25.

Shell, Alison, *Catholicism, Controversy and the English Literary Imagination 1558–1660* (Cambridge, 1999).

Sherburn, Charles Danes, *A History of the Family of Sherborn* (London, 1901).

Sitwell, G.A., 'A Crisis of Authority in English Benedictine History 1717–21', *Recusant History*, 16 (1982–3), pp. 221–80.

Skeet, F.J.A., 'The Eighth Duchess of Norfolk', *Stonyhurst Magazine*, 257 (1925), pp. 73–4.

Skeet, F.J.A., *The Life of the Rt. Hon. James Radcliffe, Third Earl of Derwentwater and Charles Radcliffe* (London, 1929).

Skeet, F.J.A., ed., *Stuart Papers, Relics, Medals and Books in the Collection of Miss Maria Widdrington* (London, 1930).

Skerpan Wheeler, Elizabeth, 'Eikon Basilike and the Rhetoric of Self-Representation', in Corns, ed., *The Royal Image*, pp. 122–40.

Skinner, Quentin, 'The Principles and Practice of Opposition: The Case of Bolingbroke versus Walpole', in Neil McKendrick, ed., *Historical Perspectives: Studies in English Thought and Society in honour of J.H. Plumb* (London, 1974), pp. 93–128.

Smith, Hannah, 'The Idea of Protestant Monarchy in Britain 1714–1760', *Past and Present*, 185 (2005), pp. 91–118.

Smith, R.J., *The Gothic Bequest: Medieval Institutions in British Thought, 1688–1833* (Cambridge, 1987).

Somerville, Johann P., 'Absolutism and Royalism', in Burns and Goldie, eds, *History of Political Thought*, pp. 347–73.

Speck, W.A., *Reluctant Revolutionaries: Englishmen and the Revolution of 1688* (Oxford, 1988).

Speck, W.A., *Stability and Strife in England 1714–60* (London, 1977).

Spence, Jonathan D., *The Memory Palace of Matteo Ricci* (London, 1985).

Starkie, Andrew, *The Birth of the Modern Church of England: The Bangorian Controversy, 1716–1721* (Woodbridge, 2007).

Stourton, Charles Botolph Joseph, Baron Mowbray, *The History of the Noble House of Stourton* (2 vols, London, 1899).

Sweet, Rosemary, *Antiquaries: The Discovery of the Past in Eighteenth-Century Britain* (London, 2004).

Szechi, Daniel, 'A Blueprint for Tyranny? Sir Edward Hales and the Catholic Jacobite Response to the Revolution of 1688', *English Historical Review*, 116 (2001), pp. 342–67.

Szechi, Daniel, 'Constructing a Jacobite: The Social and Intellectual Origins of George Lockhart of Carnwath', *Historical Journal*, 40 (1997), pp. 977–96.

Szechi, Daniel 'Defending the True Faith: Kirk, State and Catholic Missionaries in Scotland 1653–1755', *Catholic Historical Review*, 82 (1996), pp. 397–411.

Szechi, Daniel, 'The Image of the Court: Idealism, Politics and the Evolution of the Stuart Court 1689–1730', in Corp, ed., *Stuart Court in Rome*, pp. 49–64, at 49–53.

Szechi, Daniel, 'The Jacobite Revolution Settlement 1689–96', *English Historical Review*, 108 (1993), pp. 611–28.

Szechi, Daniel, 'The Jacobite Theatre of Death', in Cruickshanks and Black, eds, *The Jacobite Challenge*, pp. 57–73.

Szechi, Daniel, *The Jacobites: Britain and Europe 1688–1788* (Edinburgh, 1986).

Tabori, Paul, *The Anatomy of Exile: A Semantic and Historical Study* (London, 1972).

Tavard, George H., *The Seventeenth Century Tradition: A Study in Recusant Thought* (Leiden, 1978).

Tayler, Henrietta, *Lady Nithsdale and her Family* (London, 1939).

Taylor, Stephen, and Walsh, John, 'The Church and Anglicanism in the "Long" Eighteenth Century', in *The Church of England c.168–c.1833. From Toleration to Tractarianism*, ed. John Walsh, Colin Haydon and Stephen Taylor (Cambridge, 1993), pp. 1–64.

Thompson, A.C., 'Popery, Politics and Private Judgement in Early Hanoverian Britain', *Historical Journal*, 45 (2002), pp. 333–58.

Thompson, Andrew C., *Britain, Hanover and the Protestant Interest, 1688–1756* (Woodbridge, 2006).

Thorpe, Victoria, 'Mysterious Jacobite Iconography', in E. Corp, ed., *The Stuart Court in Rome*, pp. 95–110.

Tomaselli, Sylvana, 'Intolerance, the Virtue of Princes and Radicals', in Grell and Porter, eds, *Toleration in Enlightenment Europe*, pp. 86–101.

Trevor, Meriol, *James II: The Shadow of a Crown* (London, 1988).

Trevor Roper, Hugh, 'Toleration and Religion after 1688', in Grell, Israel and Tyacke, eds, *Persecution to Toleration*, pp. 389–408.

Tutino, Stefania, 'The Catholic Church and the English Civil War: The Case of Thomas White', *Journal of Ecclesiastical History*, 58 (2007), pp. 232–55.

Van Kley, Dale K., *The Jansenists and the Expulsion of the Jesuits from France, 1757–1765* (New Haven, 1975).

Van Kley, Dale K. 'Piety and Politics in the Century of Lights', in Mark Goldie and Robert Wokler, eds, *Cambridge History of Eighteenth-Century Political Thought* (Cambridge, 2006), pp. 119–45.

Van Strien, C.D., 'Recusant Houses in the Southern Netherlands as seen by British Tourists, c. 1650–1720', *Recusant History*, 20 (1990–1), pp. 495–511.

Walker, Claire, *Gender and Politics in Early Modern Europe: English Convents in France and the Low Countries* (Basingstoke, 2003).

Walker, Claire, 'Prayer, Patronage and Political Conspiracy: English Nuns and the Restoration', *Historical Journal*, 42 (2000), pp. 1–23.

Walsham, Alexandra, *Charitable Hatred: Tolerance and Intolerance in England, 1500–1700* (Manchester, 2006).

Walsham, Alexandra, *Church Papists: Catholicism, Conformity and Confessional Polemic in Early Modern England* (Woodbridge, 1993).

Ward, W.R., *The English Land Tax in the Eighteenth Century* (1953).

Webster, C., 'Richard Towneley and the Towneley Group', *Transactions of the Historical Society of Lancashire and Cheshire*, 118 (1960).

Wenham, L.P., *Roger Strickland of Richmond: A Jacobite Gentleman 1680–1749* (North Yorkshire CRO, 1982).

Whaley, Johann, 'Tolerant Society? Religious Toleration and the Holy Roman Empire, 1648–1806', in Porter and Grell, eds, *Toleration in Enlightenment Europe*, pp. 175–95.

Williams, Basil, *The Whig Supremacy* (2nd edn, Oxford, 1962).

Williams, John Anthony, 'Benedictine Missions in Wiltshire in the Seventeenth and Eighteenth Centuries', *Downside Review*, 78 (1960), pp. 203–13.

Williams, John Anthony, 'Bishops Giffard and Ellis and the Western Vicariate 1688–1715', *Journal of Ecclesiastical History*, 15 (1964), pp. 218–26.

Williams, John Anthony, *Catholicism in Bath* (2 vols, CRS, 1974, 1975).

Williams, John Anthony, 'Change or Decay? The Provincial Laity 1691–1781', in E. Duffy, ed., *Challoner and his Church*, pp. 27–54.

Williams, John Anthony, '"Our Patriarch": Bishop Bonaventure Giffard, 1642–1734. An Introductory Sketch', *Recusant History*, 26 (2002–3), pp. 426–87.

Williams, John Anthony, 'Sources for Recusant History in English Official Archives', *Recusant History*, 16 (1983), pp. 331–441.

Williams, Michael E., 'Origins of the English College, Lisbon', *Recusant History*, 20 (1990–1), pp. 78–92.

Wilton, R.C., 'Early Eighteenth Century Catholics in England', *Catholic Historical Review*, n.s., 4 (1924), pp. 367–87.

Winn, James A., *John Dryden and his World* (Yale, 1987).

Woolf, Daniel, *The Idea of History in Early Stuart England* (1990).

Zon, Bennett, 'Jacobitism and the Liturgy in the Eighteenth Century English Catholic Church', *Royal Stuart Society* (1992).

Zon, Bennett, 'The Origin of *Adeste Fideles*', *Early Music*, 24 (2) (1996), pp. 279–88.

Zwicker, Stephen N., 'Representing the Revolution: Politics and High Culture in 1688', in Cruickshanks, *By Force or by Default*, pp. 109–35.

Unpublished dissertations

Brown, Anthony J., 'Anglo-Irish Gallicanism 1635–1685', Cambridge University PhD thesis, 2004.

Duffy, Eamon, 'Joseph Berington and the English Cisalpine Movement 1772–1803', Cambridge University PhD thesis, 1973.

Hopkins, Paul Anthony, 'Aspects of Jacobite Conspiracy in the Reign of William III', Cambridge University PhD thesis, 1981.

MacKenzie, Niall, 'Gender, Jacobitism and Dynastic Sanctity', Cambridge University PhD thesis, 2003.

Index

291

Caryll, John (1667–1736), 56, 129
Caryll, John (1687–1718), 80
Caryll, John Baptist, 81, 84, 155
Caryll, Abbess Mary, 74, 75, 85
Caryll, Mary, née Mackenzie, 80, 201
Caryll, Philip, 141
Caryll family, 62, 63, 64, 65, 69, 72, 82, 153, 197, 253
Castlemaine, earl of, *see* Palmer, Roger
Catherine of Braganza, Queen, 31, 36, 74
Caussin, Nicholas, 95
Cavendish, William, first duke of Devonshire, 131
Cecil, James, fourth earl of Salisbury, 22, 23, 45
Cecil family, 45
Cellier, Elizabeth, 34
Chaillot, 200
Challoner, Richard, bishop and vicar apostolic, 4, 55, 65–6, 124, 219
   Britannia Sancta by, 66
   Memoirs of Missionary Priests by, 66
Champion, Justin, 7
Charles I, King, 5, 8, 29, 33, 47, 83, 95, 96, 97, 99, 100, 119, 151, 156, 205, 216
Charles II, King, 28, 29, 30, 31, 32, 33, 38, 40, 98, 102, 124, 142, 181, 182, 205, 207
   Declaration of Breda by, 207
Charles V, Emperor, 170
Charlton, Barbara, 254
Charlton family, 60, 252
Charnock, Robert, 127–8
Cheshire, 25
Chester, 22
Chesterfield, earl of, *see* Stanhope, Philip Dormer
Chichester, 28, 56
Chinnici, Joseph, 17
Church of England, 4, 7, 10, 118–19, 133
   and action against Catholics, 57–8, 123, 137
   and local relations with Catholics, 64, 66, 69
   and reign of James II, 40–1, 42, 48
   Catholic appeals to, 30, 32, 38, 47–8, 192, 207, 209, 213–15, 217, 225–6, 232–3, 255
   converts to Catholicism from, 26, 30–1, 40, 102–3
   attitude of Jacobite court to, 105–6, 109–10, 119
Churchill, John, first duke of Marlborough, 227

Churchill, Sarah, duchess of Marlborough, 155, 156
Cisalpine movement, 256, 257
Civil Wars, 8, 20, 28–29, 30, 32, 37, 47, 49, 68, 70, 83, 85, 106, 114, 124, 160
Clancy, Thomas, 6
Clarendon, earls of, *see under* Hyde
Clark, Jonathan, 1
Clarke, Samuel, 148
Clavering family, 60, 252
Claydon, Tony, 9
Clement XI, Pope, 159, 170, 176–8, 184
clergy, 3, 4, 8, 10, 14, 15, 21, 22, 55, 57, 66–7, 74–6, 80, 109, 164
   and activism in exile, 195–7, 198–9, 200–9, 215–20, 229
   and conflicts of national identity, 198–9
   and culture of Jacobitism, 194–5, 197, 200–3, 219–220
   and the English mission, 191–2, 194, 197, 205, 215–20, 222, 238
   and the exiled court, 80, 96–8, 109–10, 112, 113, 115–16, 172, 175–6, 181, 184, 185, 191, 198
   and the Jacobite Church campaign, 192, 203–20
   and the oath debate, 138–40, 173–4, 192, 203–4
   and reign of James II, 33–5, 193–4
Clifford, Lord Thomas, 66
Clifton, Sir Gervase, 24
Cliveden, 156
Cobham, Viscount, *see* Temple, Richard
Coke, Sir Edward, 100, 151
Cole, William, 214
Colley, Linda, 1
Collier, Jeremy, 213, 215
Collingwood, George, 202
Collingwood family, 56, 60, 252
Colonia, Dominique de, 228
Commissioners for Forfeited Estates, 58, 61
Conciliarism, 225
Confucianism, 231, 236, 246
Congregation of St. Edmunds, 237
Connell, Michael, 141
Connock, Sir Timon, 81
Conquest family, 130
Constable, Cuthbert, 148, 210
Constable, John, 217
Constable, Sir Marmaduke, 77, 85
Constable, Sir Philip, 56
Constable family, 197, 235
Copley, Anthony, 111
   A Fig for Fortune by, 111